VIZ GRAPHIC NOVEL

W9-AYC-060

BATTLE ANGEL

ALITA

STORY AND ART BY

YUKITO KISHIRO

CONTENTS

STORY AND ART BY YUKiTO KISHIRO

Translation/Fred Burke & Sterling Bell and Matt Thorn
Touch-Up Art & Lettering/Wayne Truman
Cover Design/Viz Graphics
Editors/Satoru Fujii & Trish Ledoux
Assistant Editor/Toshifumi Yoshida
Executive Editor/Seiji Horibuchi
Publisher/Masahiro Oga

First published as *Gunnm* by Shueisha Inc. in Japan

Printed in Canada

Published by Viz Comics
P.O. Box 77010 • San Francisco, CA 94107

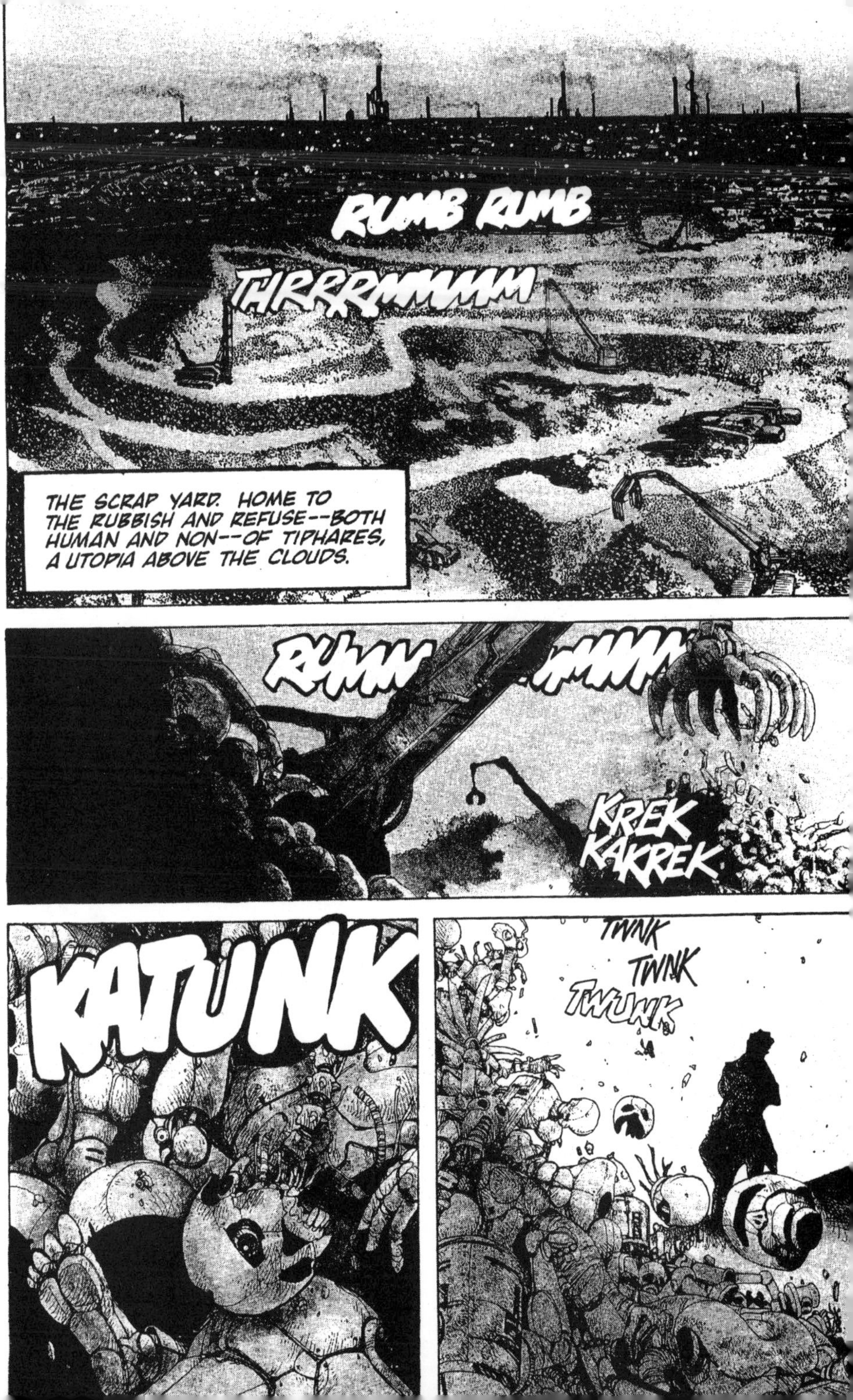
RUMB RUMB
THRRRMMMMM
THE SCRAP YARD. HOME TO THE RUBBISH AND REFUSE--BOTH HUMAN AND NON--OF TIPHARES, A UTOPIA ABOVE THE CLOUDS.
KREK KAKREK
KATUNK
TWNK
TWNK
TWUNK

RUSTY ANGEL

Battle 1 : Reclamation

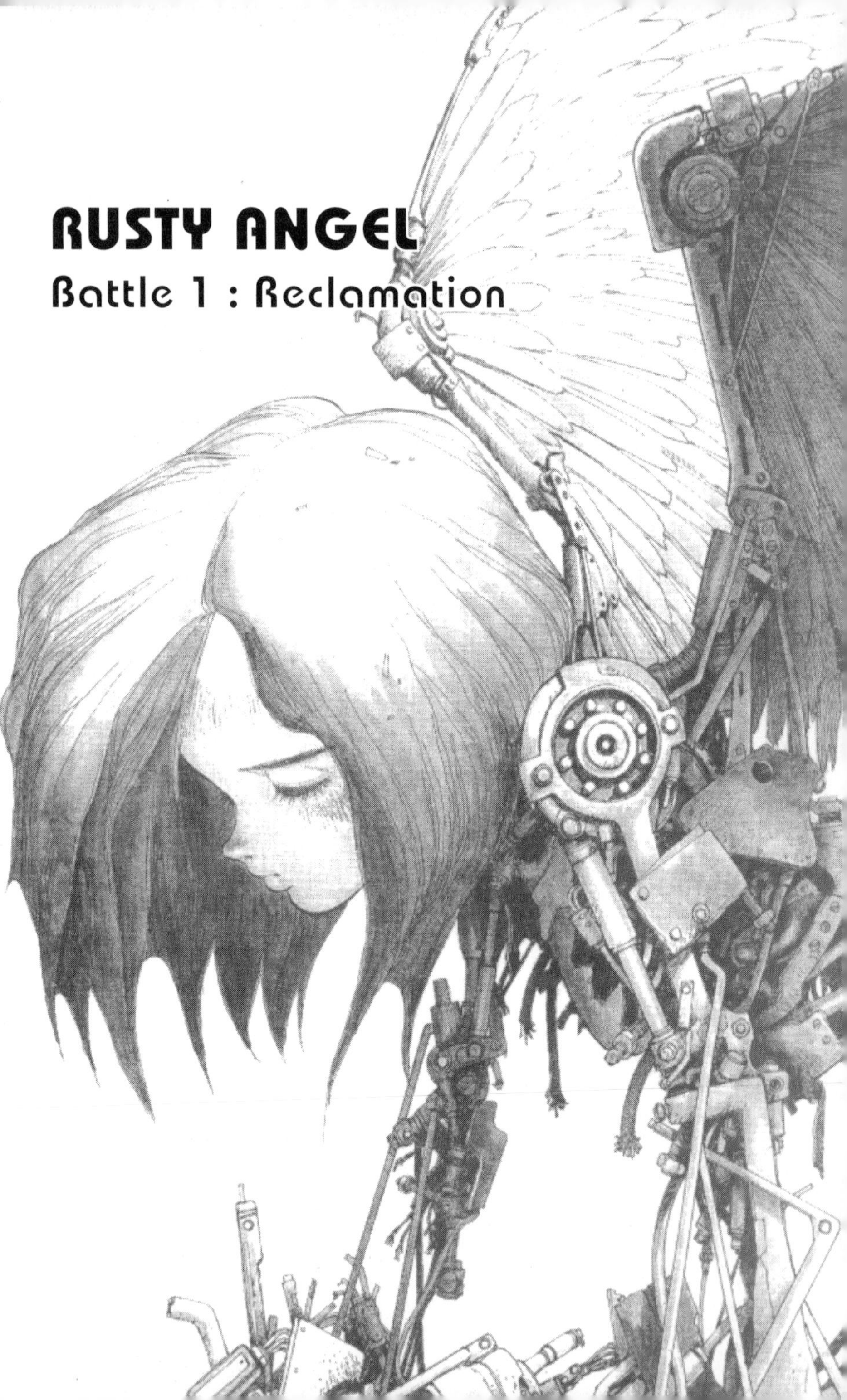

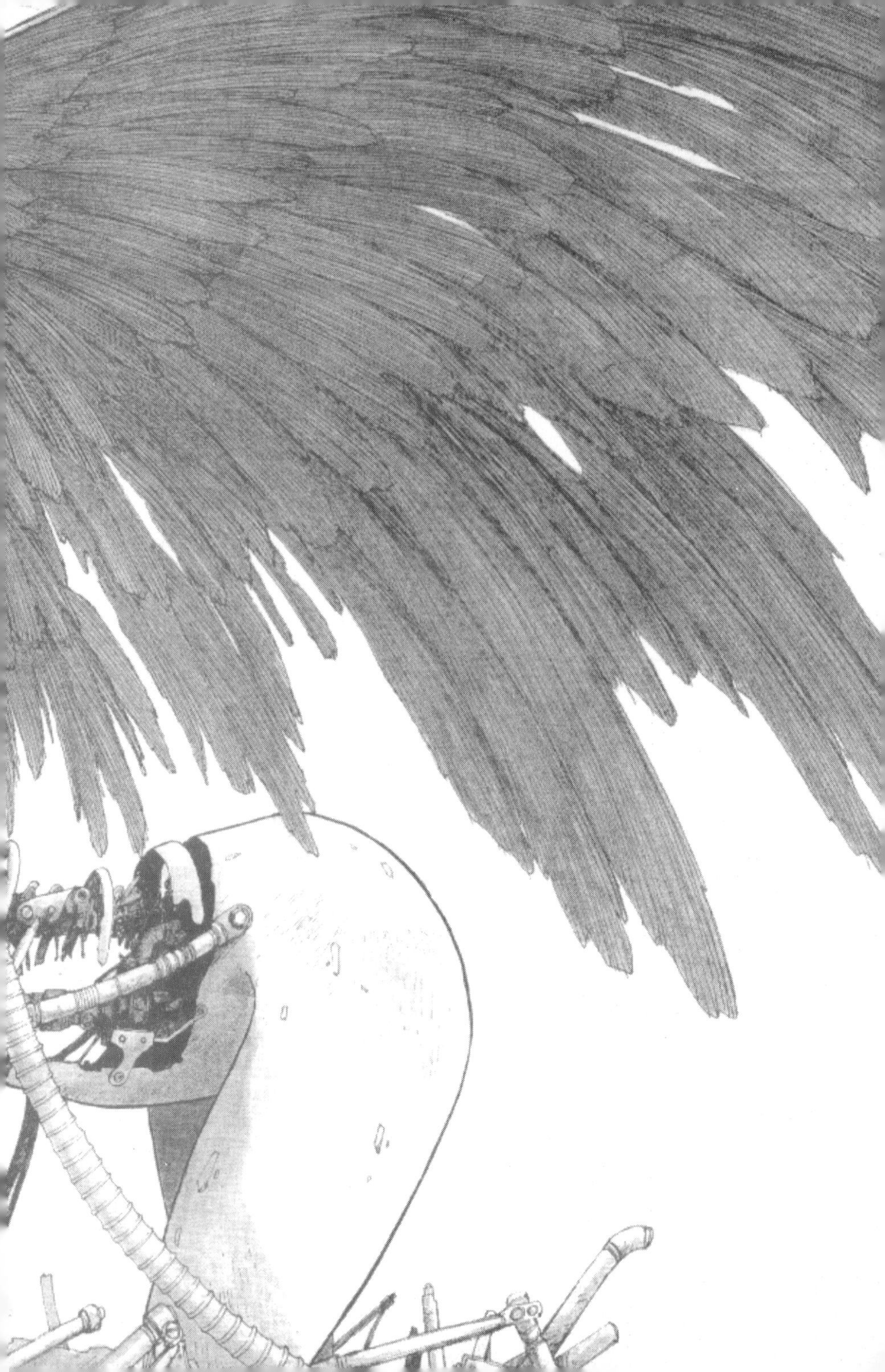

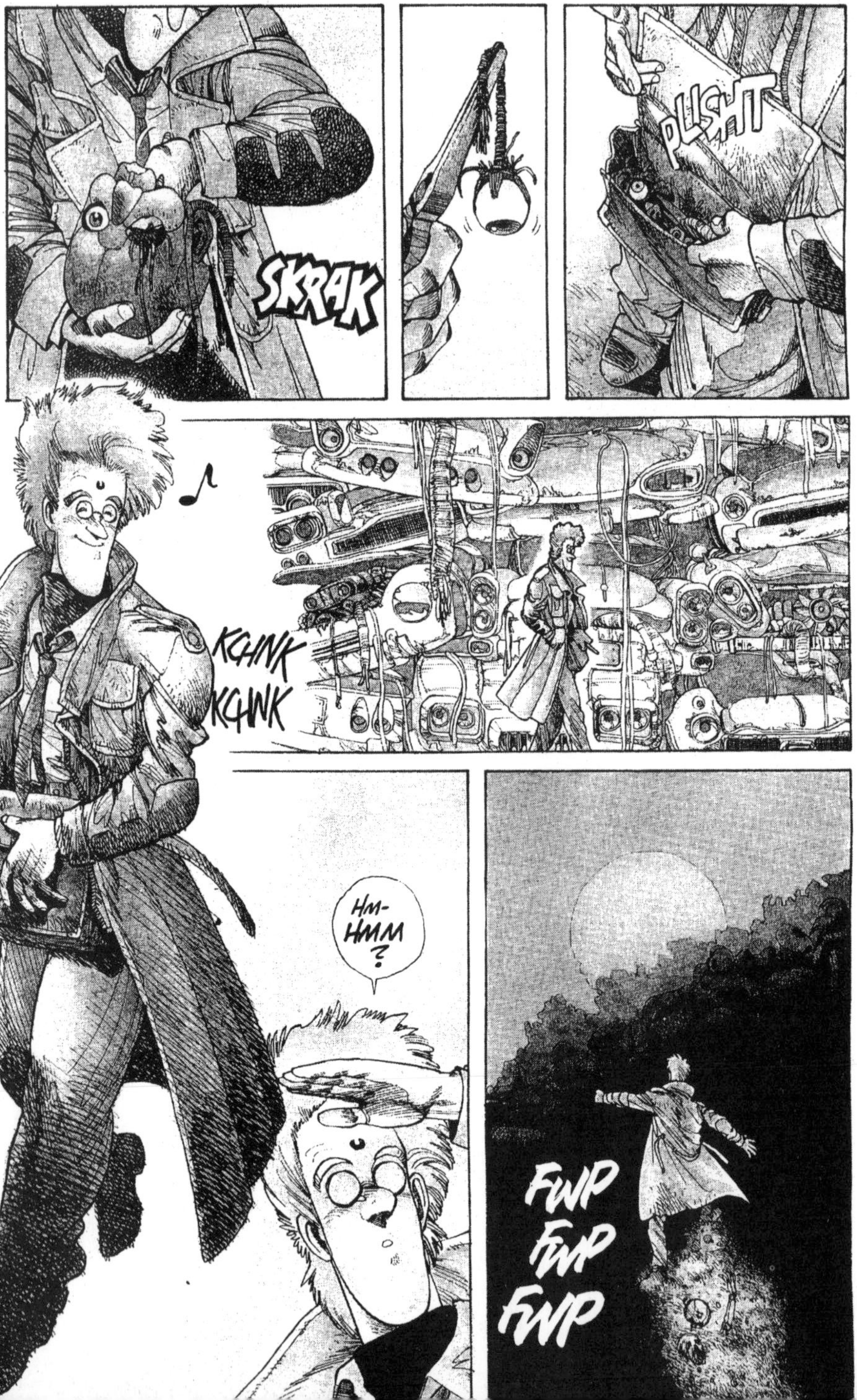
SKRAK
PLISHT
♪
KCHINK
KCHINK
HM-HMM?
FWP
FWP
FWP

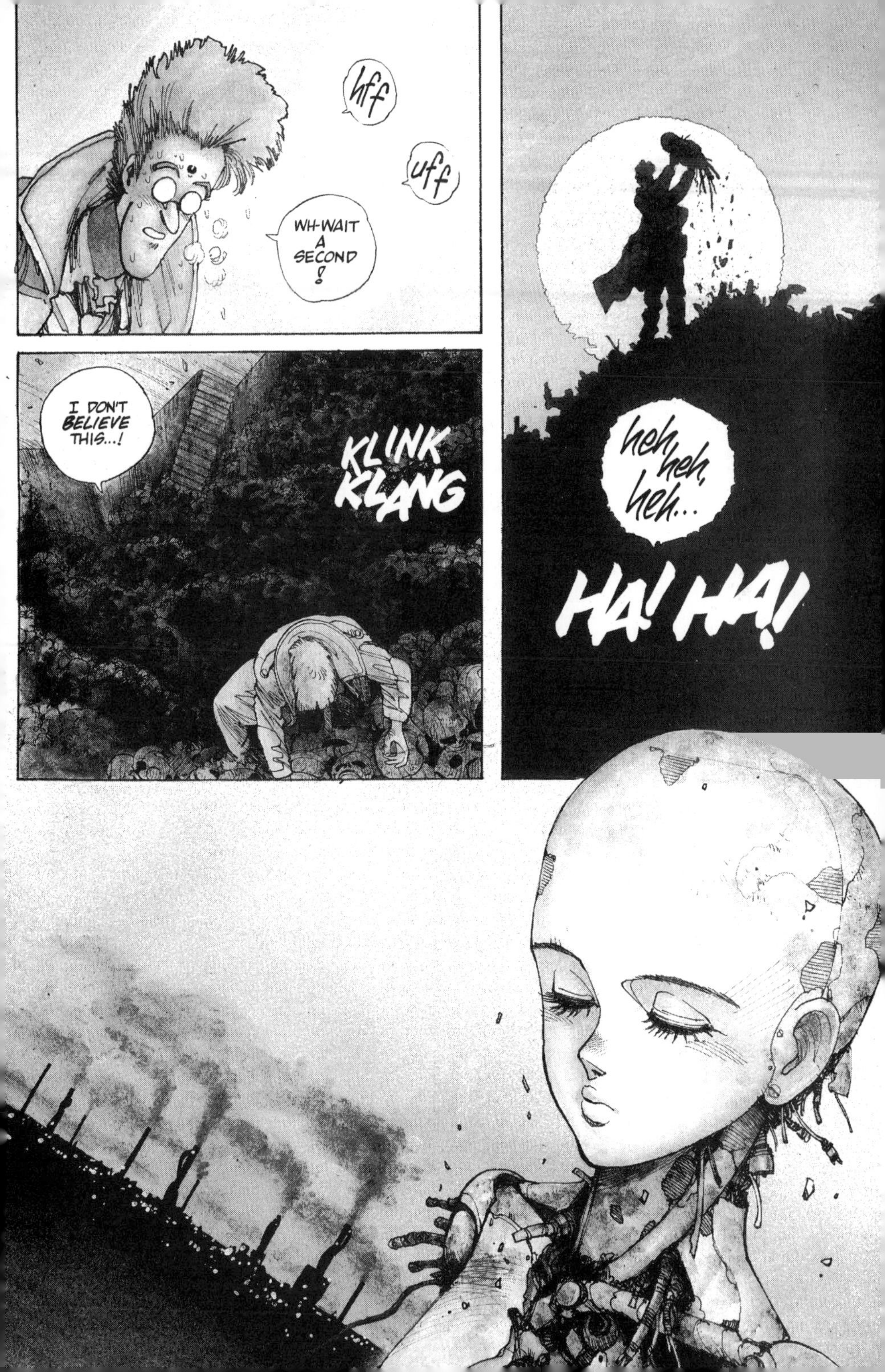
hff
uff
WH-WAIT A SECOND!
I DON'T BELIEVE THIS...!
KLINK KLANG
heh heh, heh...
HA! HA!

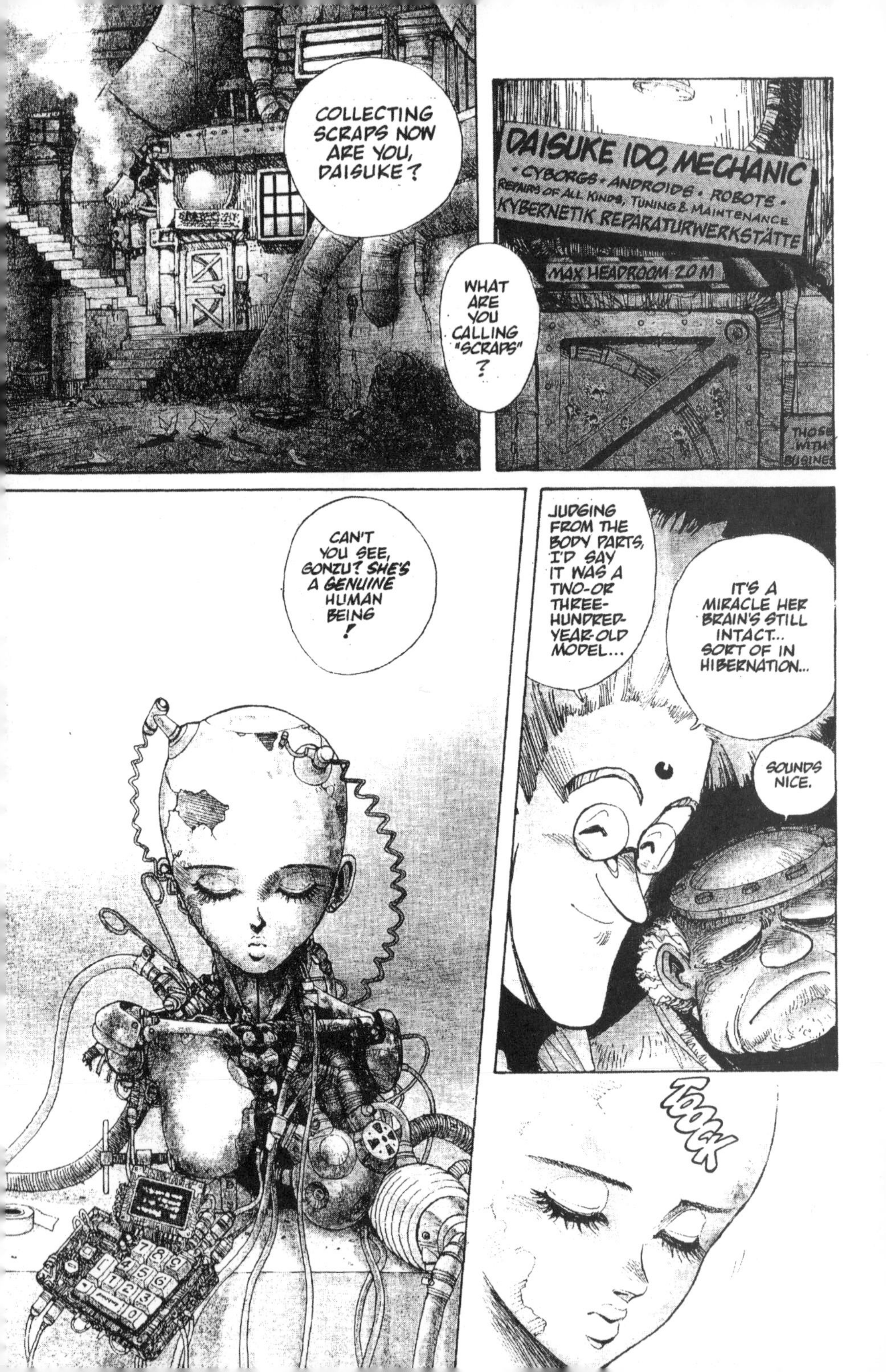

COLLECTING SCRAPS NOW ARE YOU, DAISUKE?
DAISUKE IDO, MECHANIC
• CYBORGS • ANDROIDS • ROBOTS •
REPAIRS OF ALL KINDS, TUNING & MAINTENANCE
KYBERNETIK REPARATURWERKSTÄTTE
MAX HEADROOM 2.0 M
THOSE WITH
WHAT ARE YOU CALLING "SCRAPS"?
CAN'T YOU SEE, GONZU? SHE'S A GENUINE HUMAN BEING!
JUDGING FROM THE BODY PARTS, I'D SAY IT WAS A TWO-OR THREE-HUNDRED-YEAR-OLD MODEL...
IT'S A MIRACLE HER BRAIN'S STILL INTACT... SORT OF IN HIBERNATION...
SOUNDS NICE.
TOOCK

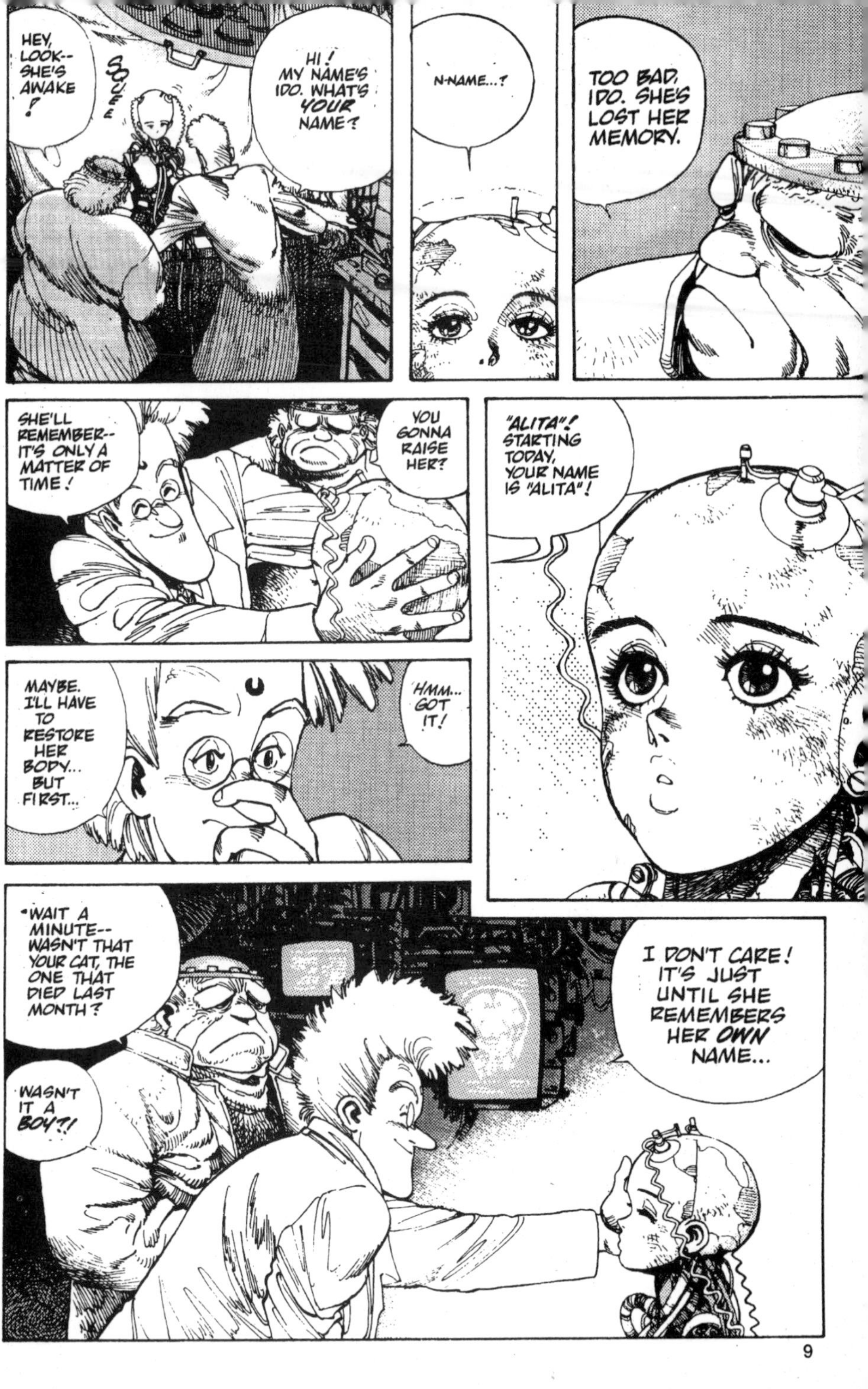
HEY, LOOK-- SHE'S AWAKE!
SQUEE
HI! MY NAME'S IDO. WHAT'S YOUR NAME?
N-NAME...?
TOO BAD, IDO. SHE'S LOST HER MEMORY.
SHE'LL REMEMBER-- IT'S ONLY A MATTER OF TIME!
YOU GONNA RAISE HER?
MAYBE. I'LL HAVE TO RESTORE HER BODY... BUT FIRST...
HMM... GOT IT!
"ALITA"! STARTING TODAY, YOUR NAME IS "ALITA"!
WAIT A MINUTE-- WASN'T THAT YOUR CAT, THE ONE THAT DIED LAST MONTH?
WASN'T IT A BOY?!
I DON'T CARE! IT'S JUST UNTIL SHE REMEMBERS HER OWN NAME...

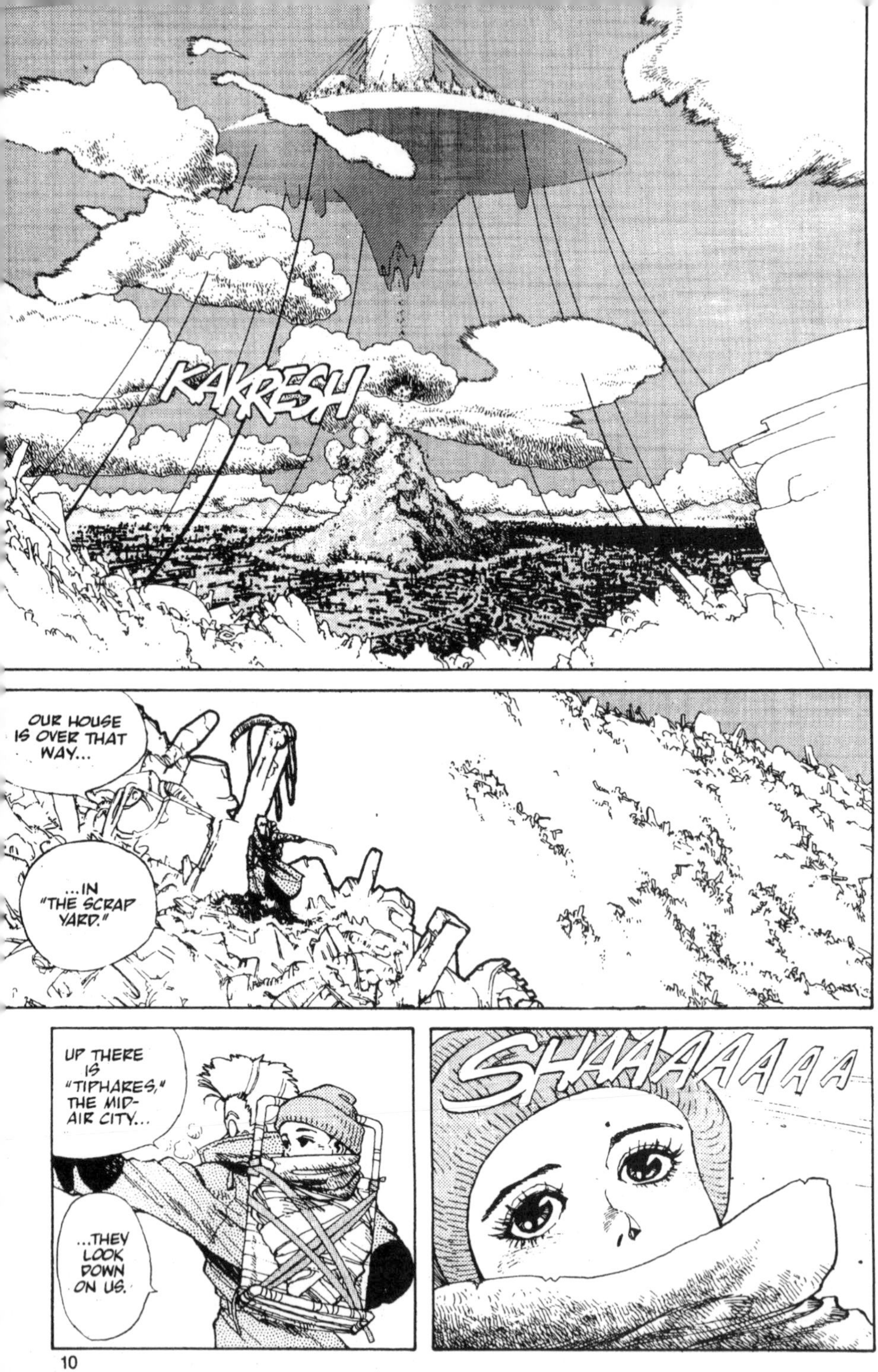
KAKRESH
OUR HOUSE IS OVER THAT WAY...
...IN "THE SCRAP YARD."
UP THERE IS "TIPHARES," THE MID-AIR CITY...
...THEY LOOK DOWN ON US.
SHAAAAAAAA

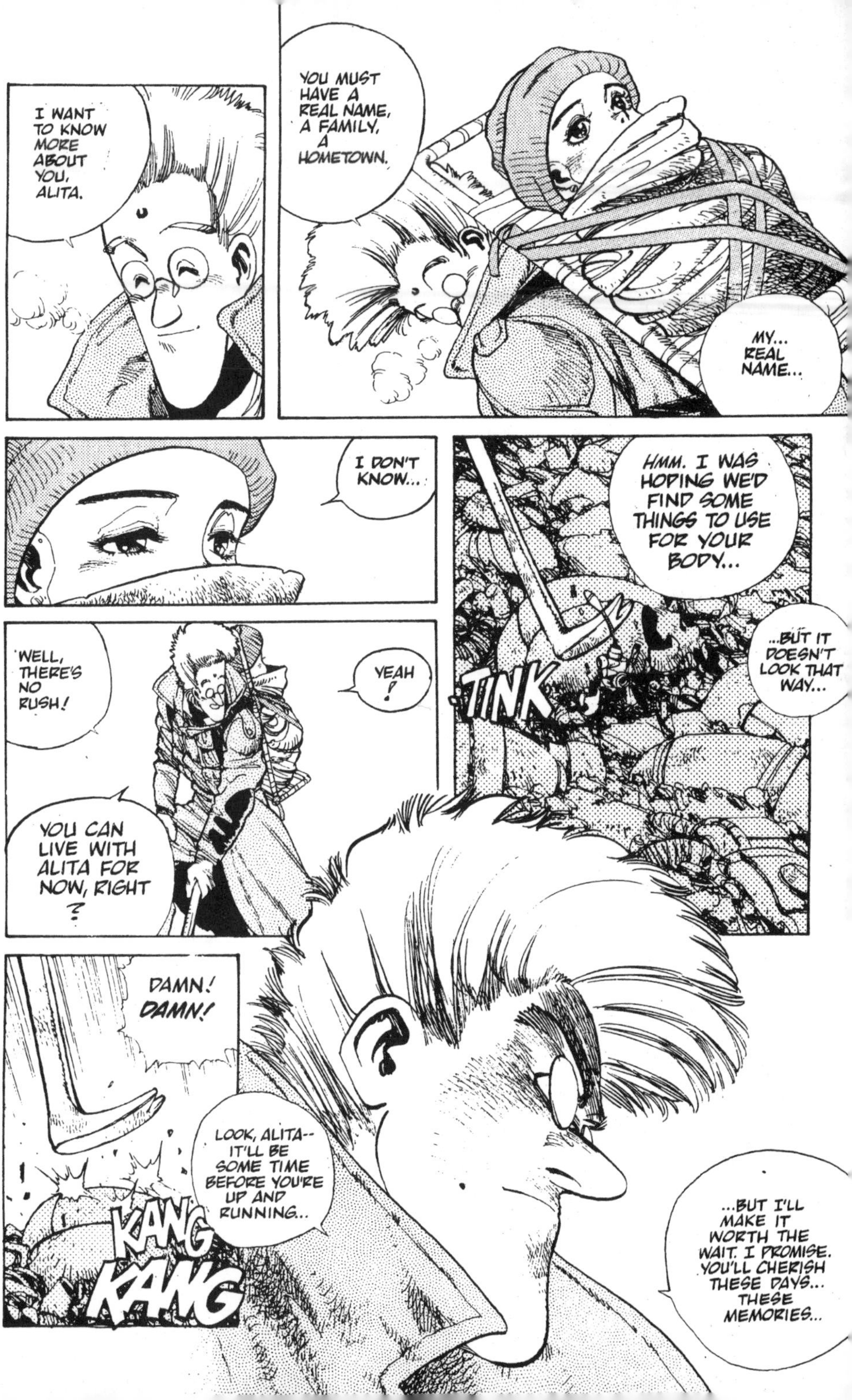
I WANT TO KNOW MORE ABOUT YOU, ALITA.
YOU MUST HAVE A REAL NAME, A FAMILY, A HOMETOWN.
MY... REAL NAME...
I DON'T KNOW...
WELL, THERE'S NO RUSH!
YEAH!
YOU CAN LIVE WITH ALITA FOR NOW, RIGHT?
HMM. I WAS HOPING WE'D FIND SOME THINGS TO USE FOR YOUR BODY...
TINK
...BUT IT DOESN'T LOOK THAT WAY...
DAMN! DAMN!
KANG KANG
LOOK, ALITA-- IT'LL BE SOME TIME BEFORE YOU'RE UP AND RUNNING...
...BUT I'LL MAKE IT WORTH THE WAIT. I PROMISE. YOU'LL CHERISH THESE DAYS... THESE MEMORIES...

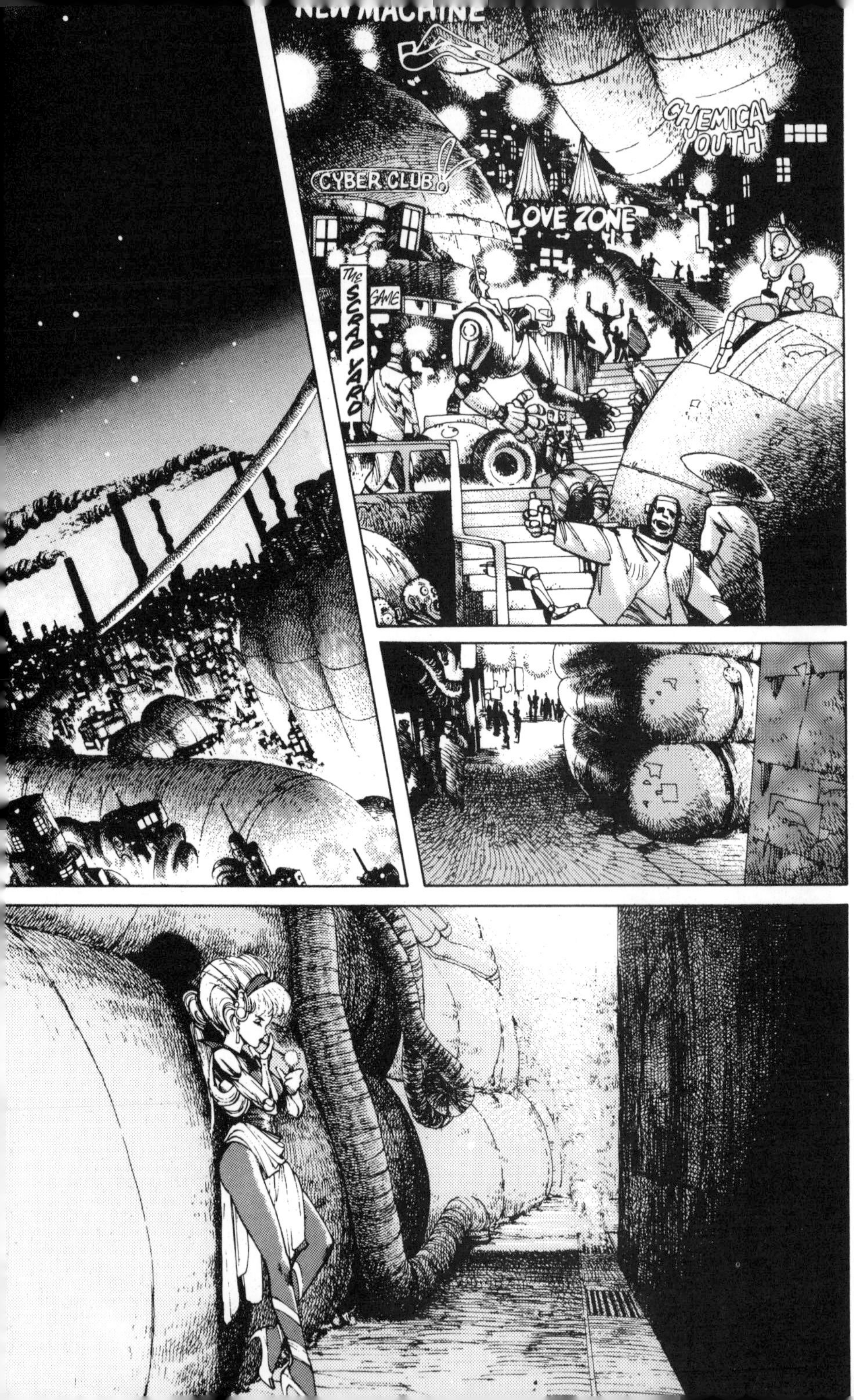
NEW MACHINE
CHEMICAL YOUTH
CYBER CLUB
LOVE ZONE
THE SCRAP YARD
GAME

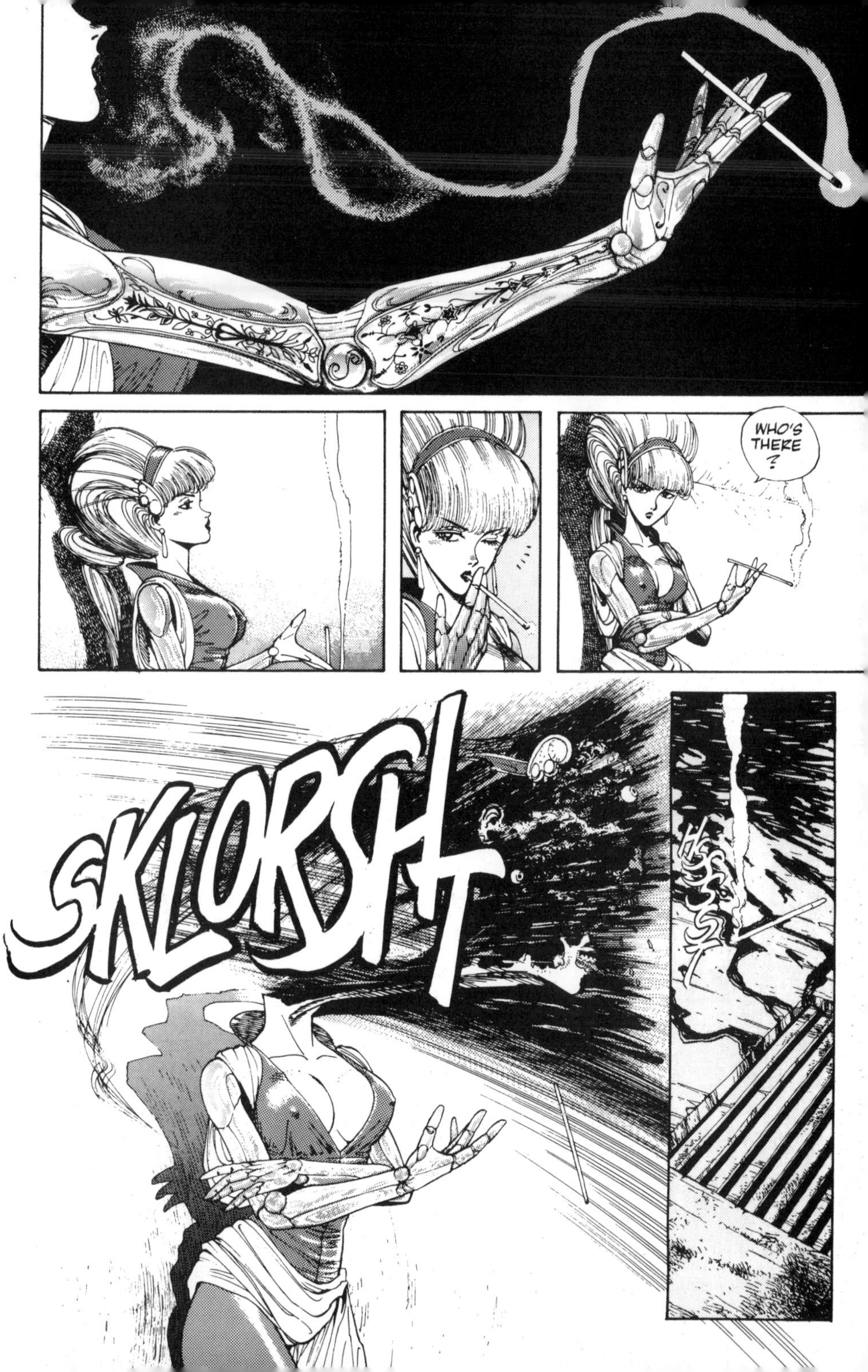
WHO'S THERE ?
SKLORSH
HSSSST

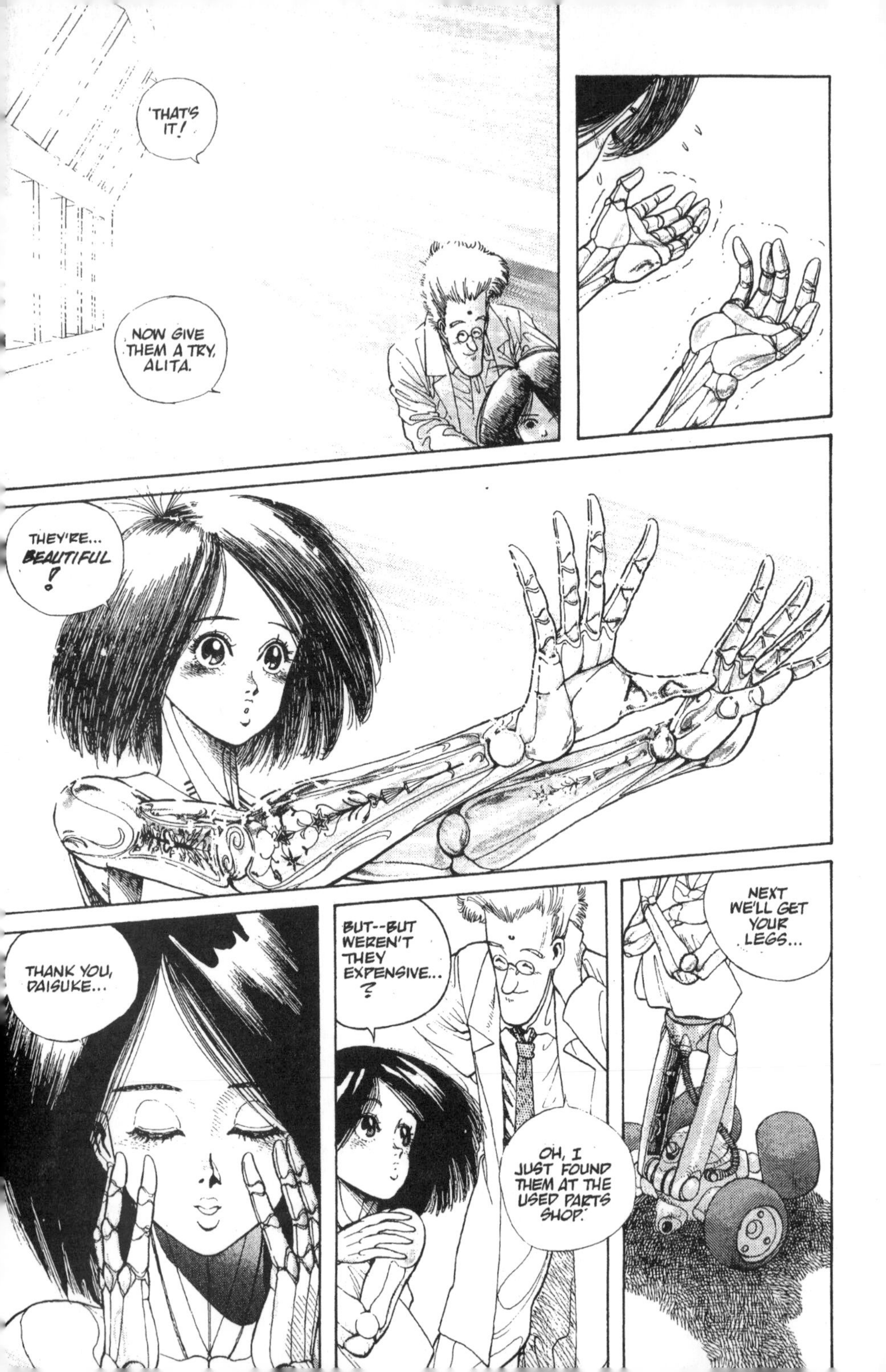
'THAT'S IT!
NOW GIVE THEM A TRY, ALITA.
THEY'RE... BEAUTIFUL!
THANK YOU, DAISUKE...
BUT--BUT WEREN'T THEY EXPENSIVE...?
OH, I JUST FOUND THEM AT THE USED PARTS SHOP.'
NEXT WE'LL GET YOUR LEGS...

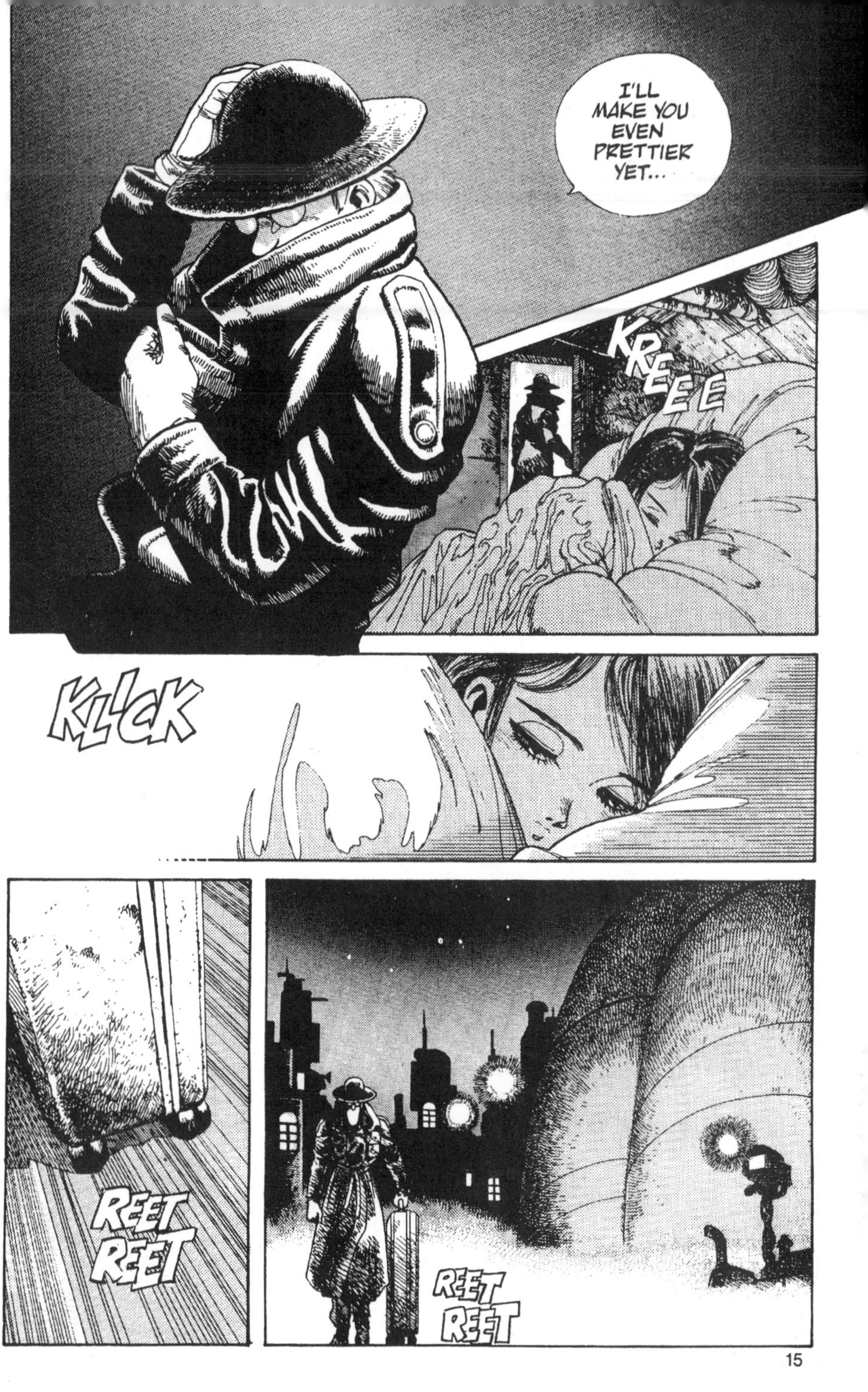
I'LL MAKE YOU EVEN PRETTIER YET...
KREEEE
KLICK
REET REET
REET REET

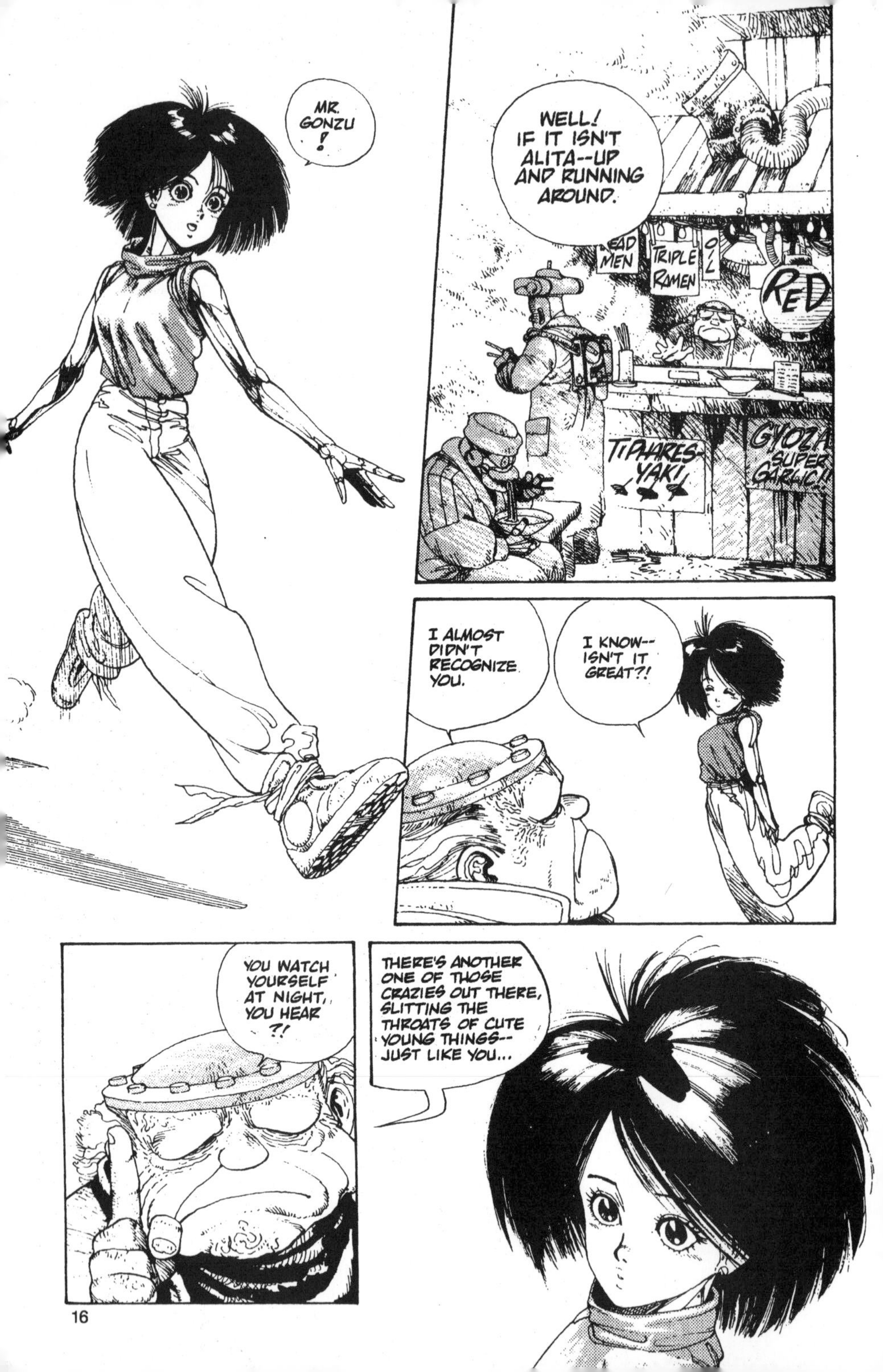
MR. GONZU !
WELL! IF IT ISN'T ALITA--UP AND RUNNING AROUND.
TRIPLE RAMEN
OIL
RED
TIPHARES-YAKI
GYOZA SUPER GARLIC!!
I ALMOST DIDN'T RECOGNIZE YOU.
I KNOW-- ISN'T IT GREAT?!
YOU WATCH YOURSELF AT NIGHT, YOU HEAR ?!
THERE'S ANOTHER ONE OF THOSE CRAZIES OUT THERE, SLITTING THE THROATS OF CUTE YOUNG THINGS-- JUST LIKE YOU...

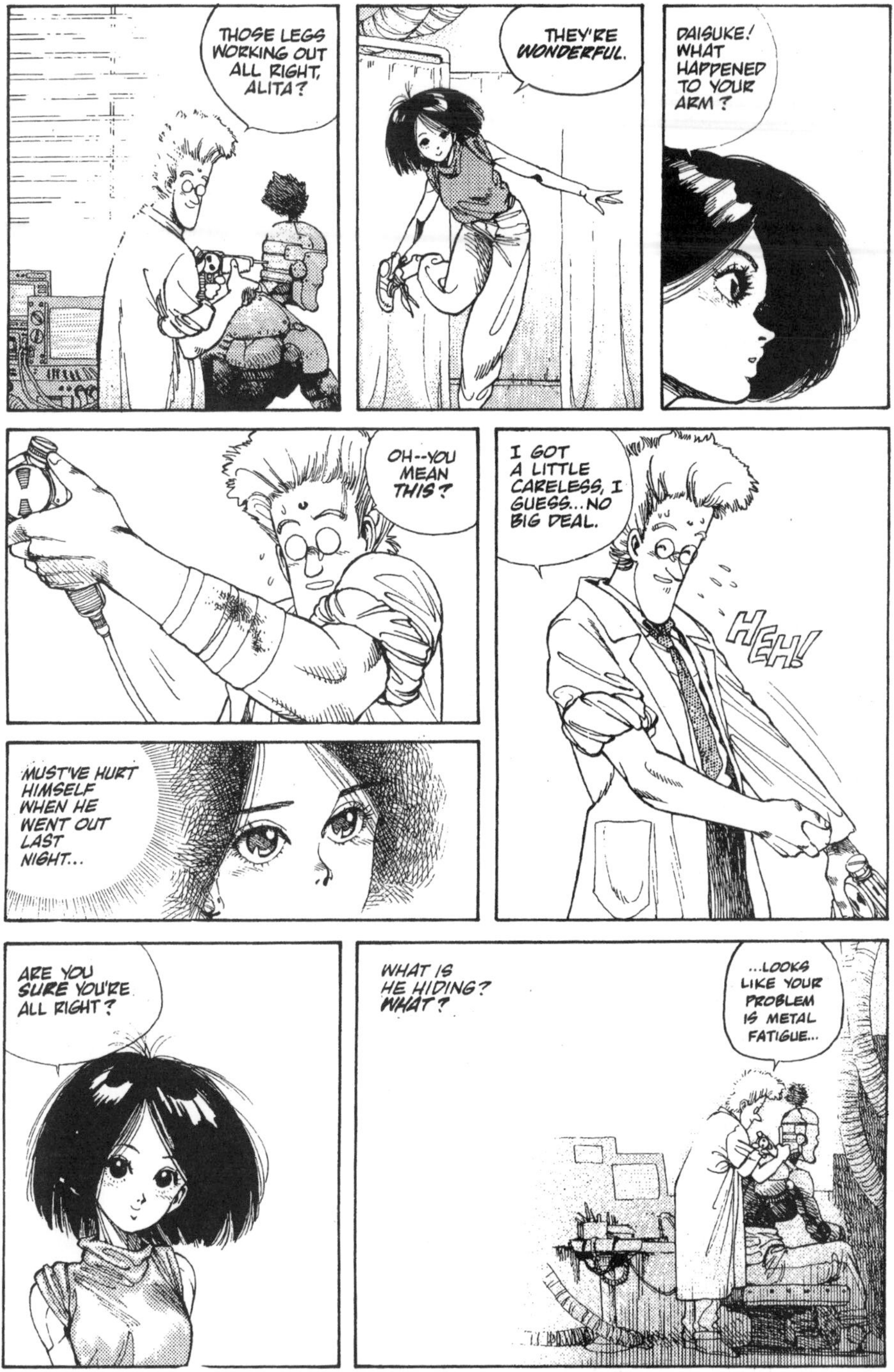
THOSE LEGS WORKING OUT ALL RIGHT, ALITA?
THEY'RE WONDERFUL.
DAISUKE! WHAT HAPPENED TO YOUR ARM?
OH--YOU MEAN THIS?
MUST'VE HURT HIMSELF WHEN HE WENT OUT LAST NIGHT...
I GOT A LITTLE CARELESS, I GUESS...NO BIG DEAL.
HEH!
ARE YOU SURE YOU'RE ALL RIGHT?
WHAT IS HE HIDING? WHAT?
...LOOKS LIKE YOUR PROBLEM IS METAL FATIGUE...

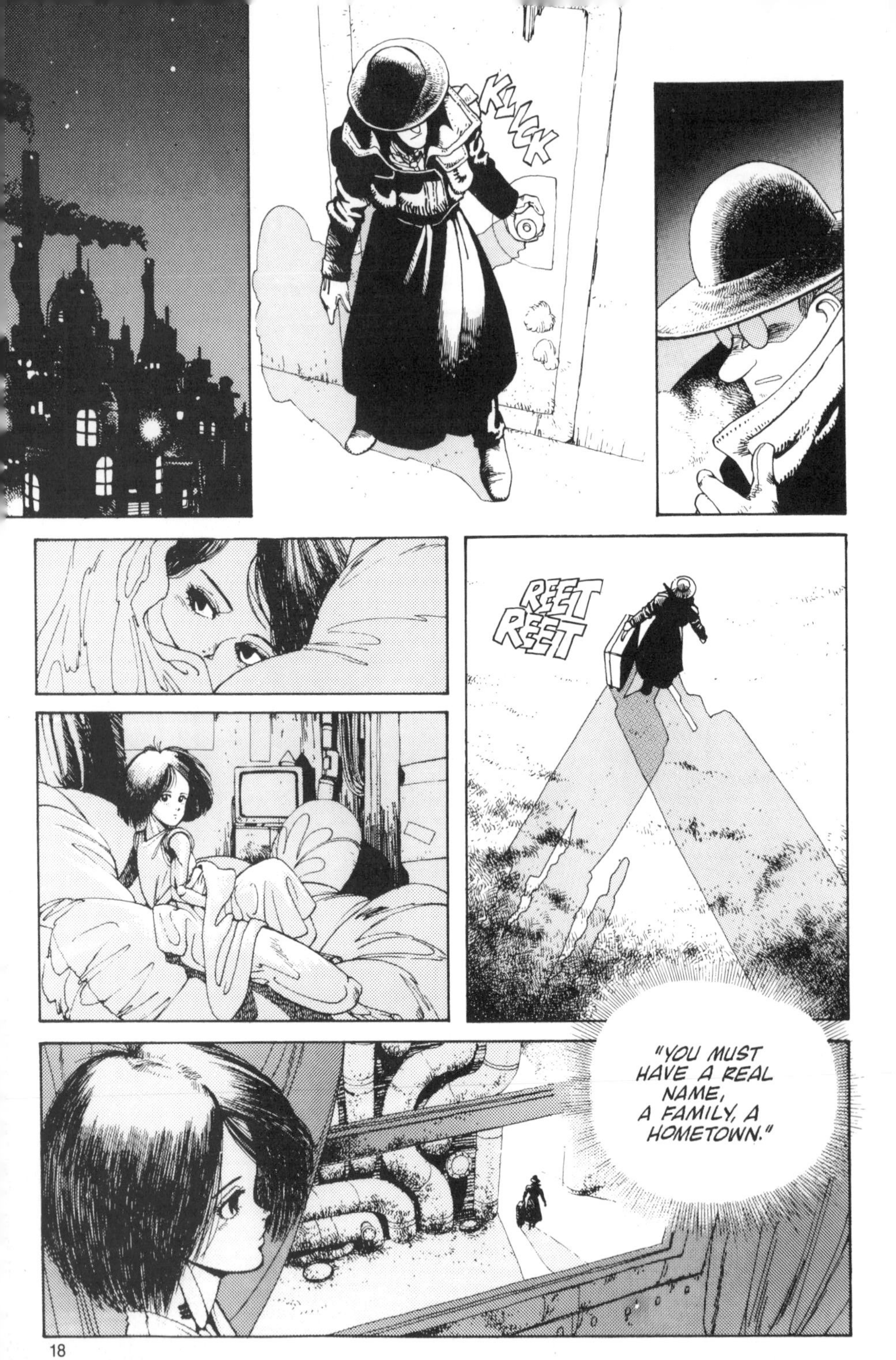
KLICK
REET REET
"YOU MUST HAVE A REAL NAME, A FAMILY, A HOMETOWN."

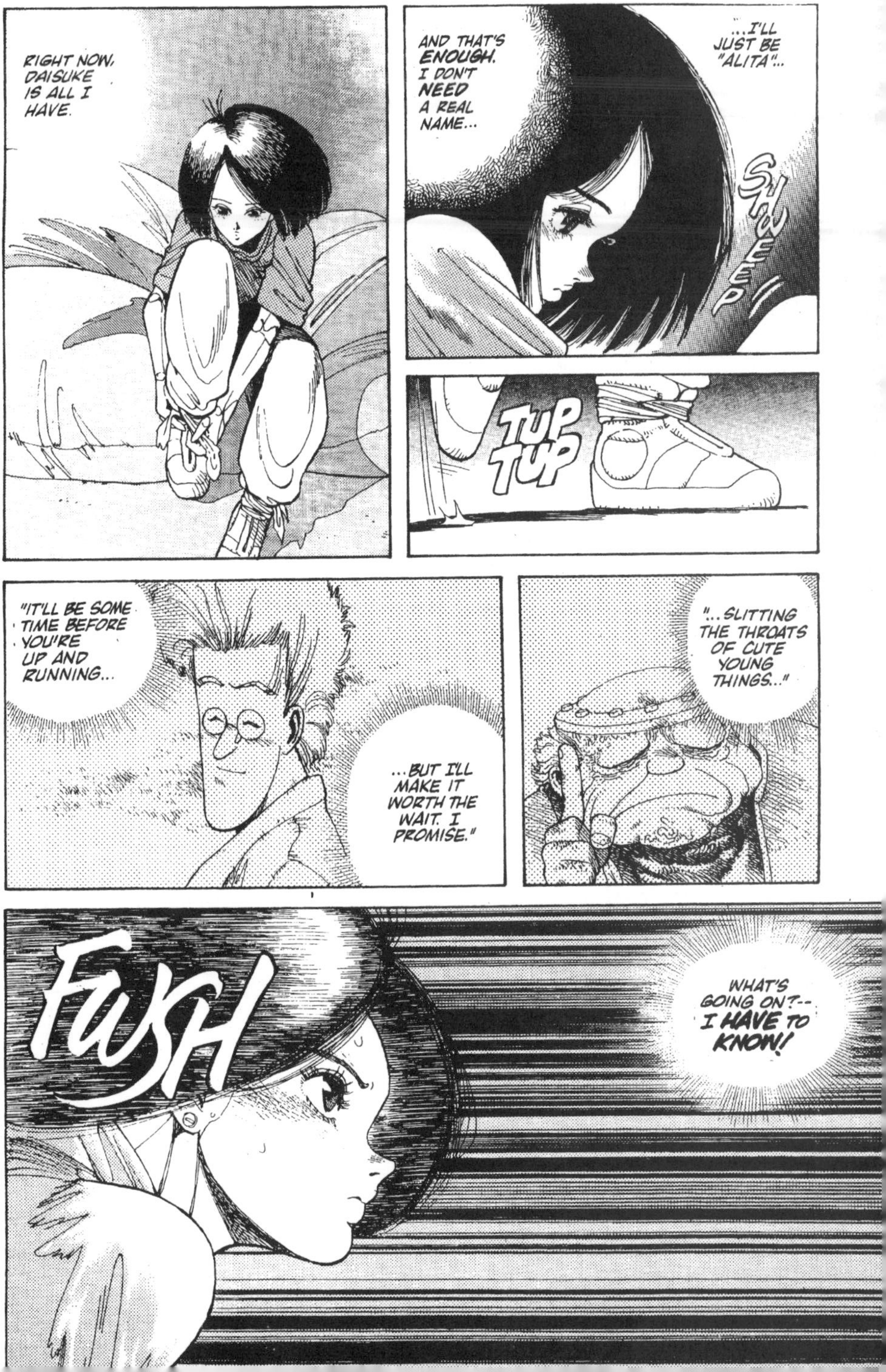
RIGHT NOW, DAISUKE IS ALL I HAVE.
AND THAT'S ENOUGH. I DON'T NEED A REAL NAME...
...I'LL JUST BE "ALITA"...
SHWEEP
TUP TUP
"IT'LL BE SOME TIME BEFORE YOU'RE UP AND RUNNING...
...BUT I'LL MAKE IT WORTH THE WAIT. I PROMISE."
"...SLITTING THE THROATS OF CUTE YOUNG THINGS..."
FUSH
WHAT'S GOING ON?-- I HAVE TO KNOW!

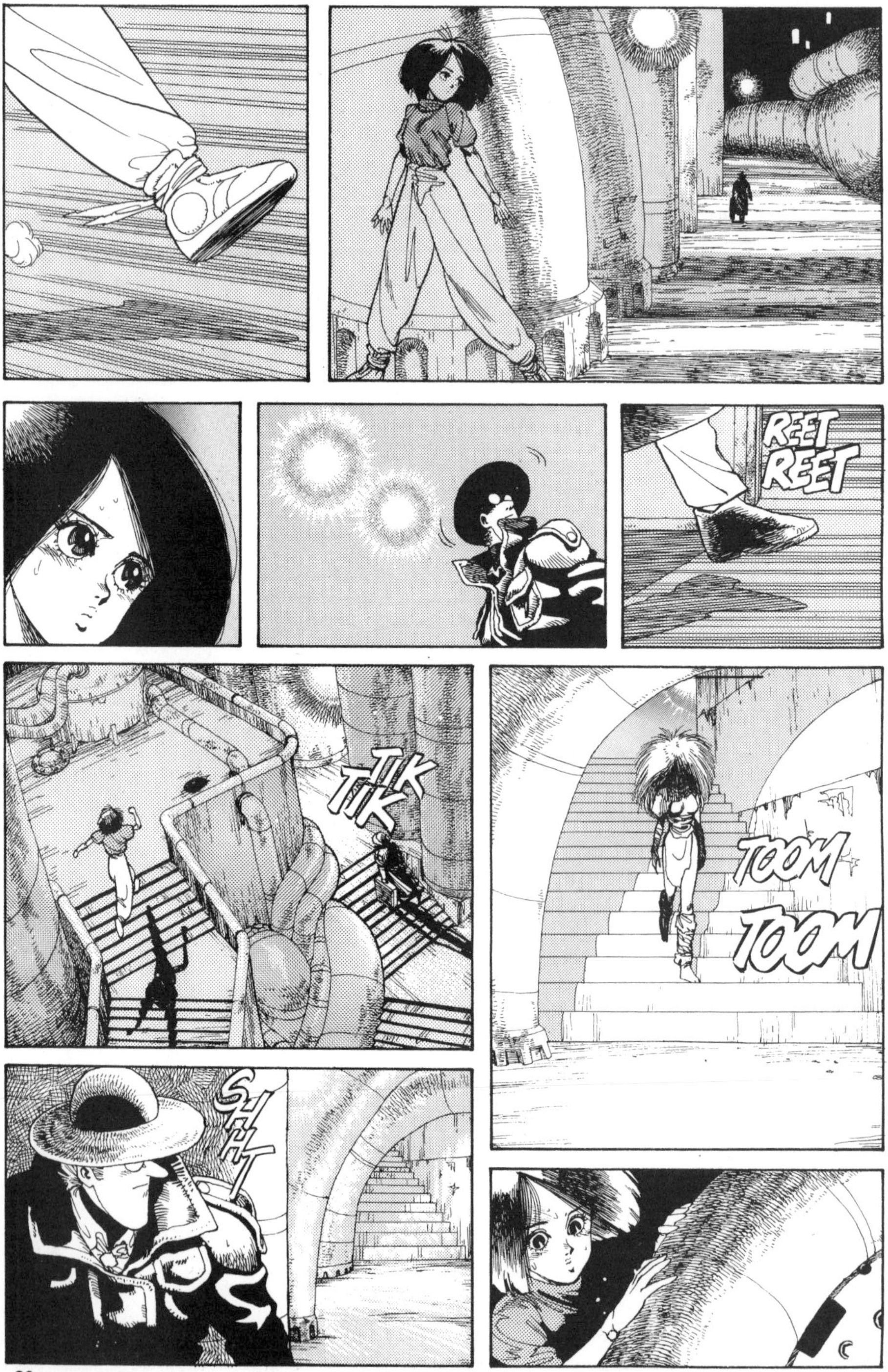
REET
REET
TIK
TIK
TOOM
TOOM
SHHT

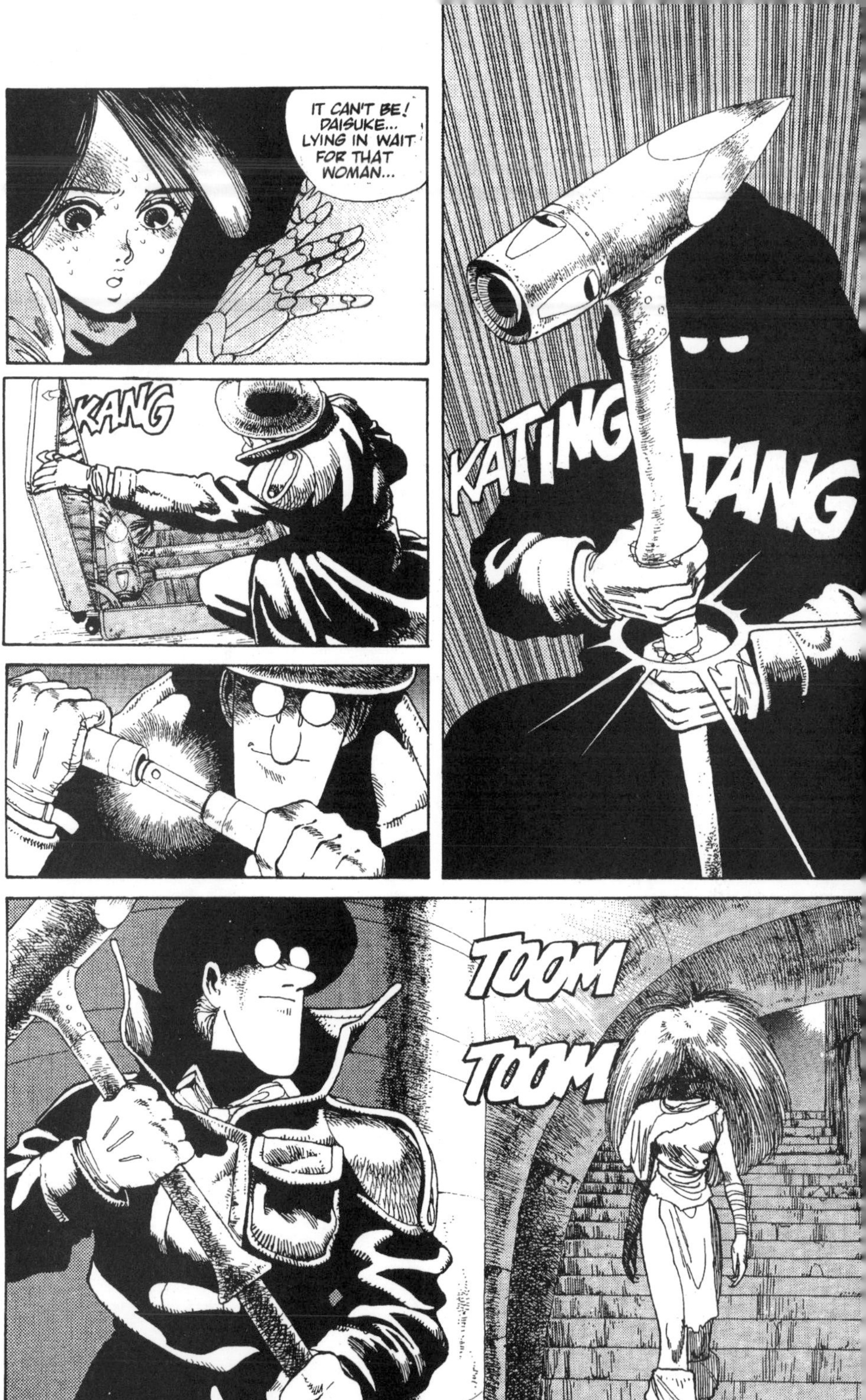
IT CAN'T BE! DAISUKE... LYING IN WAIT FOR THAT WOMAN...
KANG
KATING
TANG
TOOM
TOOM

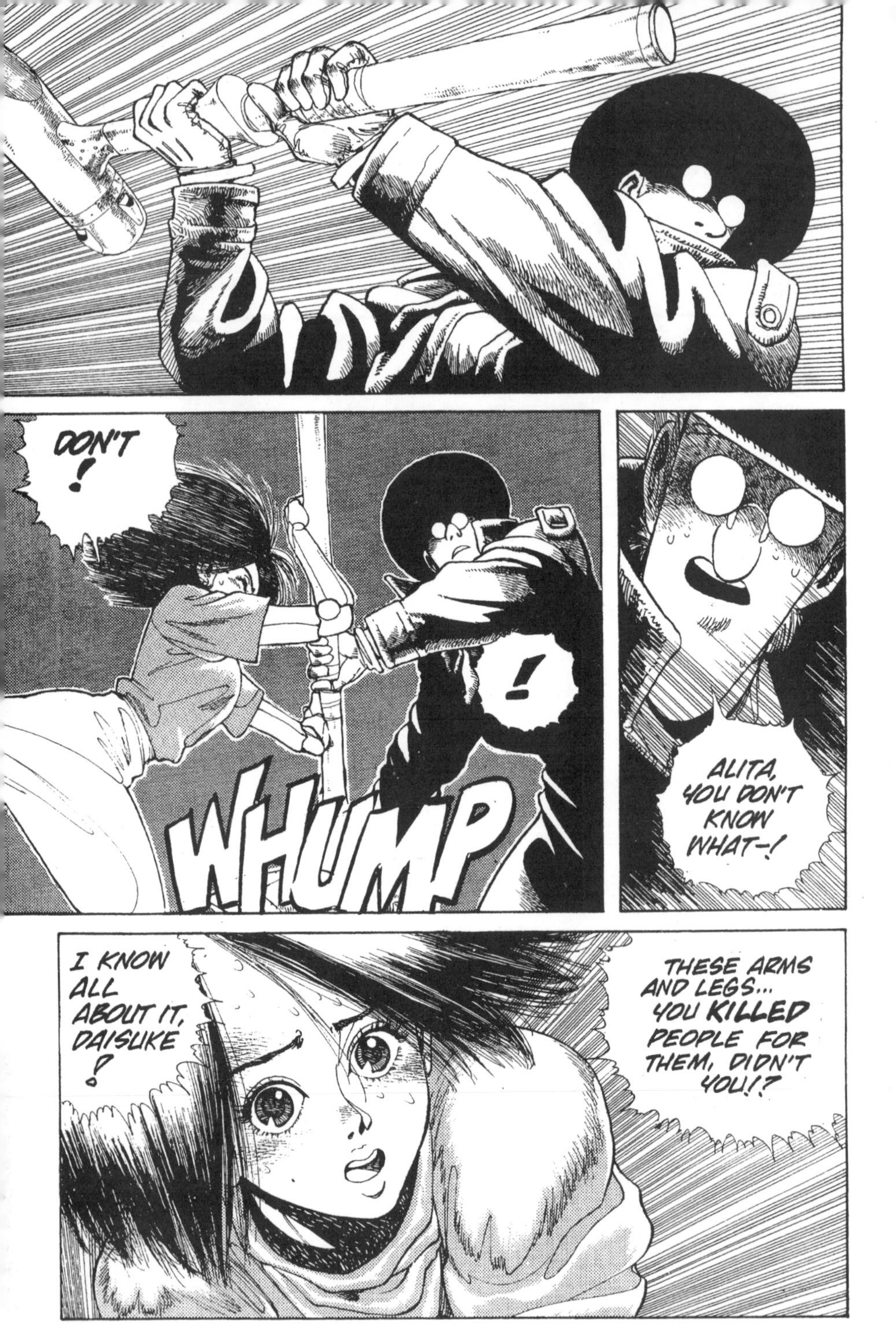
DON'T !
!
WHUMP
ALITA, YOU DON'T KNOW WHAT--!
I KNOW ALL ABOUT IT, DAISUKE !
THESE ARMS AND LEGS... YOU KILLED PEOPLE FOR THEM, DIDN'T YOU!?

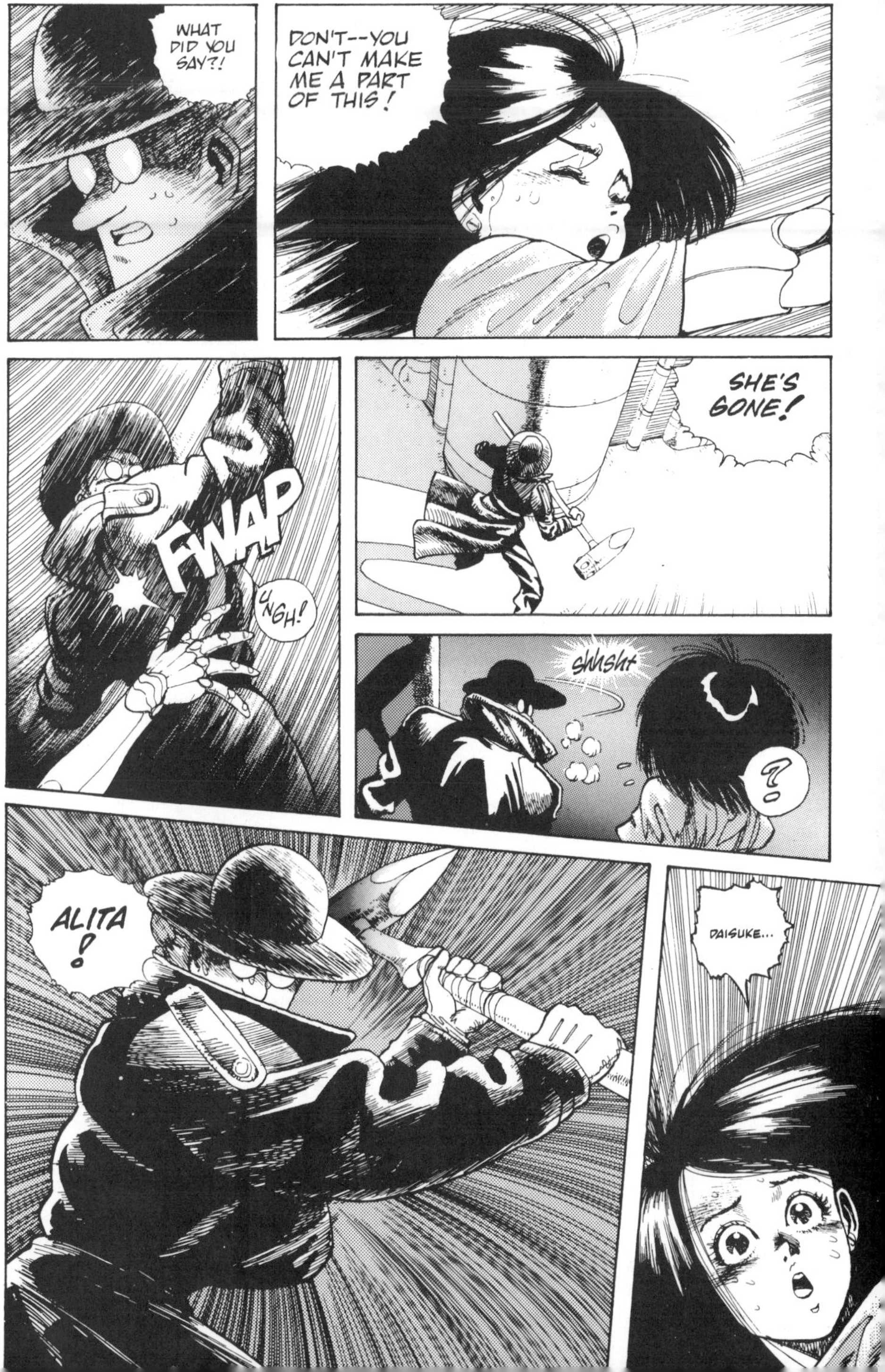
WHAT DID YOU SAY?!
DON'T--YOU CAN'T MAKE ME A PART OF THIS!
FWAP
UNGH!
SHE'S GONE!
shhsht
?
ALITA!
DAISUKE...

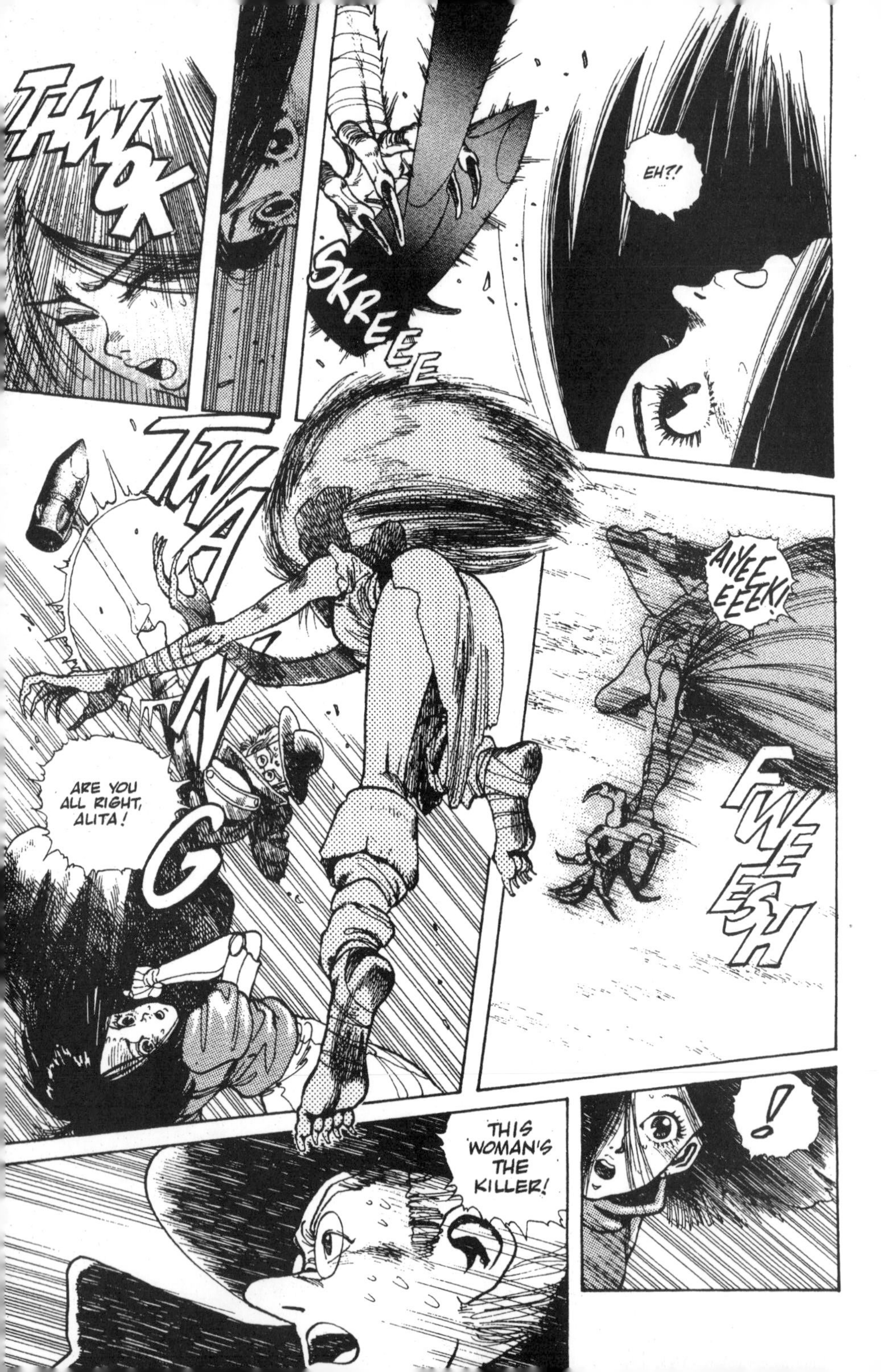
THWOK
SKREEEE
EH?!
TWAANNG
ARE YOU ALL RIGHT, ALITA!
AIYEEEEEK!
FWEESH
THIS WOMAN'S THE KILLER!
!

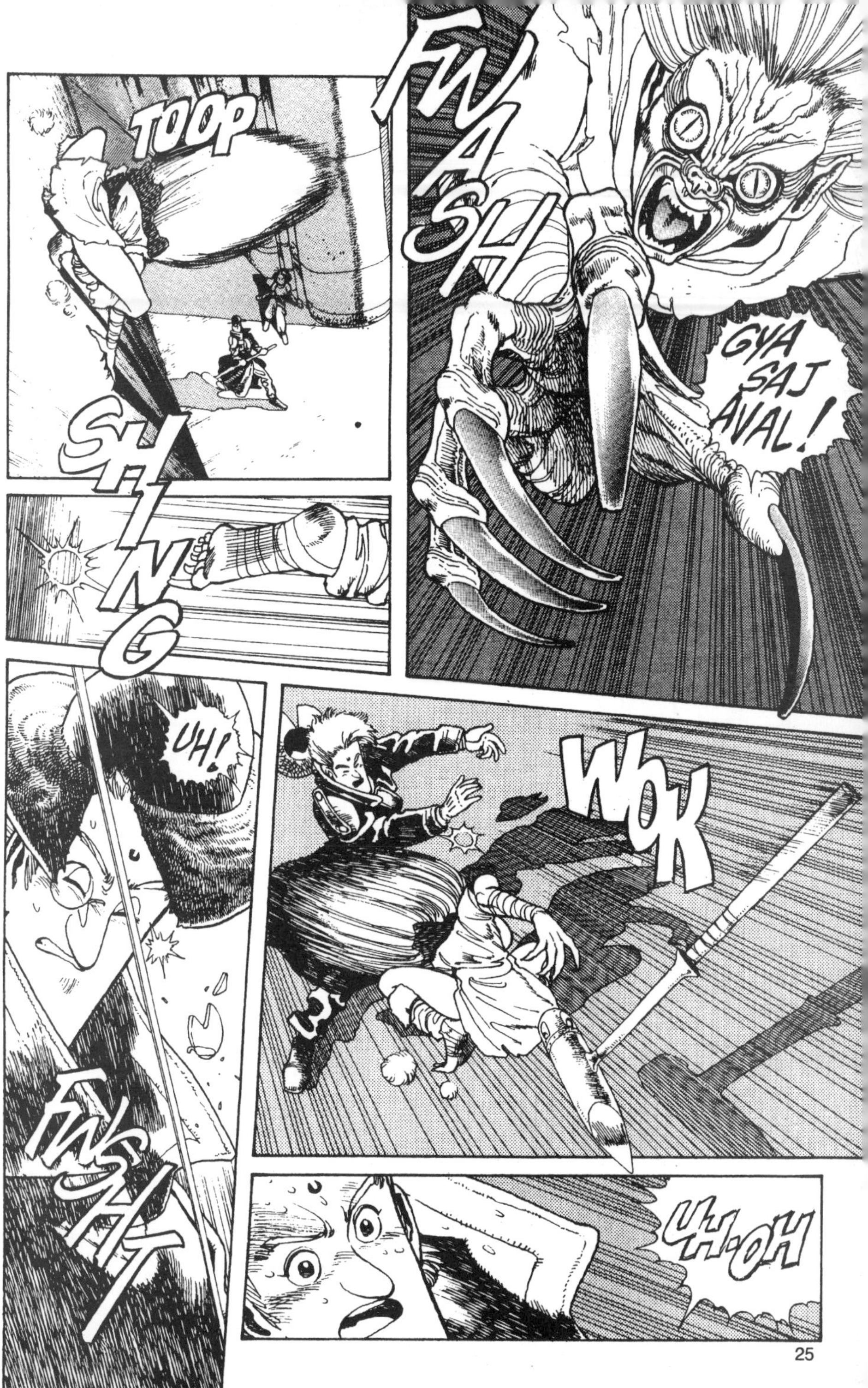
TOOP
SHING
FWASH
GYA SAJ AVAL!
UH!
FWSHT
WOK
UH-OH

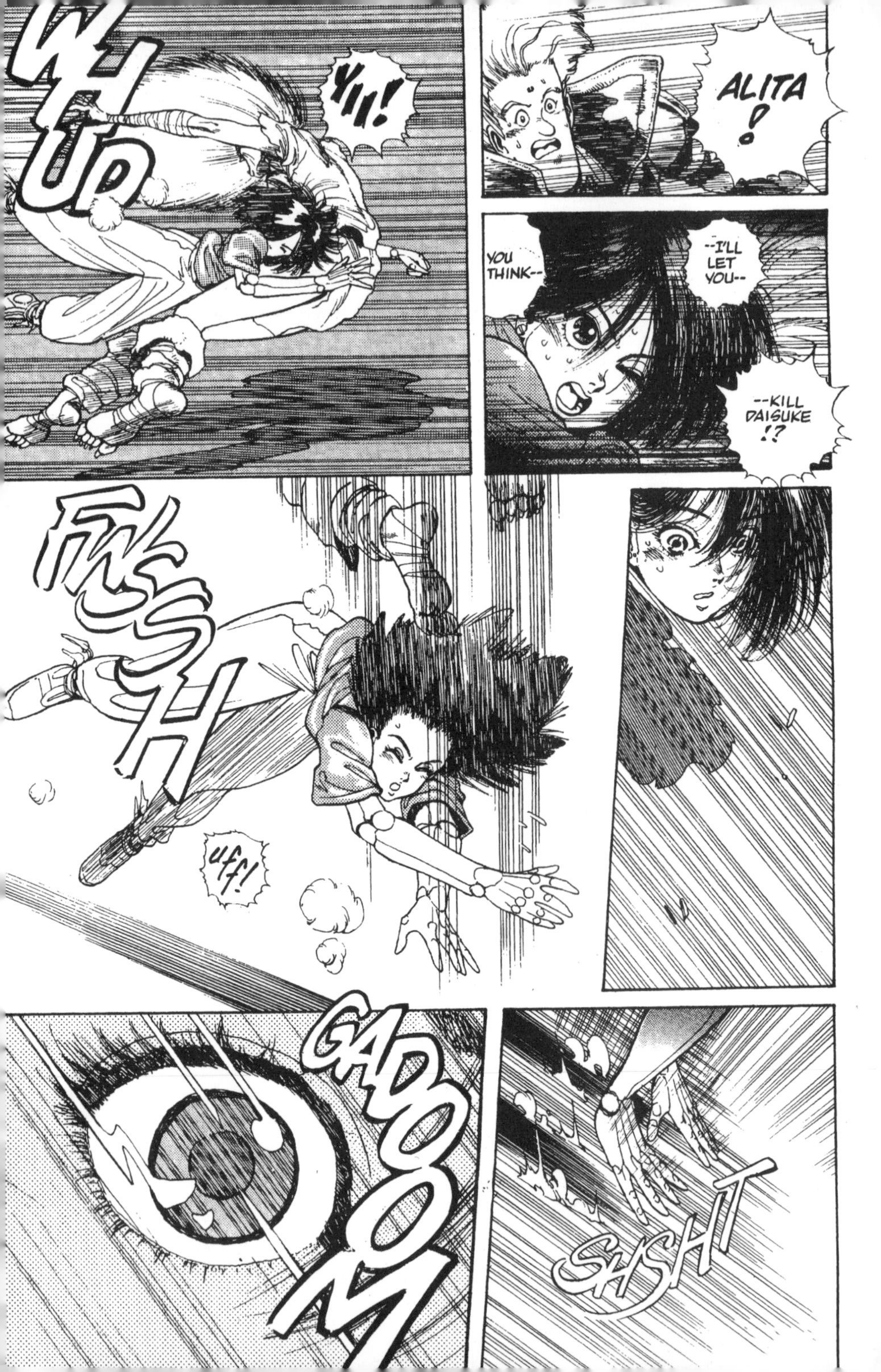
WHUD
YIII!
ALITA!
YOU THINK--
--I'LL LET YOU--
--KILL DAISUKE!?
FWSSH
uff!
GADOOOM
SHSHT

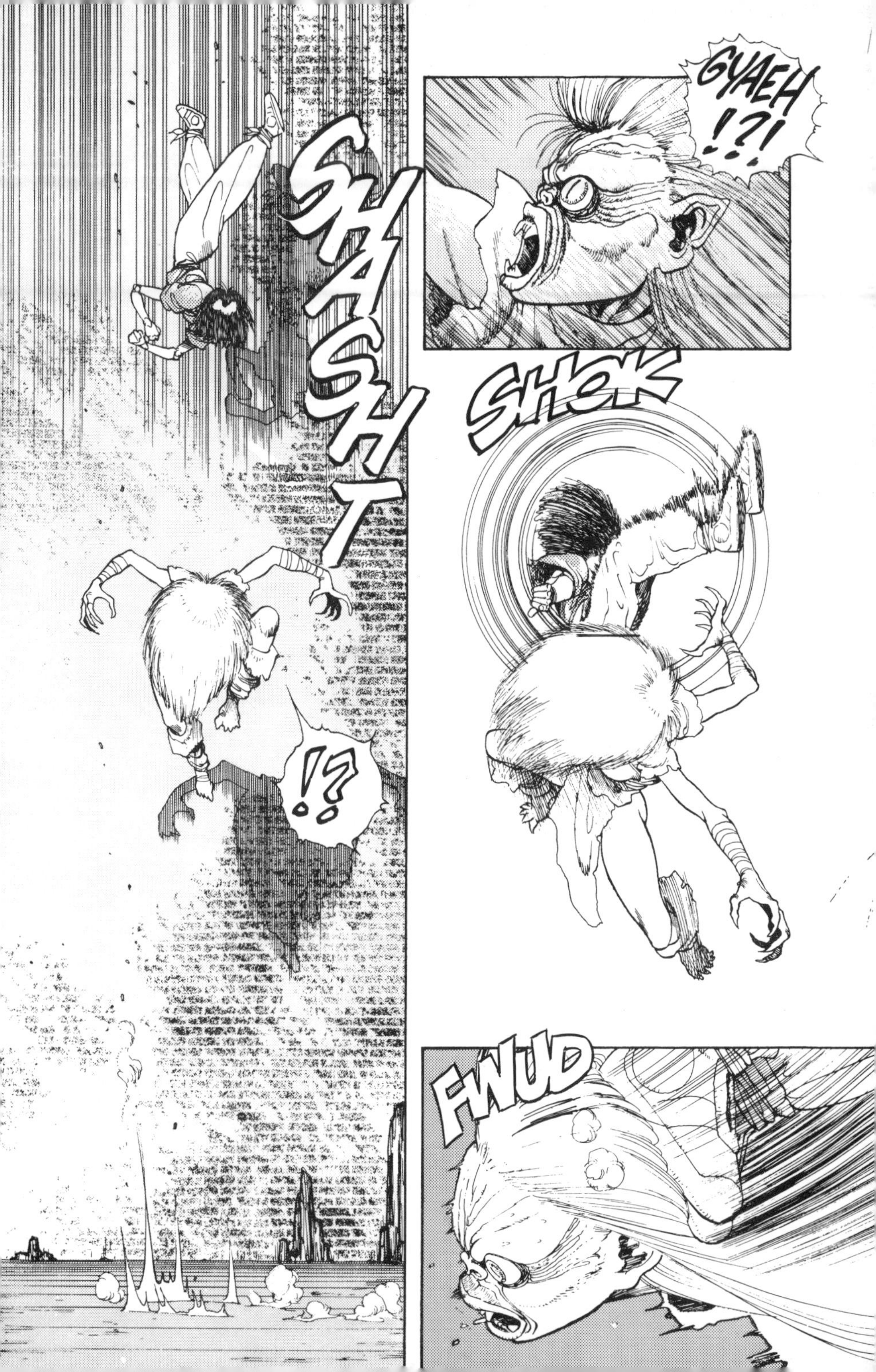
SHASHT
!?
GYAEH!?!
SHOK
FWUD

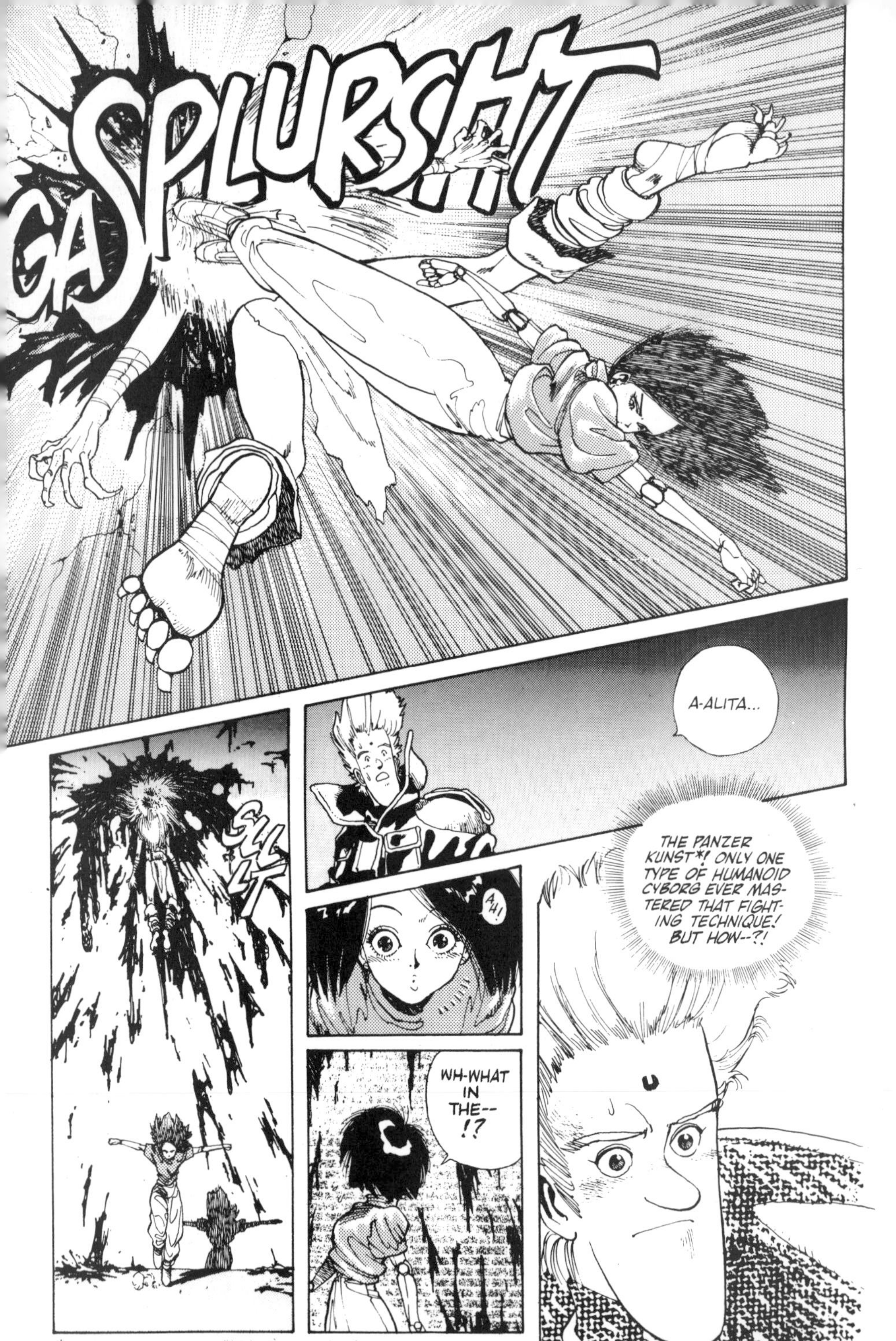
GASPLURSHT
A-ALITA...
AH!
WH-WHAT IN THE--!?
THE PANZER KUNST*! ONLY ONE TYPE OF HUMANOID CYBORG EVER MASTERED THAT FIGHTING TECHNIQUE! BUT HOW--?!

*PANZER KUNST, OR THE "ARMORED ARTS": SAID TO BE THE MOST POWERFUL OF THE VARIOUS FIGHTING TECHNIQUES DEVELOPED FOR HUMANOID CYBORGS.

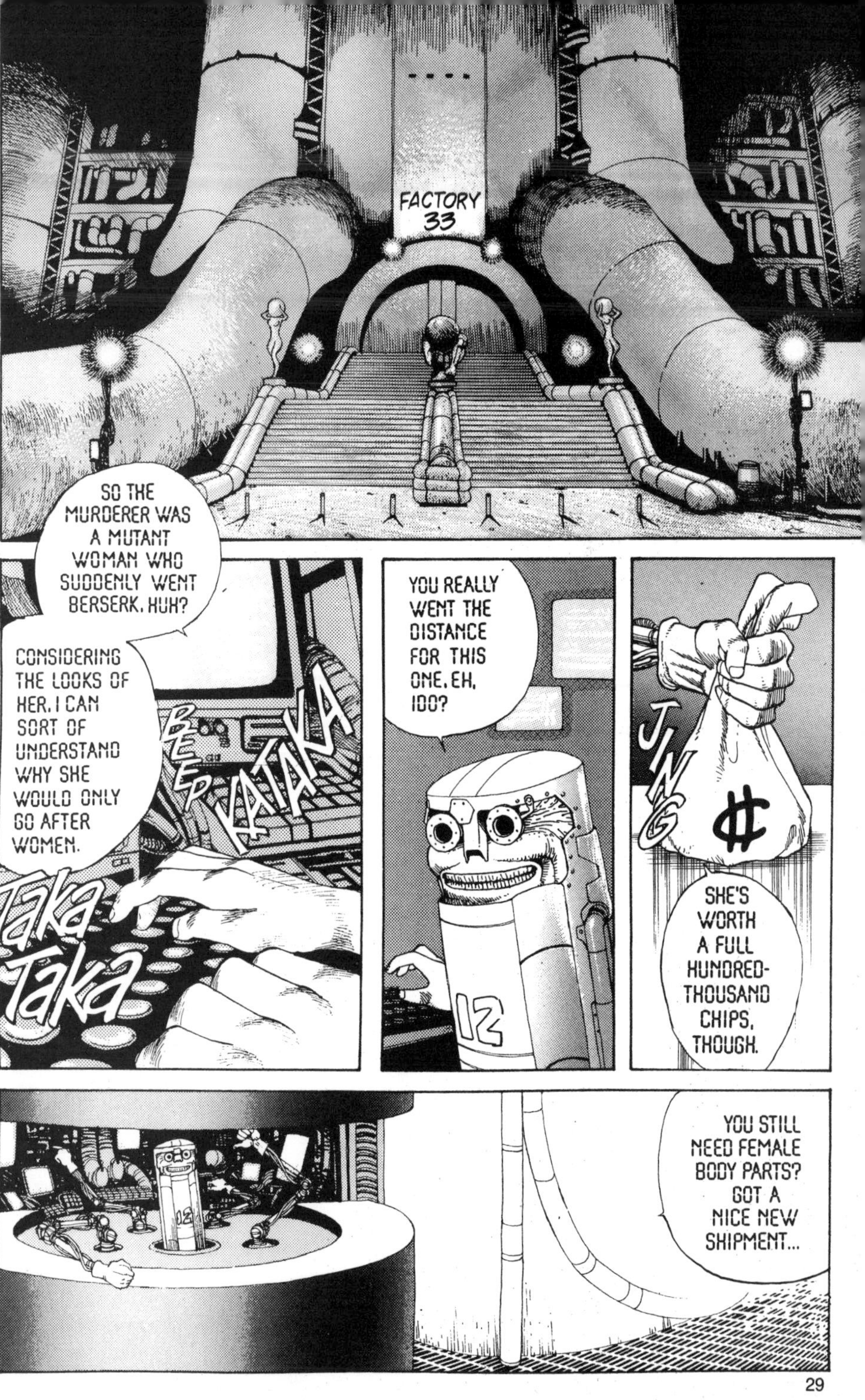
FACTORY 33
SO THE MURDERER WAS A MUTANT WOMAN WHO SUDDENLY WENT BERSERK, HUH?
CONSIDERING THE LOOKS OF HER, I CAN SORT OF UNDERSTAND WHY SHE WOULD ONLY GO AFTER WOMEN.
BEEP
KATAKA
Taka Taka
YOU REALLY WENT THE DISTANCE FOR THIS ONE, EH, IDO?
12
JING
SHE'S WORTH A FULL HUNDRED-THOUSAND CHIPS, THOUGH.
YOU STILL NEED FEMALE BODY PARTS? GOT A NICE NEW SHIPMENT...

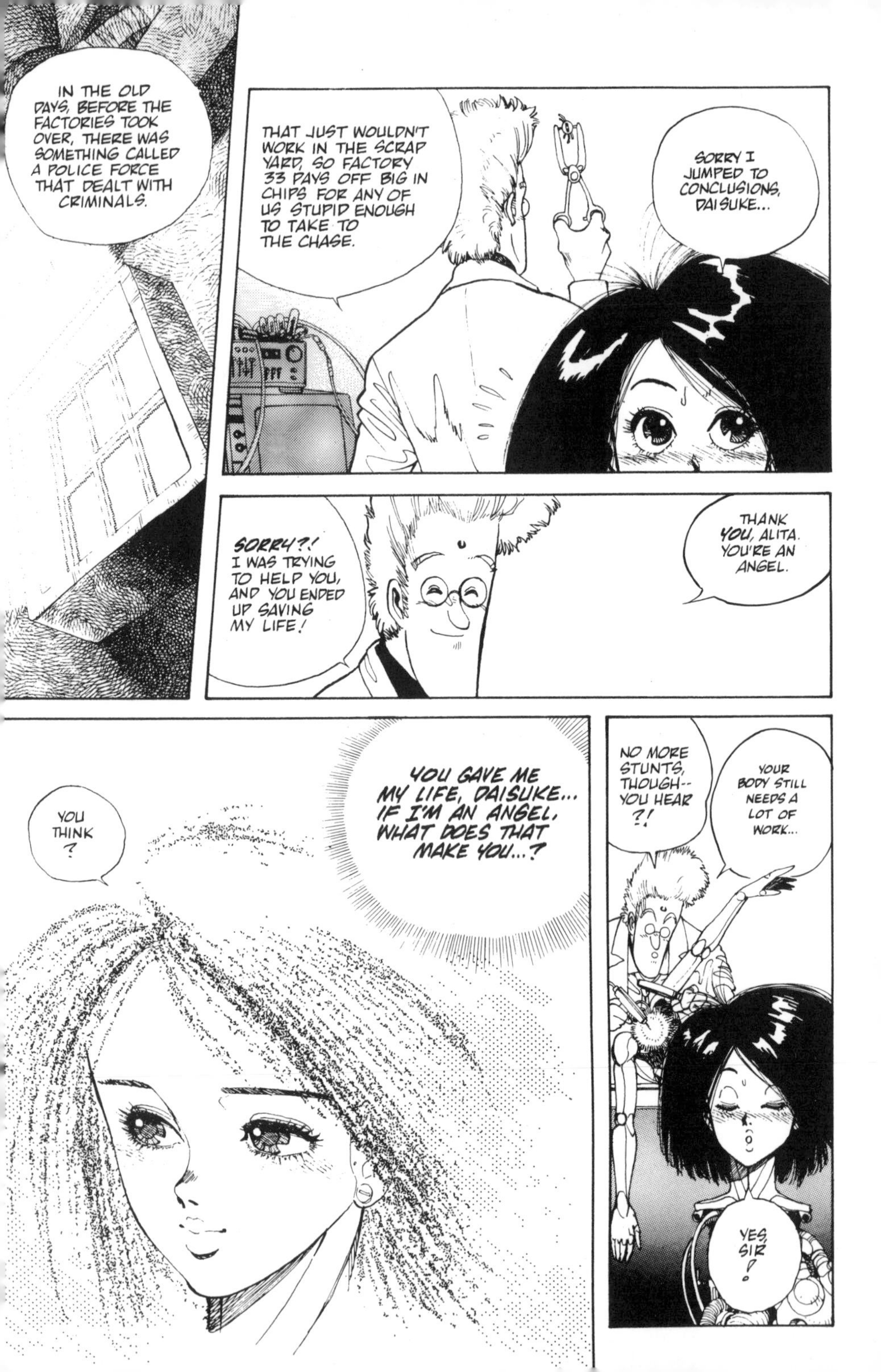
IN THE OLD DAYS, BEFORE THE FACTORIES TOOK OVER, THERE WAS SOMETHING CALLED A POLICE FORCE THAT DEALT WITH CRIMINALS.
THAT JUST WOULDN'T WORK IN THE SCRAP YARD, SO FACTORY 33 PAYS OFF BIG IN CHIPS FOR ANY OF US STUPID ENOUGH TO TAKE TO THE CHASE.
SORRY I JUMPED TO CONCLUSIONS, DAISUKE...
SORRY?! I WAS TRYING TO HELP YOU, AND YOU ENDED UP SAVING MY LIFE!
THANK YOU, ALITA. YOU'RE AN ANGEL.
YOU THINK?
YOU GAVE ME MY LIFE, DAISUKE... IF I'M AN ANGEL, WHAT DOES THAT MAKE YOU...?
NO MORE STUNTS, THOUGH-- YOU HEAR?!
YOUR BODY STILL NEEDS A LOT OF WORK...
YES, SIR!

FIGHTING BLOOD
Battle 2: Awakening

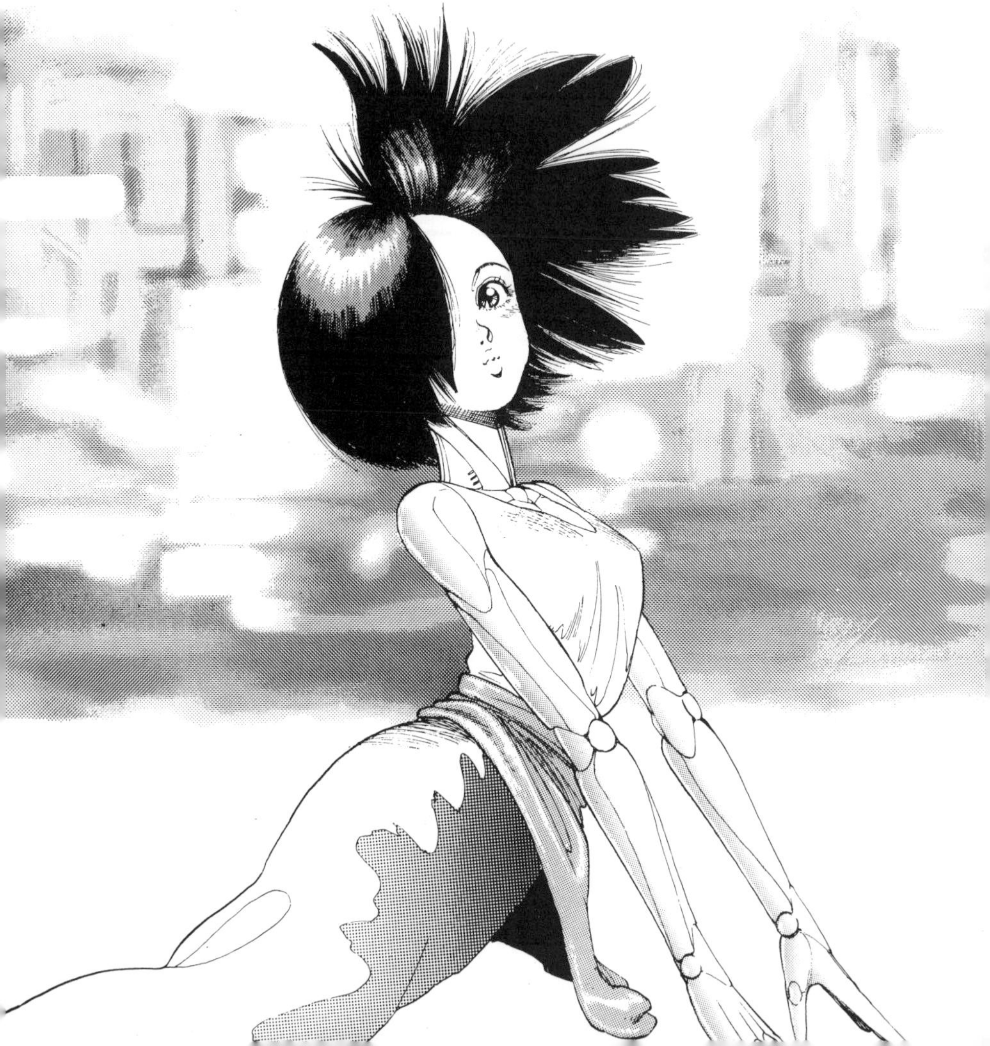

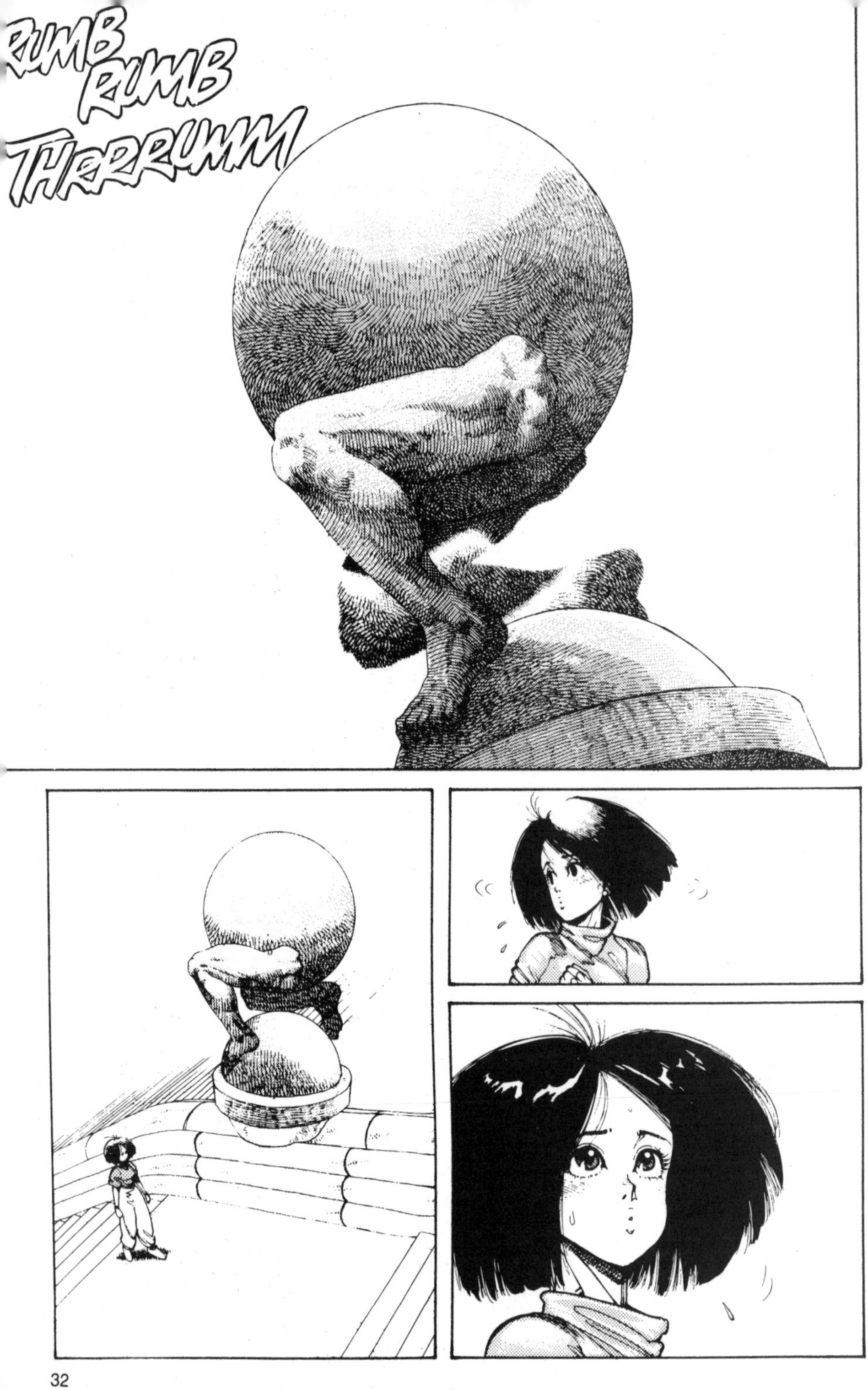
RUMB RUMB THRRRUMM

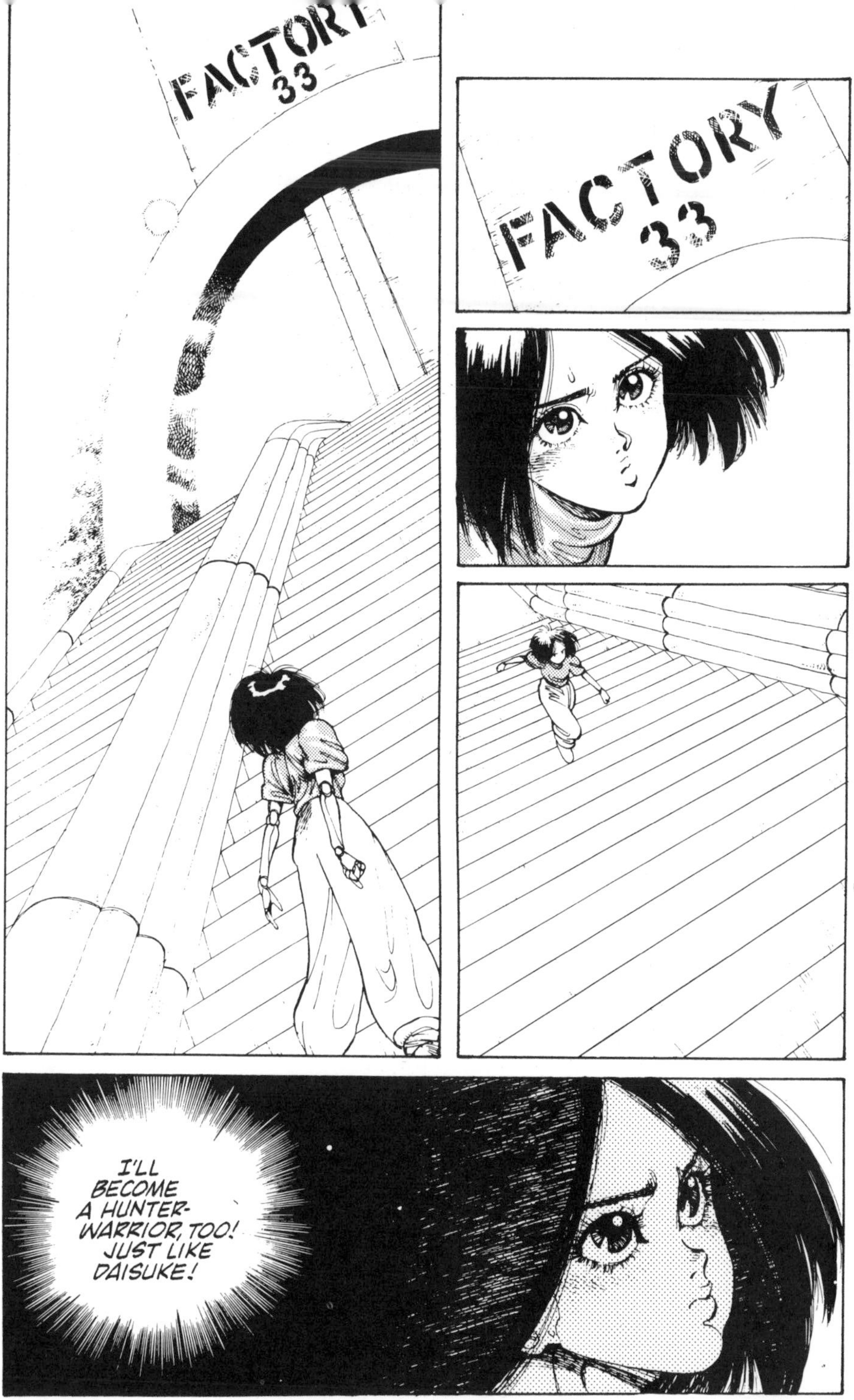
FACTORY 33
FACTORY 33
I'LL BECOME A HUNTER-WARRIOR, TOO! JUST LIKE DAISUKE!

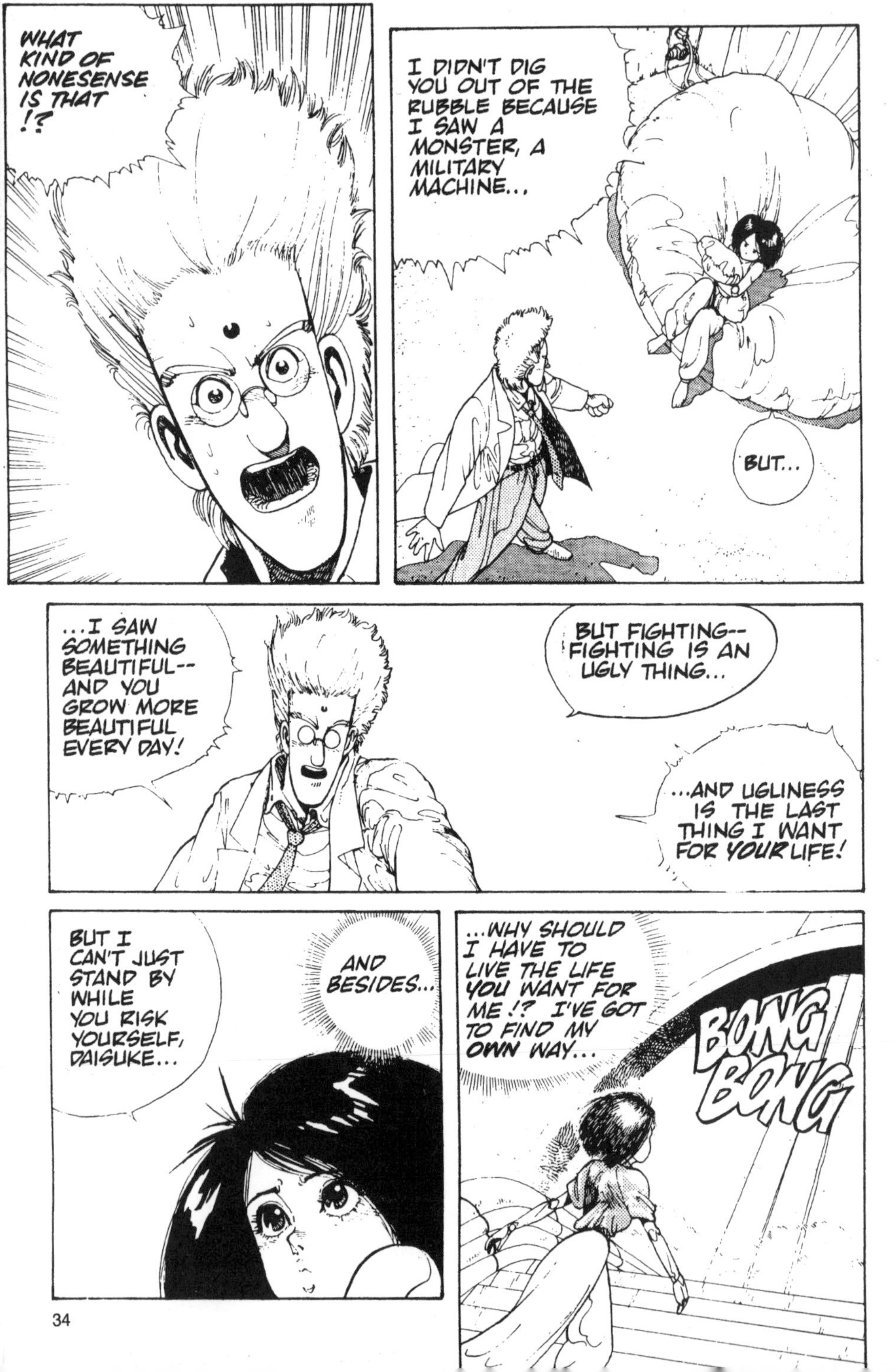
WHAT KIND OF NONESENSE IS THAT !?
I DIDN'T DIG YOU OUT OF THE RUBBLE BECAUSE I SAW A MONSTER, A MILITARY MACHINE...
BUT...
...I SAW SOMETHING BEAUTIFUL-- AND YOU GROW MORE BEAUTIFUL EVERY DAY!
BUT FIGHTING-- FIGHTING IS AN UGLY THING...
...AND UGLINESS IS THE LAST THING I WANT FOR YOUR LIFE!
BUT I CAN'T JUST STAND BY WHILE YOU RISK YOURSELF, DAISUKE...
AND BESIDES...
...WHY SHOULD I HAVE TO LIVE THE LIFE YOU WANT FOR ME !? I'VE GOT TO FIND MY OWN WAY...
BONG
BONG

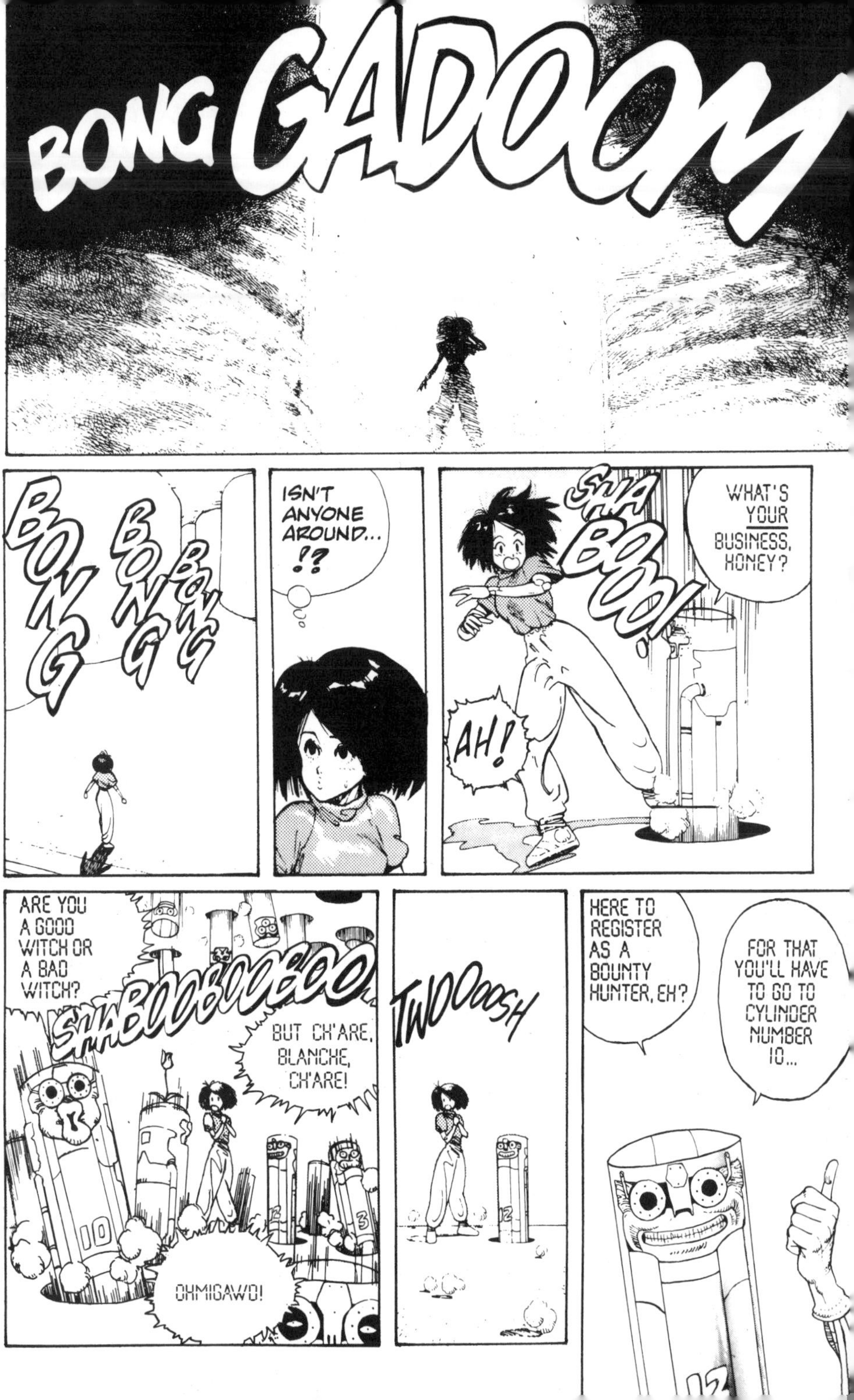
BONG GADOOM
BONG BONG BONG
ISN'T ANYONE AROUND... !?
SHA BOOO!
WHAT'S YOUR BUSINESS, HONEY?
AH!
ARE YOU A GOOD WITCH OR A BAD WITCH?
SHABOOBOOBOO
BUT CH'ARE, BLANCHE, CH'ARE!
OHMIGAWD!
TWOOOOSH
HERE TO REGISTER AS A BOUNTY HUNTER, EH?
FOR THAT YOU'LL HAVE TO GO TO CYLINDER NUMBER 10...

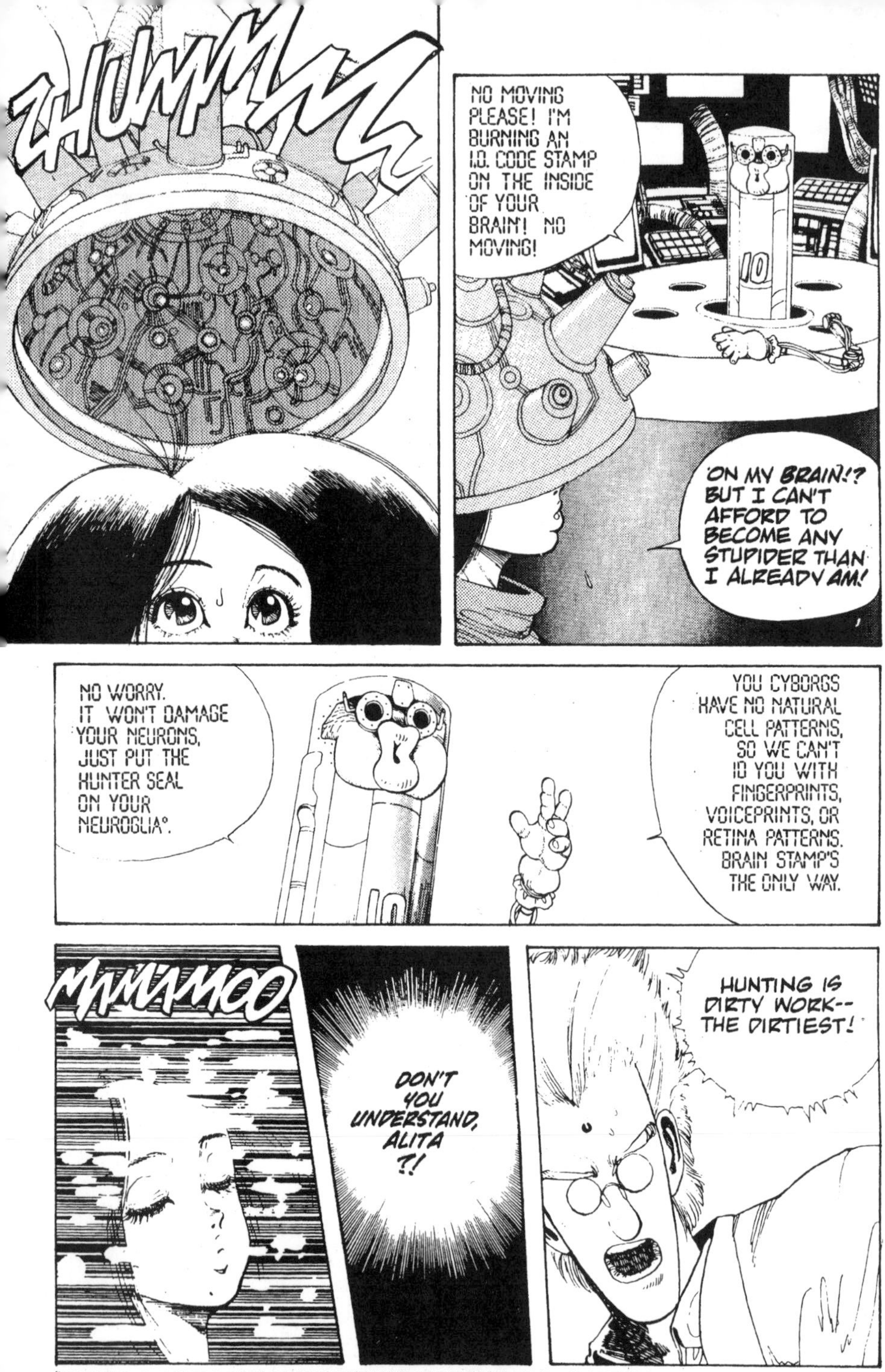
ZHUMMM
NO MOVING PLEASE! I'M BURNING AN I.D. CODE STAMP ON THE INSIDE OF YOUR BRAIN! NO MOVING!
10
ON MY BRAIN!? BUT I CAN'T AFFORD TO BECOME ANY STUPIDER THAN I ALREADY AM!
NO WORRY. IT WON'T DAMAGE YOUR NEURONS, JUST PUT THE HUNTER SEAL ON YOUR NEUROGLIA*.
YOU CYBORGS HAVE NO NATURAL CELL PATTERNS, SO WE CAN'T ID YOU WITH FINGERPRINTS, VOICEPRINTS, OR RETINA PATTERNS. BRAIN STAMP'S THE ONLY WAY.
MMMMOO
DON'T YOU UNDERSTAND, ALITA ?!
HUNTING IS DIRTY WORK-- THE DIRTIEST!

*NEUROGLIA: OF THE TWO TYPES OF CELLS THAT MAKE UP THE BRAIN, NEURONS OCCUPY A MERE 2.85% OF THE VOLUME, WITH THE GREATER PART BEING FILLED UP BY THE GLUE-LIKE NEUROGLIA.

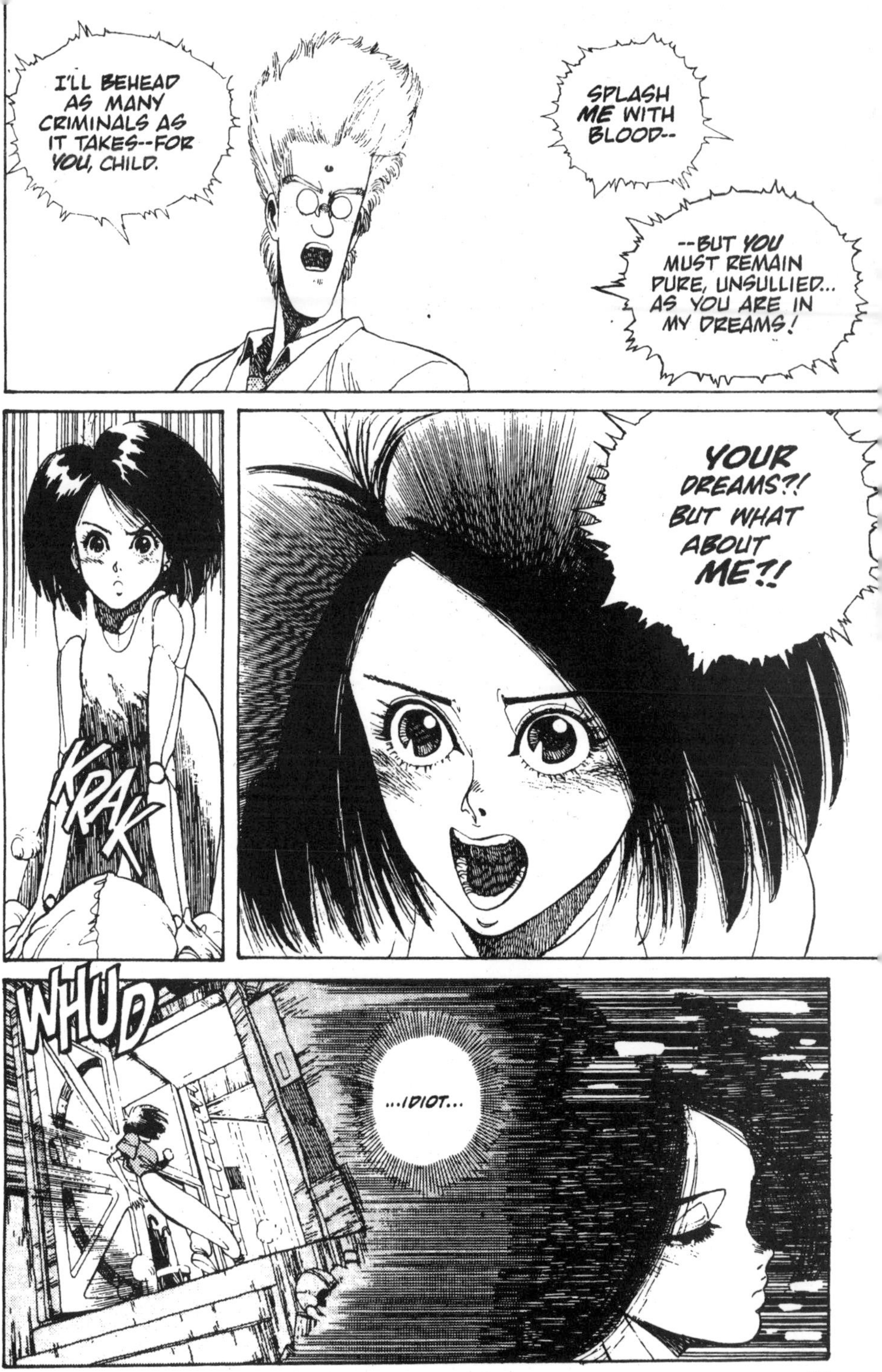
I'LL BEHEAD AS MANY CRIMINALS AS IT TAKES--FOR YOU, CHILD.
SPLASH ME WITH BLOOD--
--BUT YOU MUST REMAIN PURE, UNSULLIED... AS YOU ARE IN MY DREAMS!
KRAK
YOUR DREAMS?! BUT WHAT ABOUT ME?!
WHUD
...IDIOT...

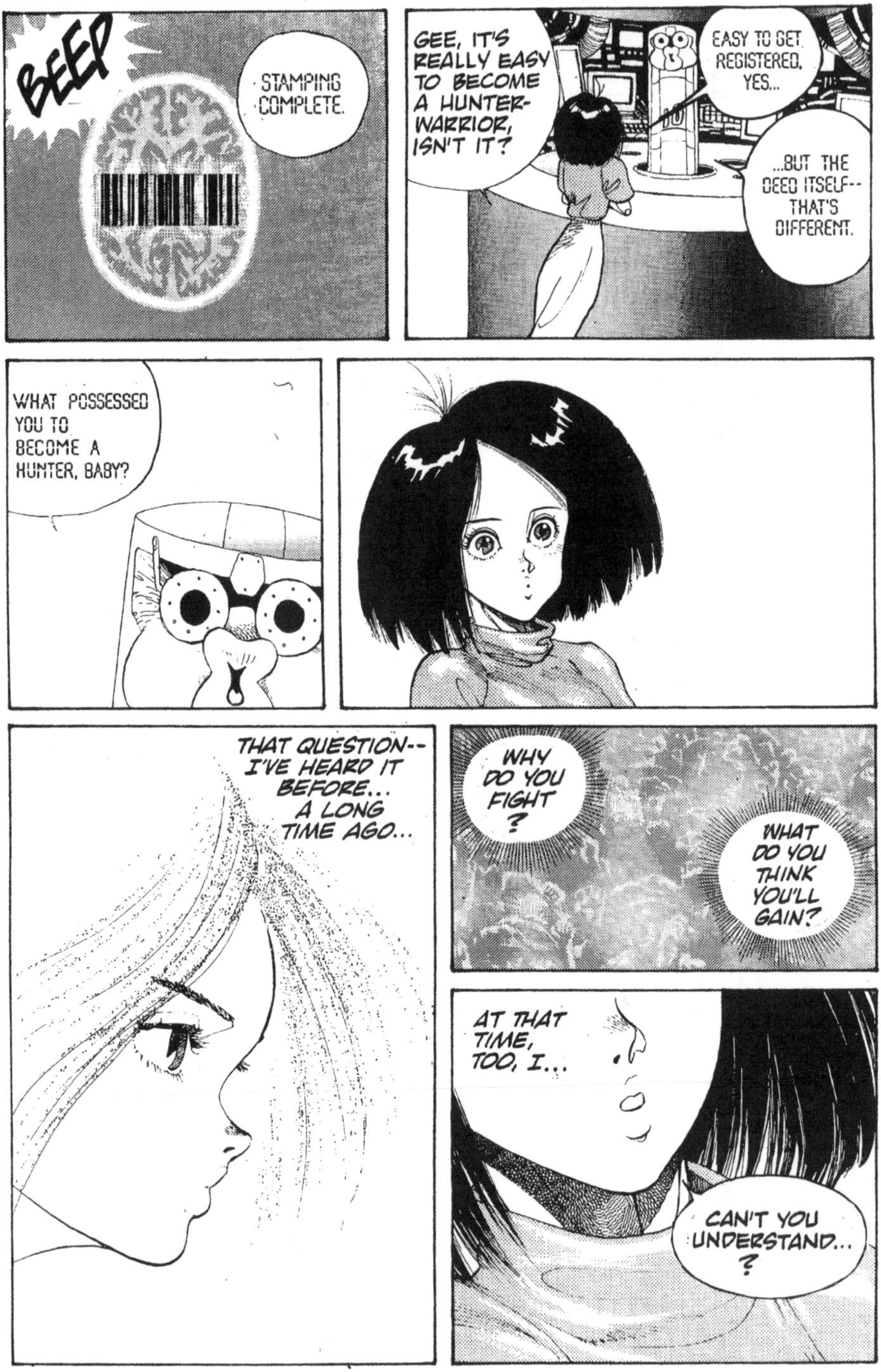
BEEP
STAMPING COMPLETE.
GEE, IT'S REALLY EASY TO BECOME A HUNTER-WARRIOR, ISN'T IT?
EASY TO GET REGISTERED, YES...
...BUT THE DEED ITSELF-- THAT'S DIFFERENT.
WHAT POSSESSED YOU TO BECOME A HUNTER, BABY?
THAT QUESTION-- I'VE HEARD IT BEFORE... A LONG TIME AGO...
WHY DO YOU FIGHT ?
WHAT DO YOU THINK YOU'LL GAIN?
AT THAT TIME, TOO, I...
CAN'T YOU UNDERSTAND... ?

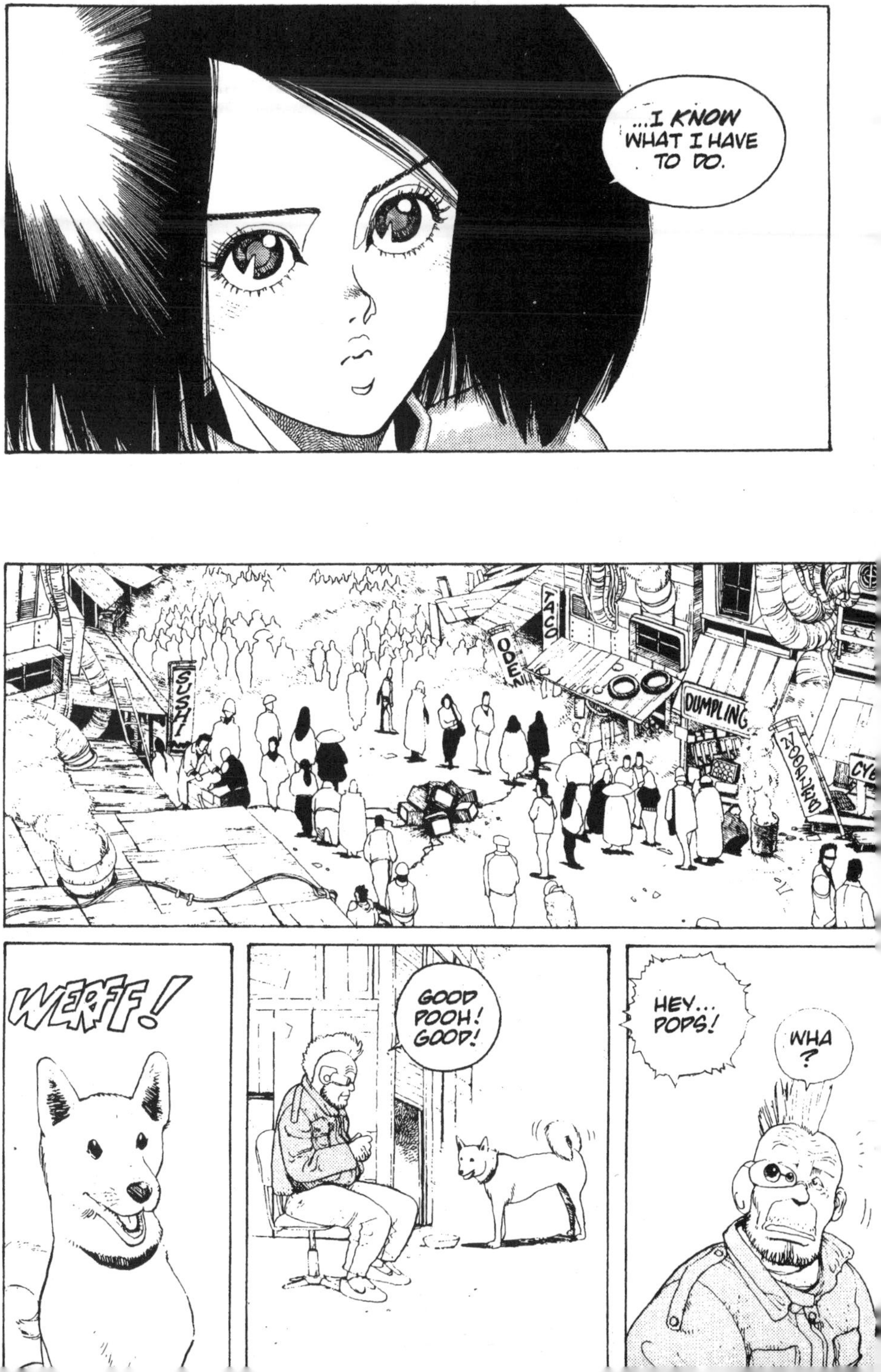
...I KNOW WHAT I HAVE TO DO.
SUSHI
TACO
ODEN
DUMPLING
WERFF!
GOOD POOH! GOOD!
HEY... POPS!
WHA?

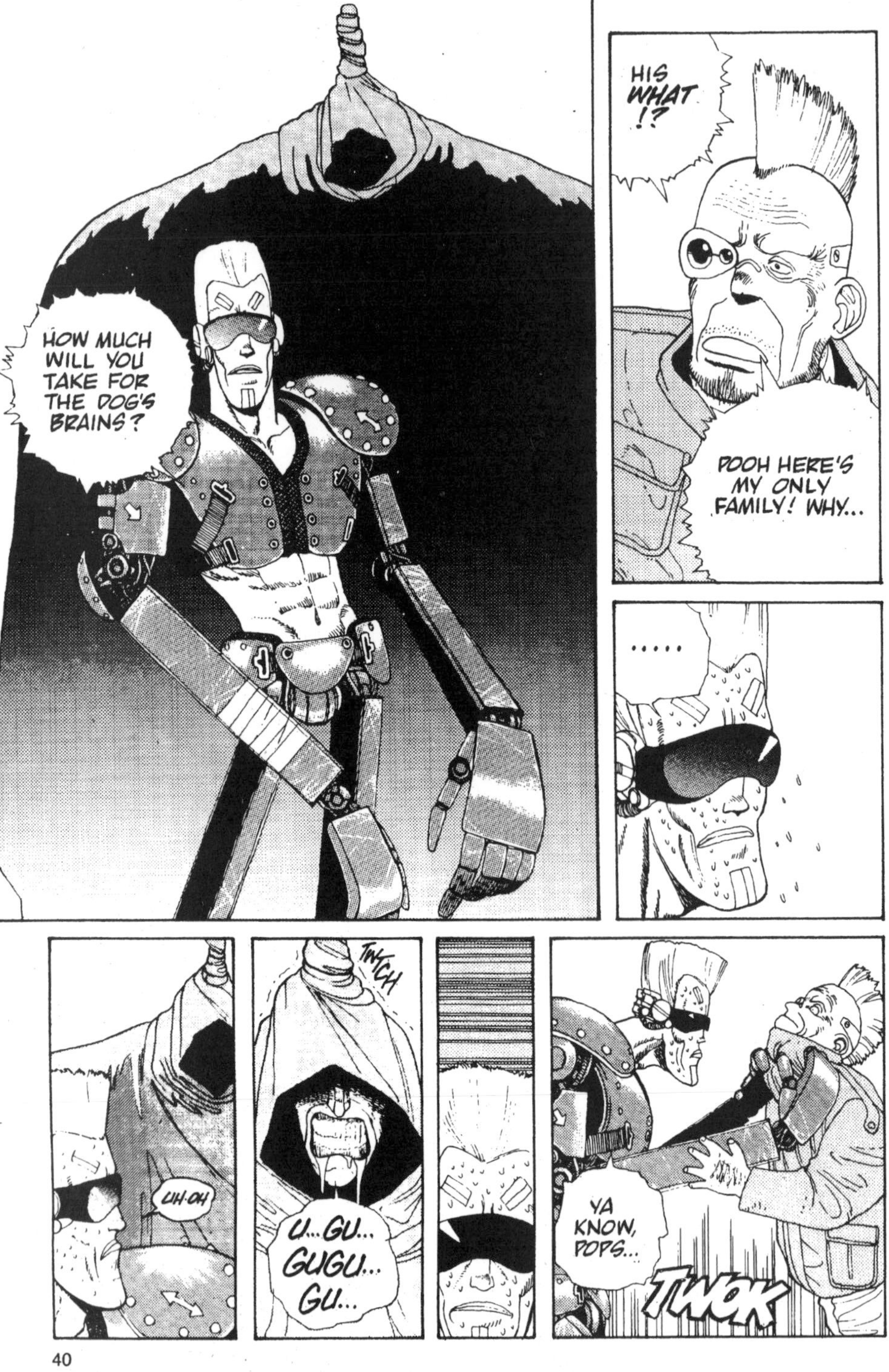
HOW MUCH WILL YOU TAKE FOR THE DOG'S BRAINS?
HIS WHAT !?
POOH HERE'S MY ONLY FAMILY! WHY...
.....
UH-OH
TWITCH
U...GU... GUGU... GU...
YA KNOW, POPS...
TWOK

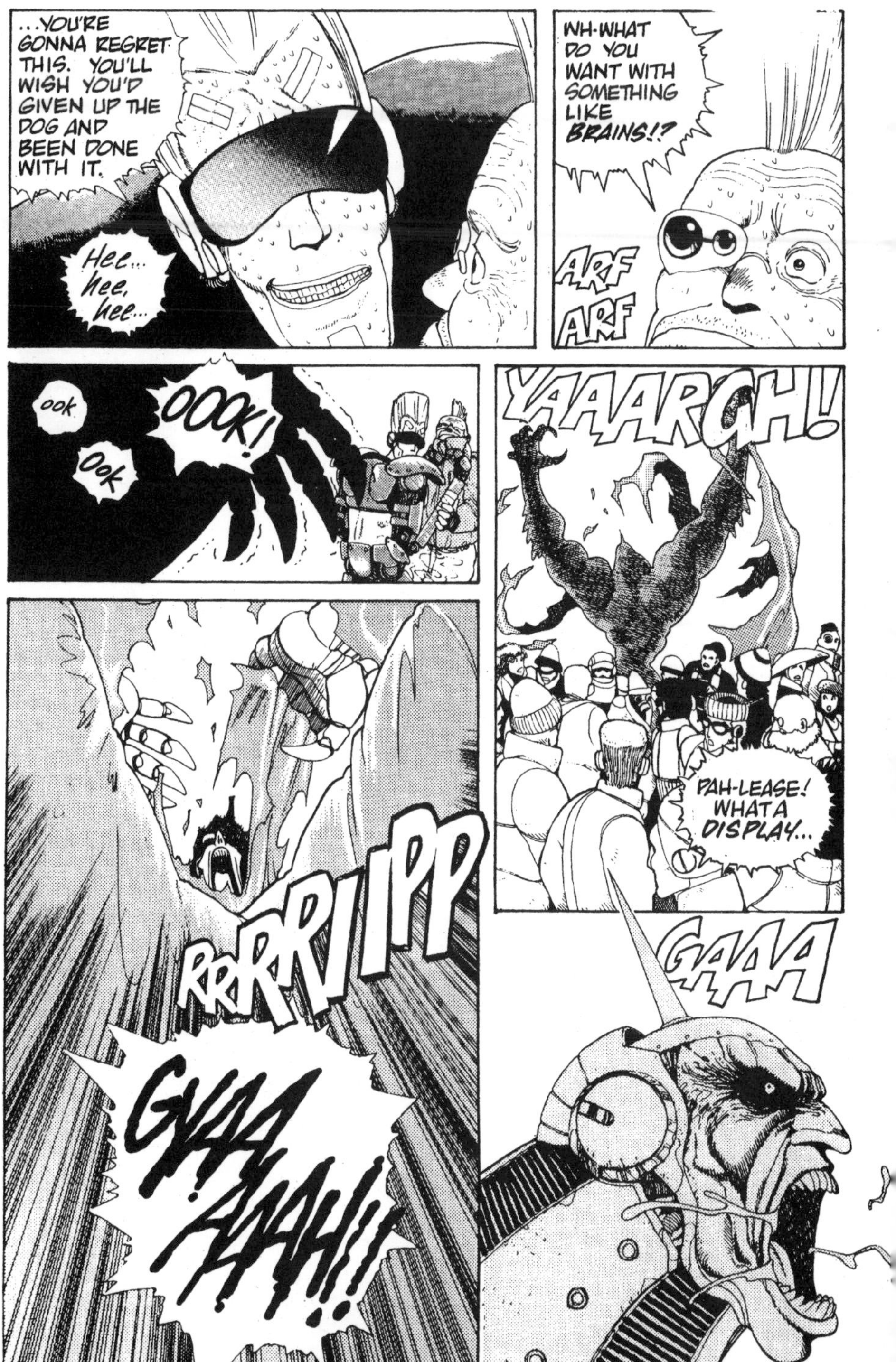
...YOU'RE GONNA REGRET THIS. YOU'LL WISH YOU'D GIVEN UP THE DOG AND BEEN DONE WITH IT.
Hee... hee, hee...
WH-WHAT DO YOU WANT WITH SOMETHING LIKE BRAINS!?
ARF ARF
ook
OOOK!
Ook
YAAARGH!
PAH-LEASE! WHATA DISPLAY...
RRRRIIPP
GAAA
GUAA AAAH!!

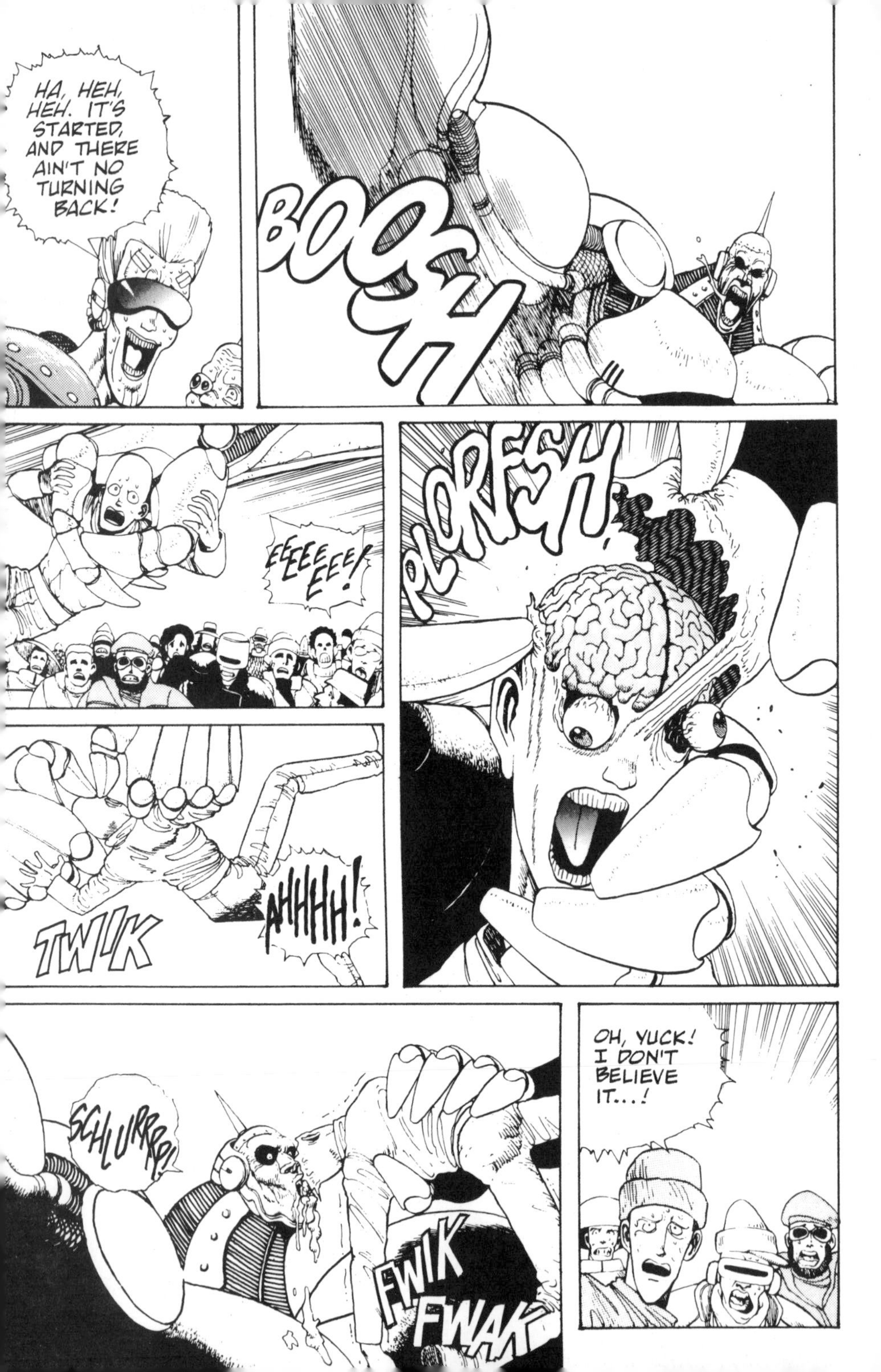
HA, HEH, HEH. IT'S STARTED, AND THERE AIN'T NO TURNING BACK!
BOOOSH
EEEEEEE!
PLORFSH
TWIK
AHHHH!
SCHLURRRP!
FWIK
FWAK
OH, YUCK! I DON'T BELIEVE IT...!

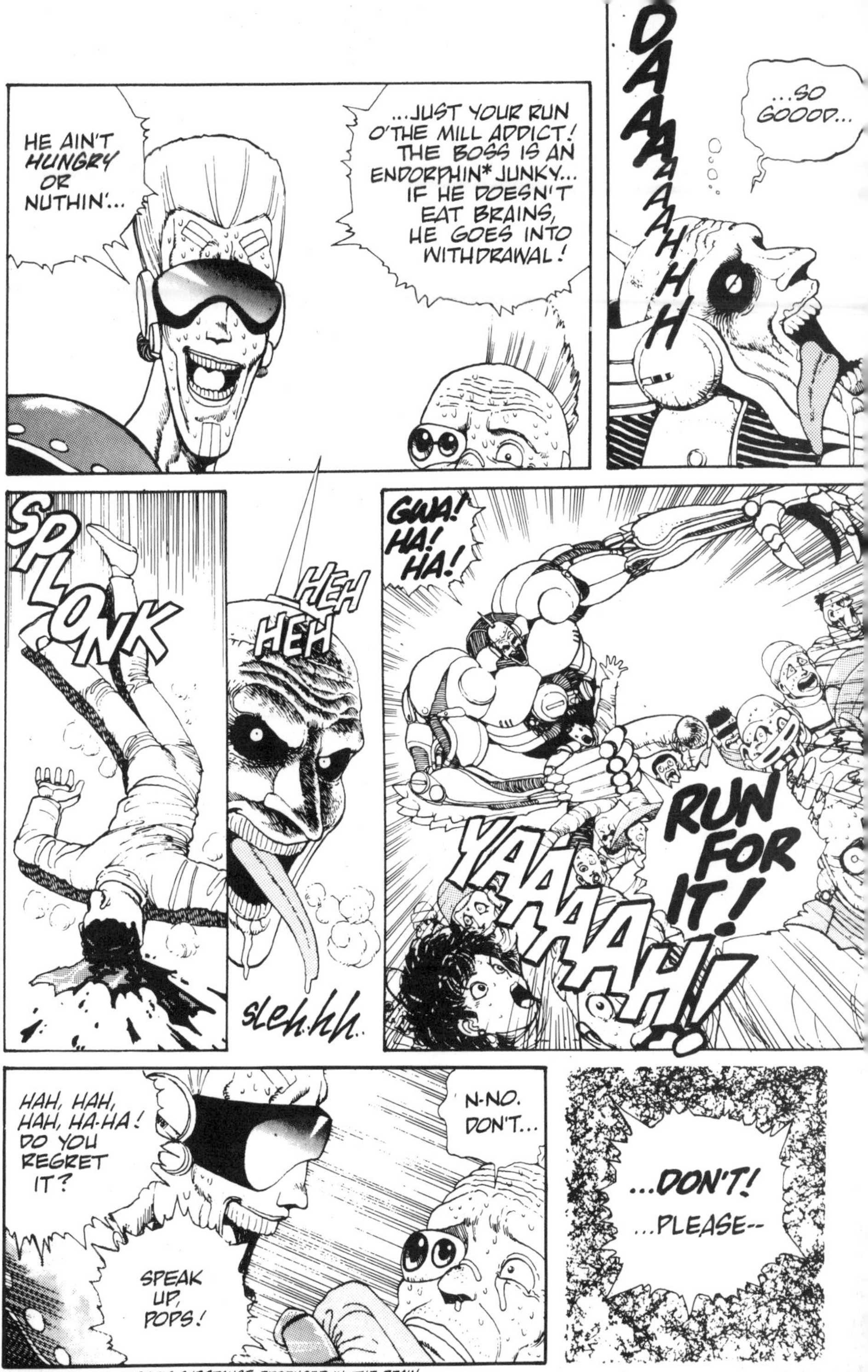
HE AIN'T HUNGRY OR NUTHIN'...
...JUST YOUR RUN O'THE MILL ADDICT! THE BOSS IS AN ENDORPHIN* JUNKY... IF HE DOESN'T EAT BRAINS, HE GOES INTO WITHDRAWAL!
OAAAAAAHHH
...SO GOOOD...
SPLONK
HEH HEH
sleh.hh..
GWA! HA! HA!
YAAAAAH!
RUN FOR IT!
HAH, HAH, HAH, HA-HA! DO YOU REGRET IT?
SPEAK UP, POPS!
N-NO. DON'T...
...DON'T!
...PLEASE--

*ENDORPHIN: A NARCOTIC SUBSTANCE PRODUCED IN THE BRAIN. ENDORPHIN MEANS LITERALLY "MORPHINE MADE INSIDE THE BODY." BETA ENDORPHINS HAVE A PAIN-RELIEVING EFFECT 6.5 TIMES THAT OF MORPHINE.

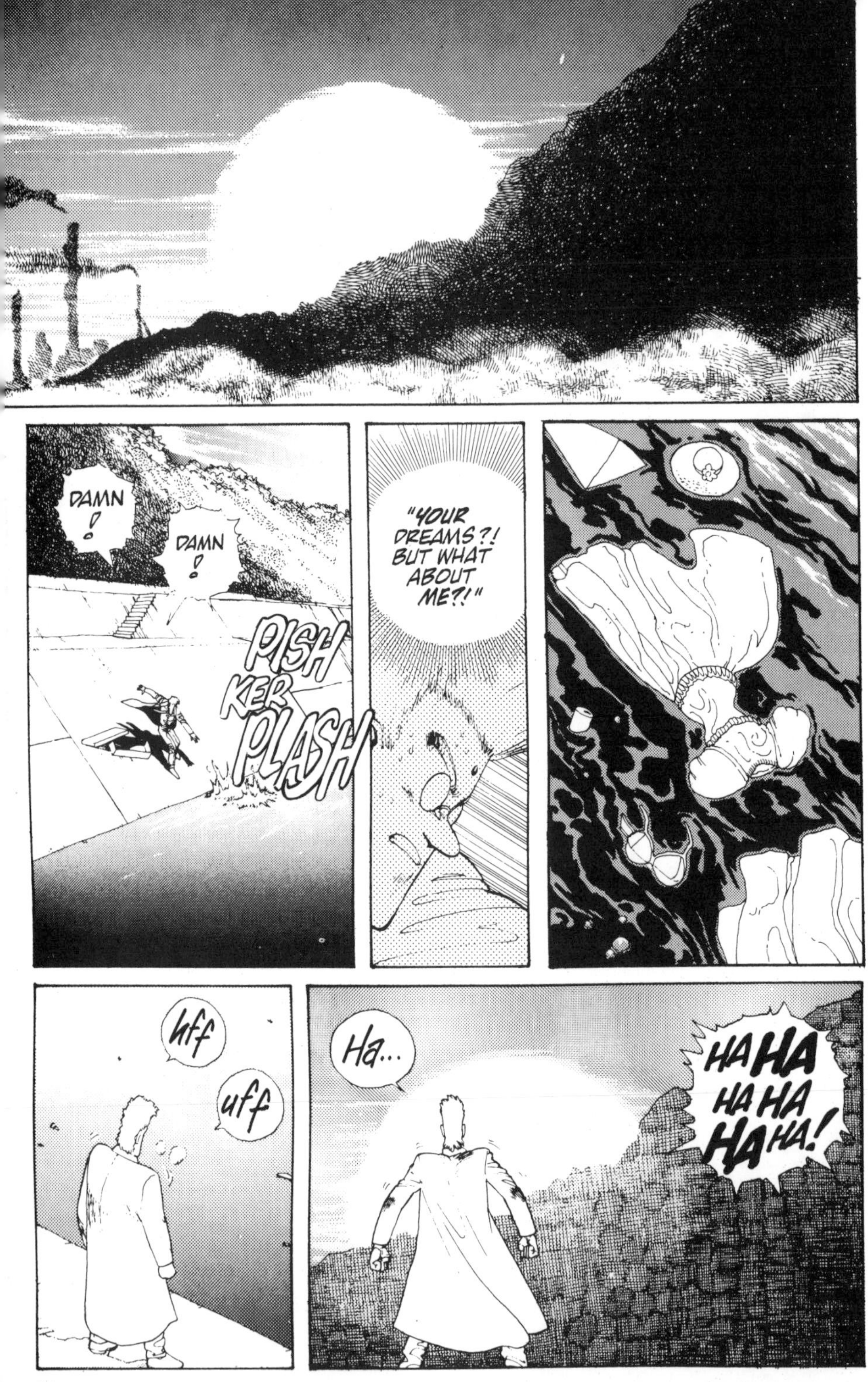

DAMN!
DAMN!
PISH KER PLASH
"YOUR DREAMS?! BUT WHAT ABOUT ME?!"
uff
uff
Ha...
HA HA HA HA HA HA HA!

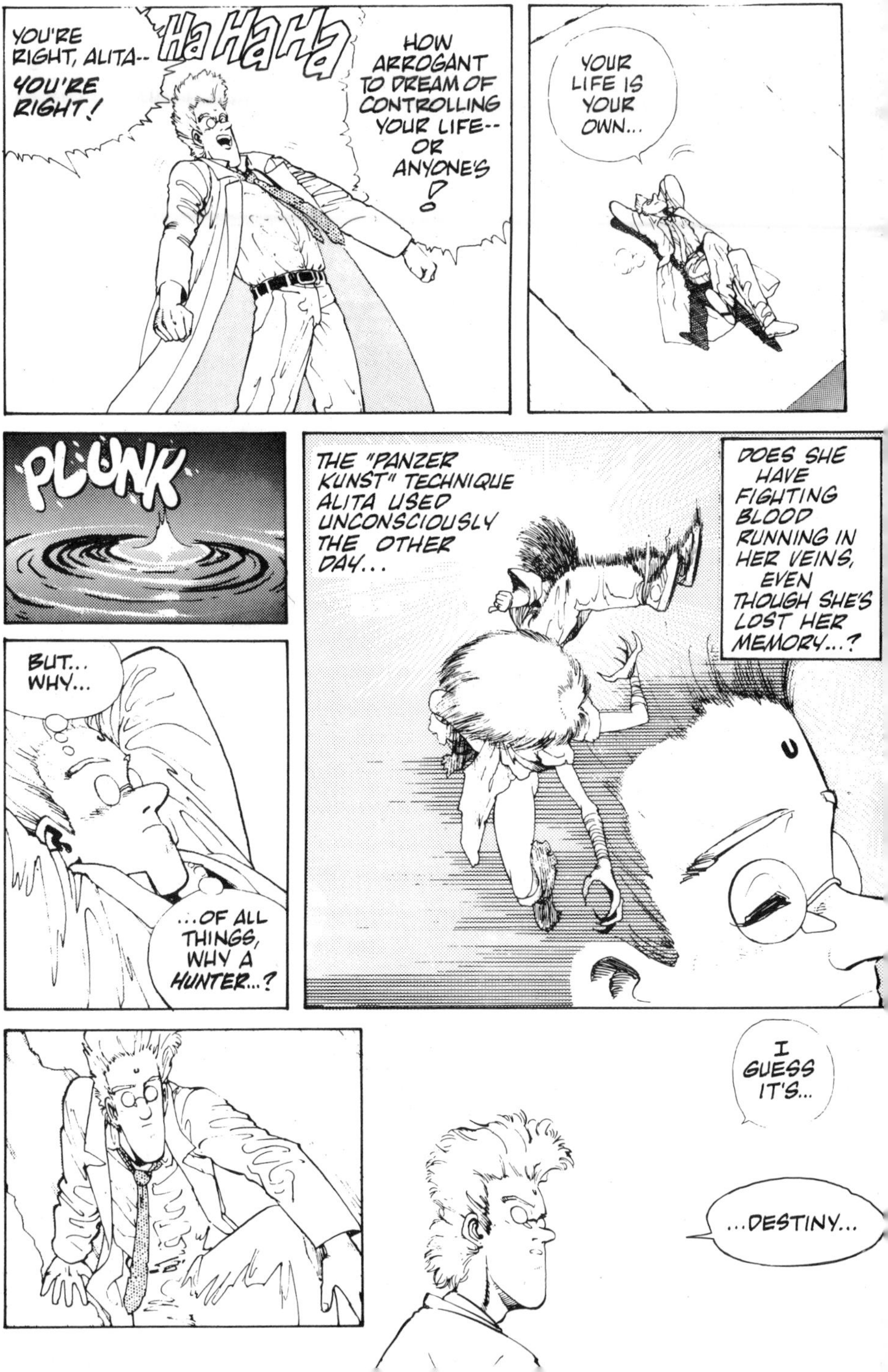
YOU'RE RIGHT, ALITA-- YOU'RE RIGHT!
Ha Ha Ha Ha
HOW ARROGANT TO DREAM OF CONTROLLING YOUR LIFE-- OR ANYONE'S!
YOUR LIFE IS YOUR OWN...
PLUNK
BUT... WHY...
...OF ALL THINGS, WHY A HUNTER...?
THE "PANZER KUNST" TECHNIQUE ALITA USED UNCONSCIOUSLY THE OTHER DAY...
DOES SHE HAVE FIGHTING BLOOD RUNNING IN HER VEINS, EVEN THOUGH SHE'S LOST HER MEMORY...?
I GUESS IT'S...
...DESTINY...

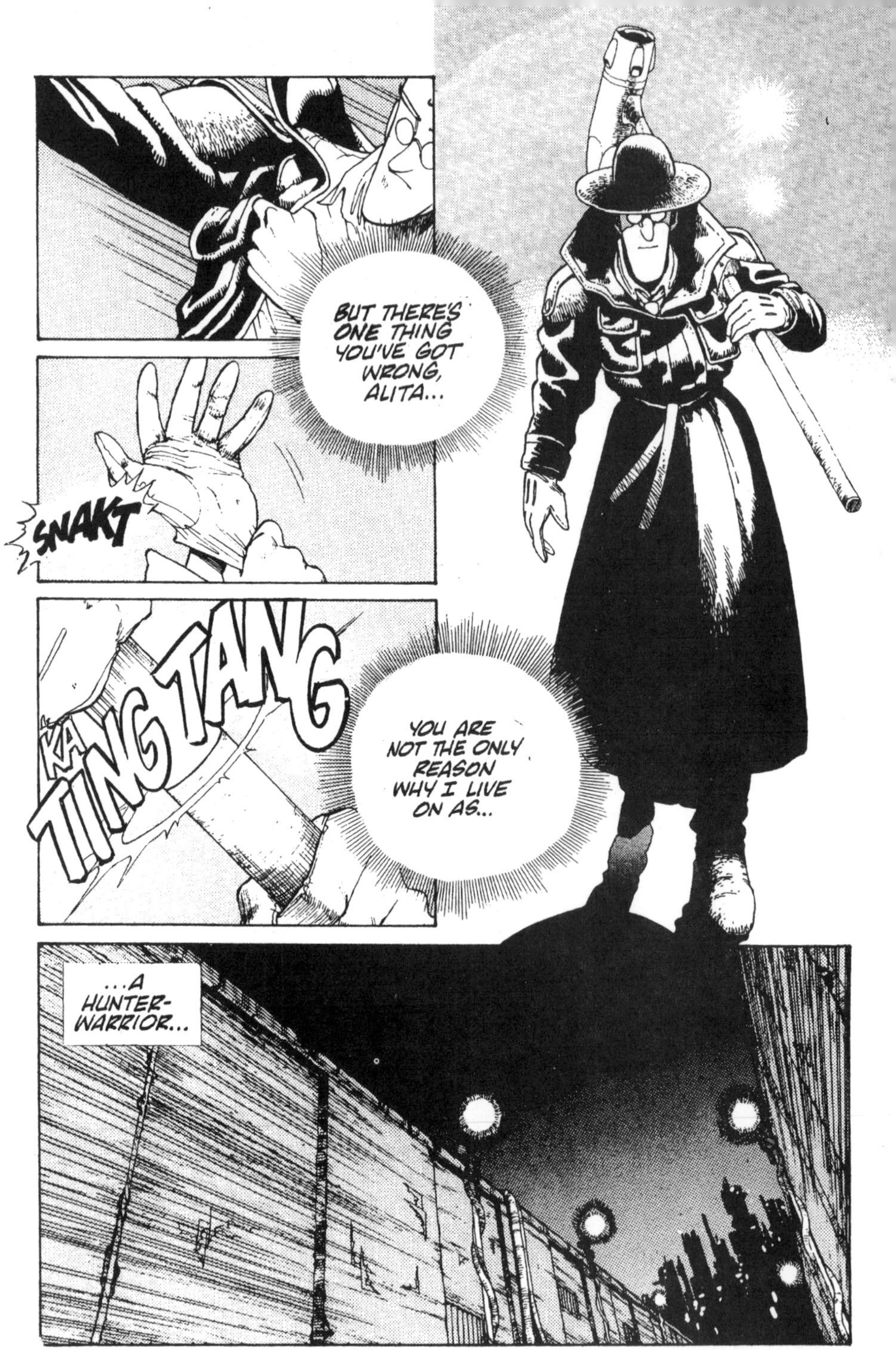
BUT THERE'S ONE THING YOU'VE GOT WRONG, ALITA...
SNAKT
KA TING TANG
YOU ARE NOT THE ONLY REASON WHY I LIVE ON AS...
...A HUNTER-WARRIOR...

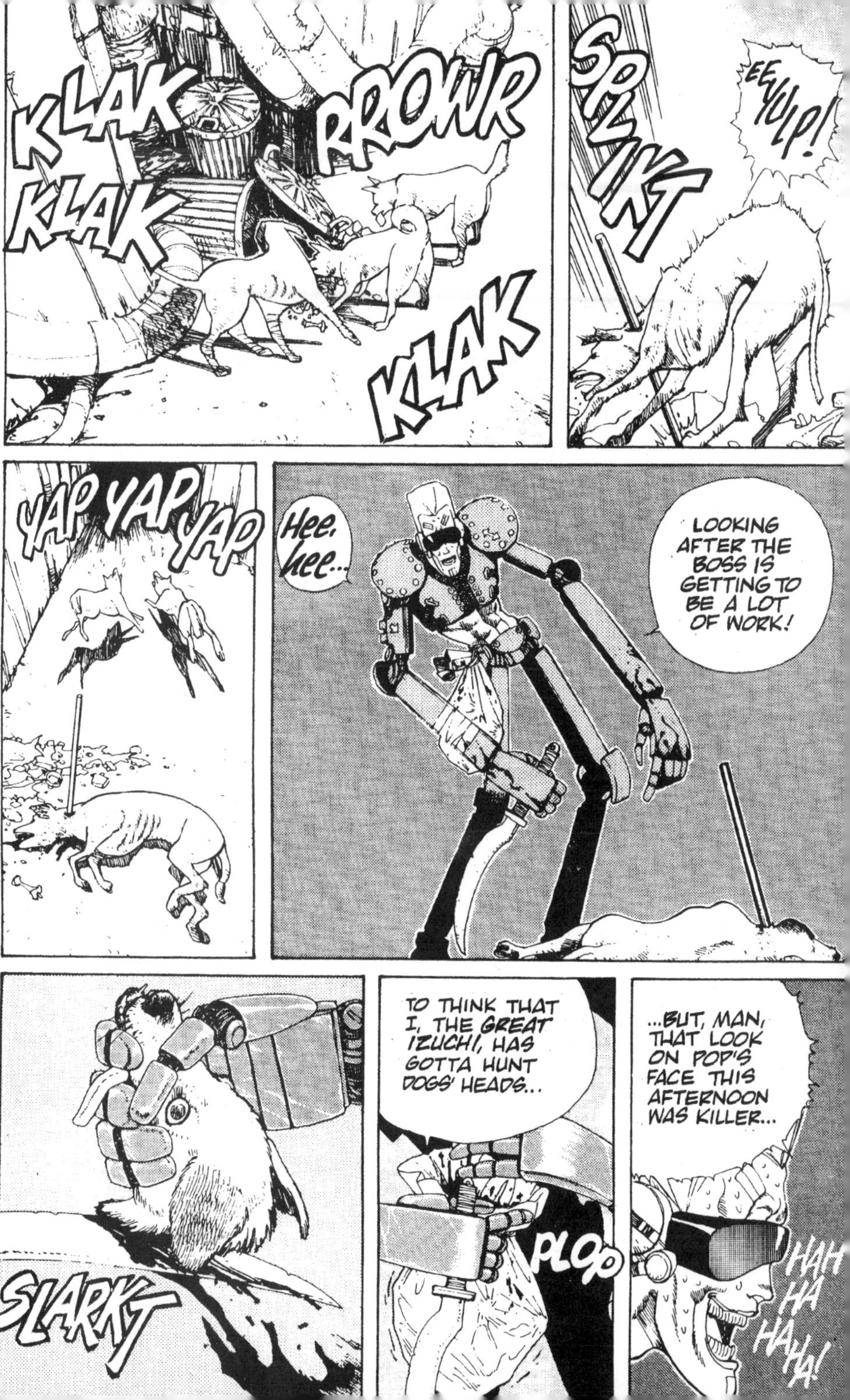
KLAK
KLAK
RROWR
KLAK
SPLIKT
EE YULP!
YAP YAP YAP
Hee. hee...
LOOKING AFTER THE BOSS IS GETTING TO BE A LOT OF WORK!
SLARKT
TO THINK THAT I, THE GREAT IZUCHI, HAS GOTTA HUNT DOGS' HEADS...
PLOP
...BUT, MAN, THAT LOOK ON POP'S FACE THIS AFTERNOON WAS KILLER...
HAH HA HA HA HA!

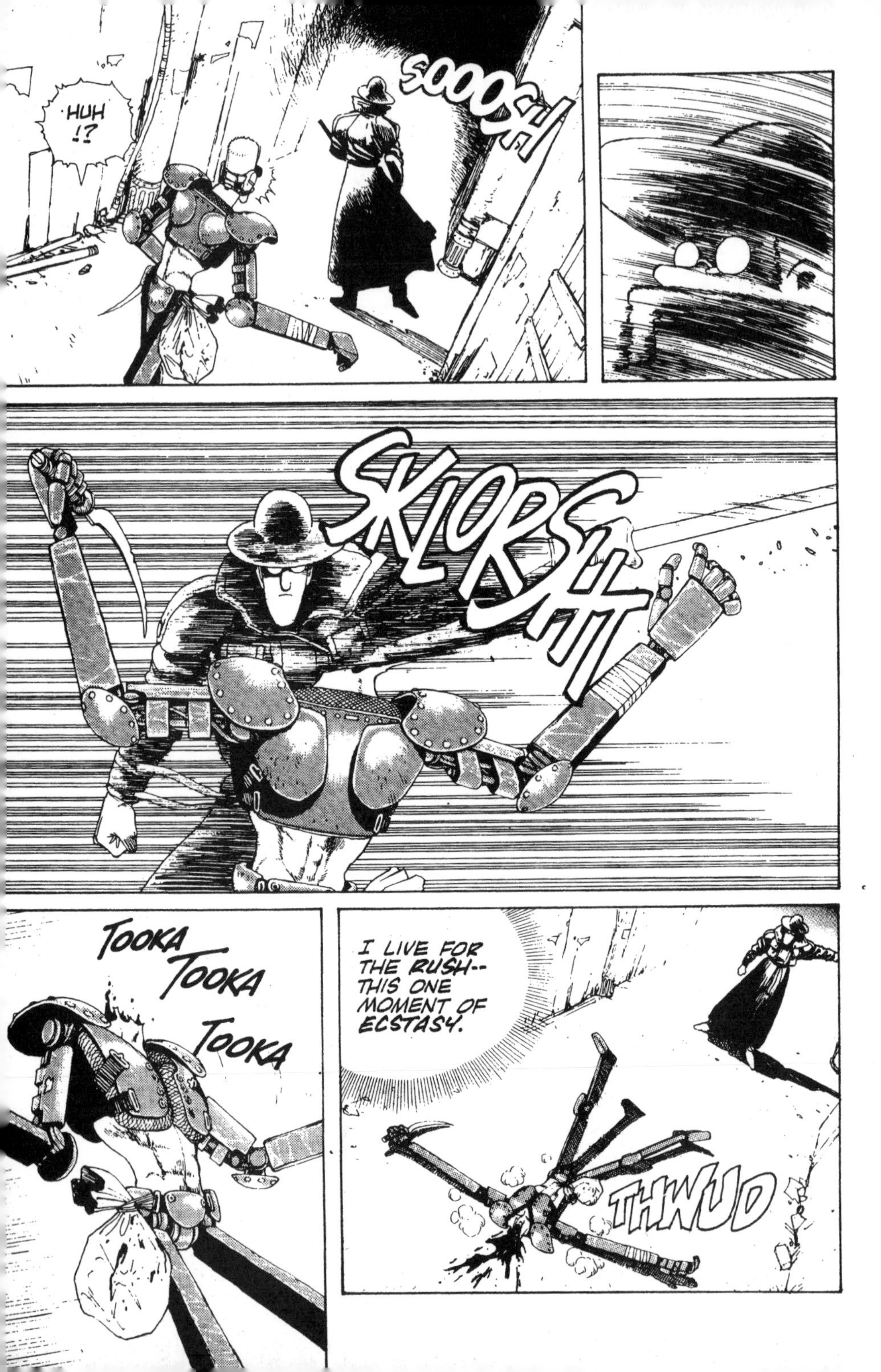
HUH !?
SOOOSH
SKLORSHT
TOOKA
TOOKA
TOOKA
I LIVE FOR THE RUSH-- THIS ONE MOMENT OF ECSTASY.
THWUD

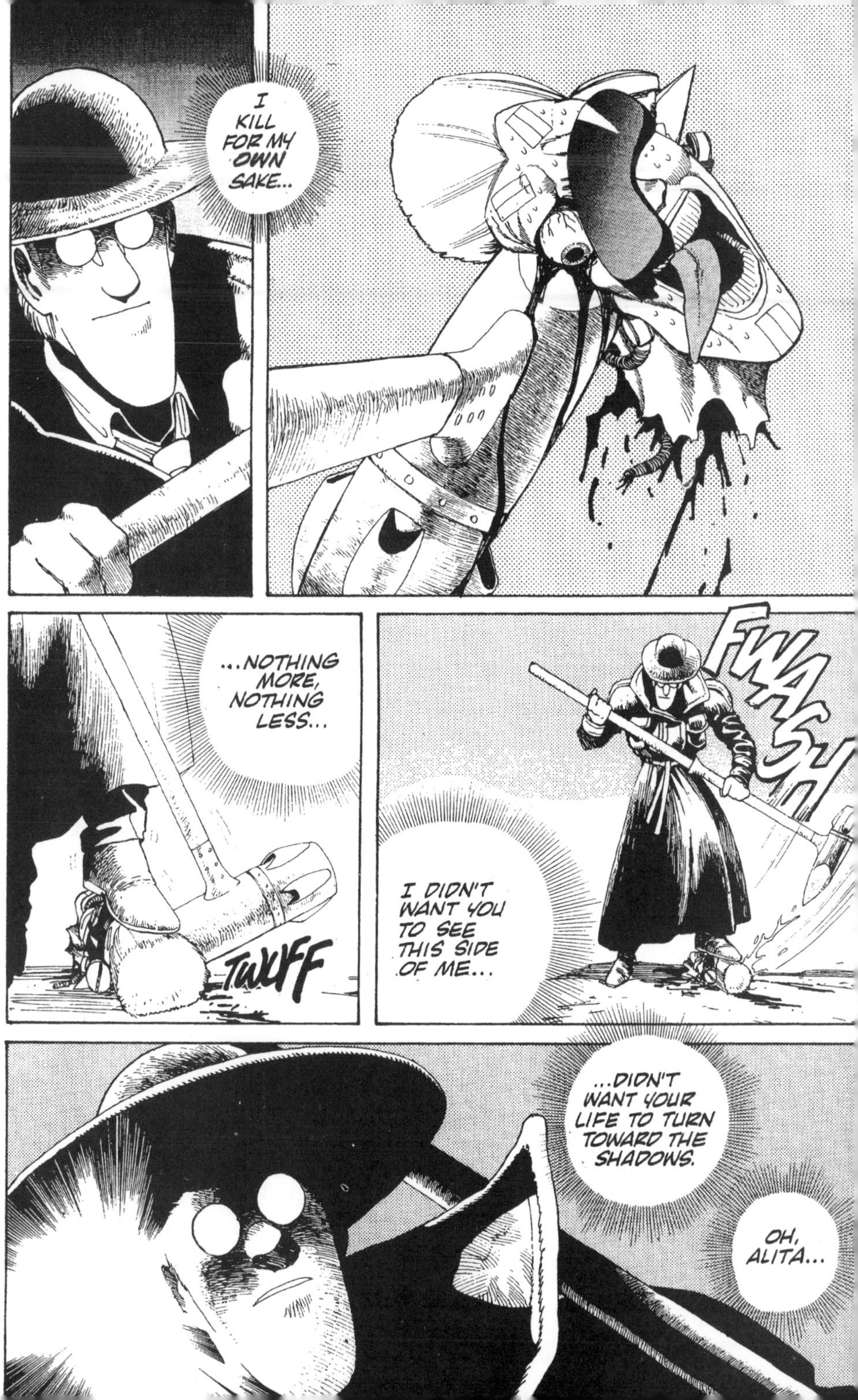
I KILL FOR MY OWN SAKE...
...NOTHING MORE, NOTHING LESS...
TWUFF
FWASH
I DIDN'T WANT YOU TO SEE THIS SIDE OF ME...
...DIDN'T WANT YOUR LIFE TO TURN TOWARD THE SHADOWS.
OH, ALITA...

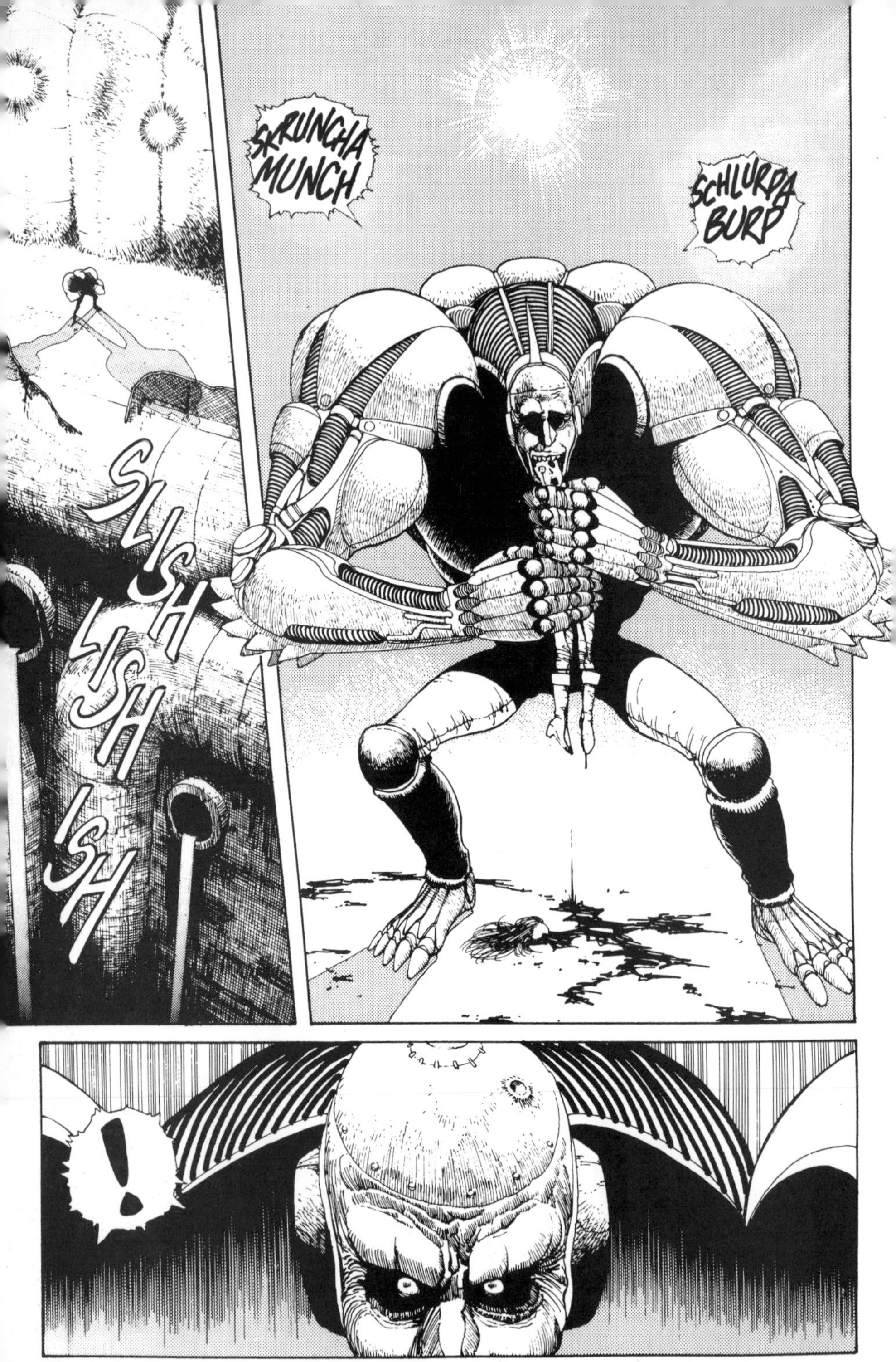
SLISH LISH ISH ISH
SKRUNCHA MUNCH
SCHLURPA BURP
!

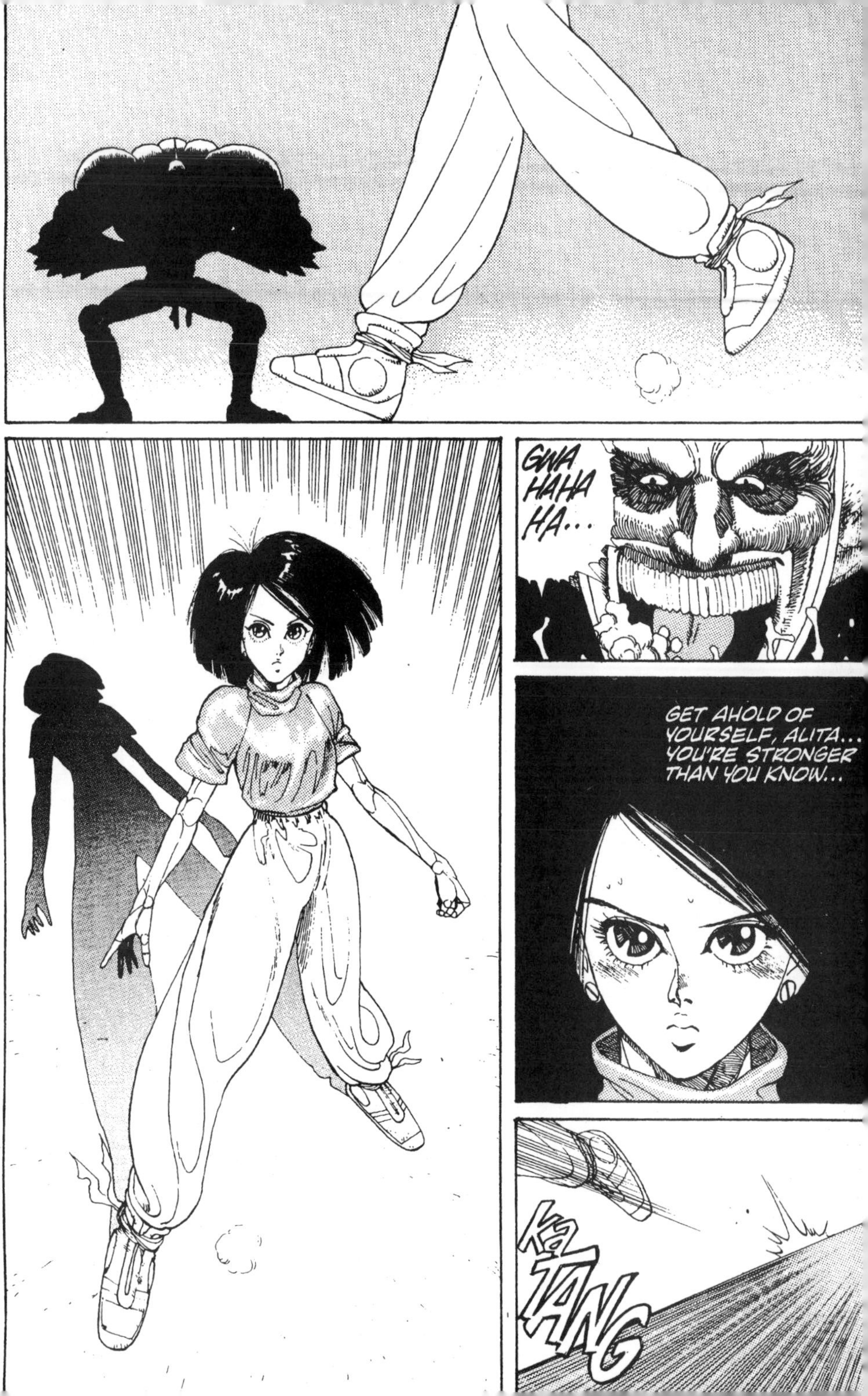
GWA HAHAHA HA...
GET AHOLD OF YOURSELF, ALITA... YOU'RE STRONGER THAN YOU KNOW...
KaTANG

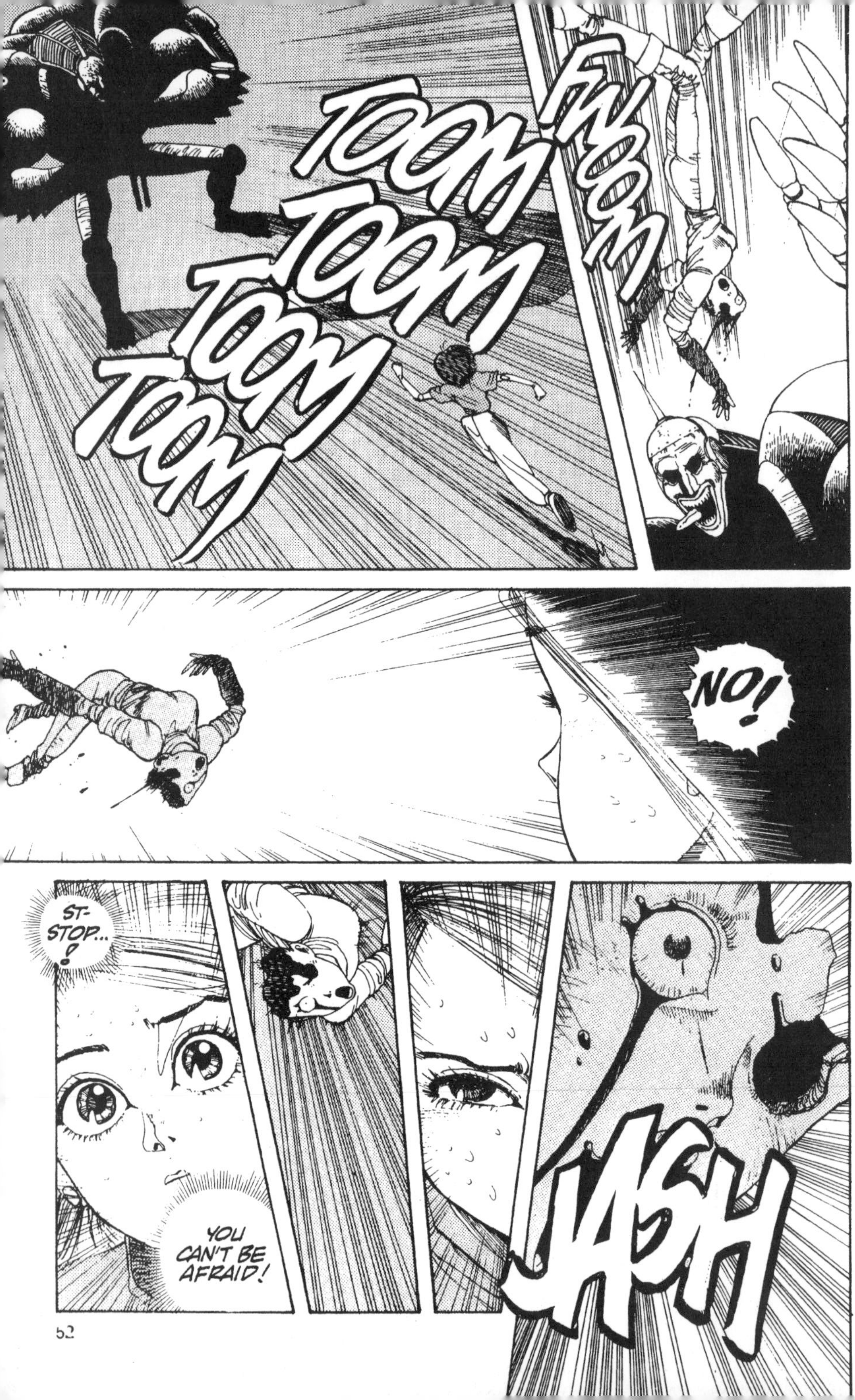
TOOM TOOM TOOM TOOM
FWOOM
NO!
ST- STOP...!
YOU CAN'T BE AFRAID!
JASH

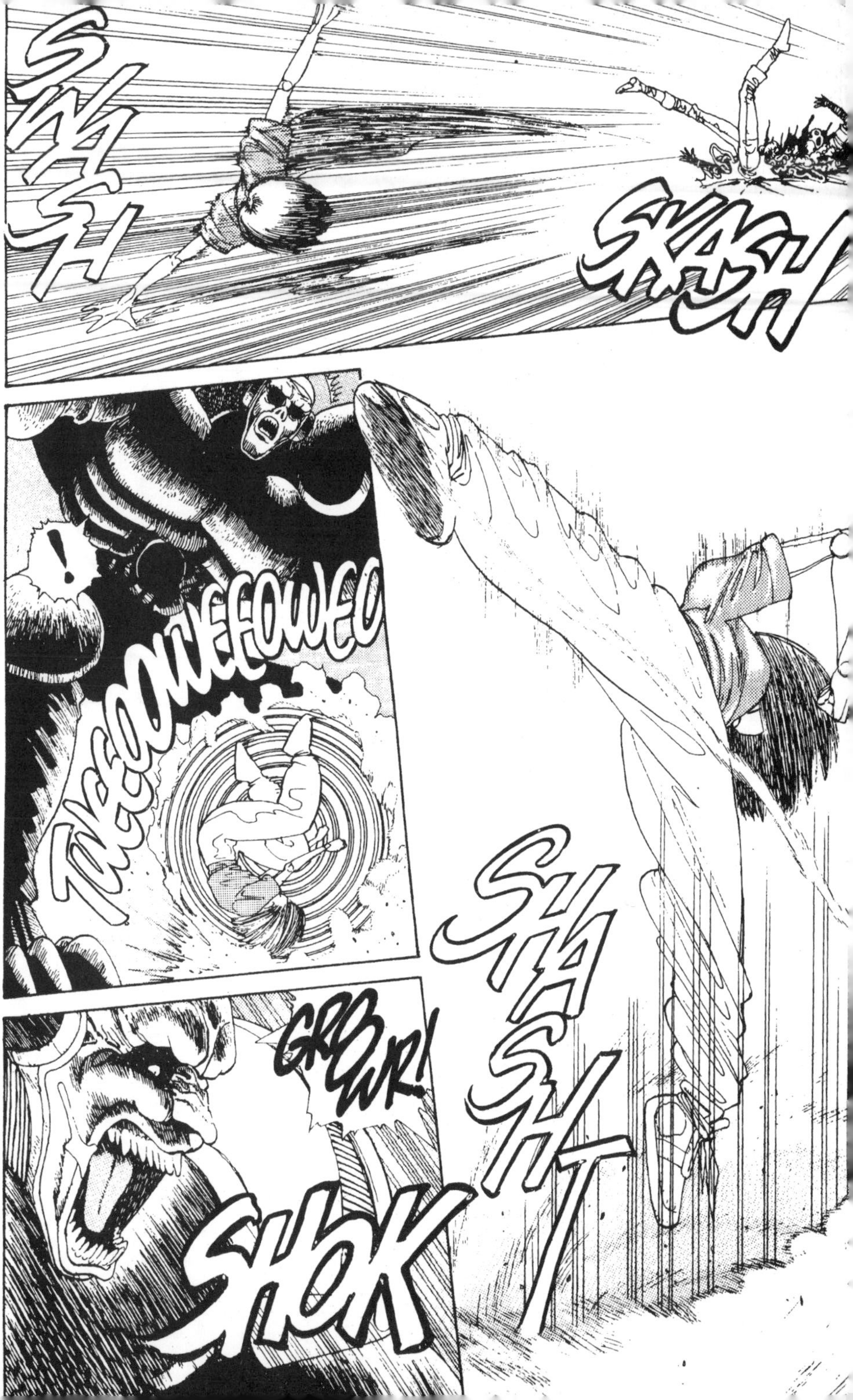
SHASH
SKASH
!
SHASHT
GROOWR!
SHOK

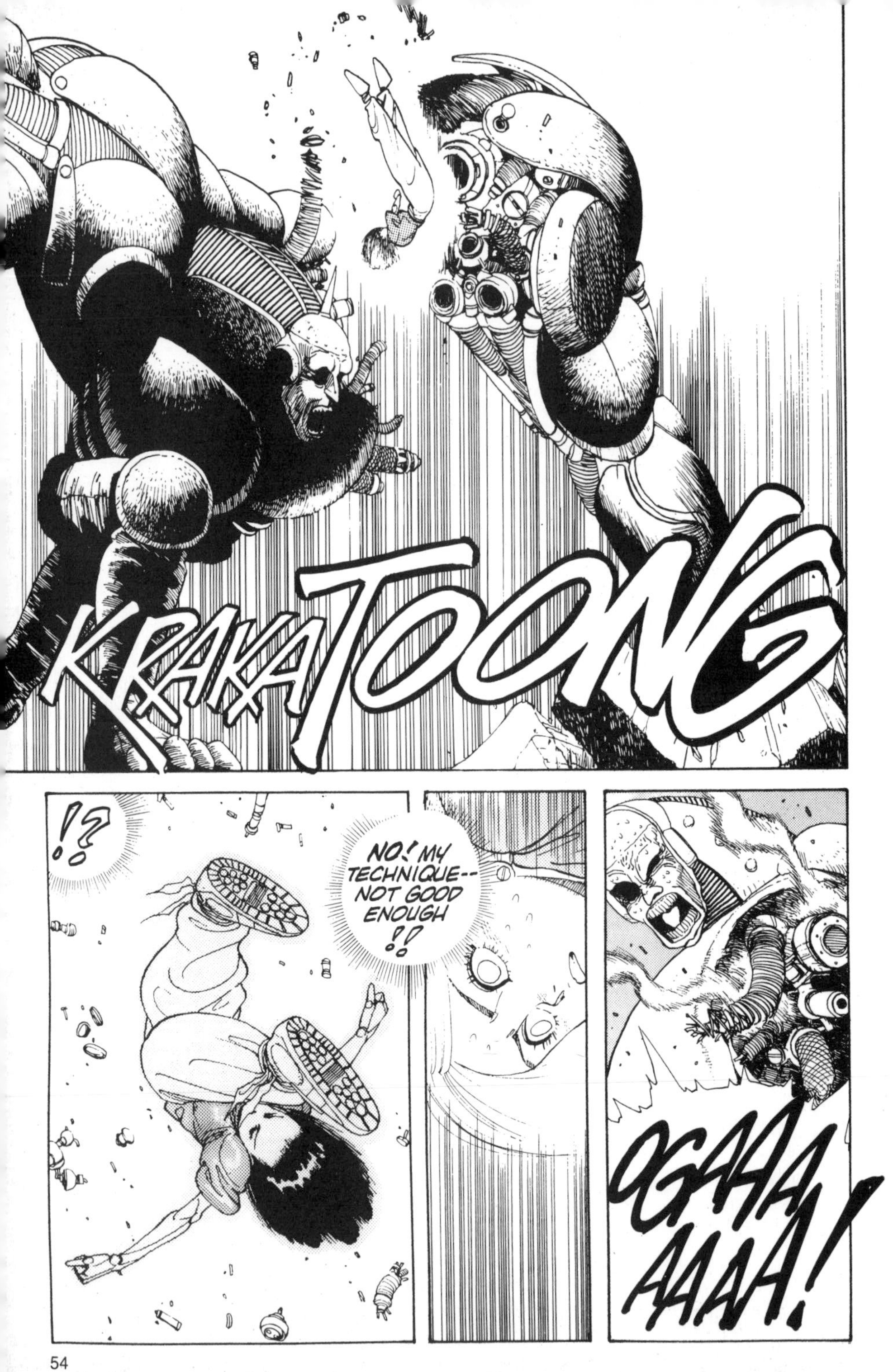
KRAKATOONG
!?
NO! MY TECHNIQUE-- NOT GOOD ENOUGH !!
OGAHAAAAA!

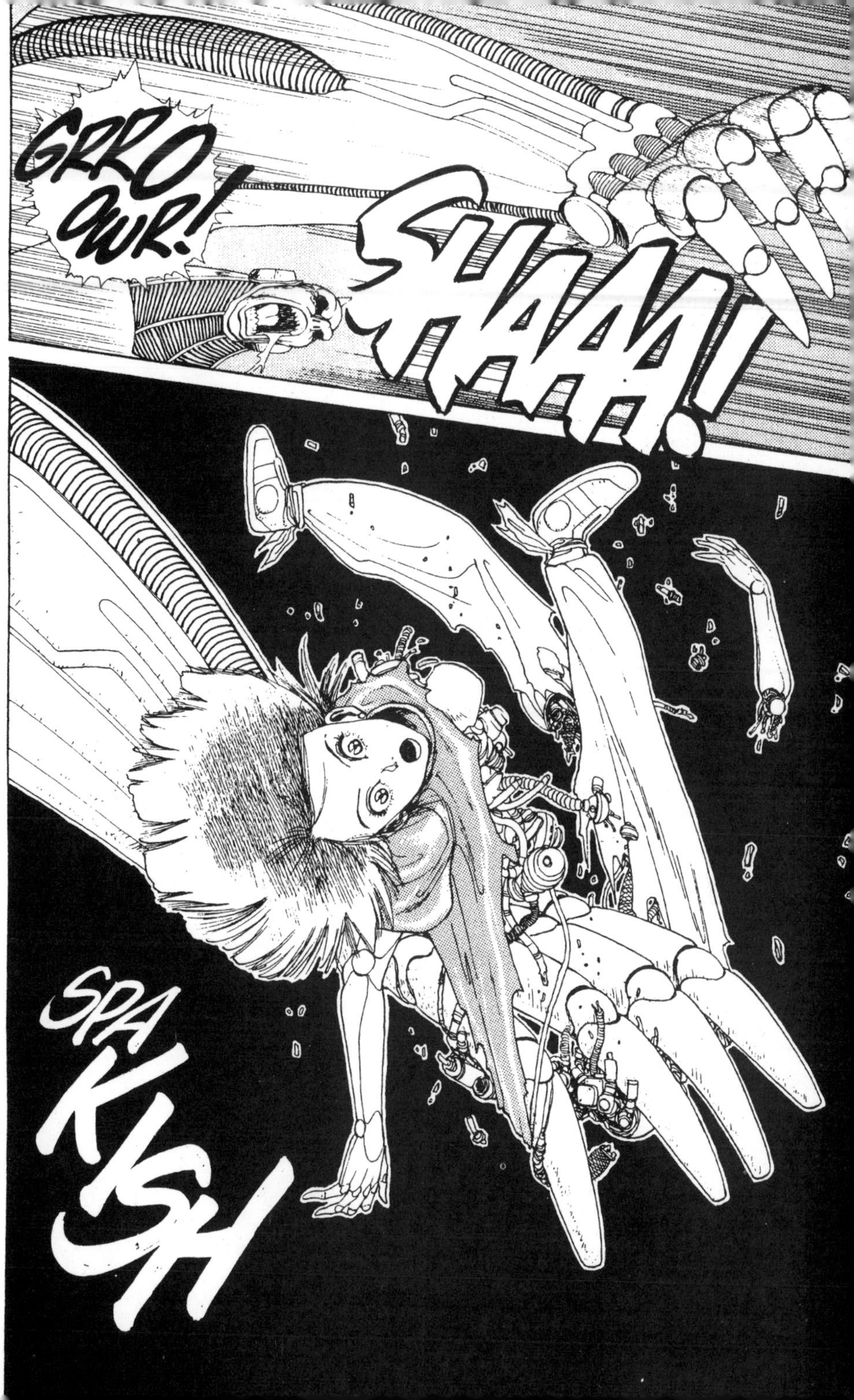
GRRO OWR!
SHAAA!
SPA KISH

TORN ASUNDER
Battle 3: Values

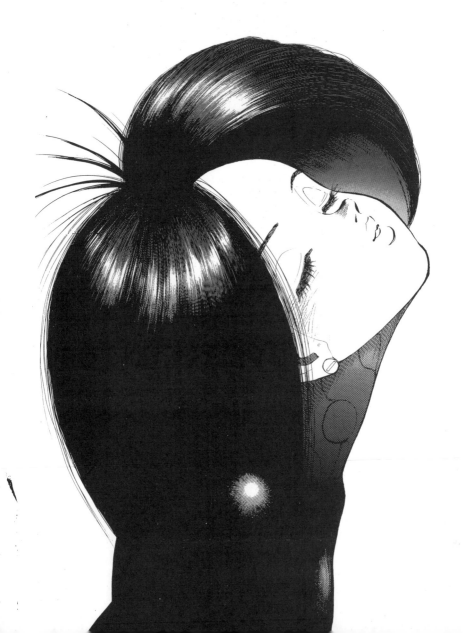

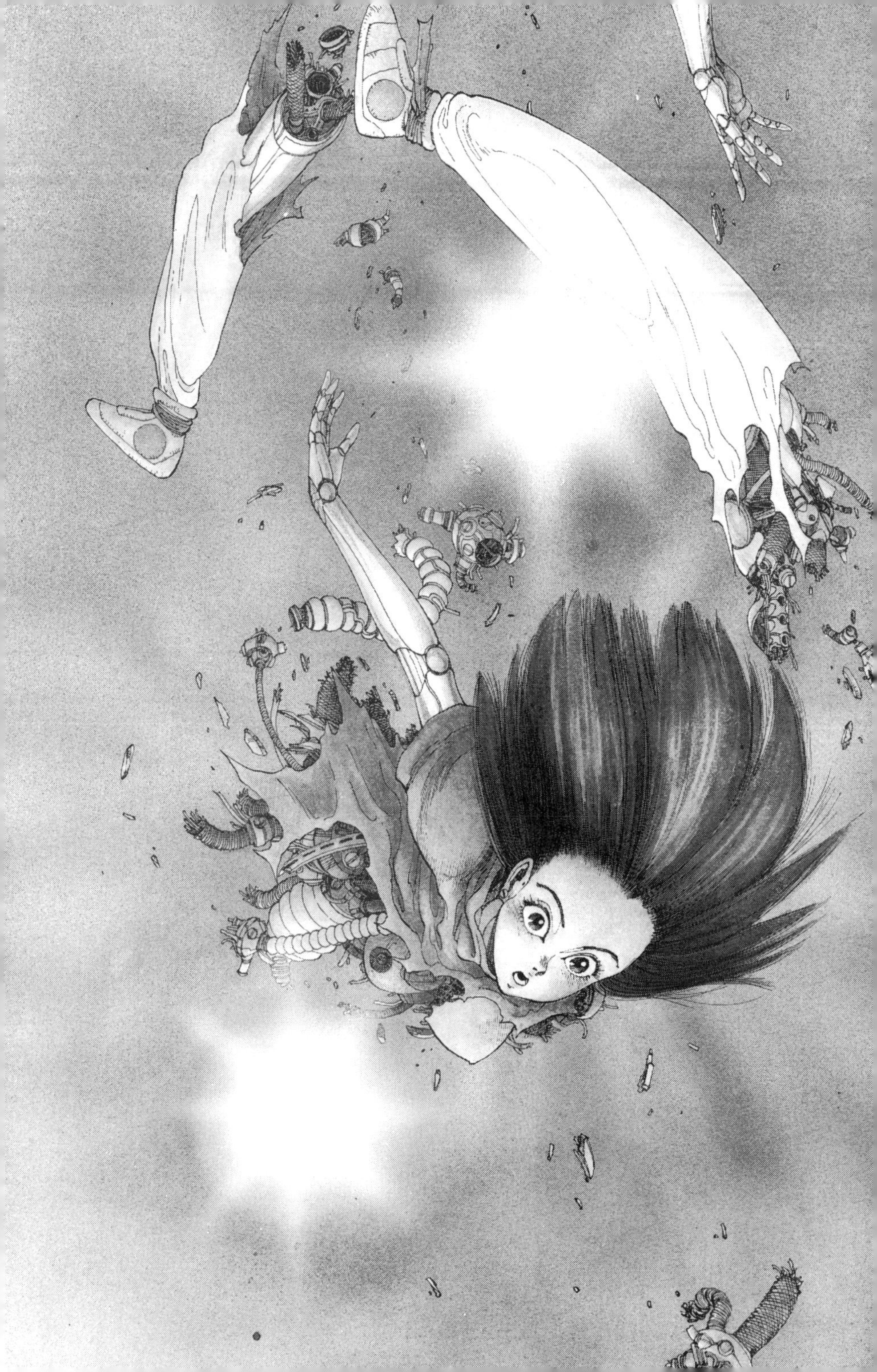

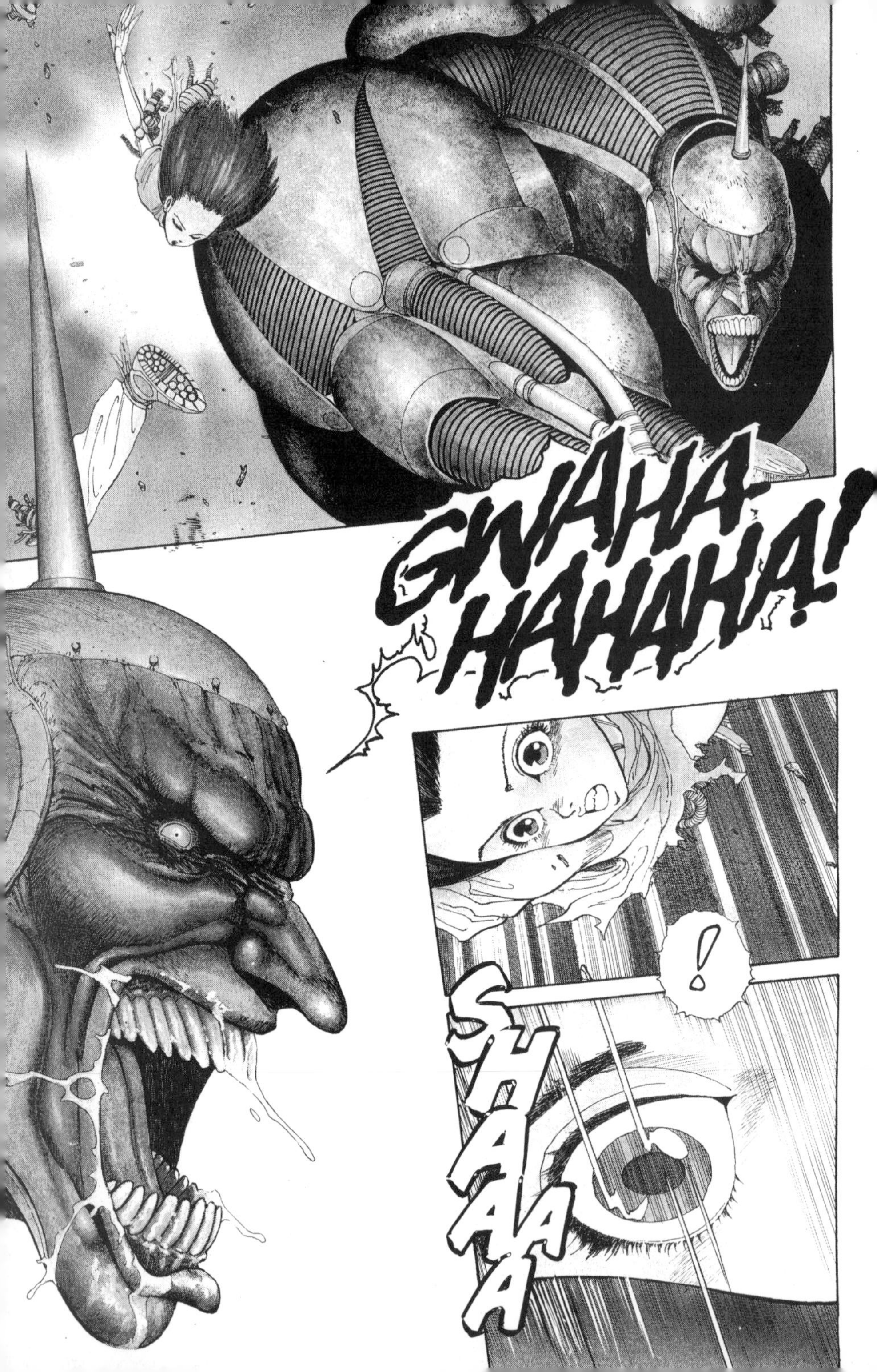
GWAHA-HAHAHA!
!
SHAAAAA

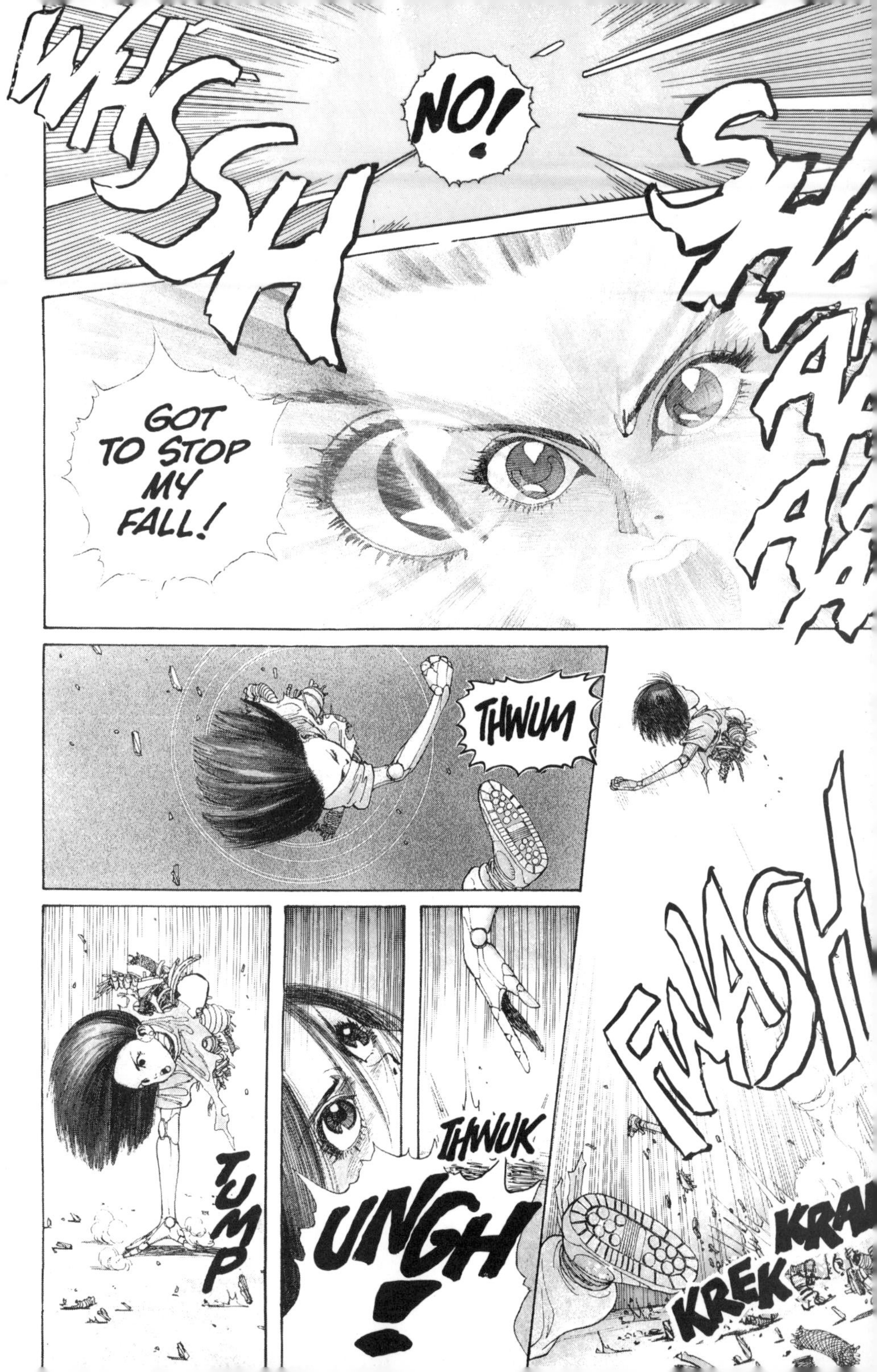
WHSH
NO!
SHAAAA
GOT TO STOP MY FALL!
THWUM
FWASH
TUMP
THWUK
UNGH!
KRA
KREK

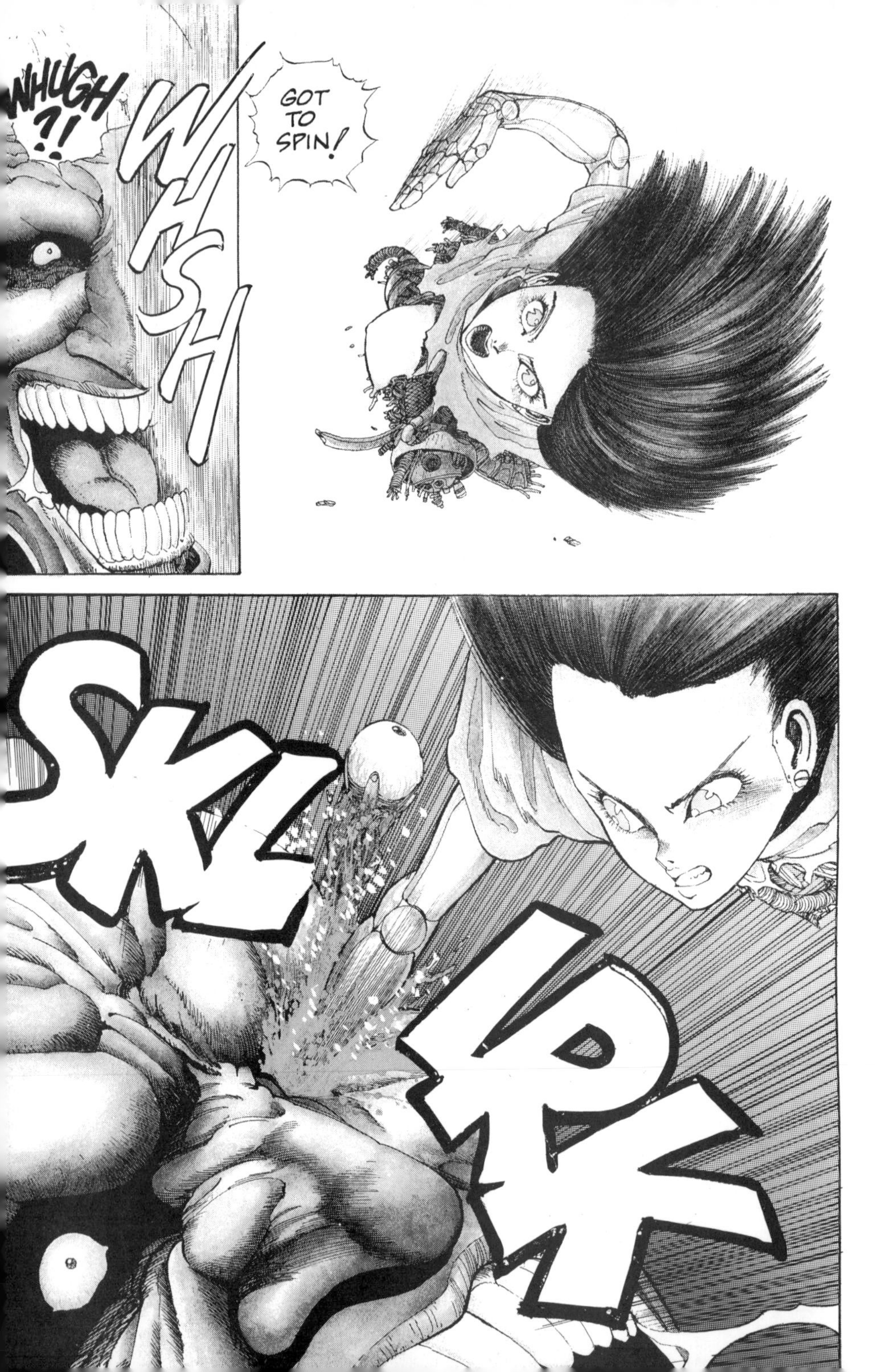

WHUGH ?!
WHSH
GOT TO SPIN!
SKLURK

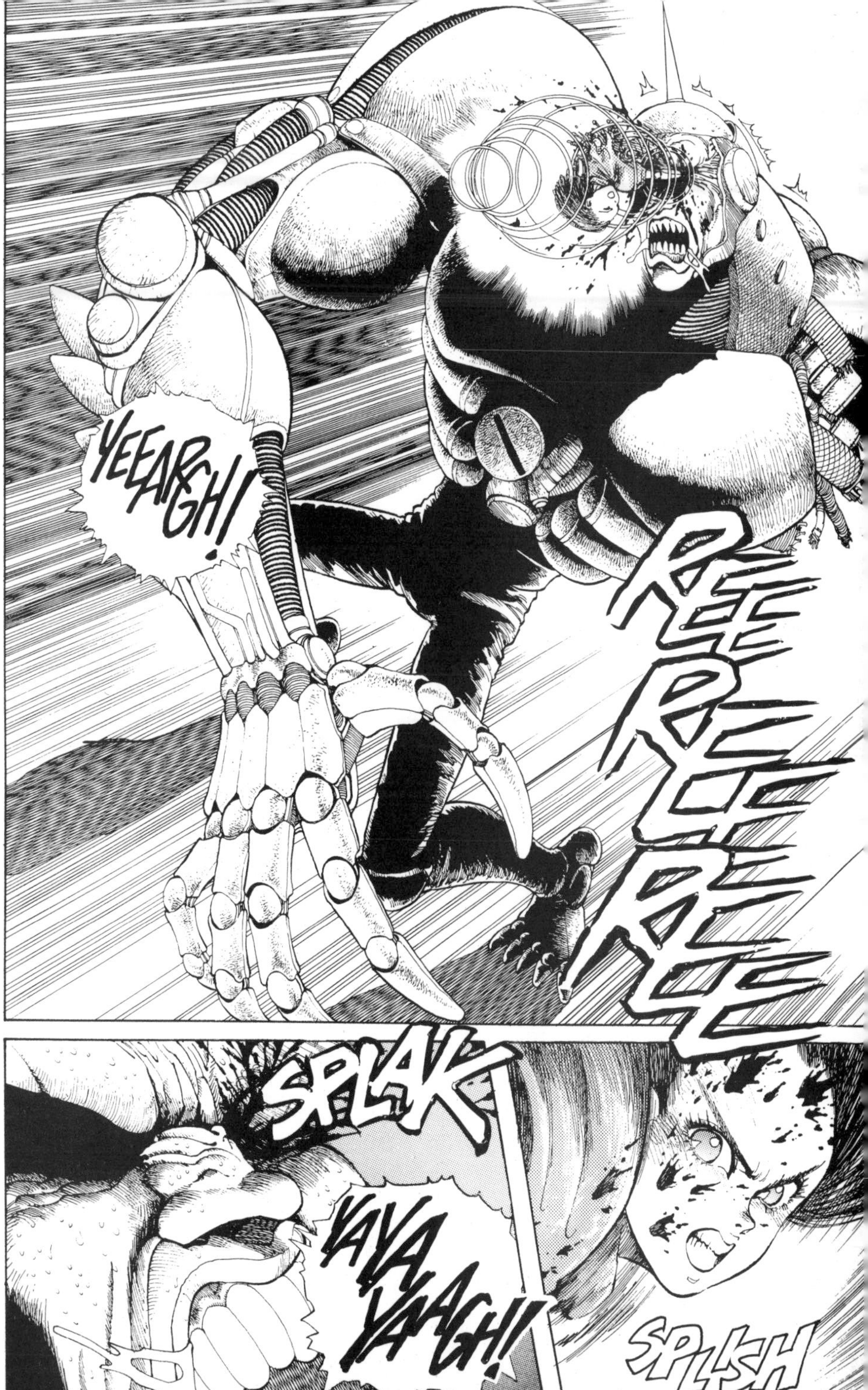
YEEARGH!
REEEREEEREEE
SPLAK
YAYAYAYAAGH!
SPLISH

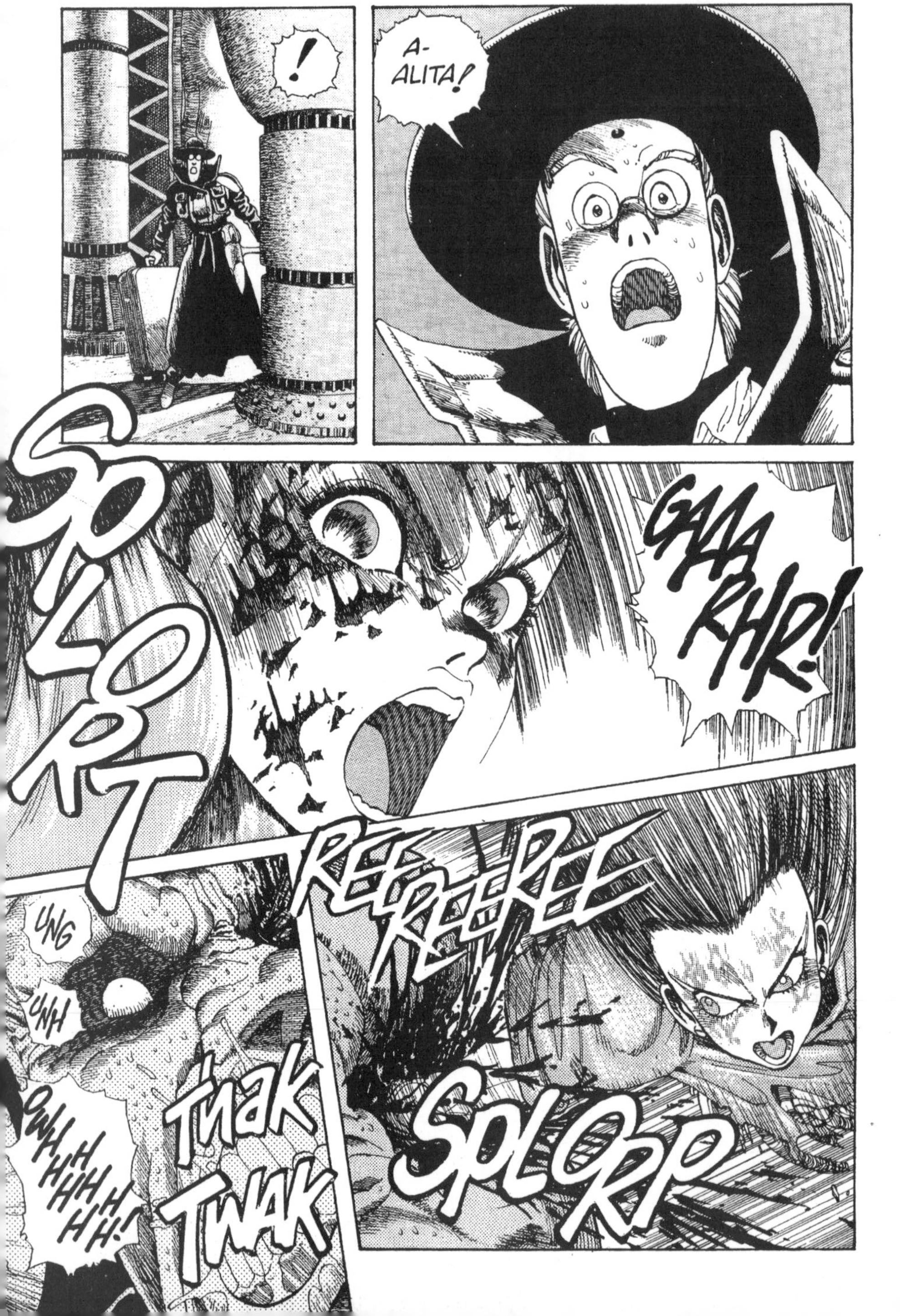
!
A-
ALITA!
SPLORT
GAAARHR!
REEEREEEREEE
UNG
UNH
OWHHHHHH!
THAK
TWAK
SPLORP

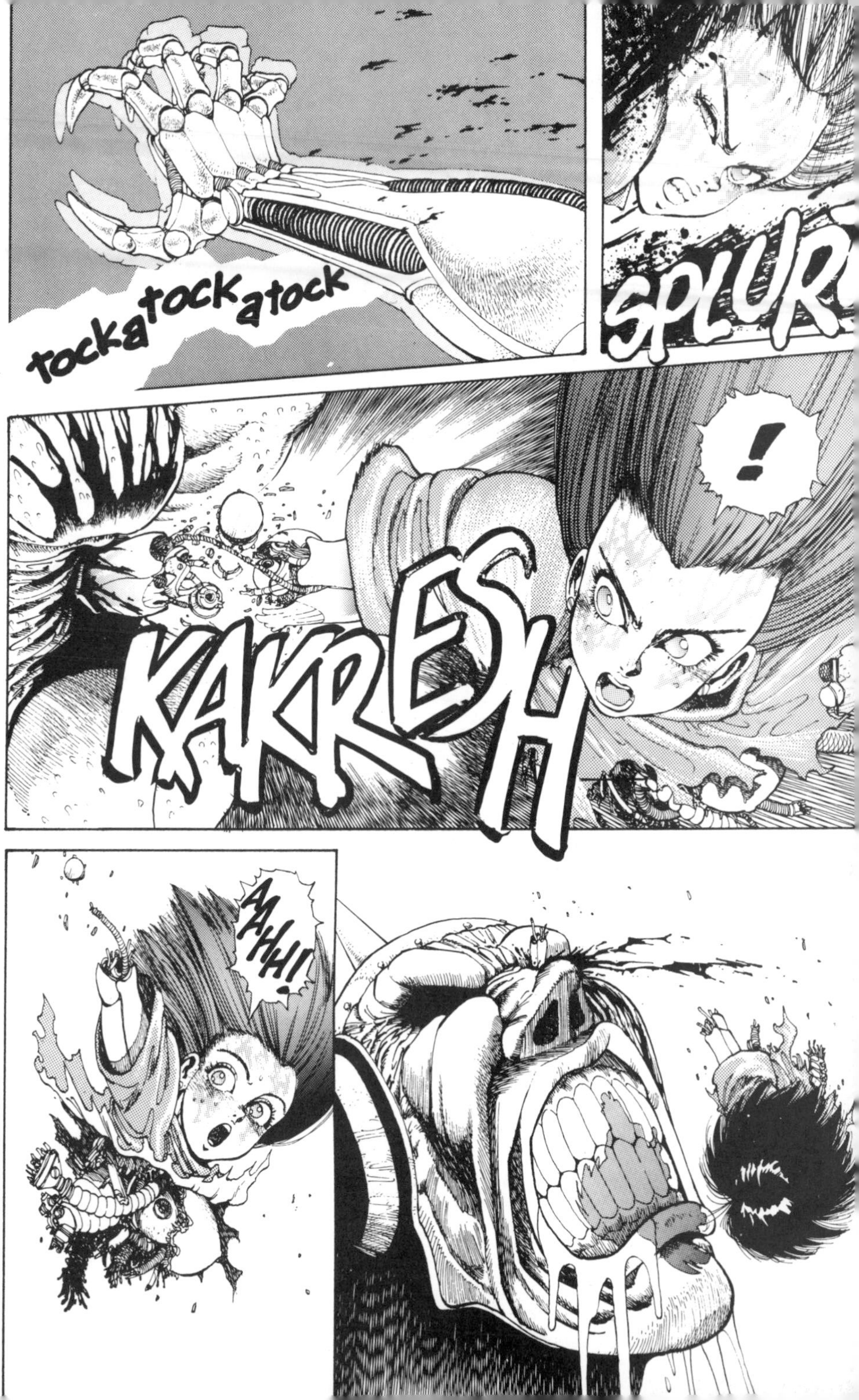
tockatockatock
SPLUR
!
KAKRESH
AAAHHH!

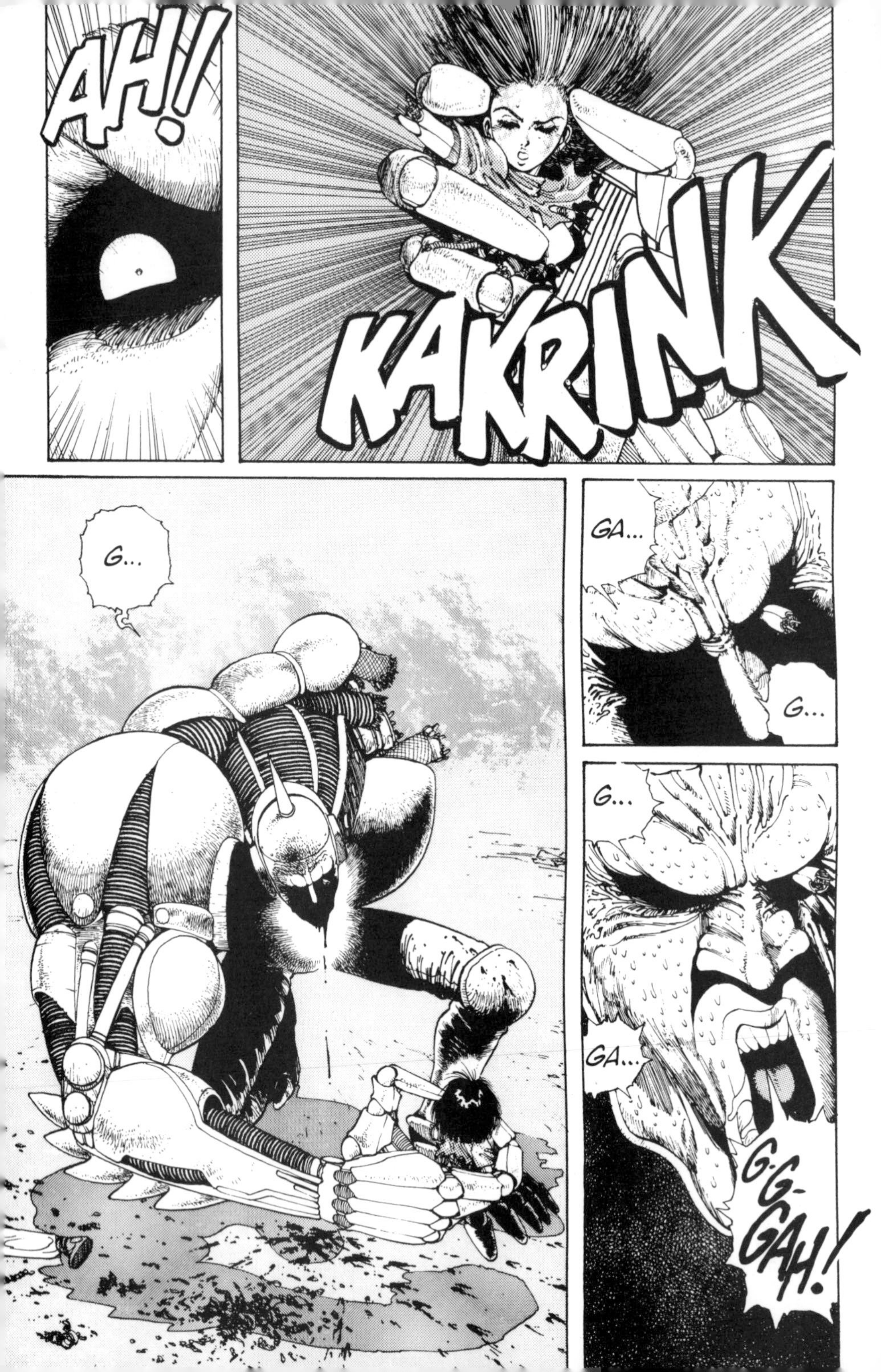
AH!!
KAKRINK
G...
GA...
G...
G...
GA...
G-G-GAH!

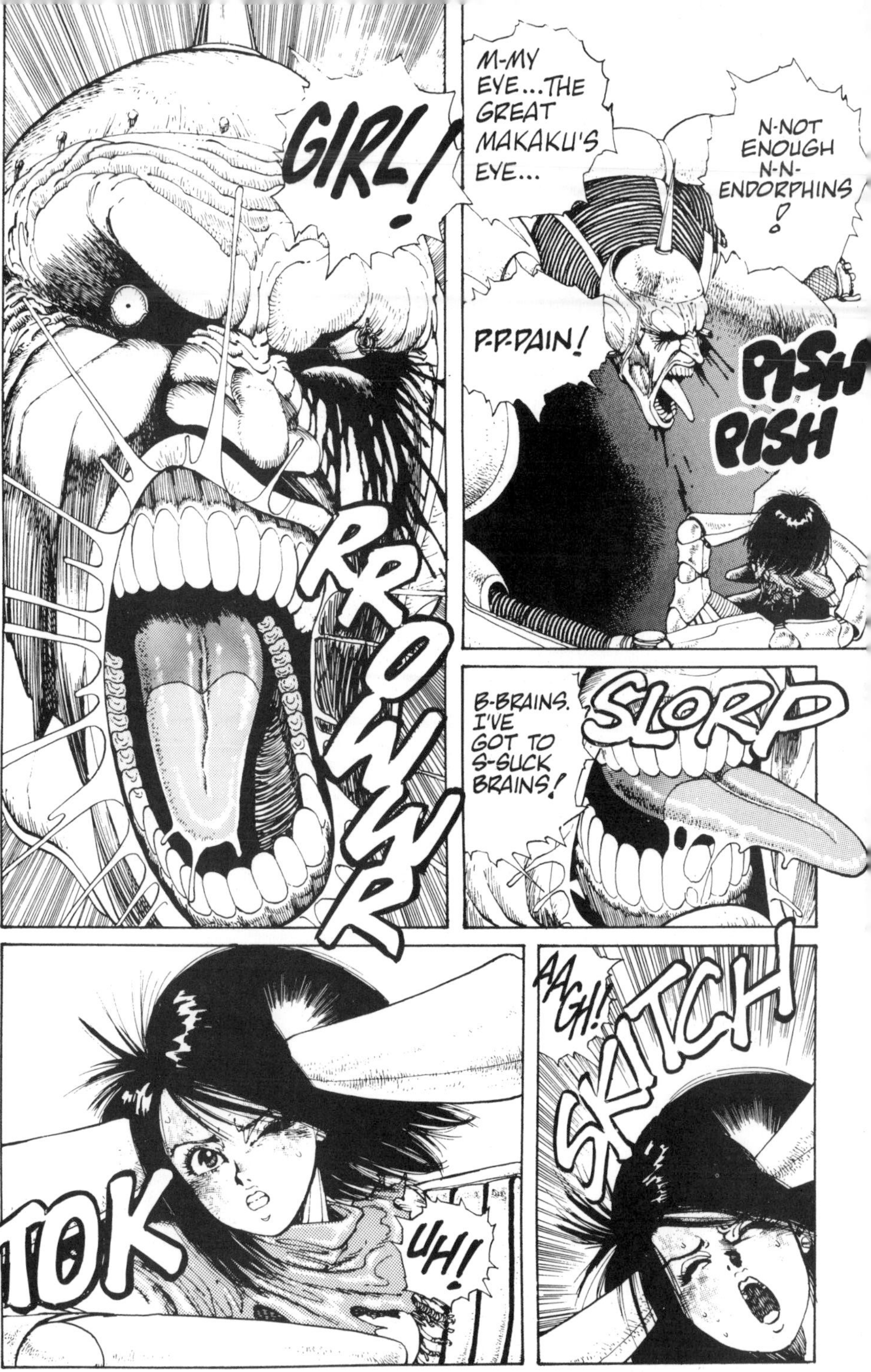
GIRL!
RROWWR
M-MY EYE...THE GREAT MAKAKU'S EYE...
N-NOT ENOUGH N-N-ENDORPHINS!
P-P-PAIN!
PISH PISH
B-BRAINS. I'VE GOT TO S-SUCK BRAINS!
SLORP
TOK
UH!
AAGH!
SKITCH

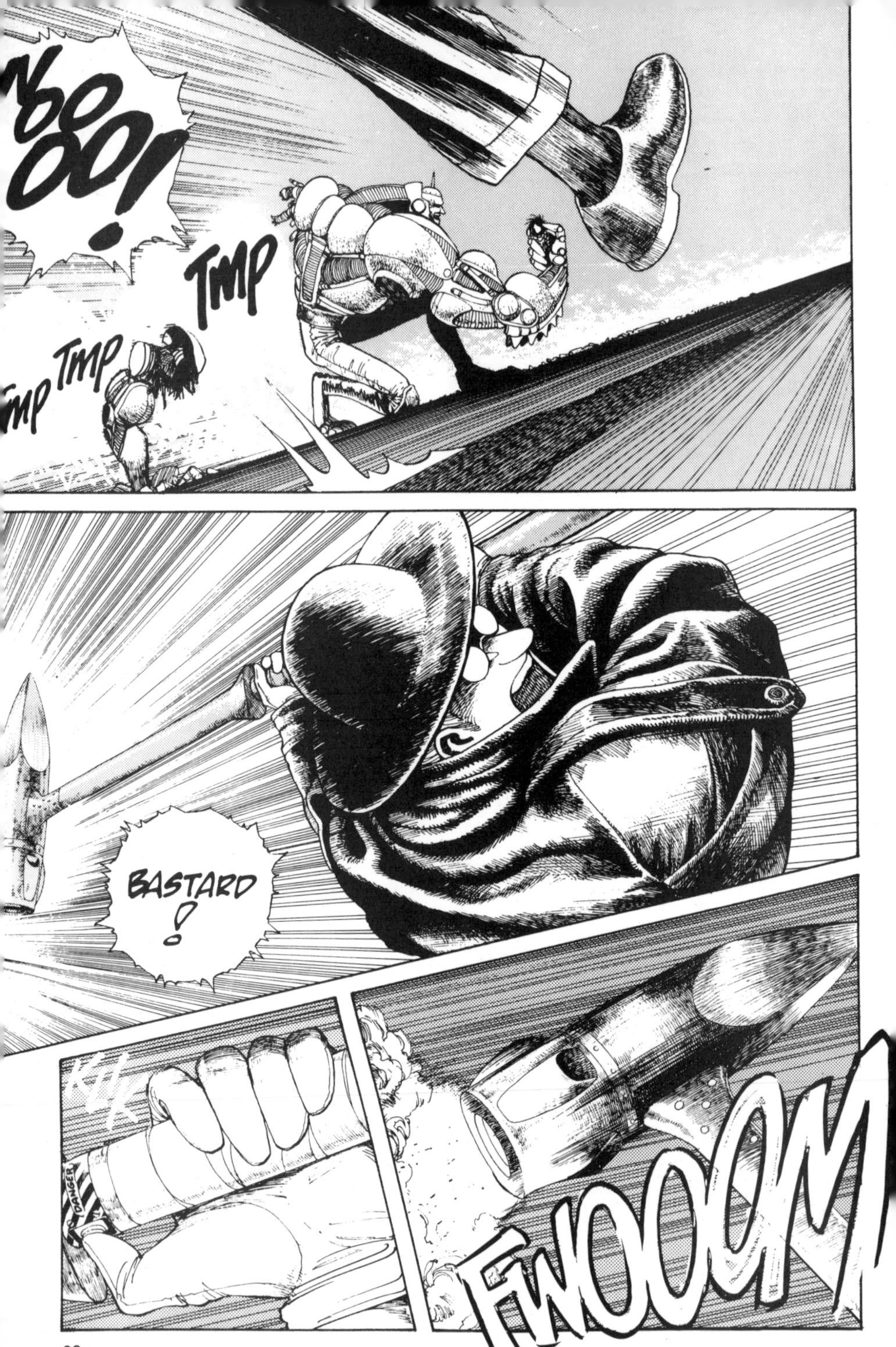
NOOOO!
TMP
TMP TMP
BASTARD!
DANGER
FWOOOM

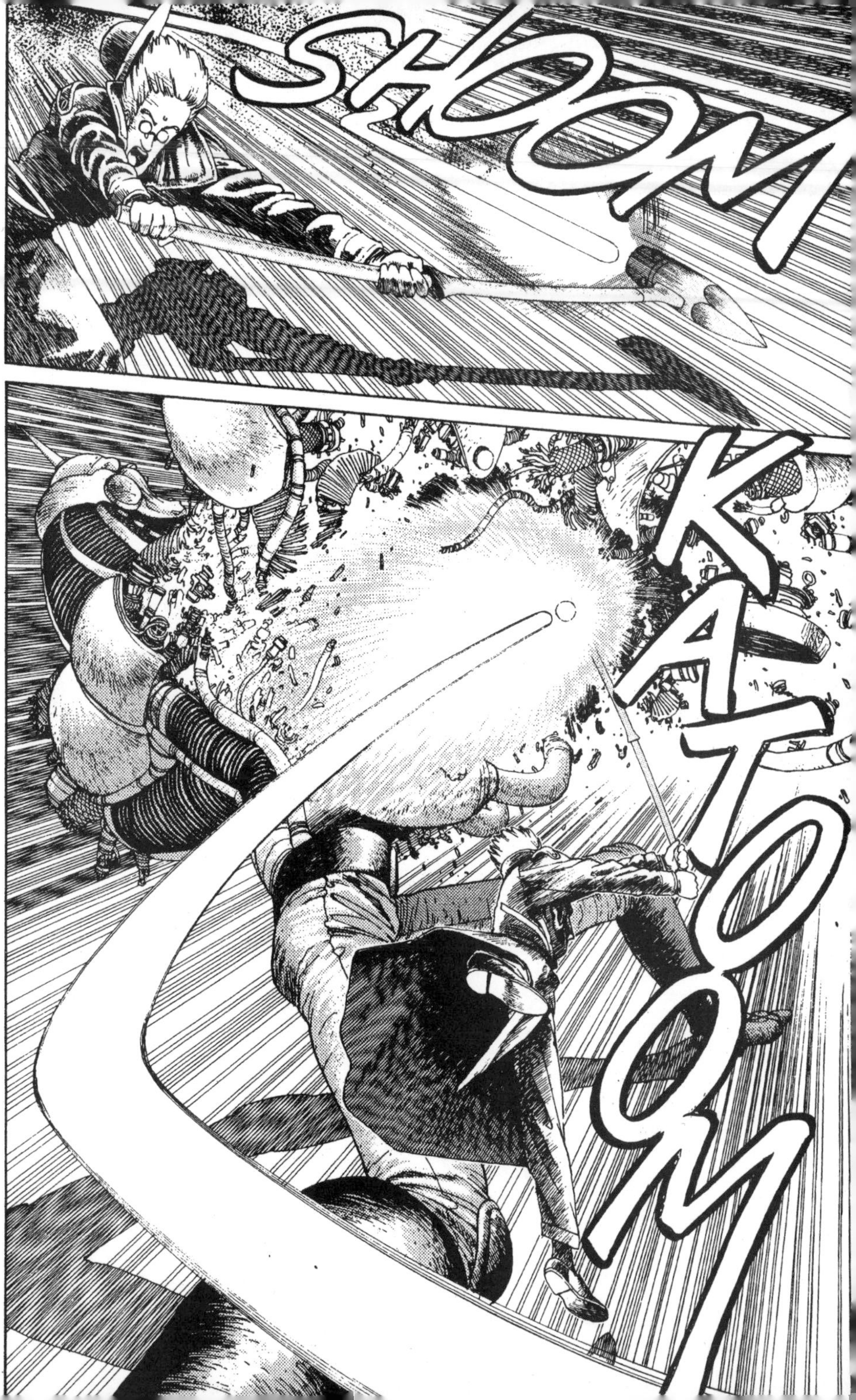
SHOOM
KATOOM

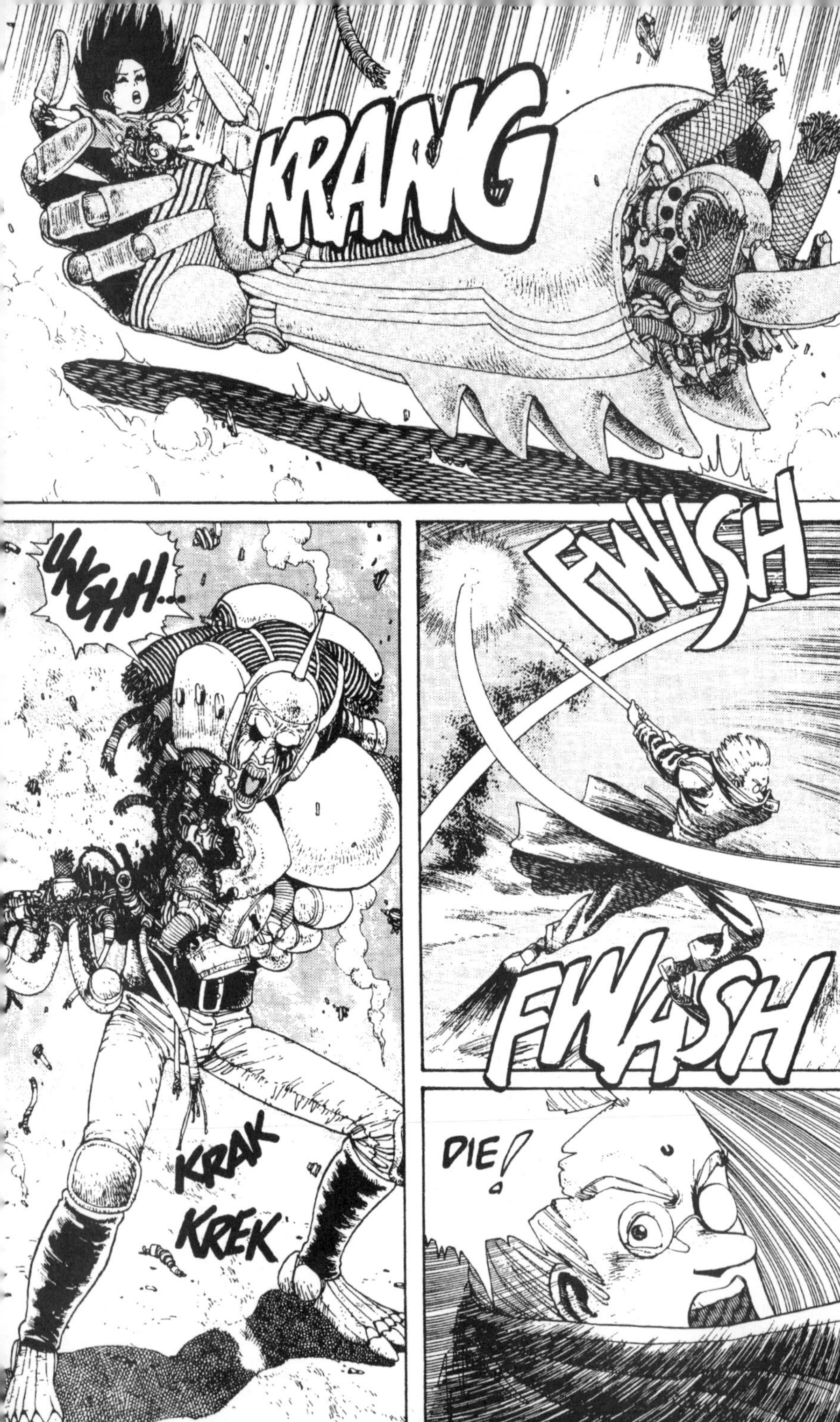
KRAANG
UNGHH...
KRAK
KREK
FWISH
FWASH
DIE!

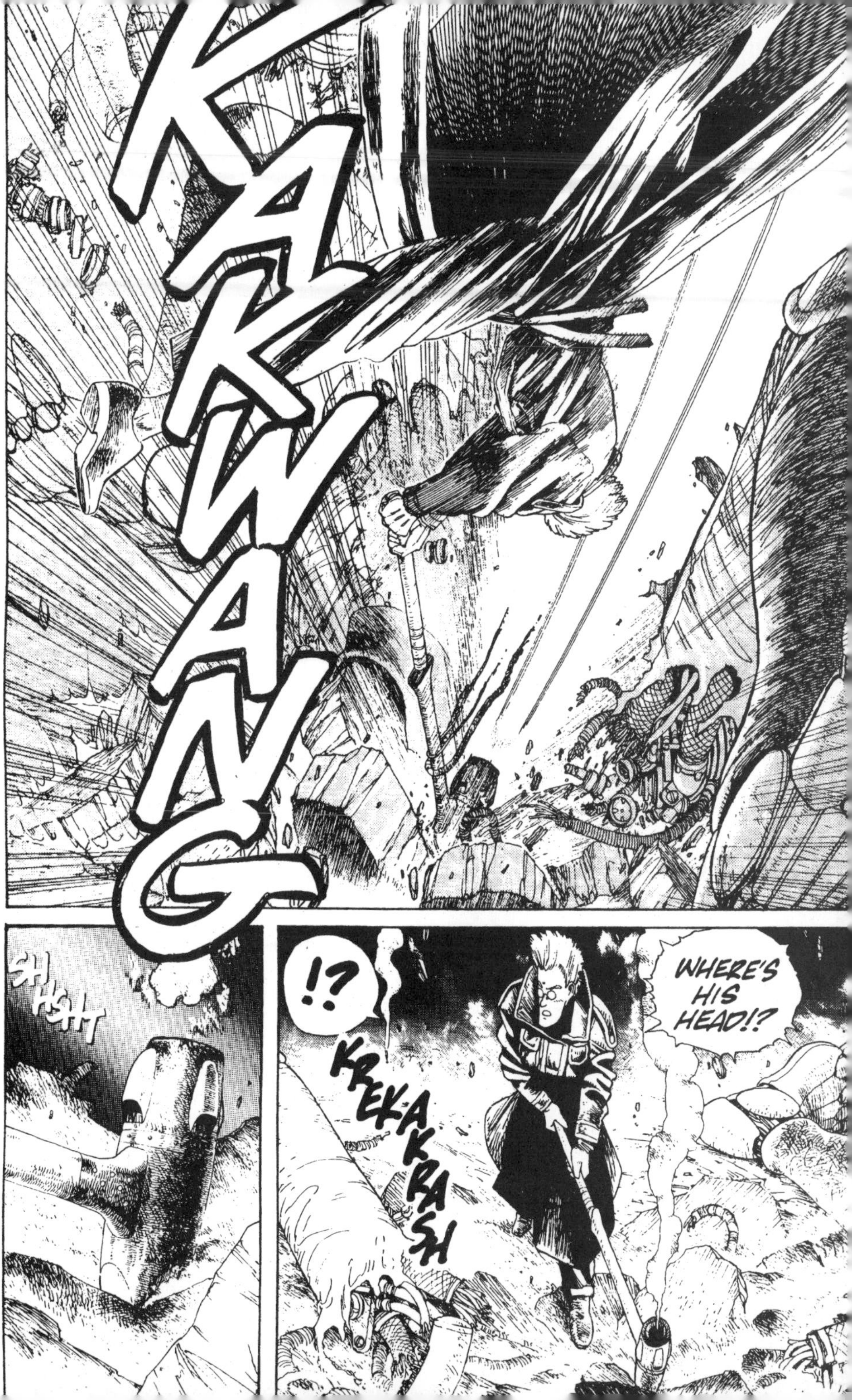
KAKWANG
SHHSHT
!?
KREKAKRASH
WHERE'S HIS HEAD!?

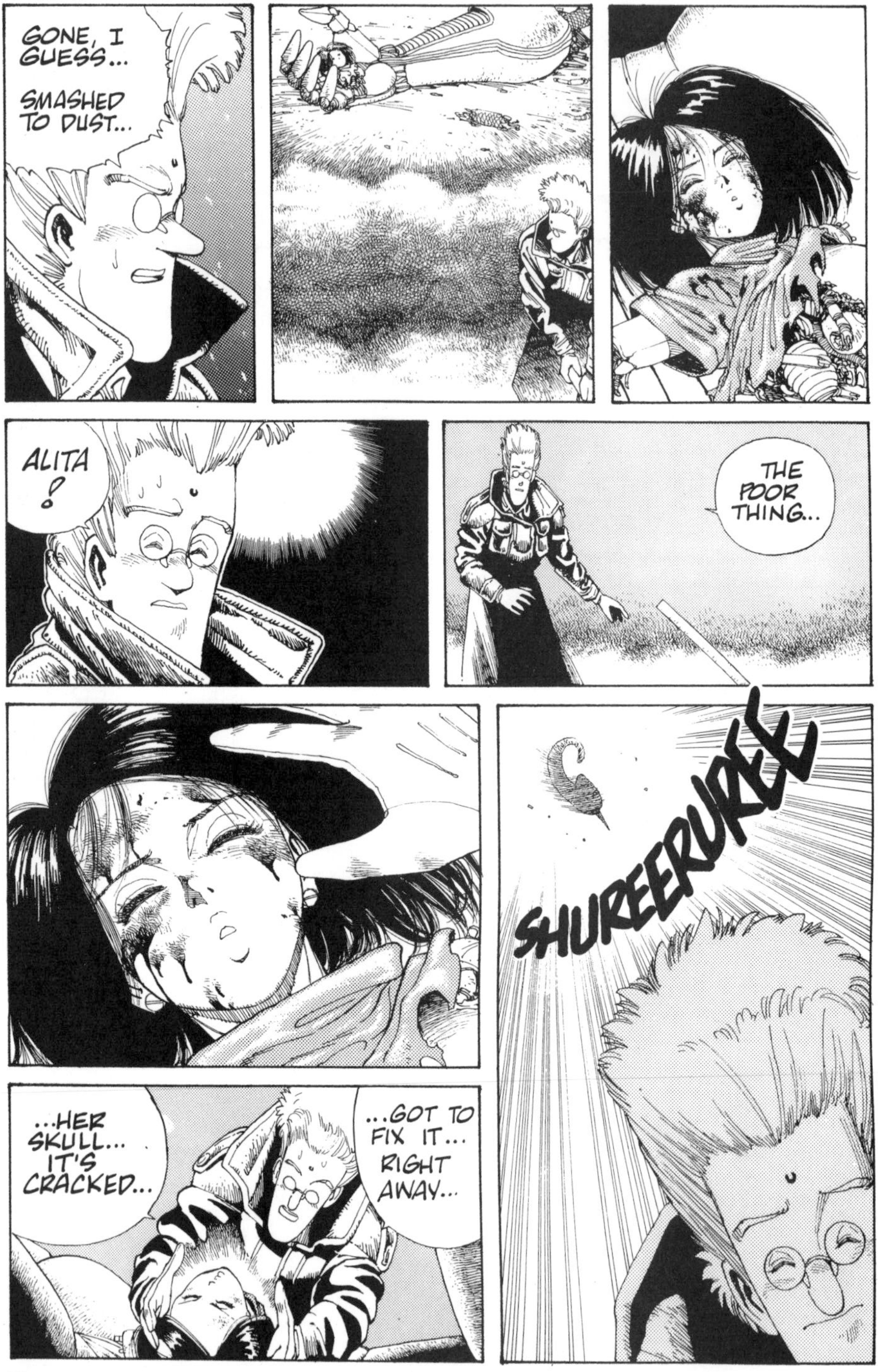
GONE, I GUESS...
SMASHED TO DUST...
ALITA!
THE POOR THING...
...HER SKULL... IT'S CRACKED...
...GOT TO FIX IT... RIGHT AWAY...
SHUREERUREE

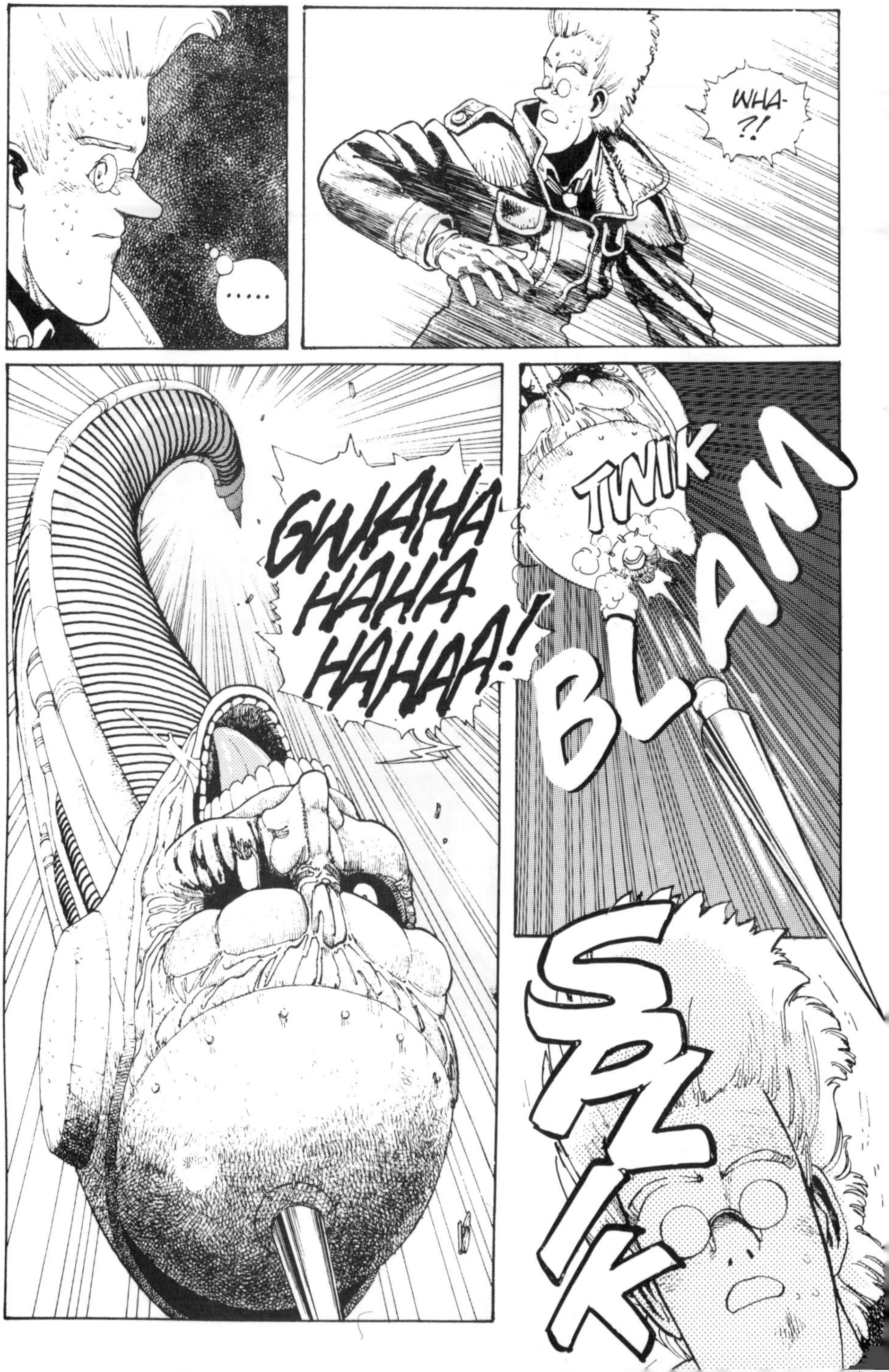
......
WHA-?!
GWAHA HAHA HAHAA!
TWIK
BLAM
SPLNK

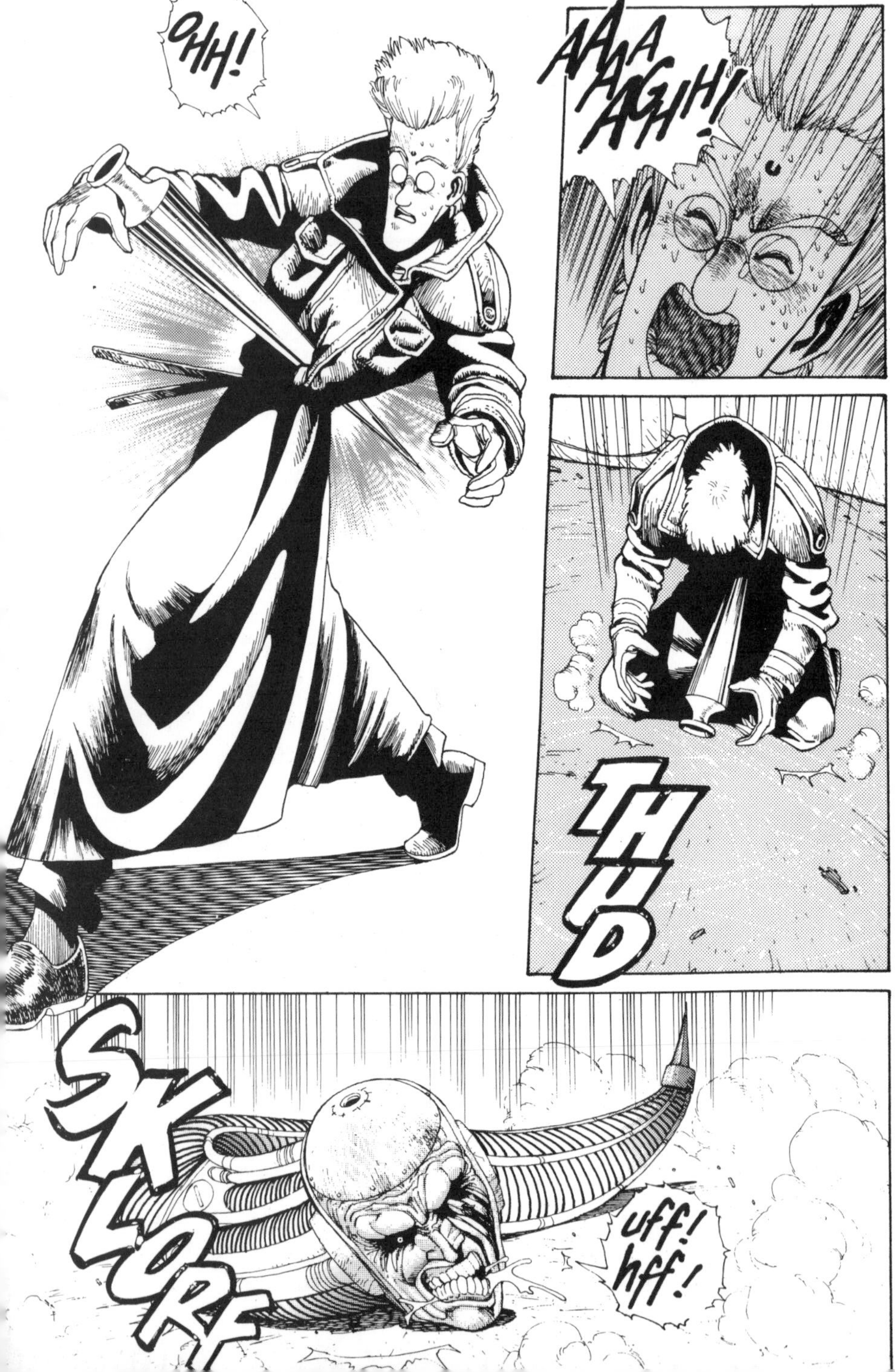
OHH!
AAAAAGHH!
THUD
SKLORK
uff! hff!

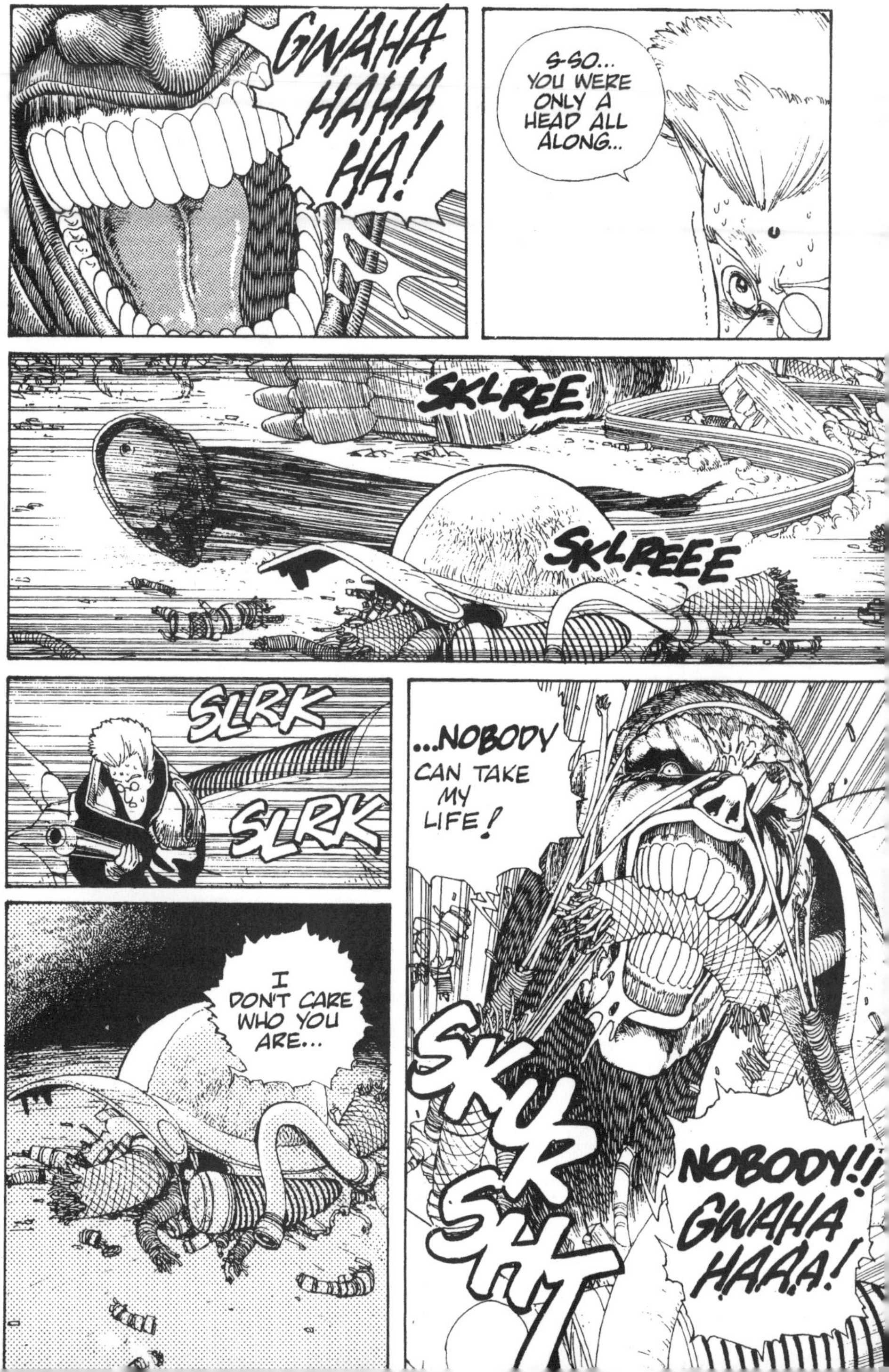
GWAHA HAHA HA!
S-SO... YOU WERE ONLY A HEAD ALL ALONG...
SKLREE
SKLREEE
SLRK
SLRK
I DON'T CARE WHO YOU ARE...
...NOBODY CAN TAKE MY LIFE!
SKURSHT
NOBODY!! GWAHA HAAAA!

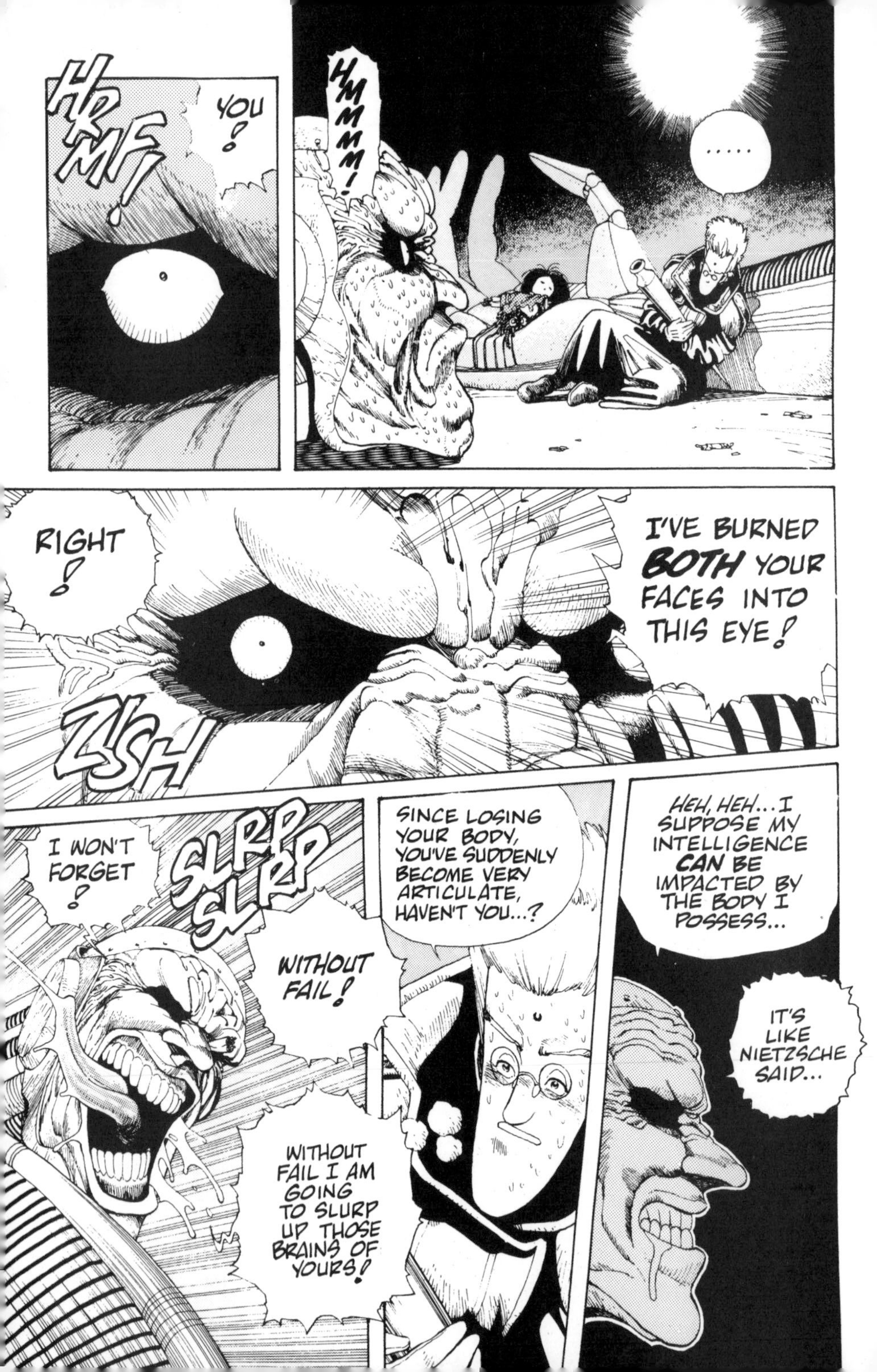
HRMF!
YOU!
HMMMMM!
......
RIGHT!
I'VE BURNED BOTH YOUR FACES INTO THIS EYE!
ZISH
I WON'T FORGET!
SLRP SLRP
WITHOUT FAIL!
WITHOUT FAIL I AM GOING TO SLURP UP THOSE BRAINS OF YOURS!
SINCE LOSING YOUR BODY, YOU'VE SUDDENLY BECOME VERY ARTICULATE, HAVEN'T YOU...?
HEH, HEH...I SUPPOSE MY INTELLIGENCE CAN BE IMPACTED BY THE BODY I POSSESS...
IT'S LIKE NIETZSCHE SAID...

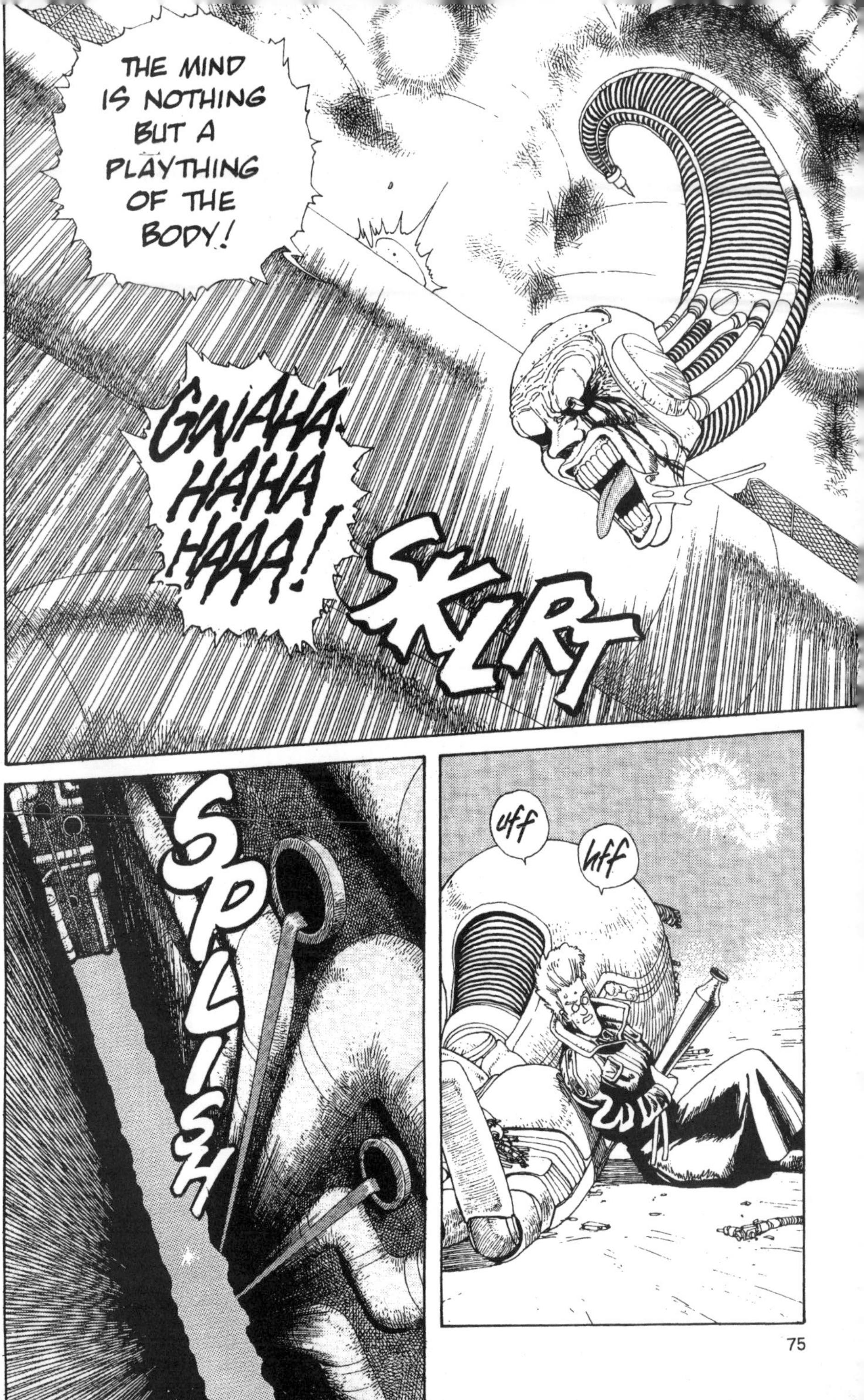
THE MIND IS NOTHING BUT A PLAYTHING OF THE BODY!
GWAHAHAHAHAHAAA!
SKLRT
SPLISH
uff
huff

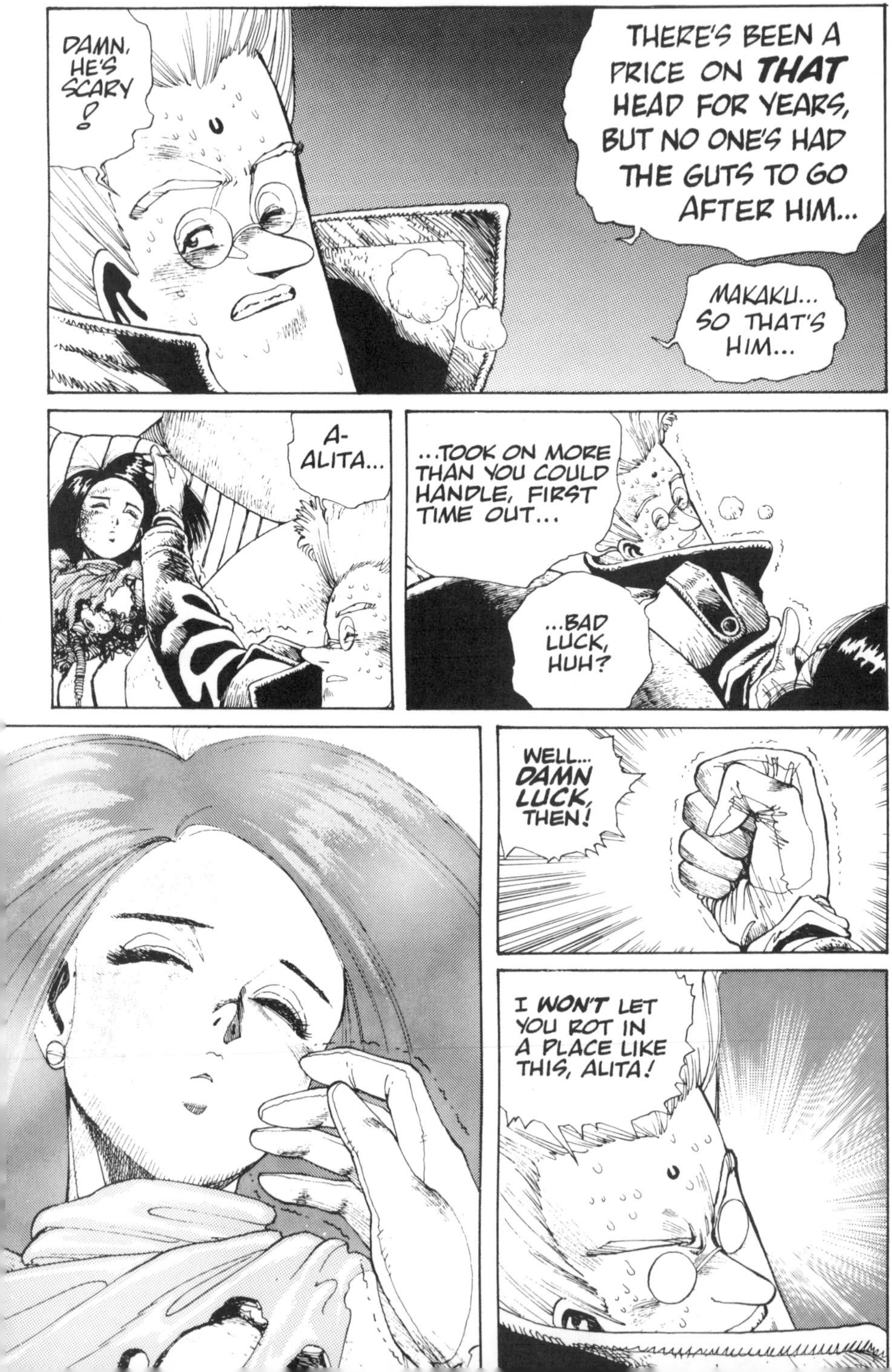
DAMN, HE'S SCARY !
THERE'S BEEN A PRICE ON **THAT** HEAD FOR YEARS, BUT NO ONE'S HAD THE GUTS TO GO AFTER HIM...
MAKAKU... SO THAT'S HIM...
A- ALITA...
...TOOK ON MORE THAN YOU COULD HANDLE, FIRST TIME OUT...
...BAD LUCK, HUH?
WELL... ***DAMN LUCK***, THEN!
I ***WON'T*** LET YOU ROT IN A PLACE LIKE THIS, ALITA!

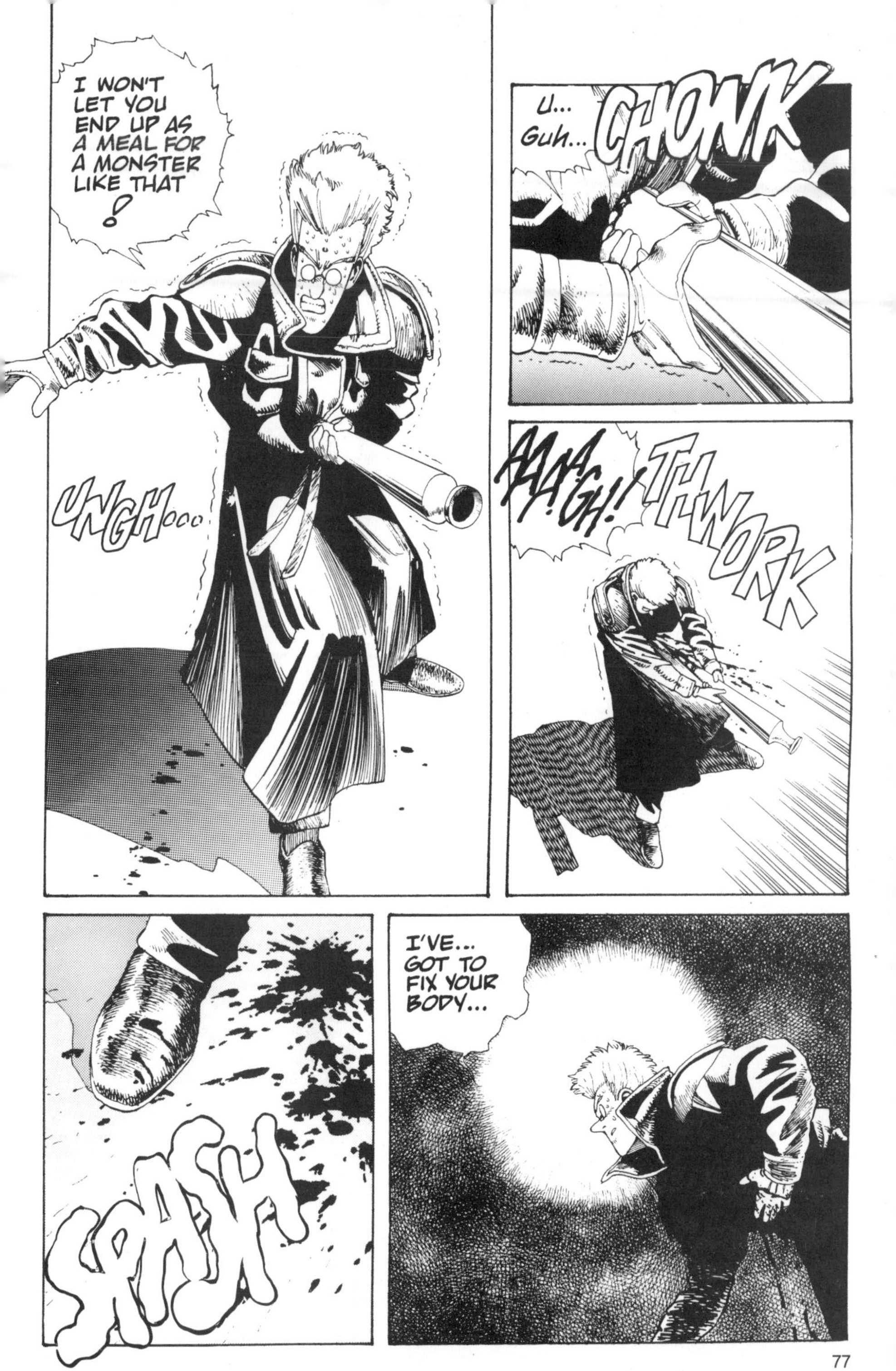
I WON'T LET YOU END UP AS A MEAL FOR A MONSTER LIKE THAT!
UNGH...
U... Guh...
CHONK
AAAAGH!!
THWORK
SPASH
I'VE... GOT TO FIX YOUR BODY...

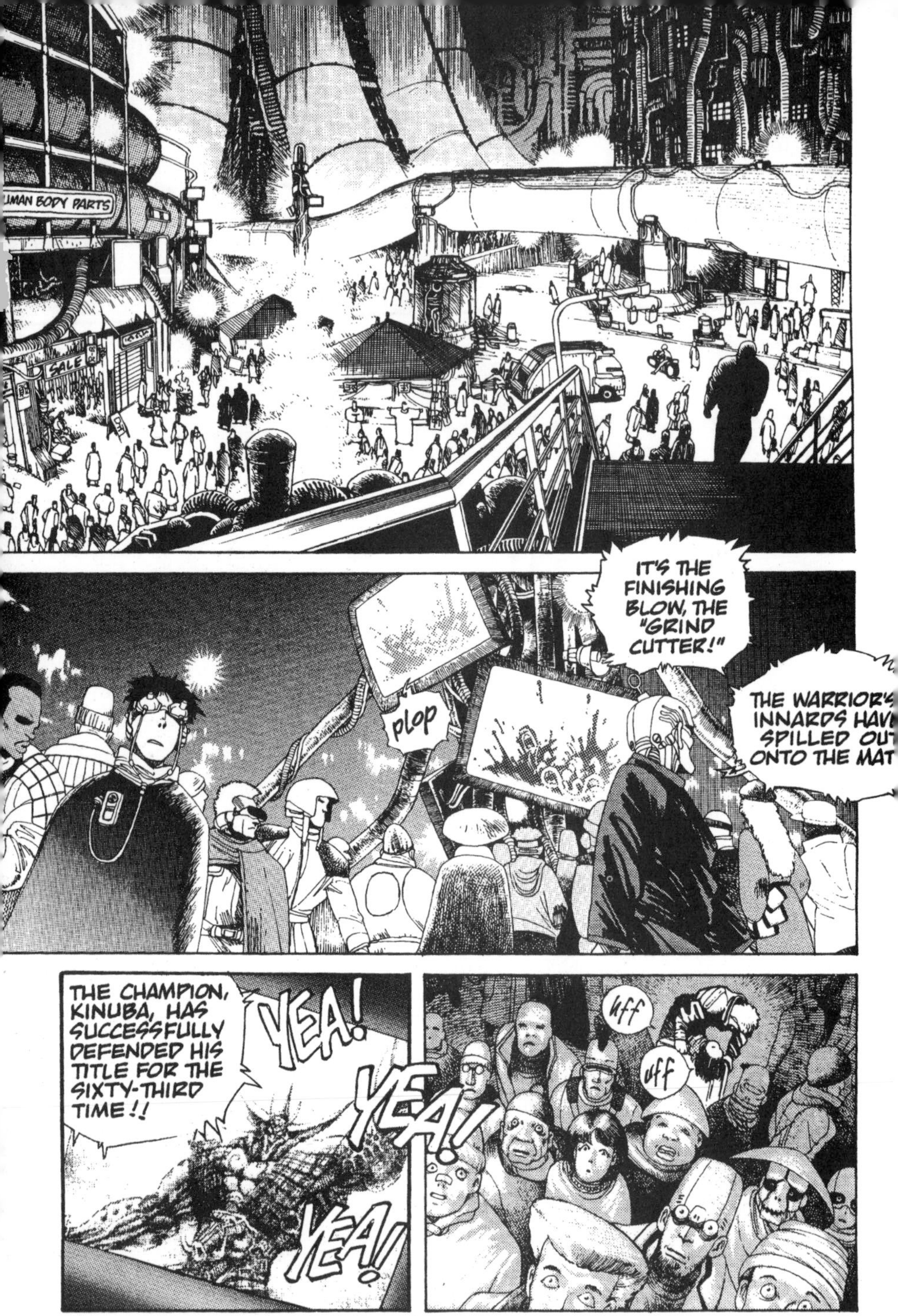
UMAN BODY PARTS
SALE
IT'S THE FINISHING BLOW, THE "GRIND CUTTER!"
plop
THE WARRIOR'S INNARDS HAVE SPILLED OUT ONTO THE MAT
THE CHAMPION, KINUBA, HAS SUCCESSFULLY DEFENDED HIS TITLE FOR THE SIXTY-THIRD TIME!!
YEA!
YEA!!
YEA!!
uff
uff

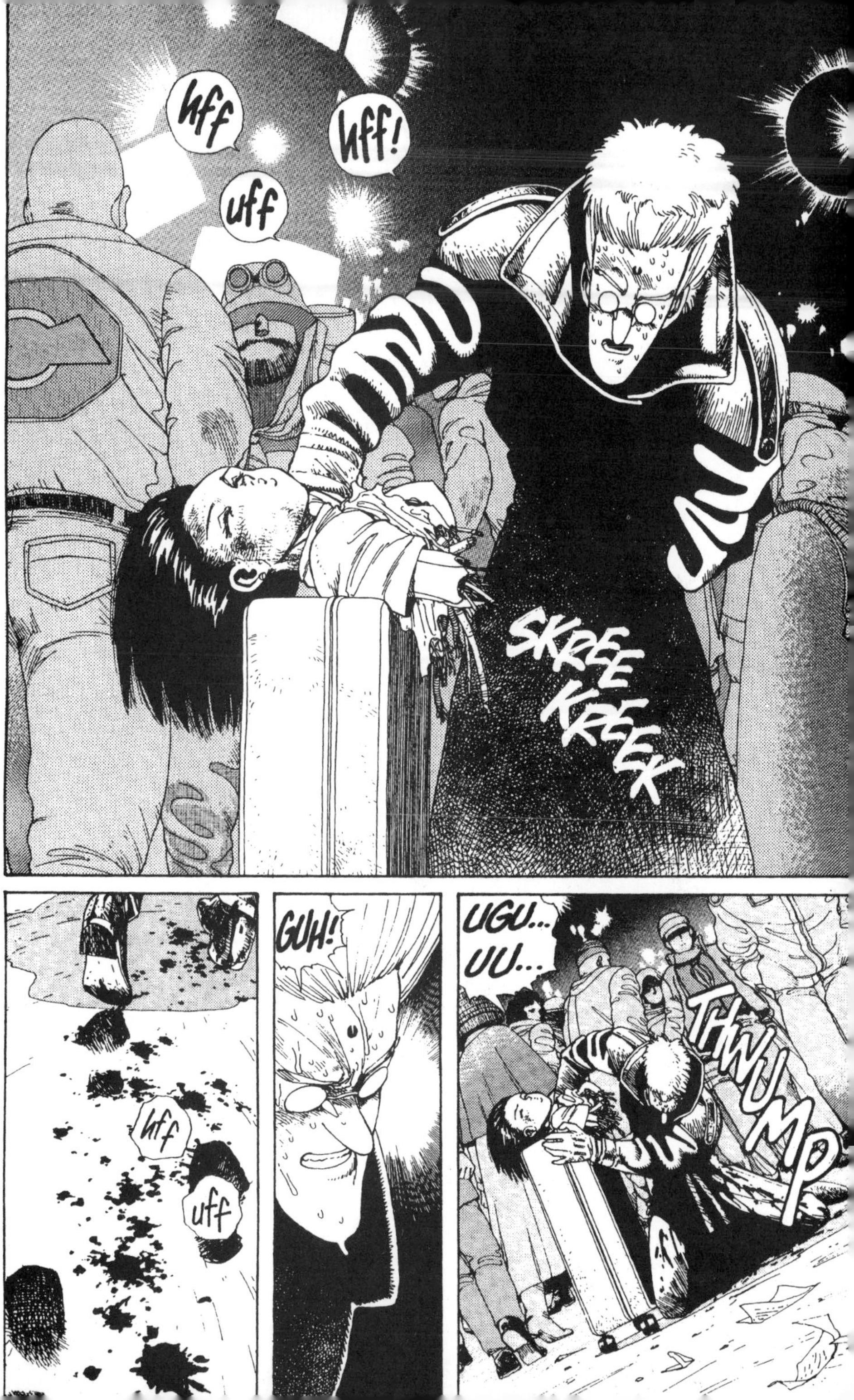
hff
hff!
uff
SKREE KREEK
hff
uff
GUH!
UGU...
UU...
THWUMP

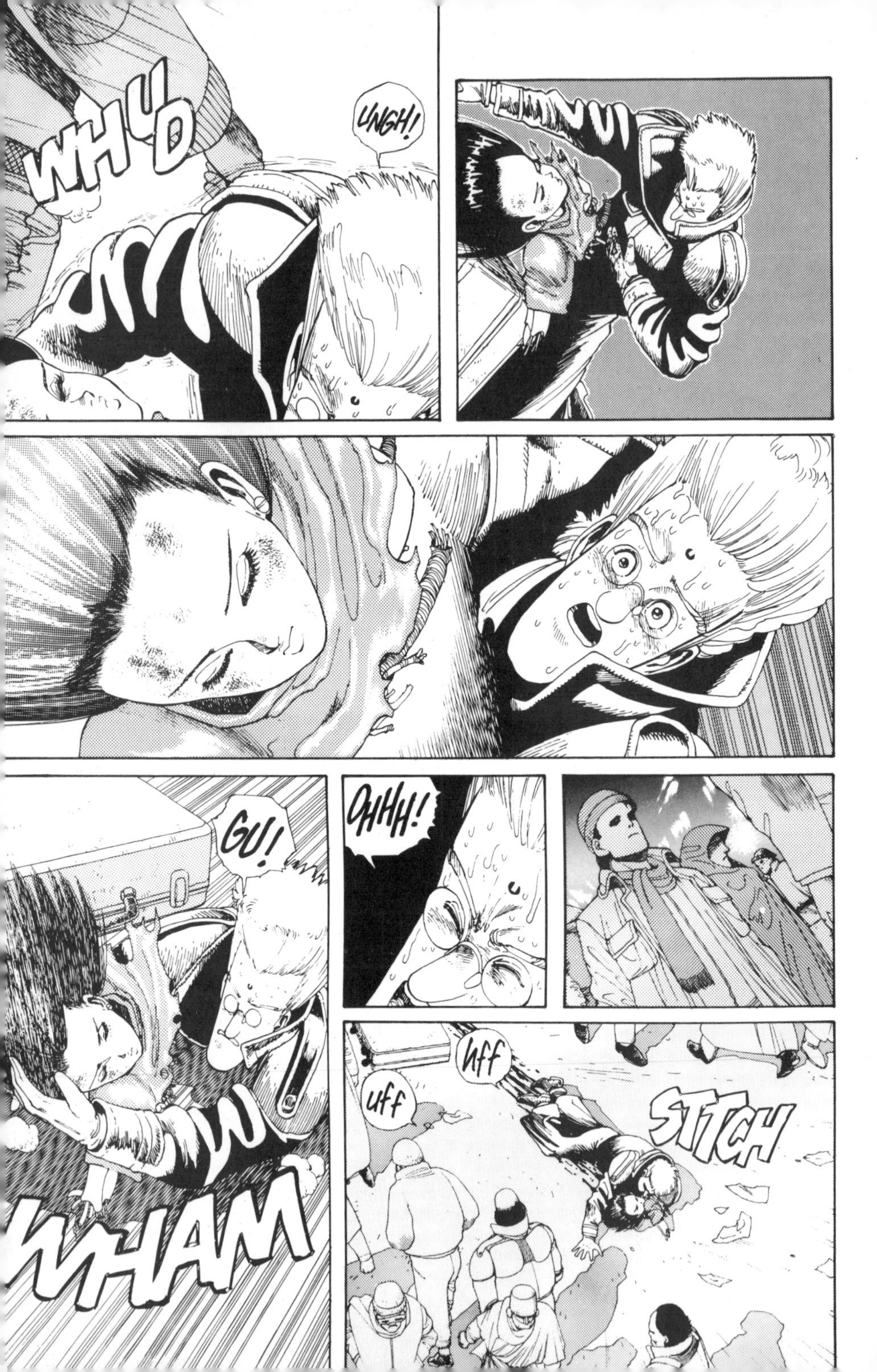

WHUD
UNGH!
OHHH!
GU!
WHAM
uff
uff
STITCH

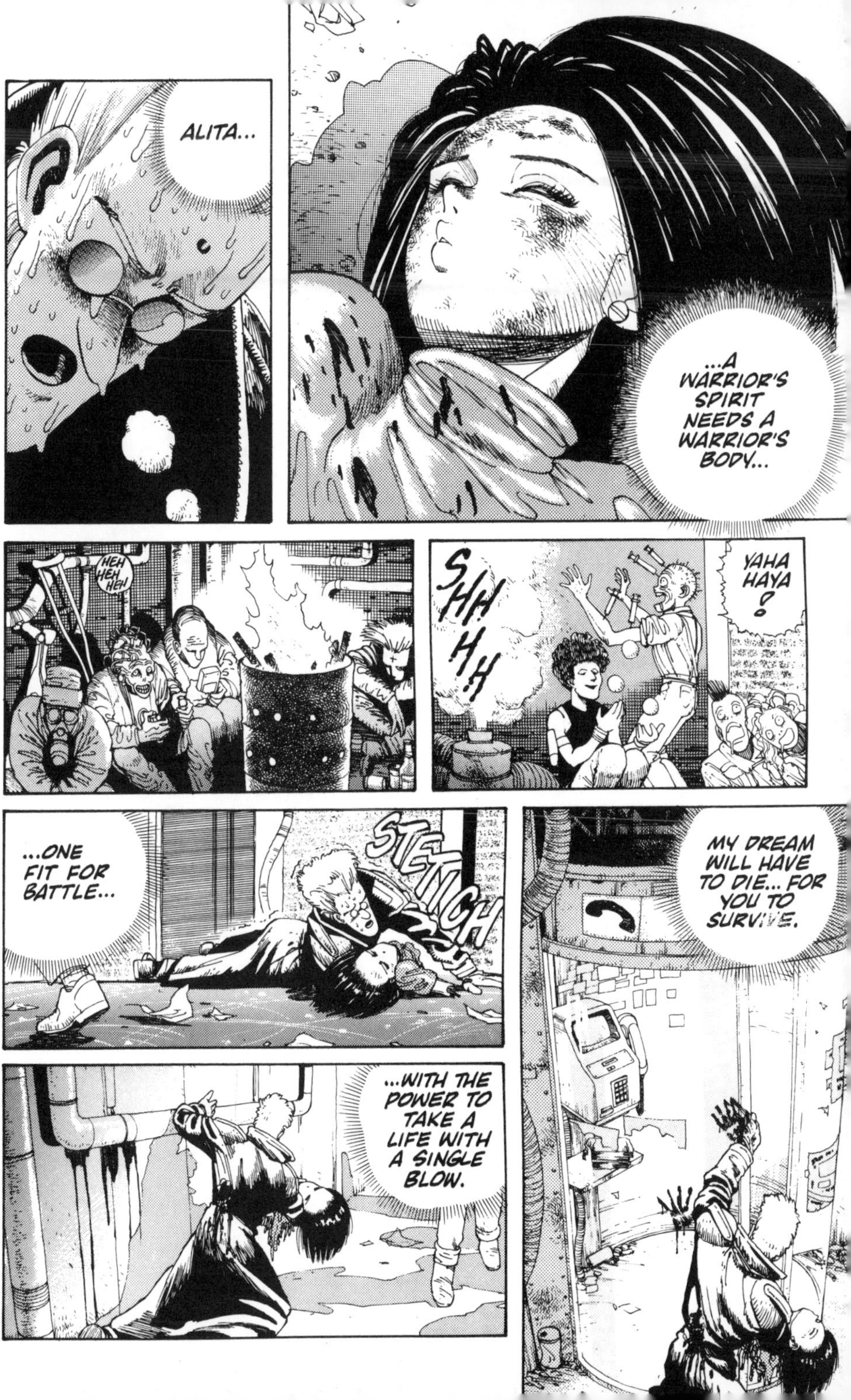
ALITA...
...A WARRIOR'S SPIRIT NEEDS A WARRIOR'S BODY...
HEH HEH HEH
SHHHH
YAHA HAYA!
...ONE FIT FOR BATTLE...
STETCH
MY DREAM WILL HAVE TO DIE... FOR YOU TO SURVIVE.
...WITH THE POWER TO TAKE A LIFE WITH A SINGLE BLOW.

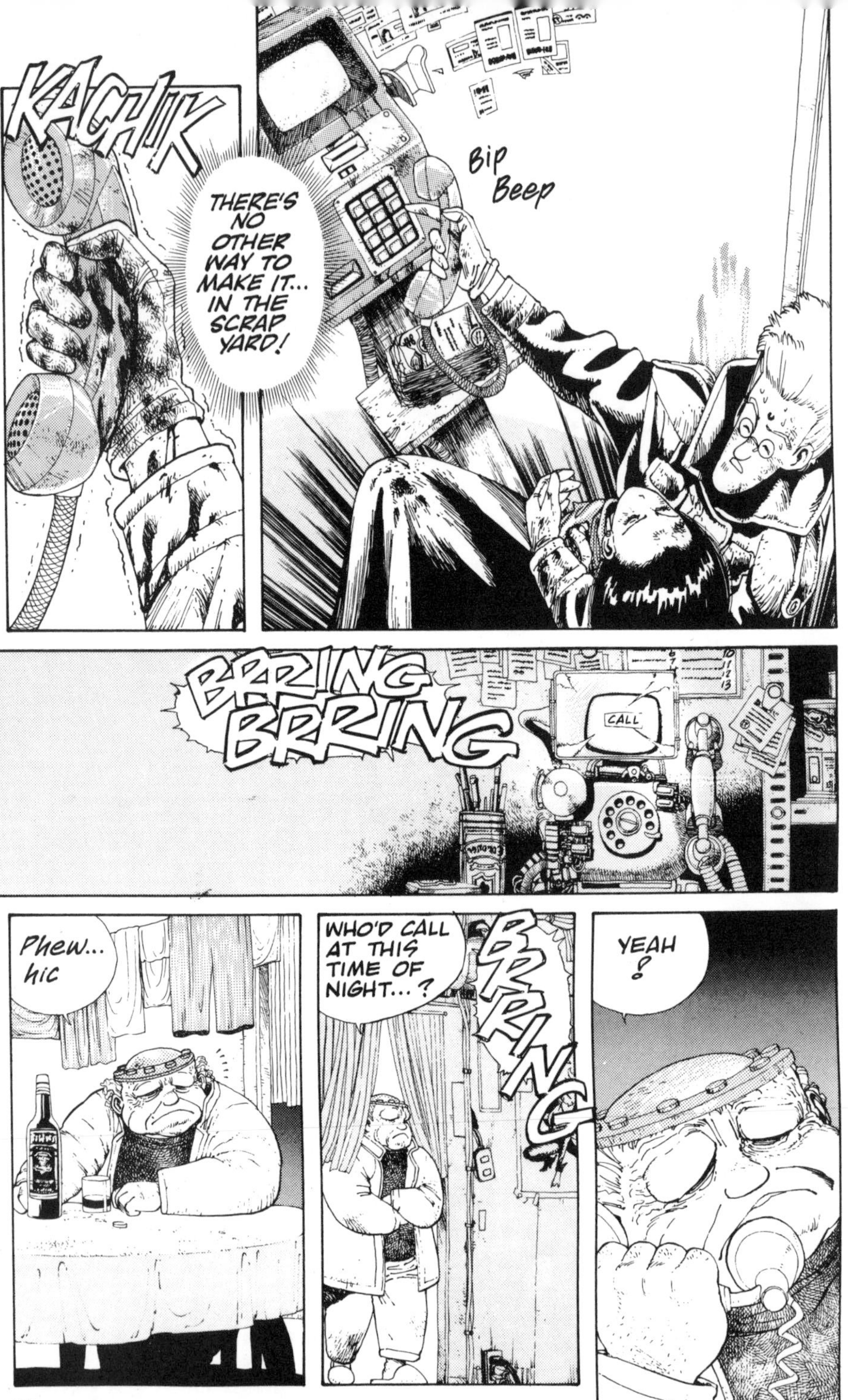
KACHIK
THERE'S NO OTHER WAY TO MAKE IT... IN THE SCRAP YARD!
Bip Beep
BRRING BRRING
CALL
Phew... hic
WHO'D CALL AT THIS TIME OF NIGHT...?
BRRRING
YEAH?

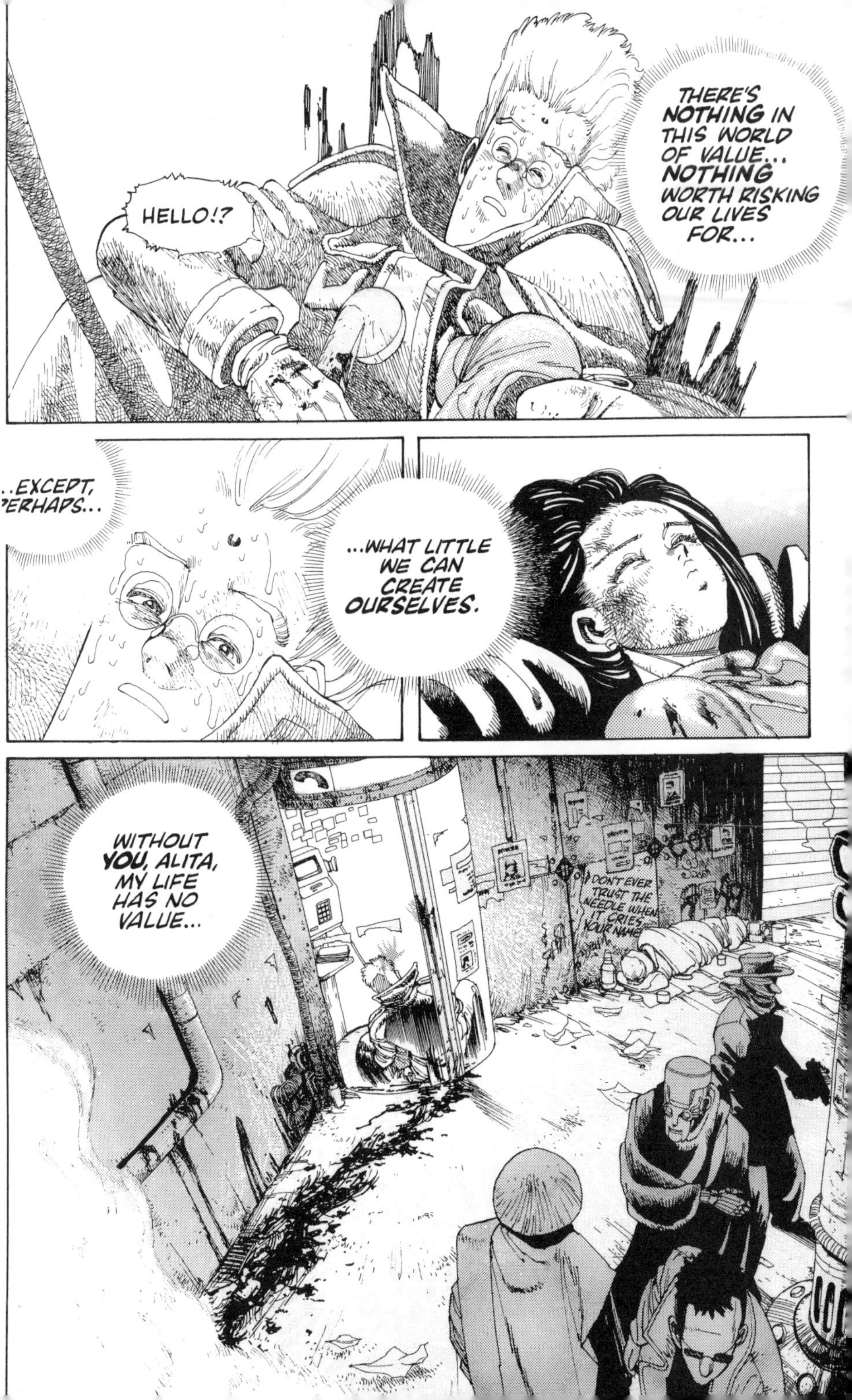
HELLO!?
THERE'S NOTHING IN THIS WORLD OF VALUE... NOTHING WORTH RISKING OUR LIVES FOR...
...EXCEPT, PERHAPS...
...WHAT LITTLE WE CAN CREATE OURSELVES.
WITHOUT YOU, ALITA, MY LIFE HAS NO VALUE...
DON'T EVER TRUST THE NEEDLE WHEN IT CRIES YOUR NAME

BERSERKERS REBORN

Battle 4: Resurgence

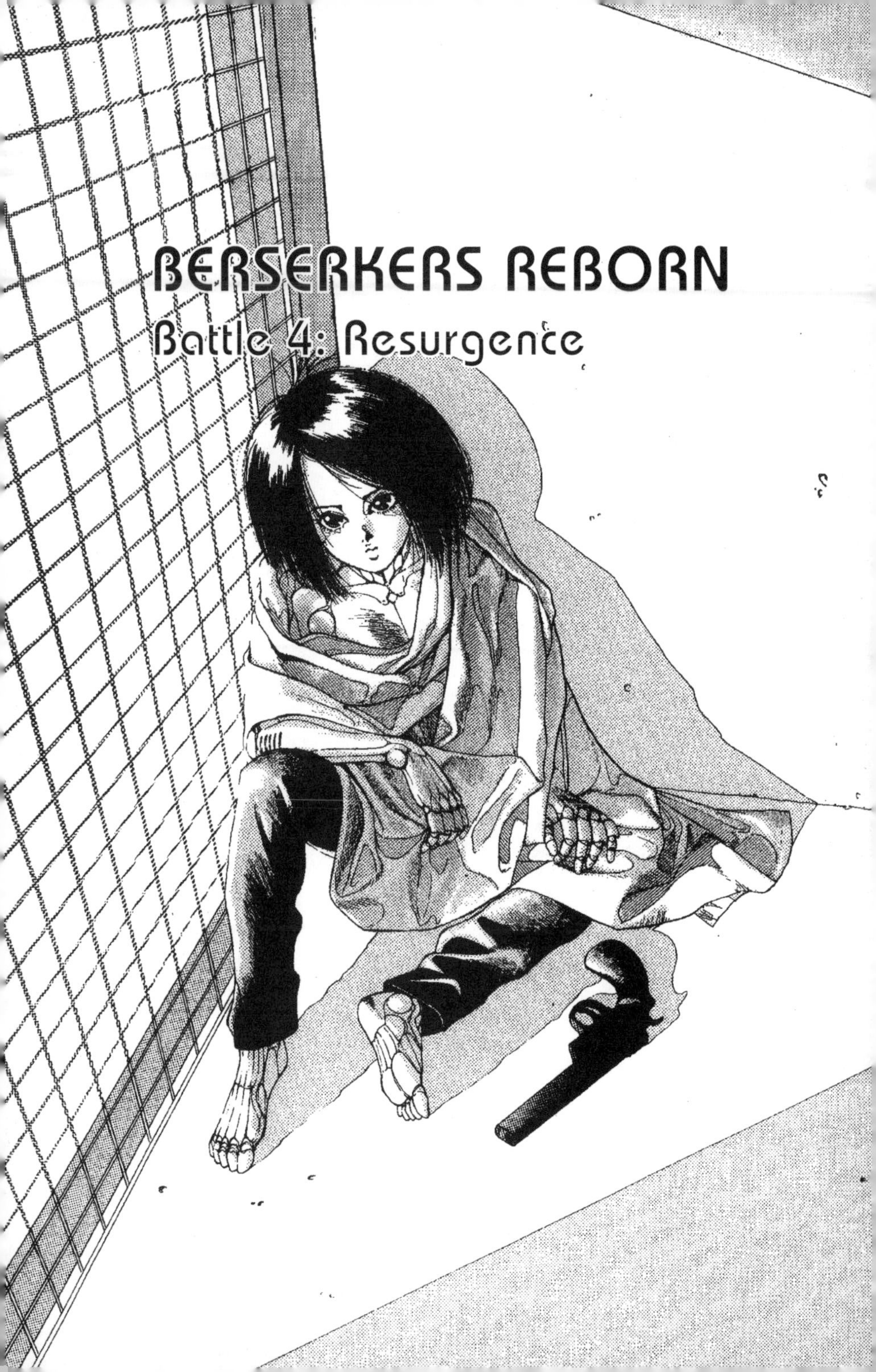

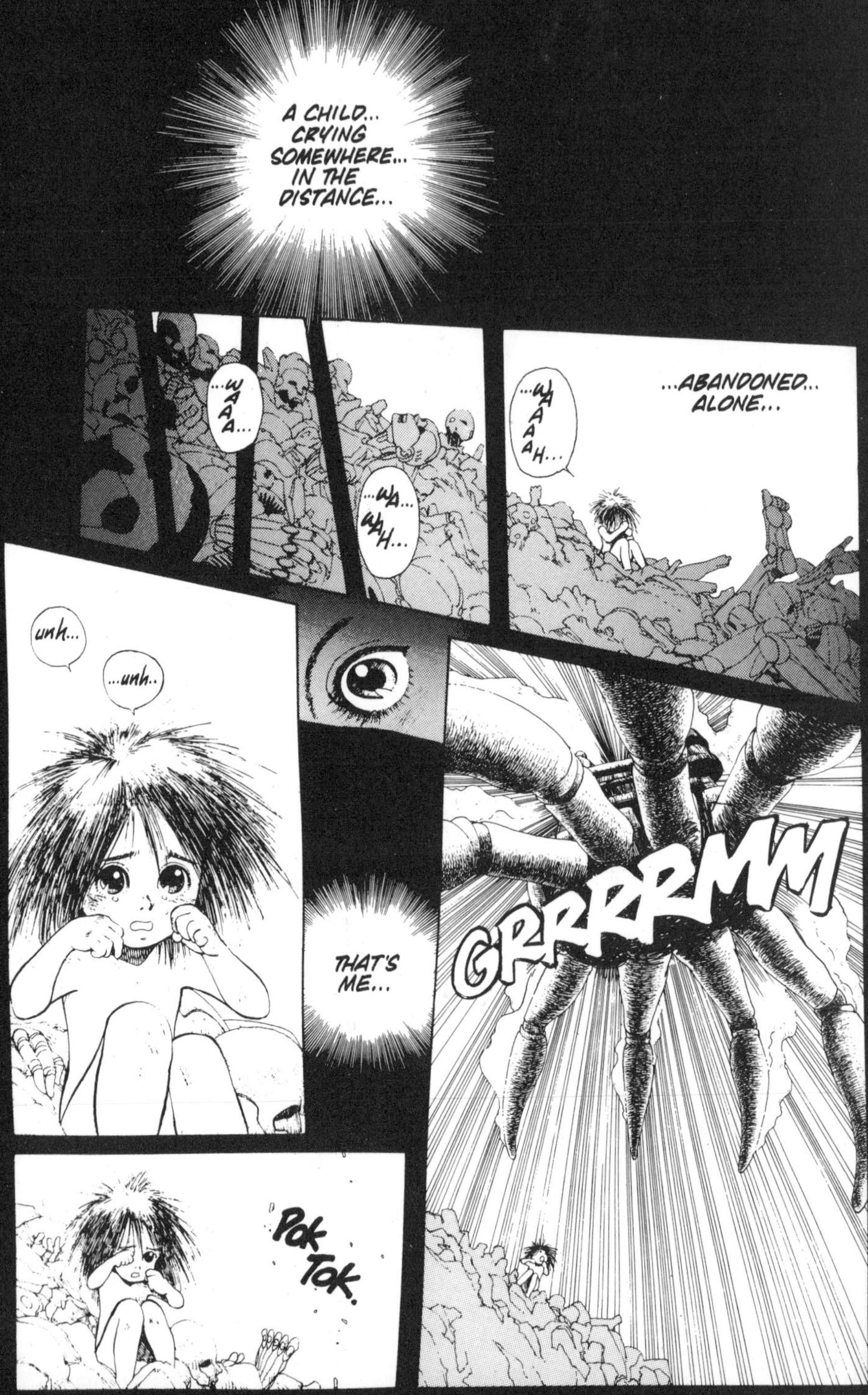
A CHILD... CRYING SOMEWHERE... IN THE DISTANCE...
...WAAA...
...WA... WAH...
...WAAAAH...
...ABANDONED... ALONE...
unh...
...unh...
THAT'S ME...
GRRRRMM
POK TOK

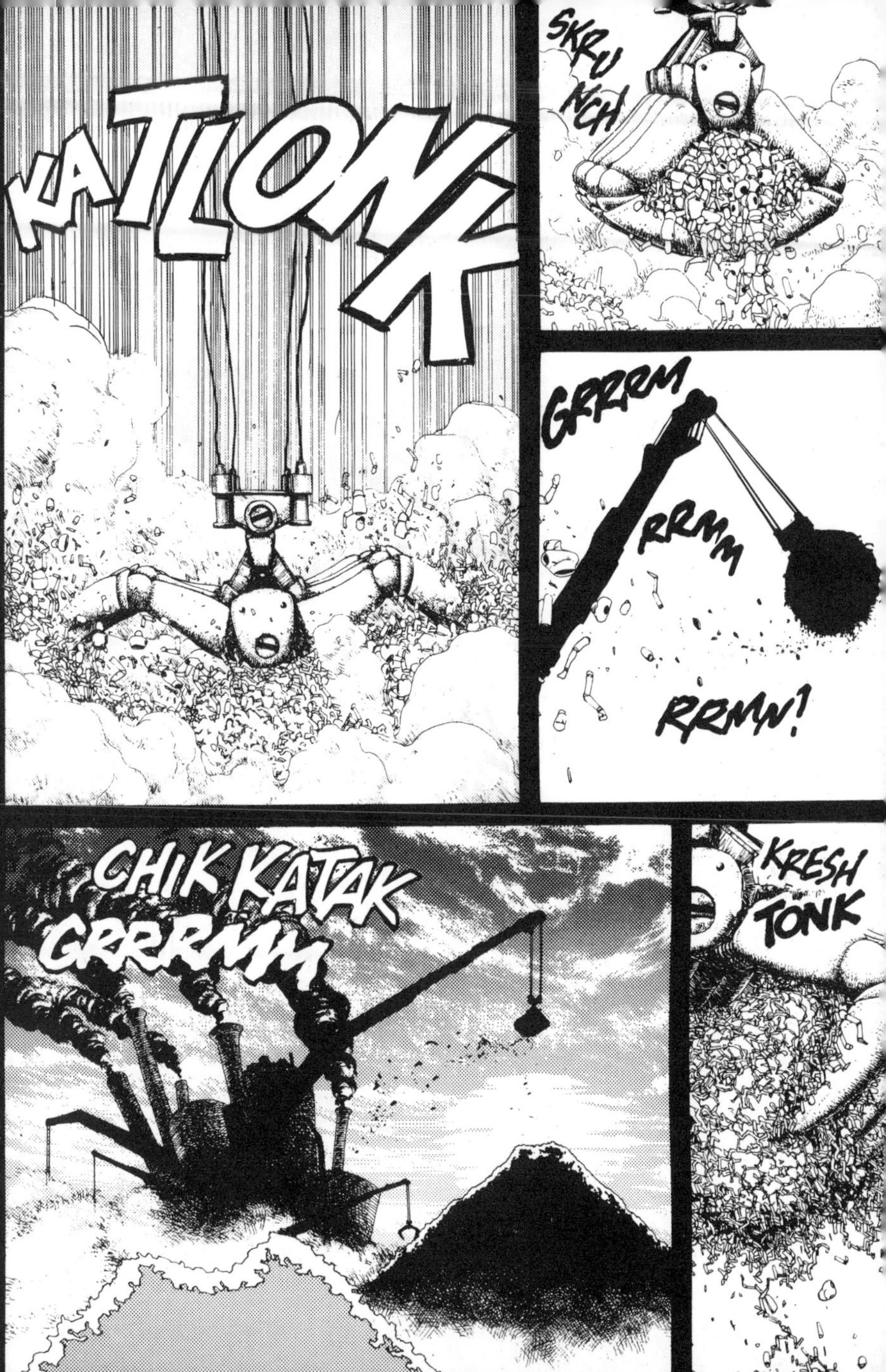
KATLONK
SKRUNCH
GRRRM
RRMM
RRMN!
CHIK KATAK
GRRRMM
KRESH
TONK

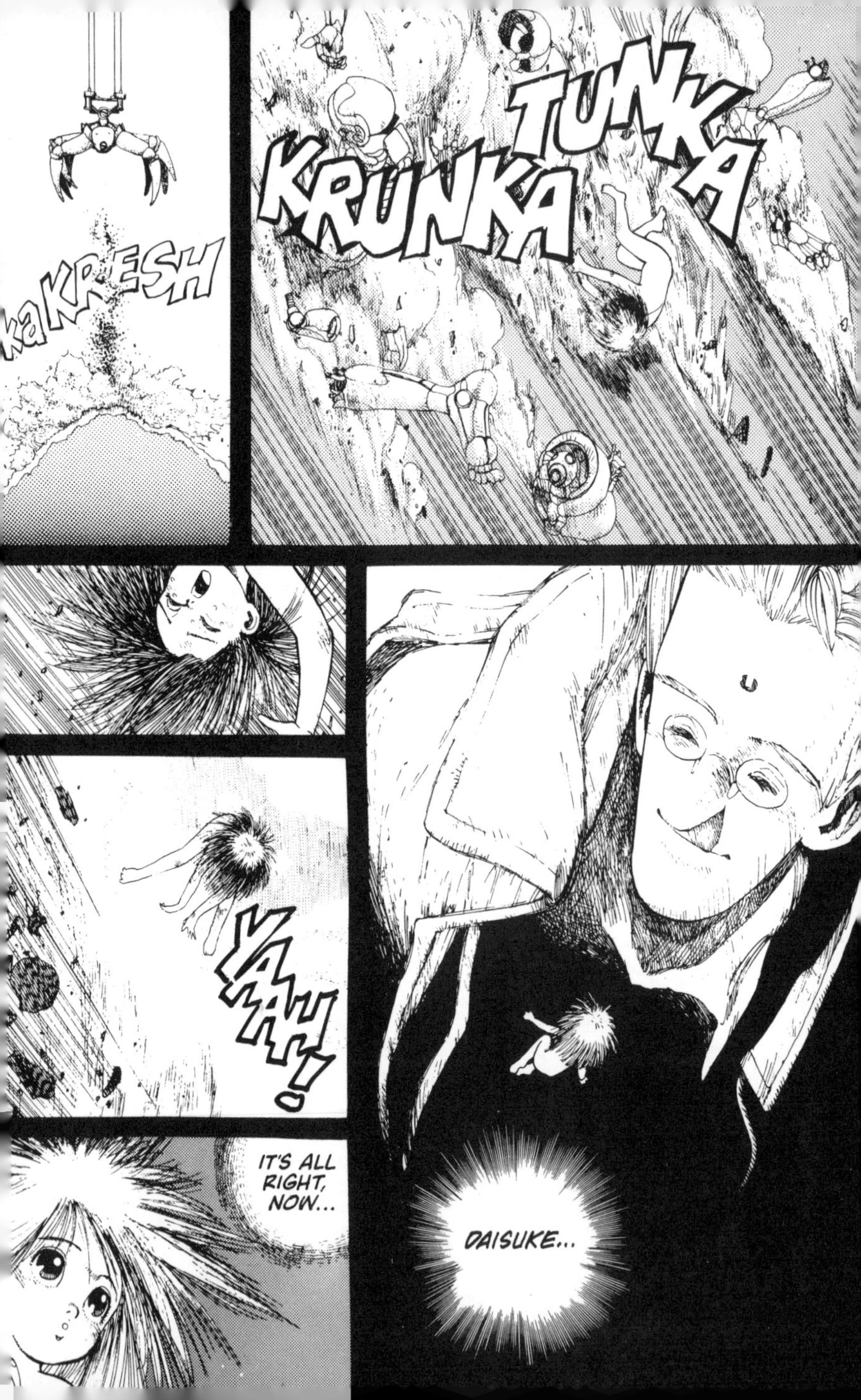
kaKRESH
KRUNKA
TUNKA
YAAAH!
IT'S ALL RIGHT, NOW...
DAISUKE...

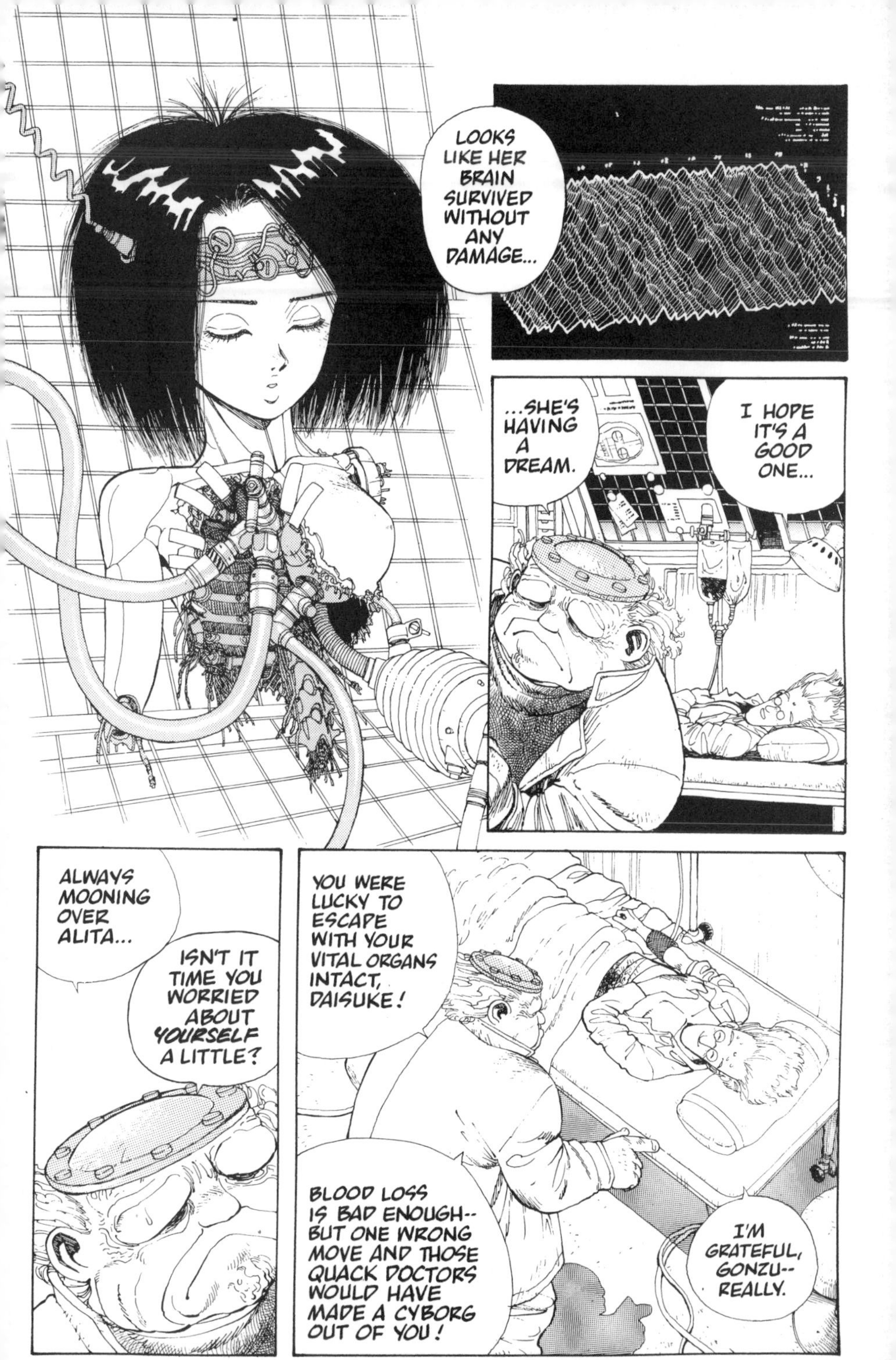
LOOKS LIKE HER BRAIN SURVIVED WITHOUT ANY DAMAGE...
...SHE'S HAVING A DREAM.
I HOPE IT'S A GOOD ONE...
ALWAYS MOONING OVER ALITA...
ISN'T IT TIME YOU WORRIED ABOUT YOURSELF A LITTLE?
YOU WERE LUCKY TO ESCAPE WITH YOUR VITAL ORGANS INTACT, DAISUKE!
BLOOD LOSS IS BAD ENOUGH-- BUT ONE WRONG MOVE AND THOSE QUACK DOCTORS WOULD HAVE MADE A CYBORG OUT OF YOU!
I'M GRATEFUL, GONZU-- REALLY.

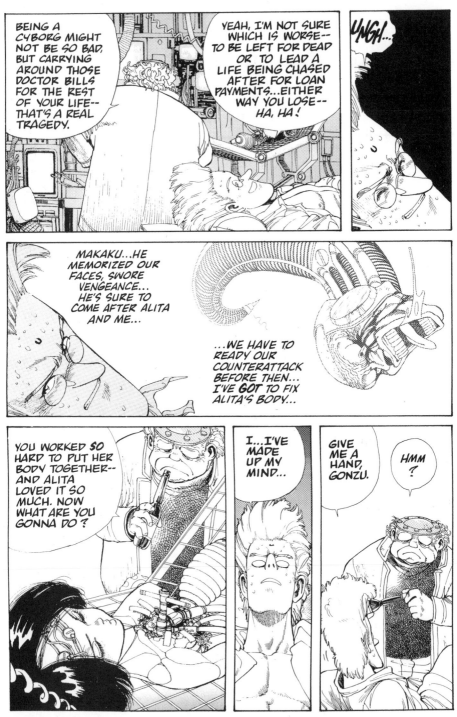

BEING A CYBORG MIGHT NOT BE SO BAD, BUT CARRYING AROUND THOSE DOCTOR BILLS FOR THE REST OF YOUR LIFE-- THAT'S A REAL TRAGEDY.

YEAH, I'M NOT SURE WHICH IS WORSE-- TO BE LEFT FOR DEAD OR TO LEAD A LIFE BEING CHASED AFTER FOR LOAN PAYMENTS...EITHER WAY YOU LOSE-- HA, HA!

UNGH...

MAKAKU...HE MEMORIZED OUR FACES, SWORE VENGEANCE... HE'S SURE TO COME AFTER ALITA AND ME...

...WE HAVE TO READY OUR COUNTERATTACK BEFORE THEN... I'VE **GOT** TO FIX ALITA'S BODY...

YOU WORKED SO HARD TO PUT HER BODY TOGETHER-- AND ALITA LOVED IT SO MUCH. NOW WHAT ARE YOU GONNA DO?

I...I'VE MADE UP MY MIND...

GIVE ME A HAND, GONZU.

HMM?

90

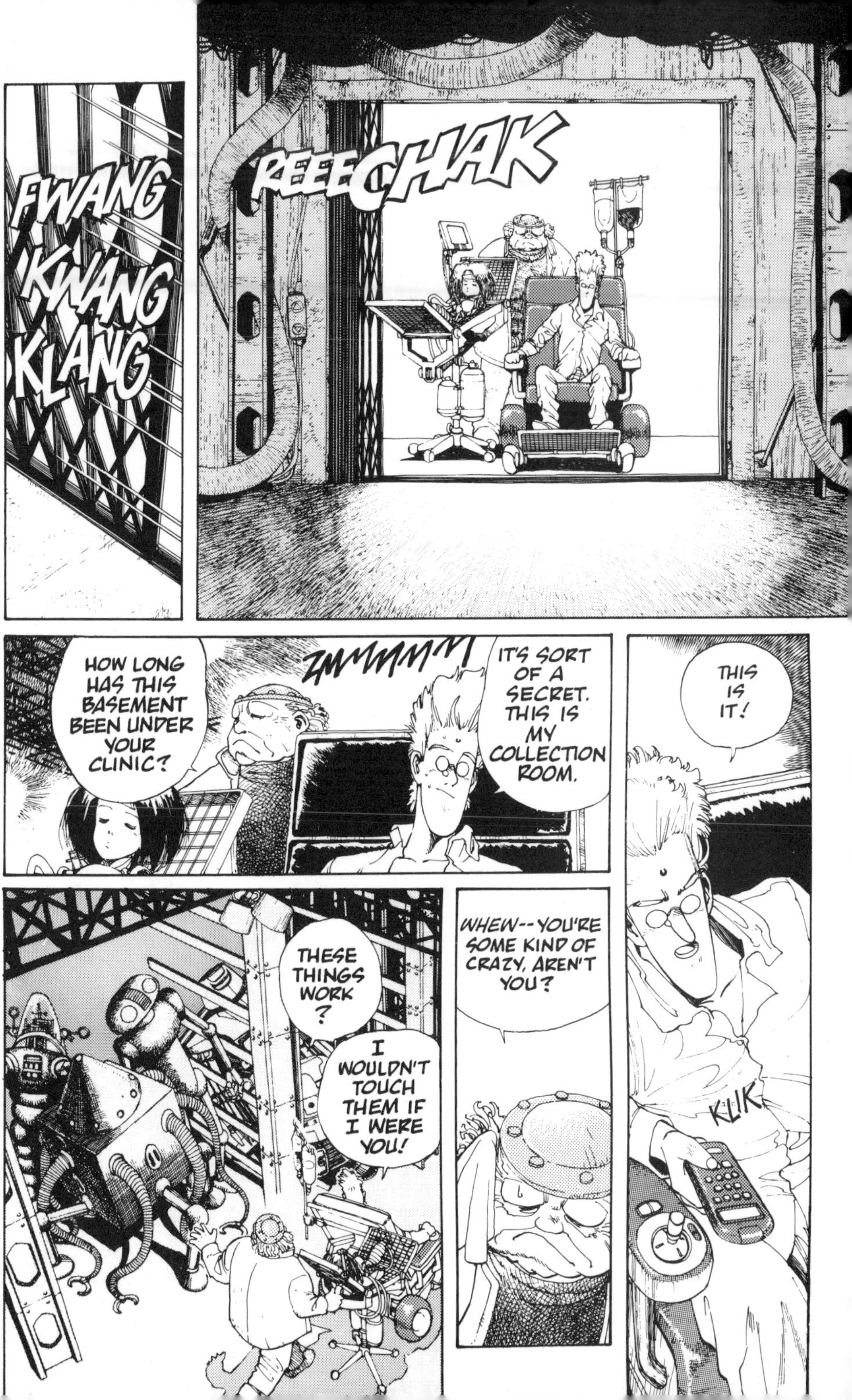
FWANG
KWANG
KLANG
REEECHAK
HOW LONG HAS THIS BASEMENT BEEN UNDER YOUR CLINIC?
ZMMMMM
IT'S SORT OF A SECRET. THIS IS MY COLLECTION ROOM.
THESE THINGS WORK?
I WOULDN'T TOUCH THEM IF I WERE YOU!
WHEW--YOU'RE SOME KIND OF CRAZY, AREN'T YOU?
THIS IS IT!
KLIK

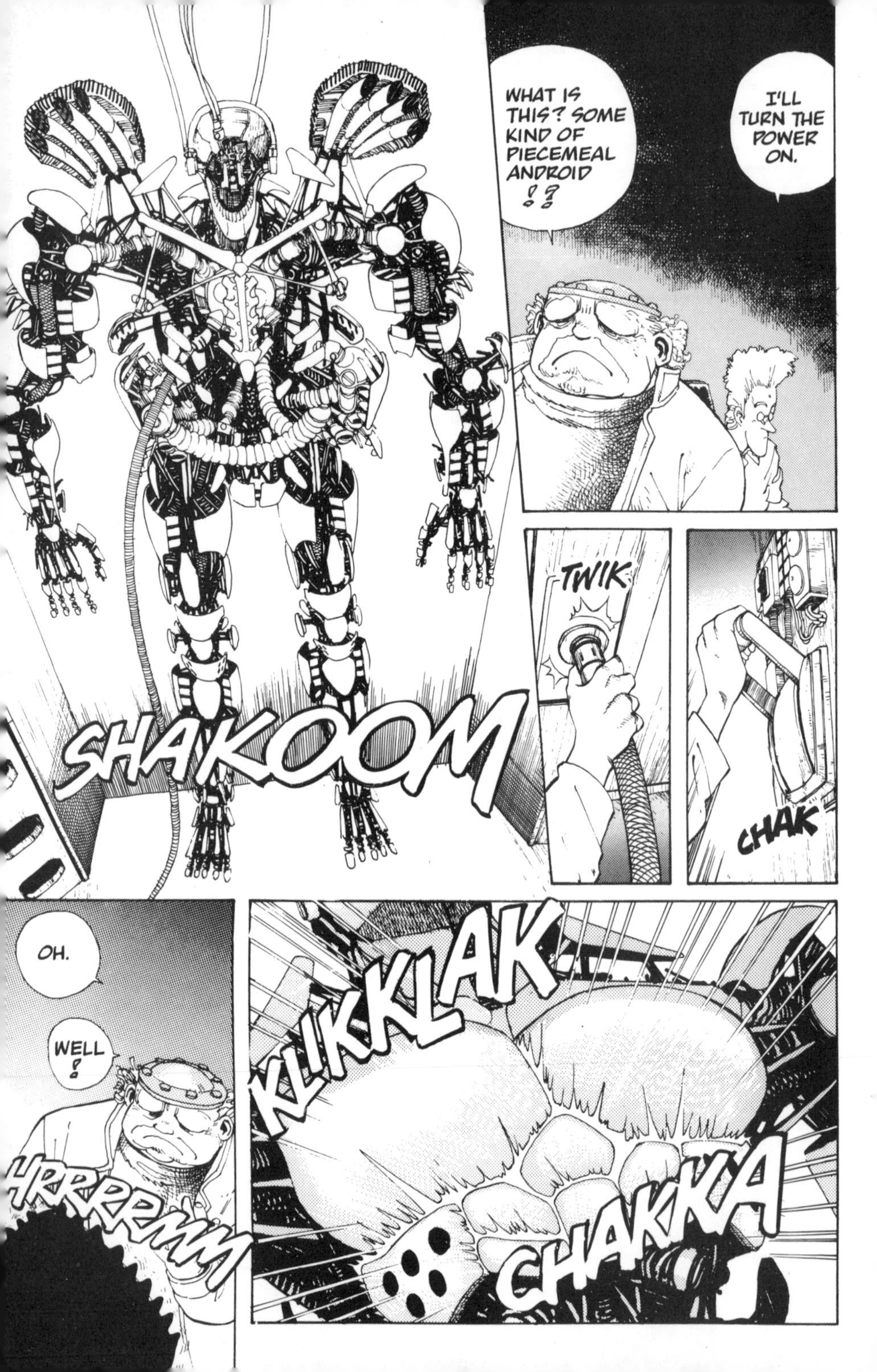
SHAKOOM
WHAT IS THIS? SOME KIND OF PIECEMEAL ANDROID !?
I'LL TURN THE POWER ON.
TWIK
CHAK
OH.
WELL !?
HRRRRMMM
KLIKKLAK
CHAKKA

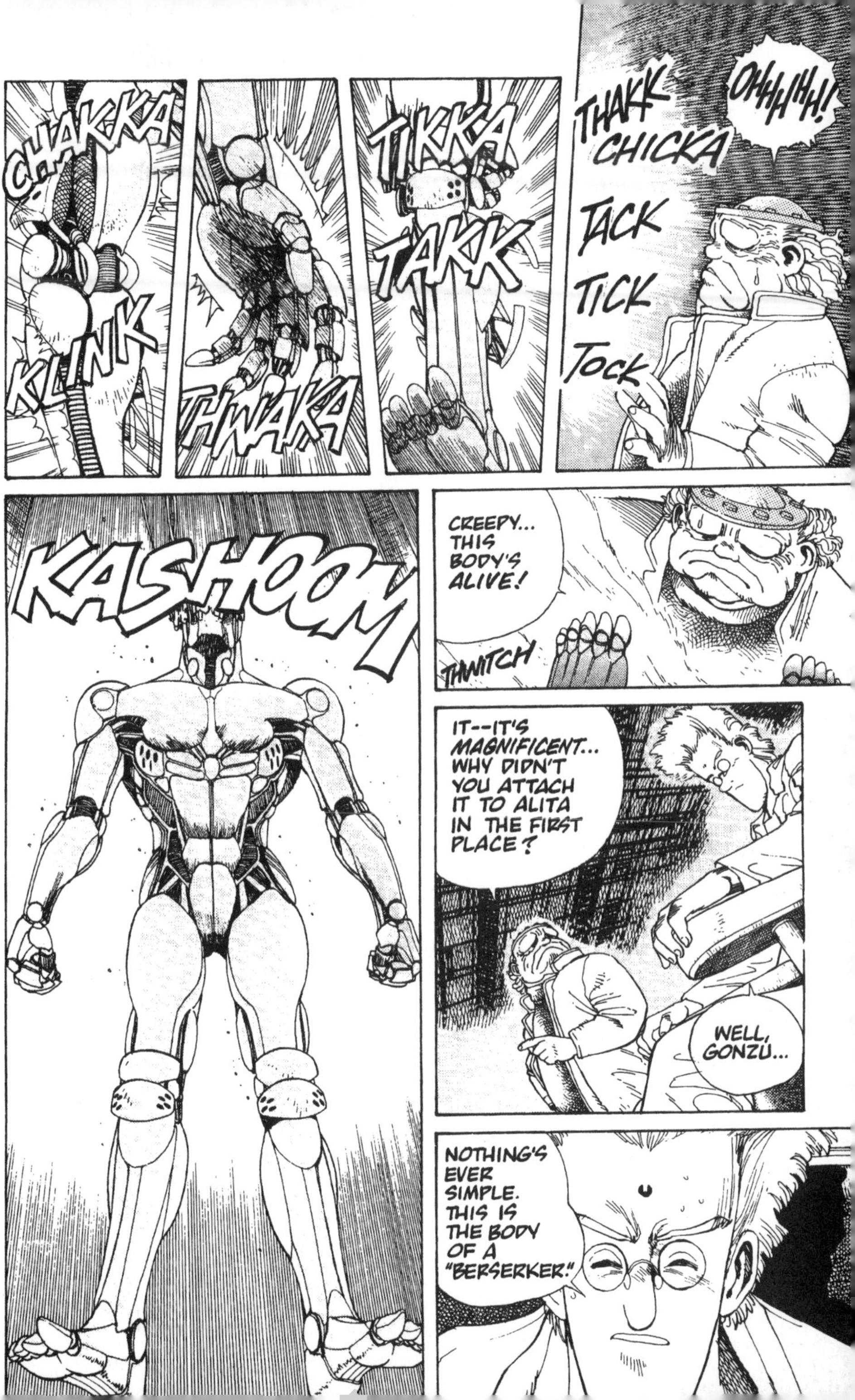

CHAKKA
KLINK
THWAKA
TIKKA
TAKK
THAKK
CHICKA
TACK
TICK
TOCK
OHHHHH!
KASHOOM
CREEPY... THIS BODY'S ALIVE!
THWITCH
IT--IT'S MAGNIFICENT... WHY DIDN'T YOU ATTACH IT TO ALITA IN THE FIRST PLACE?
WELL, GONZU...
NOTHING'S EVER SIMPLE. THIS IS THE BODY OF A "BERSERKER."

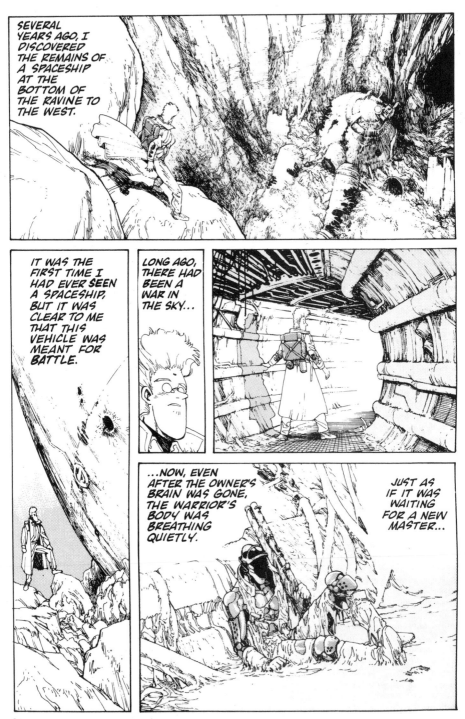

SEVERAL YEARS AGO, I DISCOVERED THE REMAINS OF A SPACESHIP AT THE BOTTOM OF THE RAVINE TO THE WEST.

IT WAS THE FIRST TIME I HAD EVER SEEN A SPACESHIP, BUT IT WAS CLEAR TO ME THAT THIS VEHICLE WAS MEANT FOR BATTLE.

LONG AGO, THERE HAD BEEN A WAR IN THE SKY...

...NOW, EVEN AFTER THE OWNER'S BRAIN WAS GONE, THE WARRIOR'S BODY WAS BREATHING QUIETLY.

JUST AS IF IT WAS WAITING FOR A NEW MASTER...

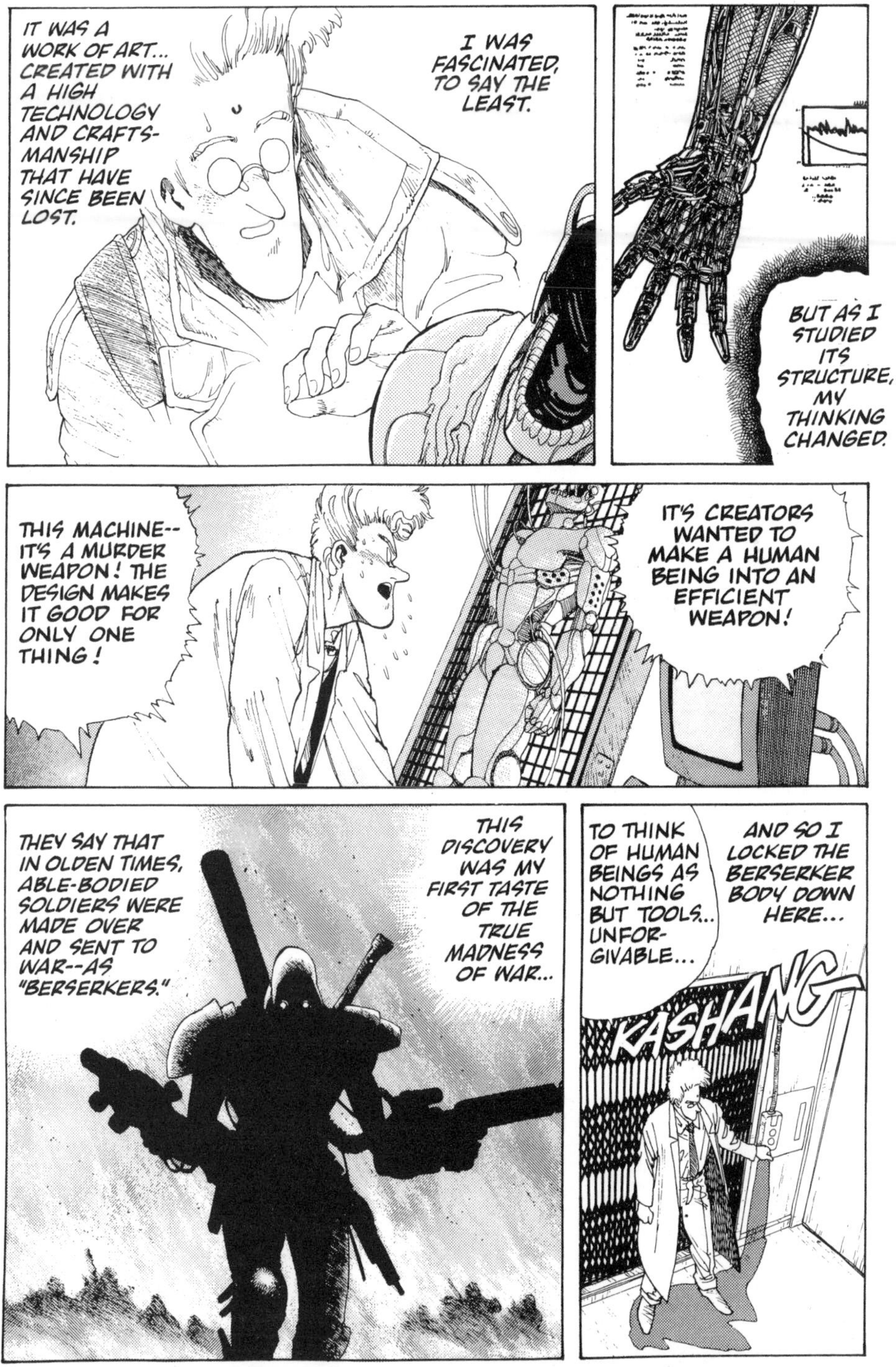
IT WAS A WORK OF ART... CREATED WITH A HIGH TECHNOLOGY AND CRAFTS-MANSHIP THAT HAVE SINCE BEEN LOST.
I WAS FASCINATED, TO SAY THE LEAST.
BUT AS I STUDIED ITS STRUCTURE, MY THINKING CHANGED.
THIS MACHINE-- IT'S A MURDER WEAPON! THE DESIGN MAKES IT GOOD FOR ONLY ONE THING!
IT'S CREATORS WANTED TO MAKE A HUMAN BEING INTO AN EFFICIENT WEAPON!
THEY SAY THAT IN OLDEN TIMES, ABLE-BODIED SOLDIERS WERE MADE OVER AND SENT TO WAR--AS "BERSERKERS."
THIS DISCOVERY WAS MY FIRST TASTE OF THE TRUE MADNESS OF WAR...
TO THINK OF HUMAN BEINGS AS NOTHING BUT TOOLS... UNFOR-GIVABLE...
AND SO I LOCKED THE BERSERKER BODY DOWN HERE...
KASHANG

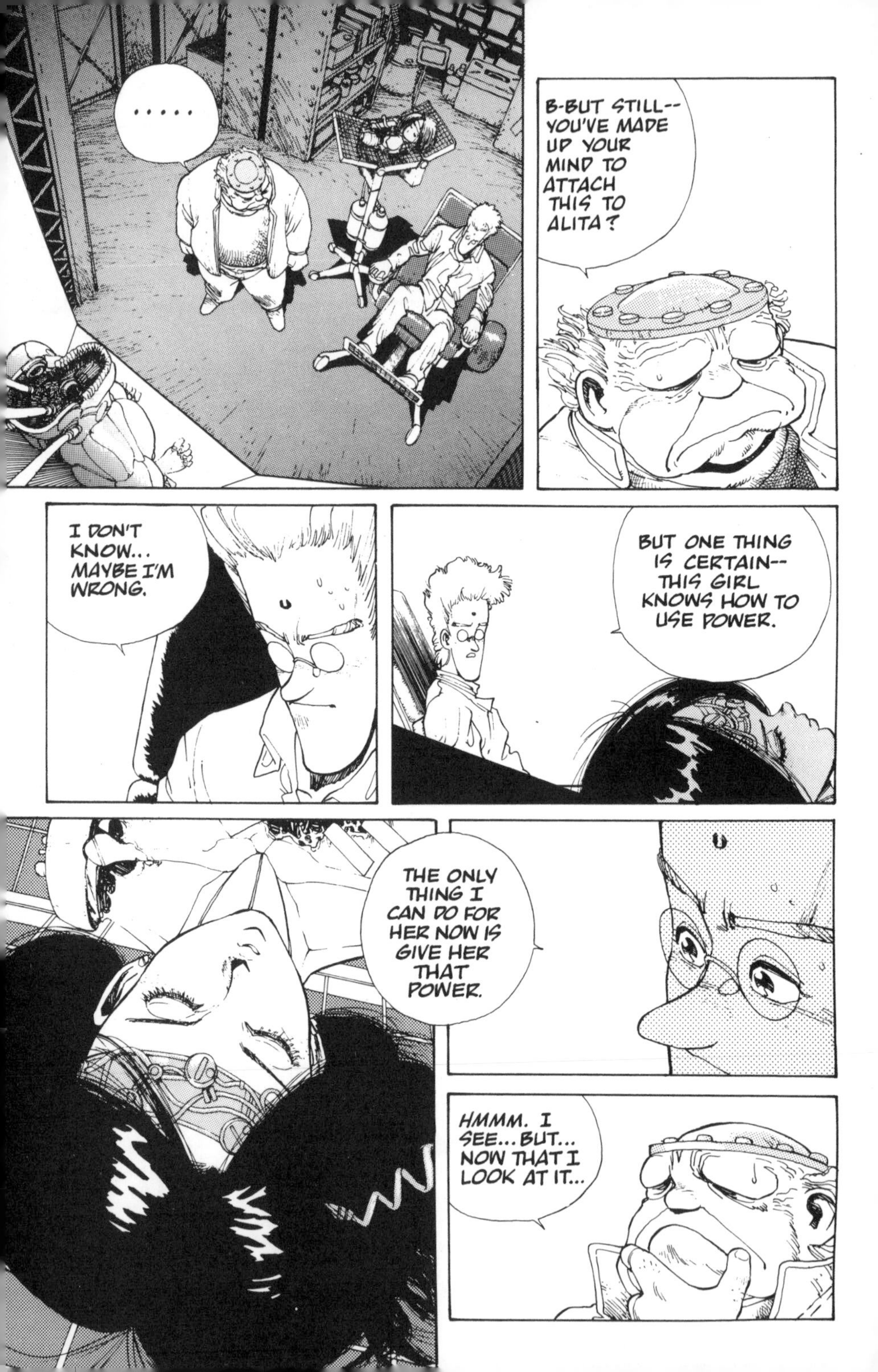
. . . . .
B-BUT STILL-- YOU'VE MADE UP YOUR MIND TO ATTACH THIS TO ALITA?
I DON'T KNOW... MAYBE I'M WRONG.
BUT ONE THING IS CERTAIN-- THIS GIRL KNOWS HOW TO USE POWER.
THE ONLY THING I CAN DO FOR HER NOW IS GIVE HER THAT POWER.
HMMM. I SEE... BUT... NOW THAT I LOOK AT IT...

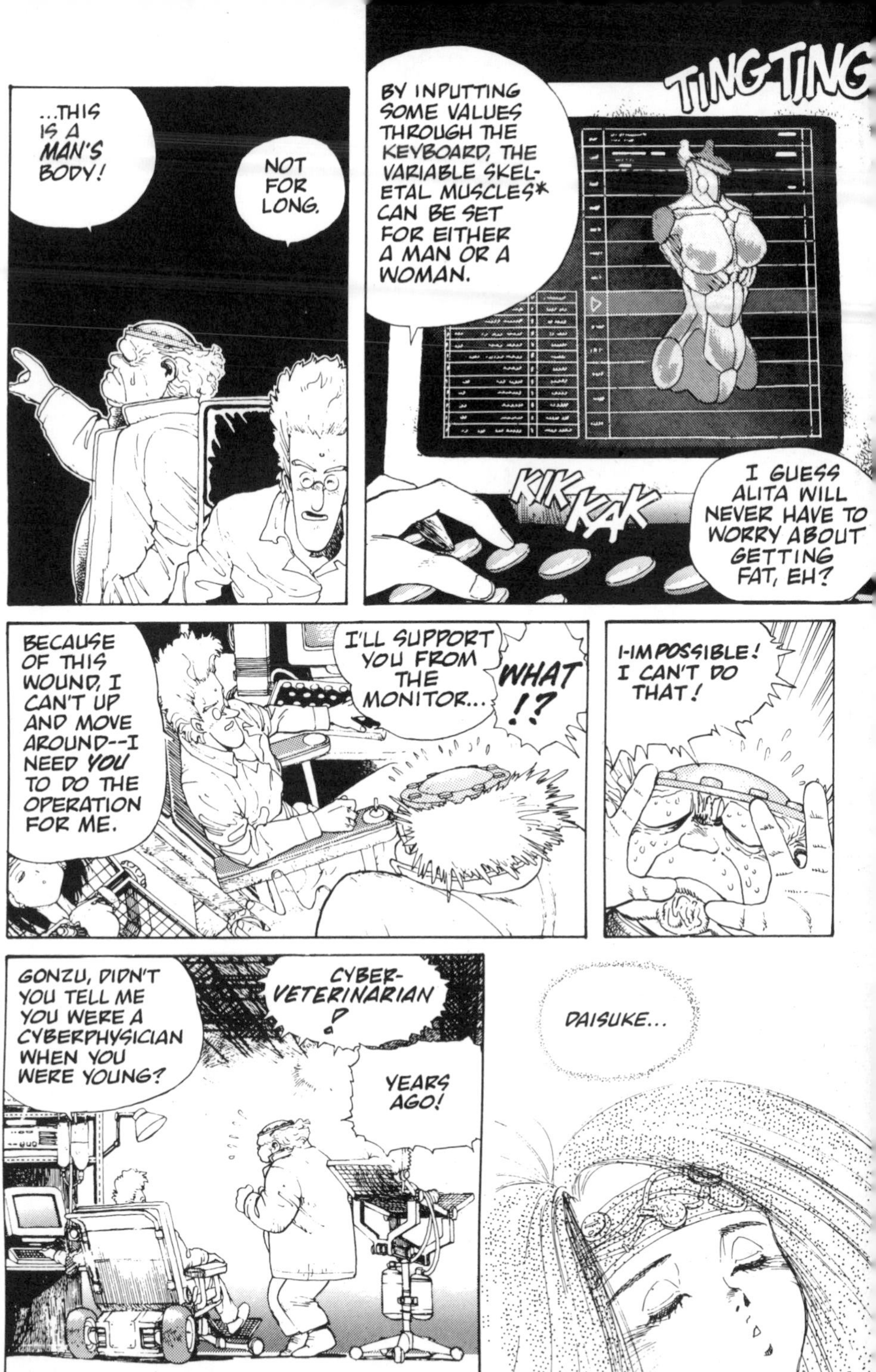
...THIS IS A MAN'S BODY!
NOT FOR LONG.
TING TING
BY INPUTTING SOME VALUES THROUGH THE KEYBOARD, THE VARIABLE SKEL-ETAL MUSCLES* CAN BE SET FOR EITHER A MAN OR A WOMAN.
KIK KAK
I GUESS ALITA WILL NEVER HAVE TO WORRY ABOUT GETTING FAT, EH?
BECAUSE OF THIS WOUND, I CAN'T UP AND MOVE AROUND--I NEED YOU TO DO THE OPERATION FOR ME.
I'LL SUPPORT YOU FROM THE MONITOR...
WHAT!?
I-IMPOSSIBLE! I CAN'T DO THAT!
GONZU, DIDN'T YOU TELL ME YOU WERE A CYBERPHYSICIAN WHEN YOU WERE YOUNG?
CYBER-VETERINARIAN?
YEARS AGO!
DAISUKE...

*VARIABLE SKELETAL MUSCLES: BECAUSE THEY ARE COMPOSED OF FINE METAL ELEMENTS, THEY ARE STRONG AND SOFT, AND HAVE THE ABILITY TO CHANGE THEIR SHAPE.

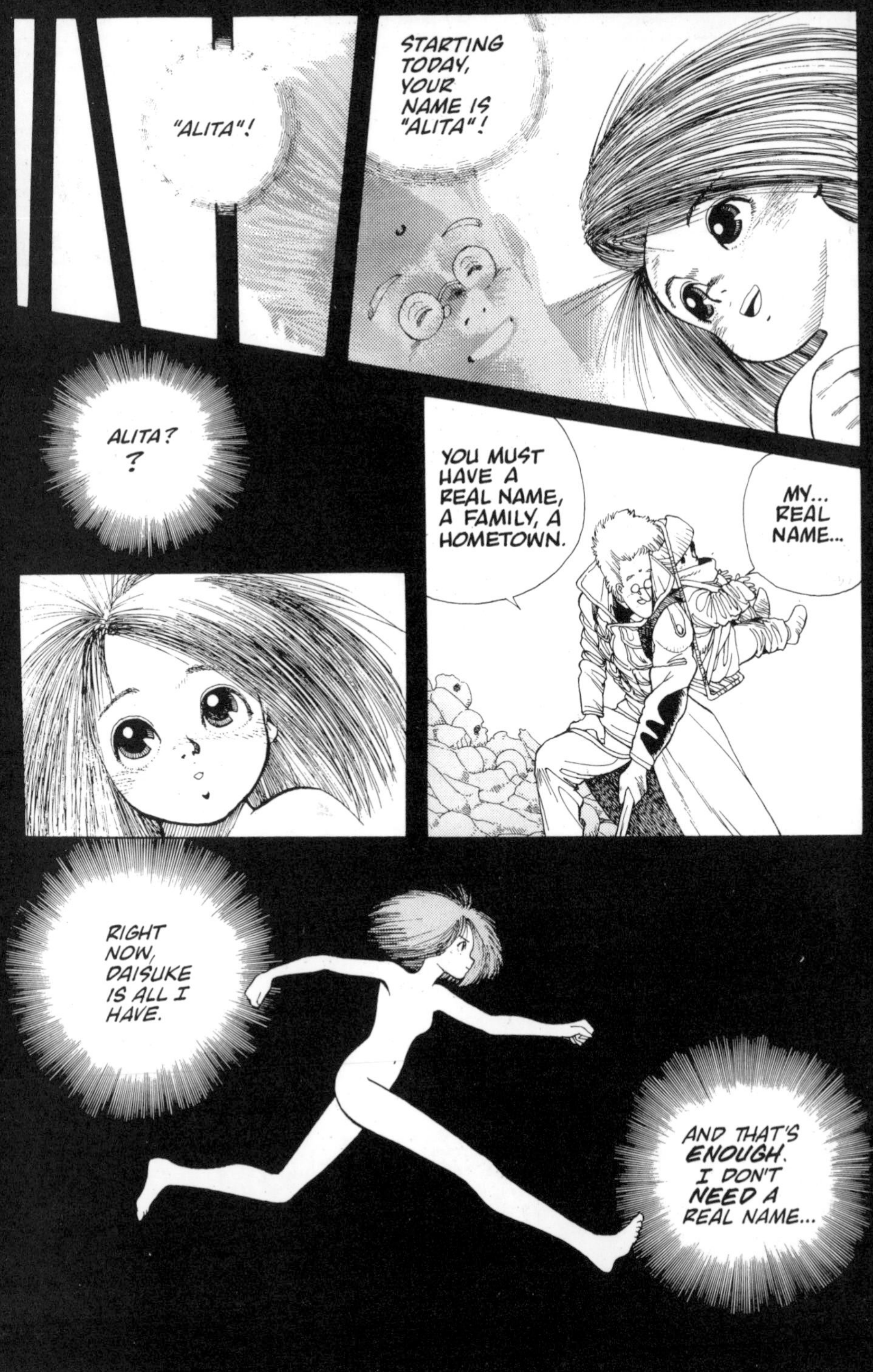
"ALITA"!
STARTING TODAY, YOUR NAME IS "ALITA"!
ALITA? ?
YOU MUST HAVE A REAL NAME, A FAMILY, A HOMETOWN.
MY... REAL NAME...
RIGHT NOW, DAISUKE IS ALL I HAVE.
AND THAT'S ENOUGH. I DON'T NEED A REAL NAME...

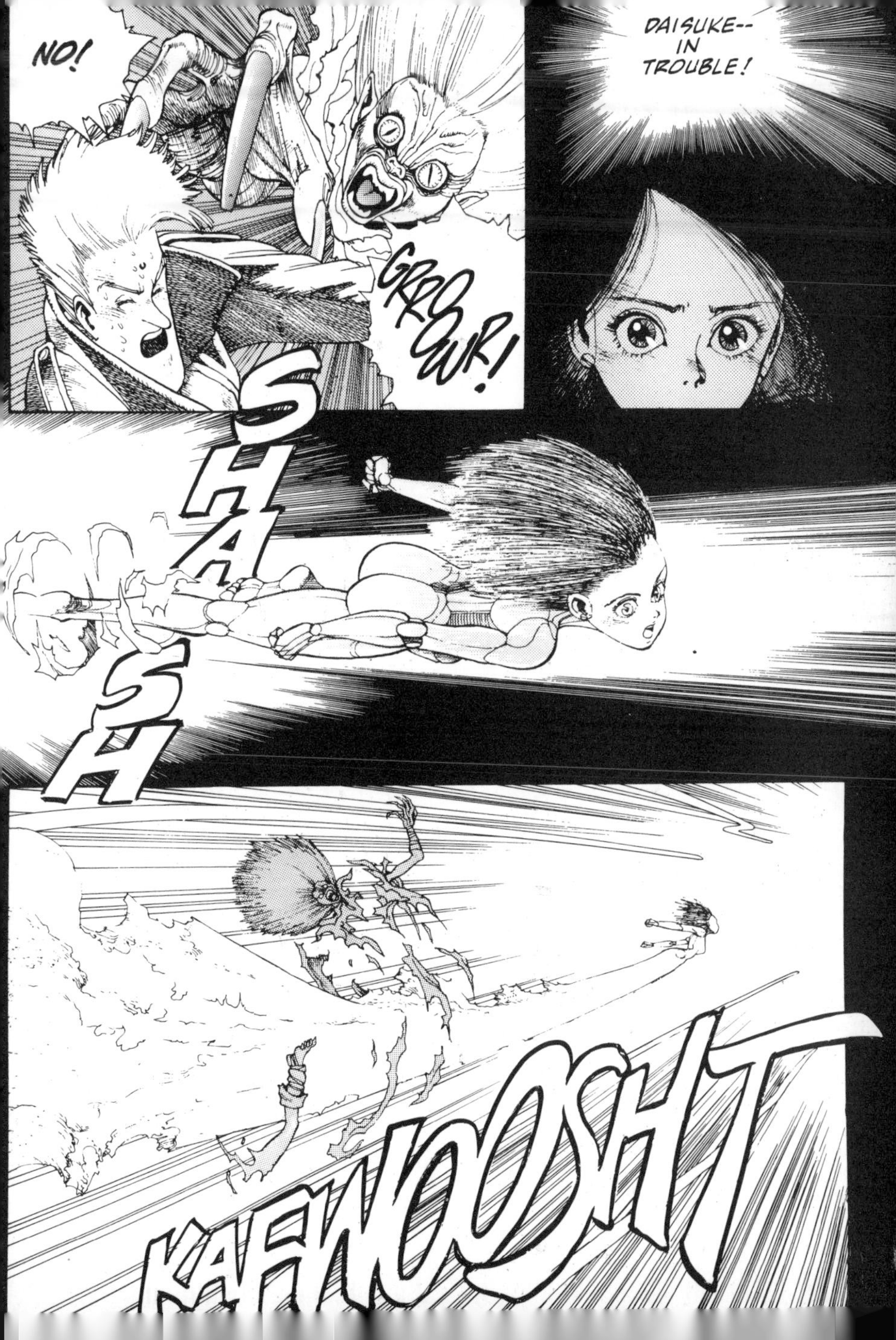
NO!
GRROOWR!
DAISUKE--
IN
TROUBLE!
SHASH
KAFWOOSHT

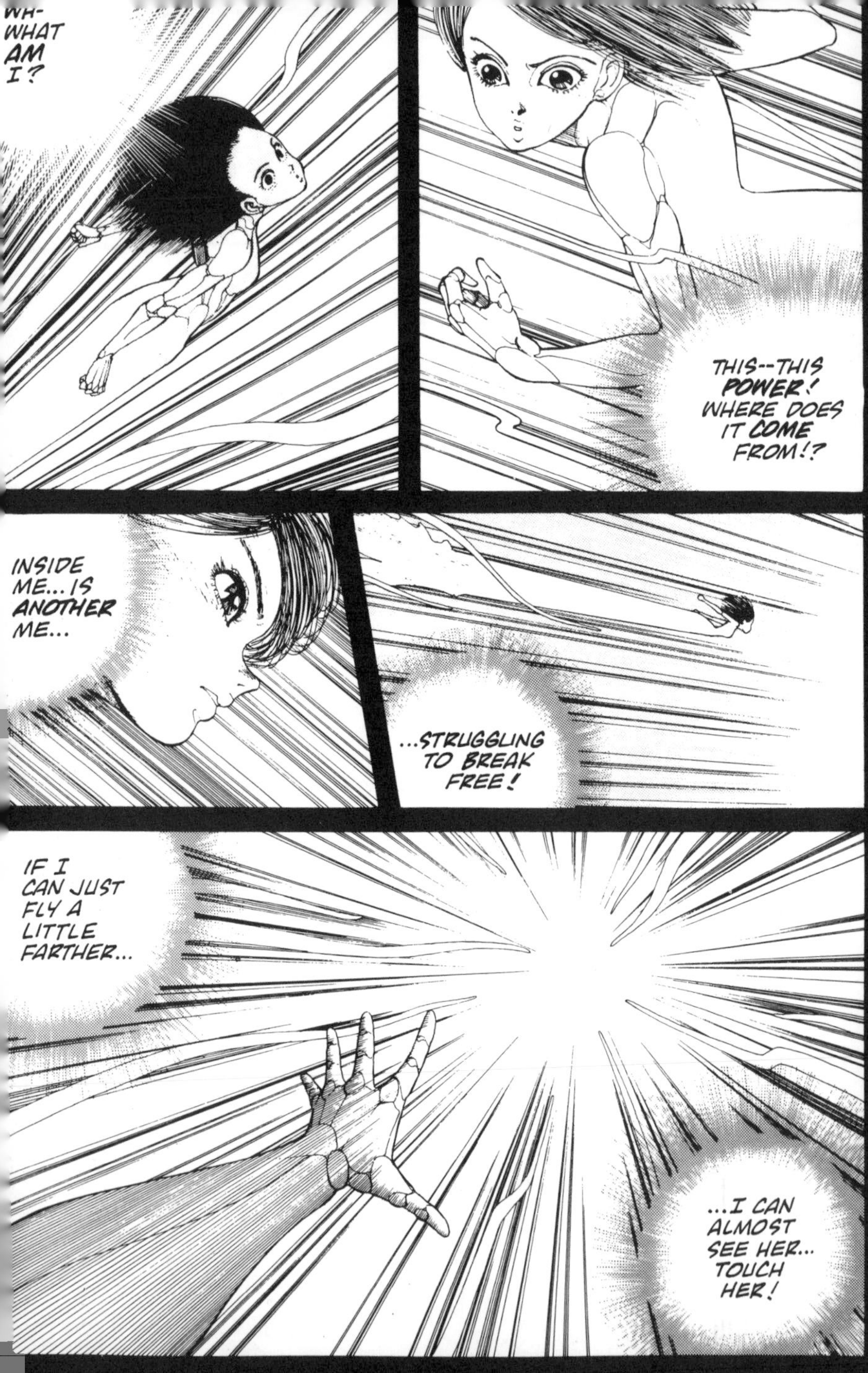
WH-WHAT AM I?
THIS--THIS POWER! WHERE DOES IT COME FROM!?
INSIDE ME...IS ANOTHER ME...
...STRUGGLING TO BREAK FREE!
IF I CAN JUST FLY A LITTLE FARTHER...
...I CAN ALMOST SEE HER... TOUCH HER!

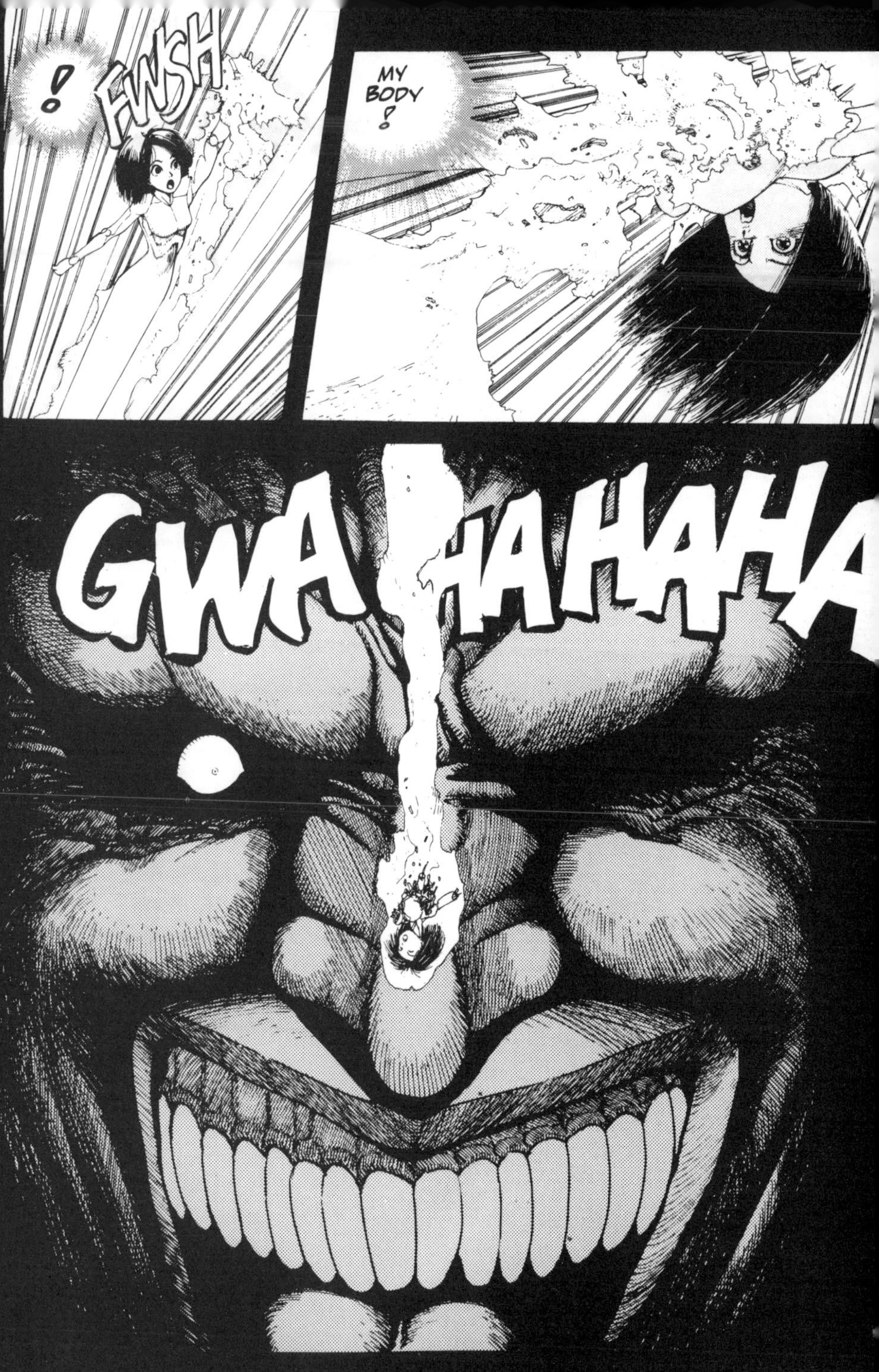
!
FWSH
MY BODY !
GWAHAHAHAHA

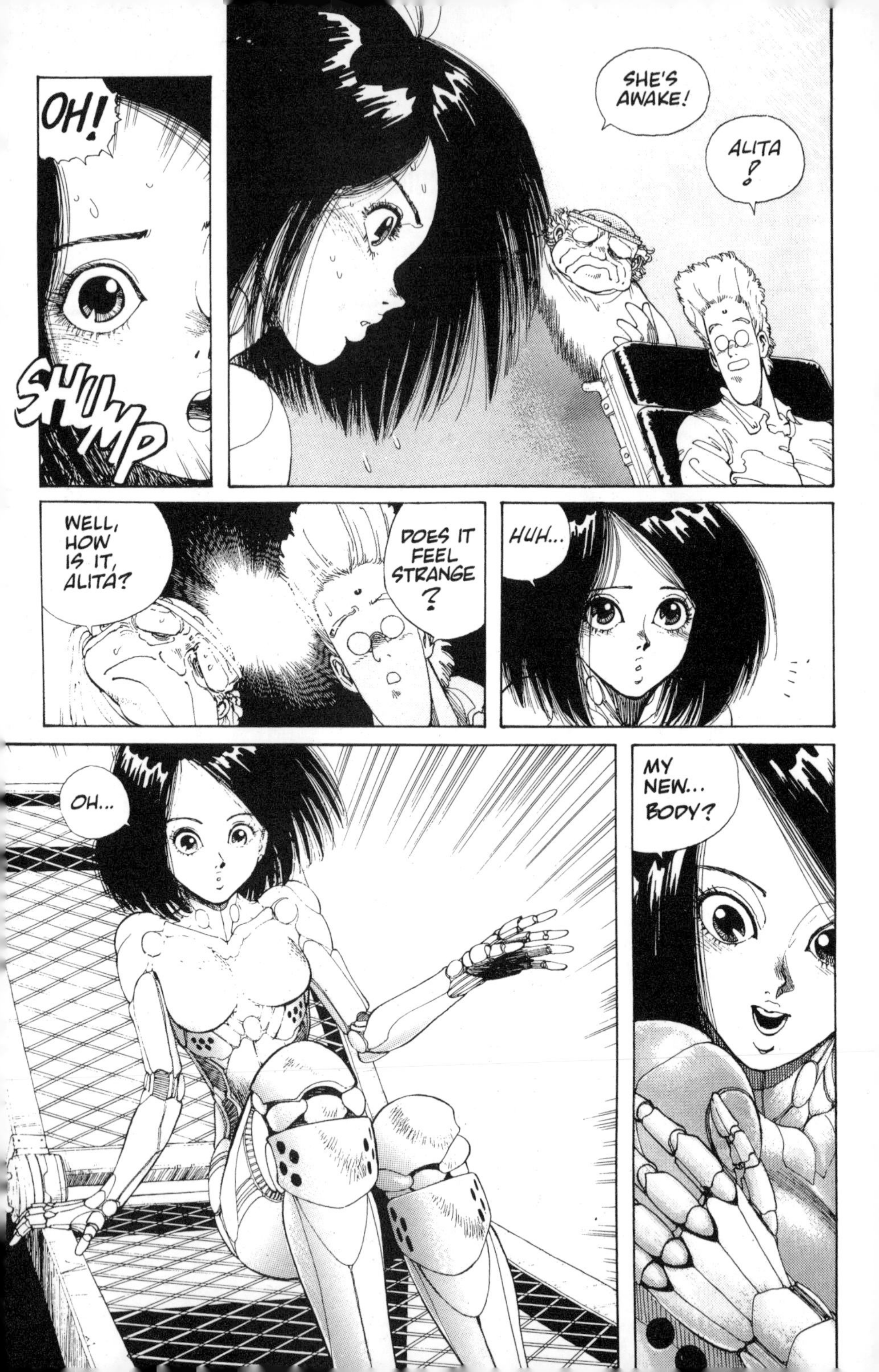
OH!
SHUMP
SHE'S AWAKE!
ALITA?
WELL, HOW IS IT, ALITA?
DOES IT FEEL STRANGE?
HUH...
OH...
MY NEW... BODY?

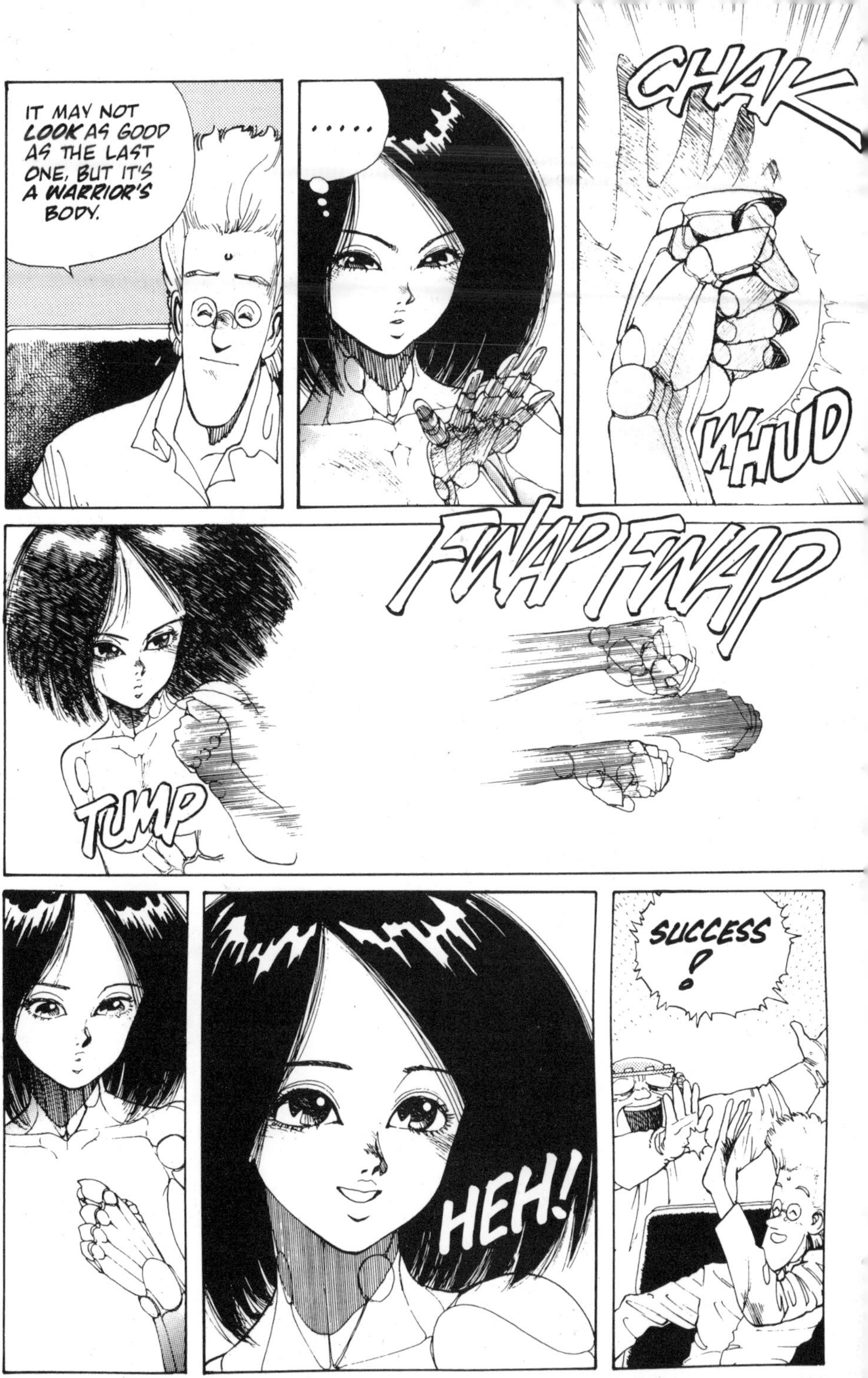
IT MAY NOT LOOK AS GOOD AS THE LAST ONE, BUT IT'S A WARRIOR'S BODY.
.....
CHAK
WHUD
FWAP FWAP
TUMP
HEH!
SUCCESS!

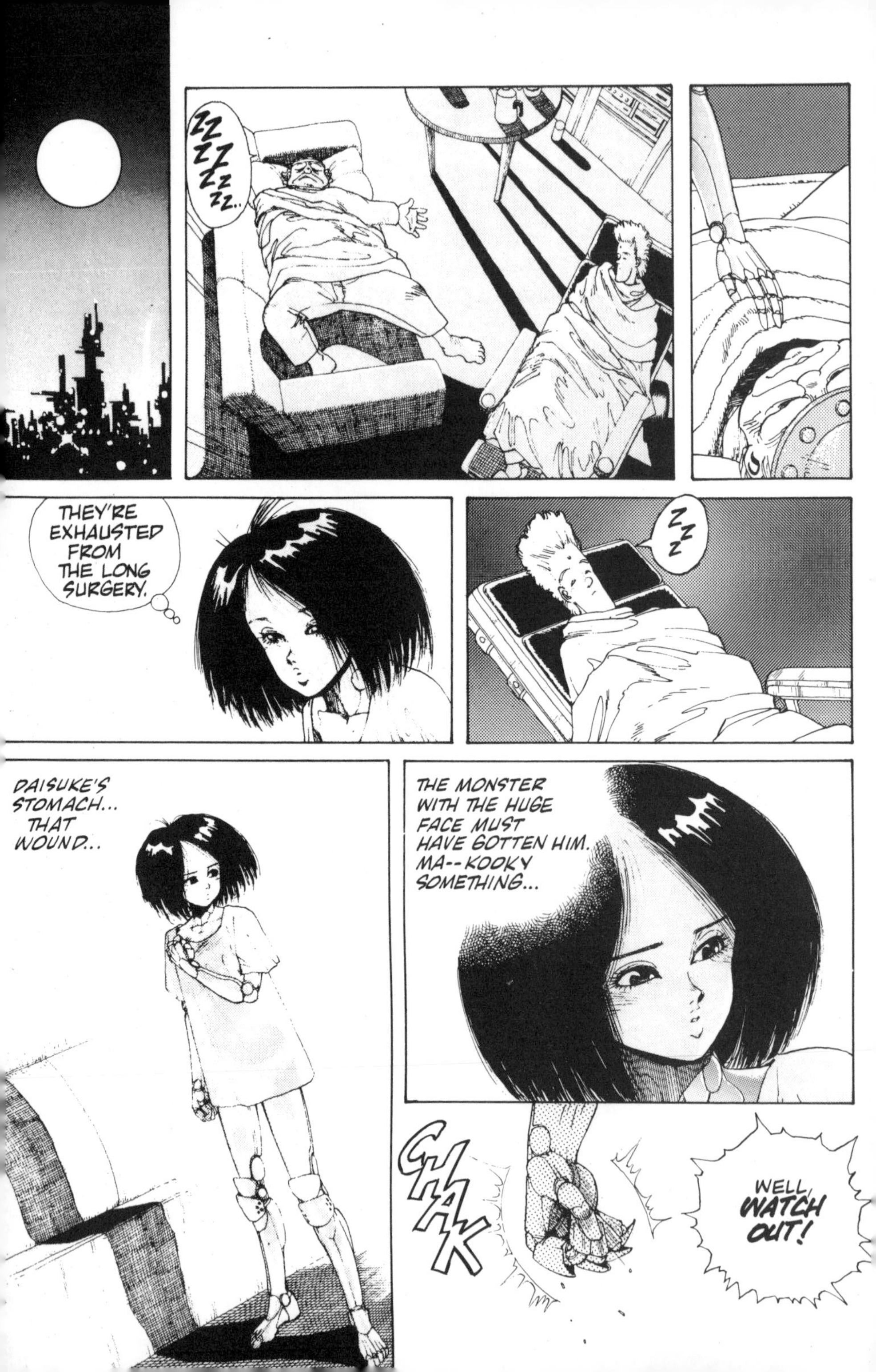
ZZZZZZ..
THEY'RE EXHAUSTED FROM THE LONG SURGERY.
ZZZ
DAISUKE'S STOMACH... THAT WOUND...
THE MONSTER WITH THE HUGE FACE MUST HAVE GOTTEN HIM. MA--KOOKY SOMETHING...
CHAK
WELL, WATCH OUT!

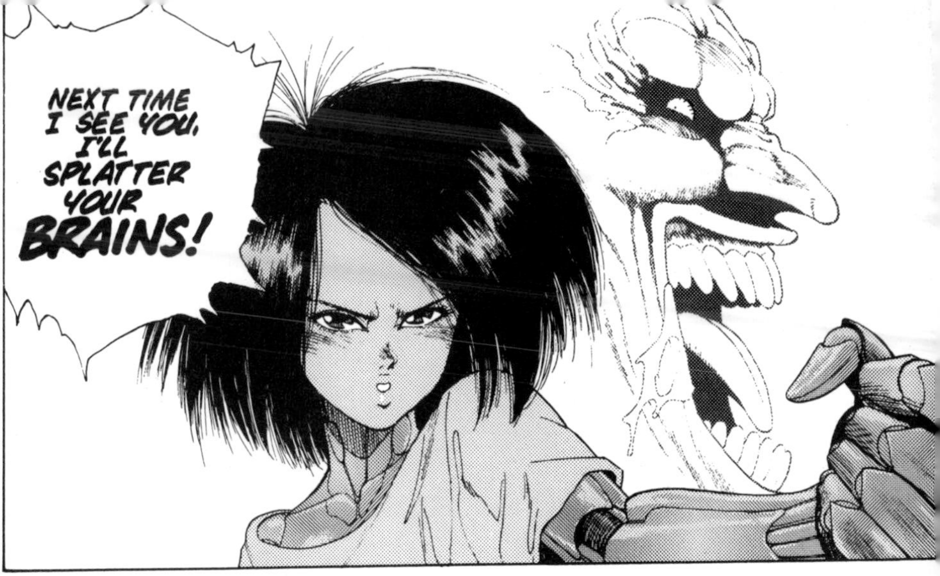
NEXT TIME I SEE YOU, I'LL SPLATTER YOUR BRAINS!

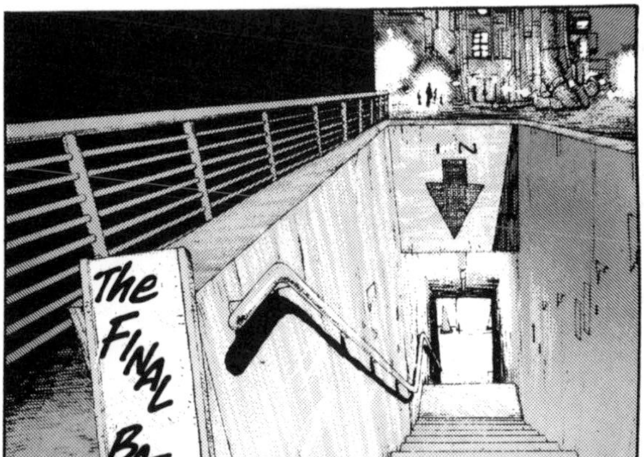
IN
The FINAL BATTLE

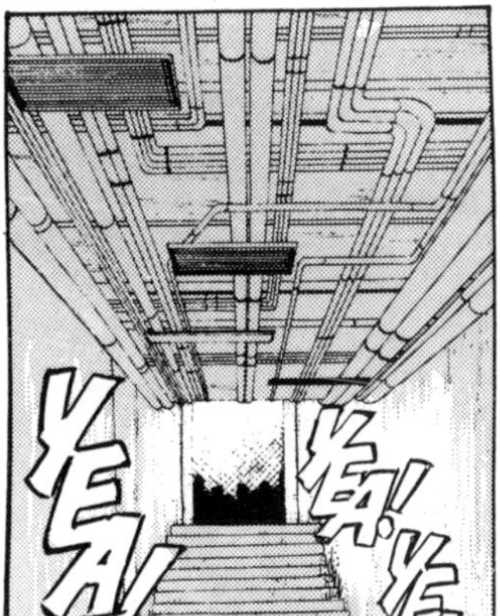
YEA!
YEA! YEA!

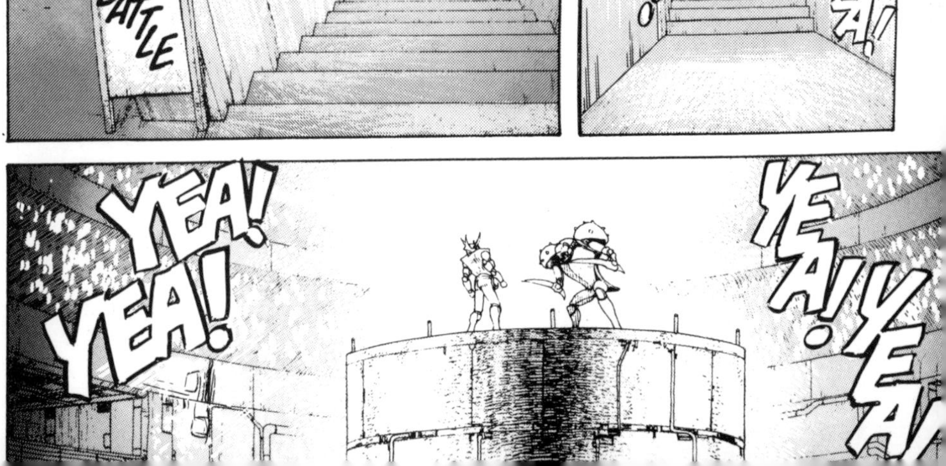
YEA! YEA!
YEA! YEA

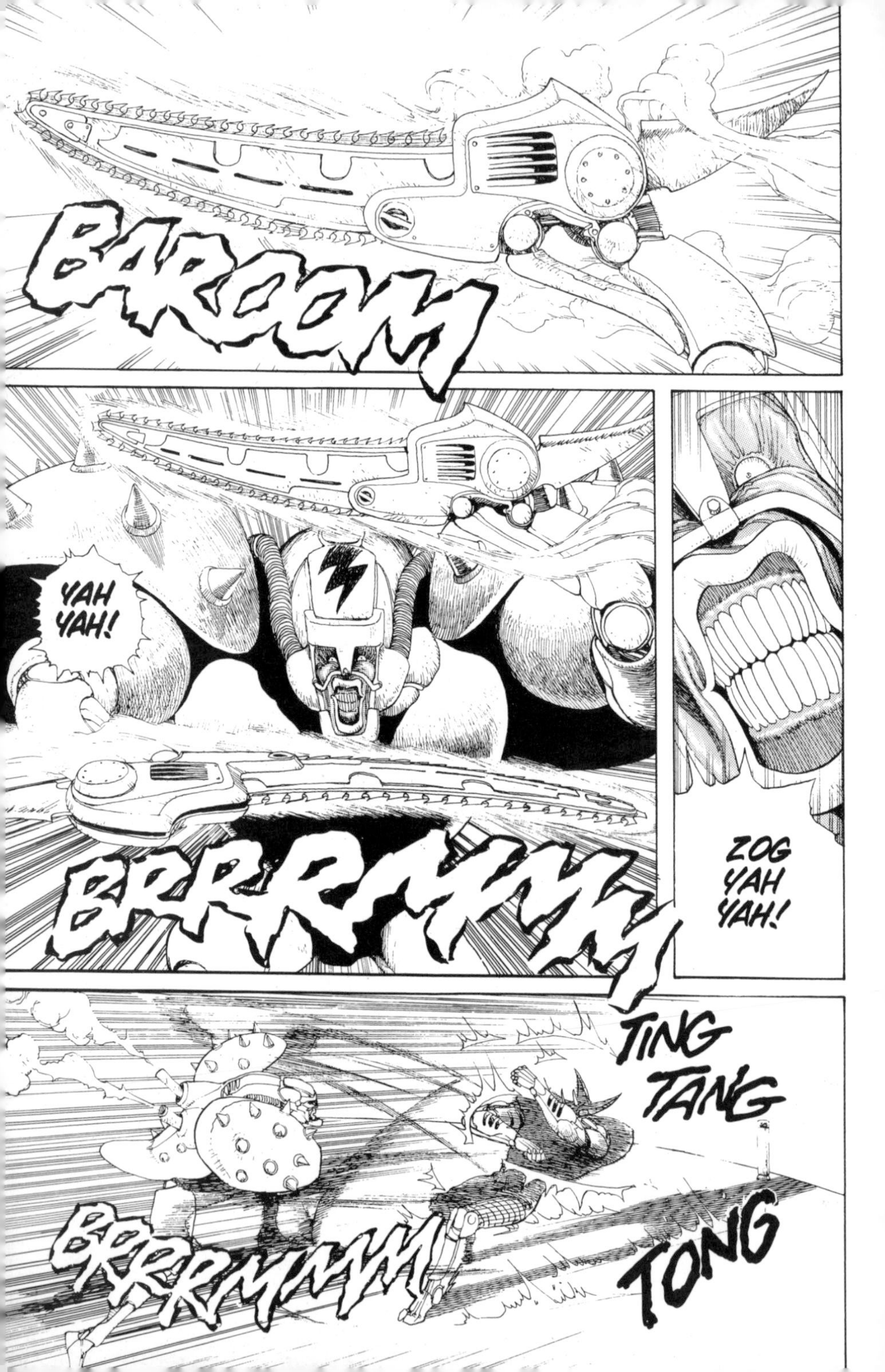
BAROOM
YAH YAH!
BRRRMMM
ZOG YAH YAH!
TING
TANG
BRRRMMM
TONG

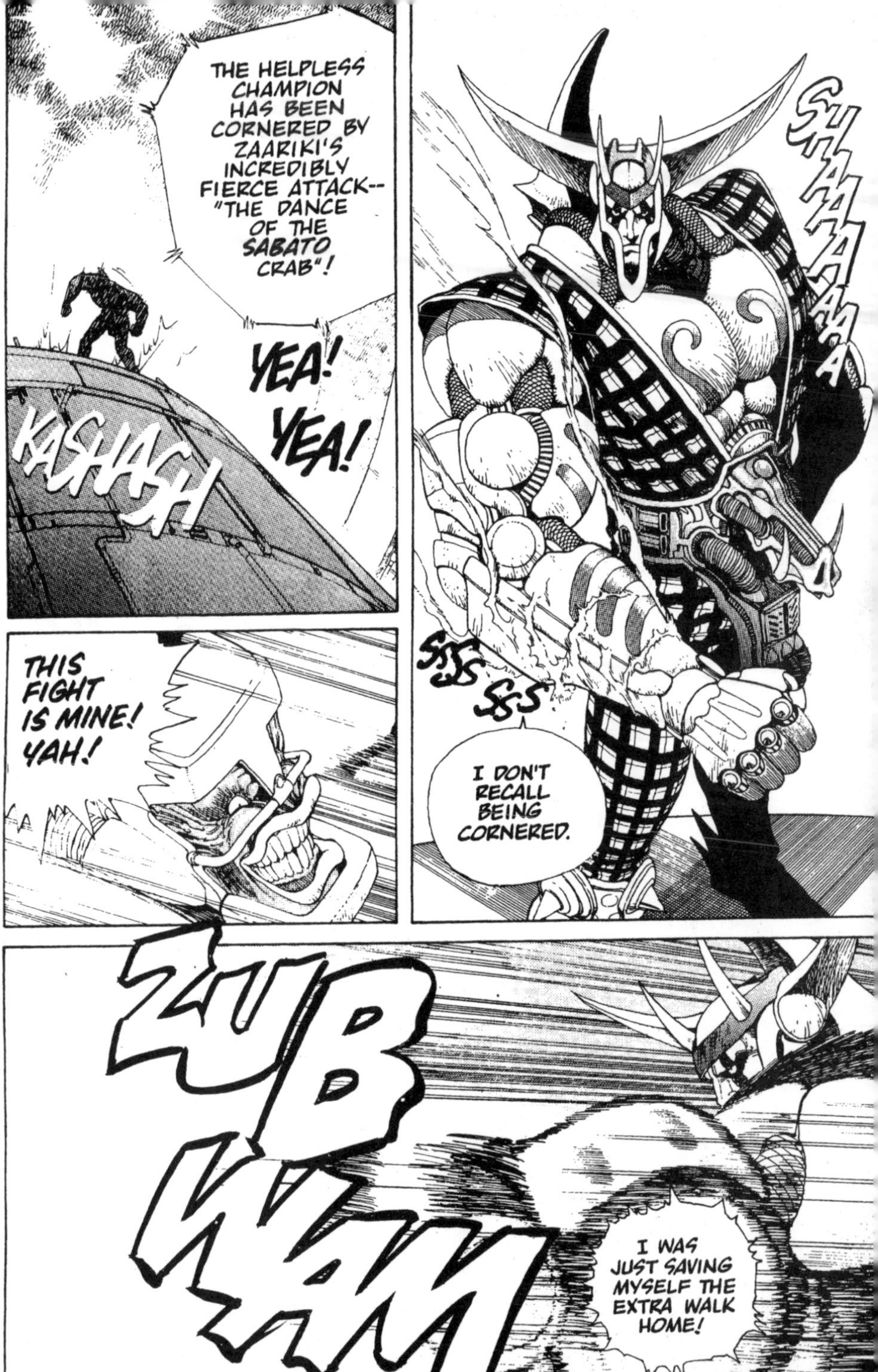
THE HELPLESS CHAMPION HAS BEEN CORNERED BY ZAARIKI'S INCREDIBLY FIERCE ATTACK-- "THE DANCE OF THE SABATO CRAB"!
YEA! YEA!
KASHASH
SHAAAAAAAA
THIS FIGHT IS MINE! YAH!
SSS SSS
I DON'T RECALL BEING CORNERED.
ZUB WAM
I WAS JUST SAVING MYSELF THE EXTRA WALK HOME!

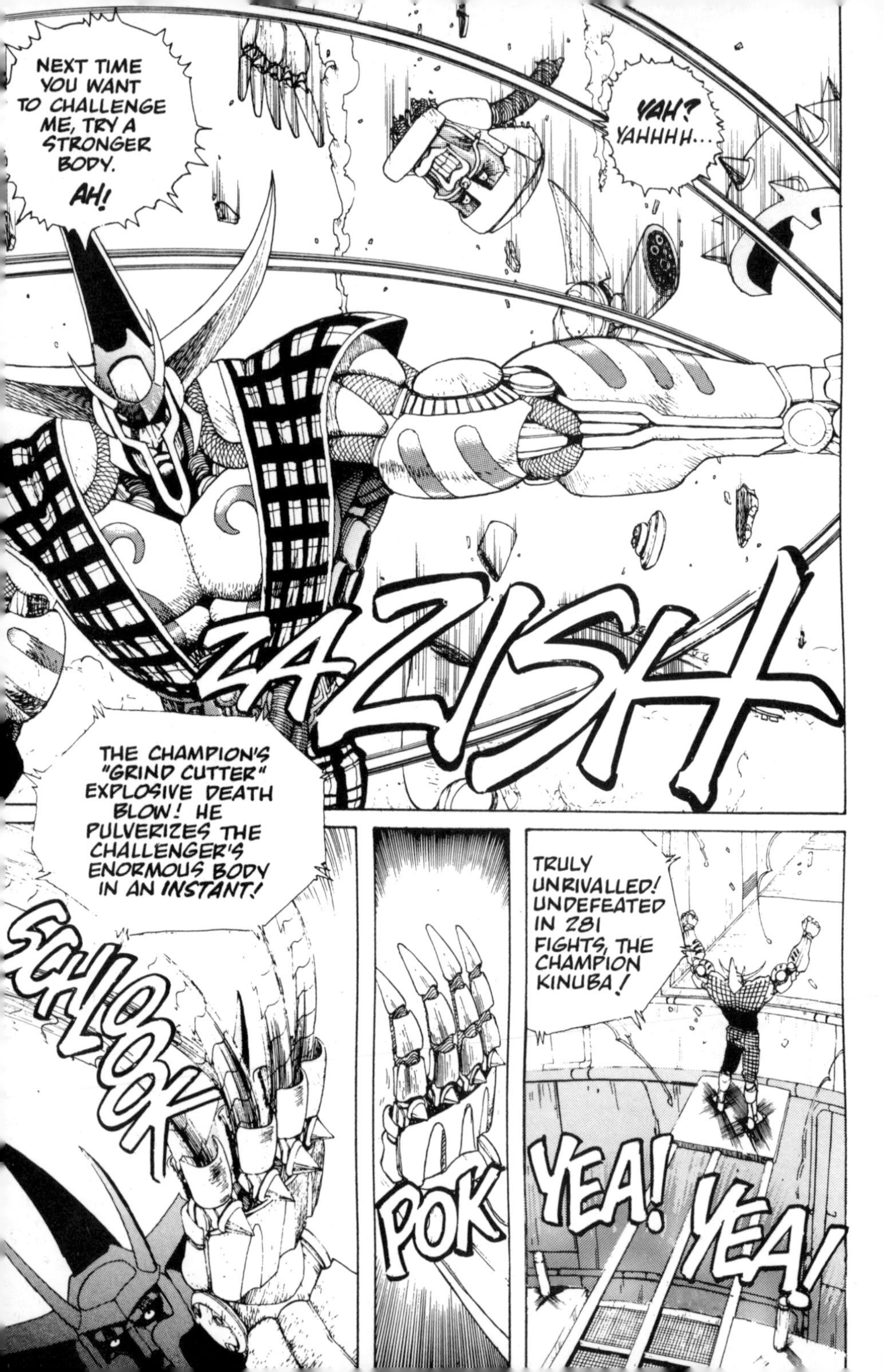
NEXT TIME YOU WANT TO CHALLENGE ME, TRY A STRONGER BODY.
AH!
YAH? YAHHHH...
ZAZISH
THE CHAMPION'S "GRIND CUTTER" EXPLOSIVE DEATH BLOW! HE PULVERIZES THE CHALLENGER'S ENORMOUS BODY IN AN INSTANT!
SCHLOOK
POK
TRULY UNRIVALLED! UNDEFEATED IN 281 FIGHTS, THE CHAMPION KINUBA!
YEA! YEA!

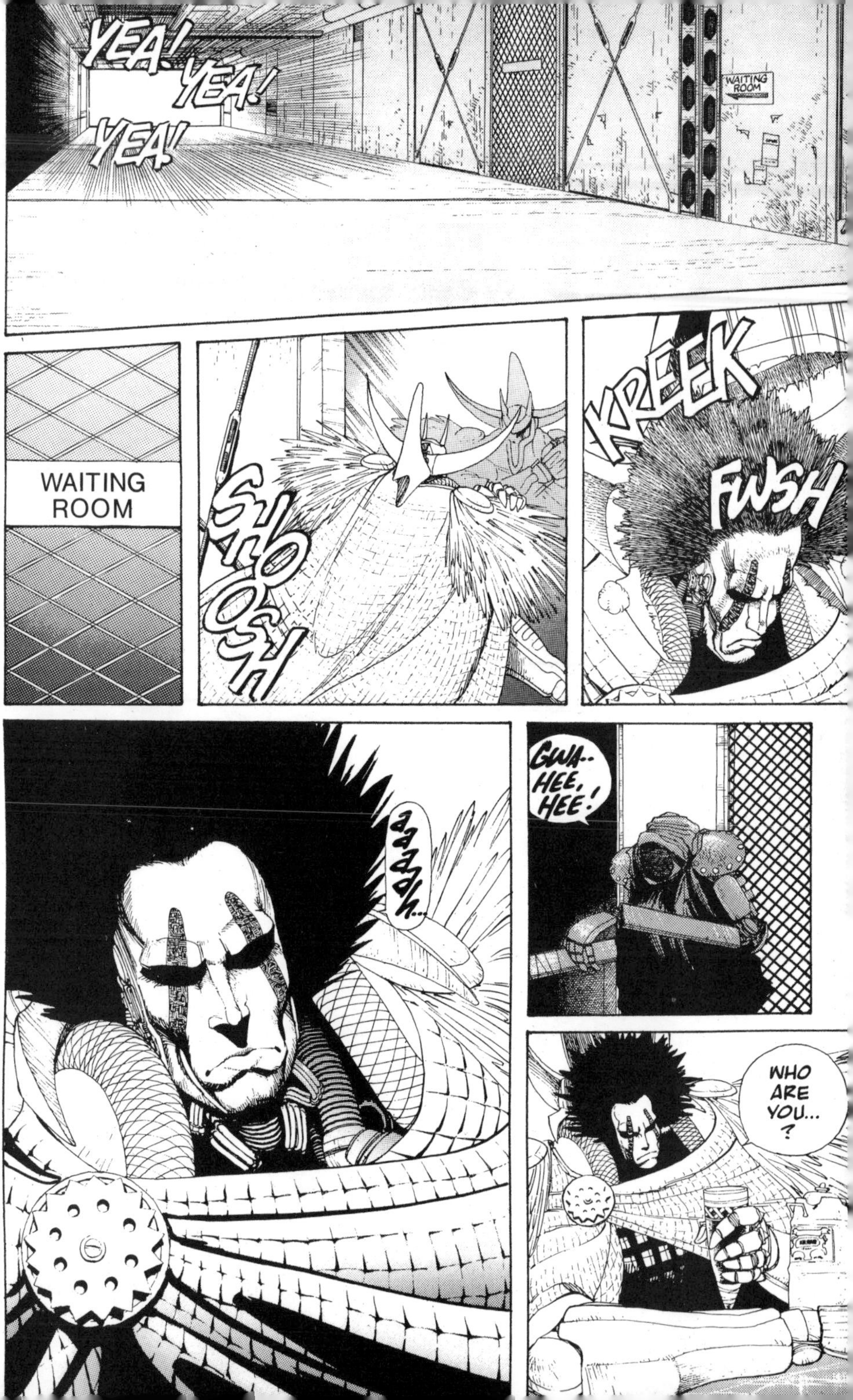
YEA! YEA! YEA!
WAITING ROOM
WAITING ROOM
SHOOSH
KREEK
FWSH
aaaahh...
GWA.. HEE, HEE!
WHO ARE YOU... ?

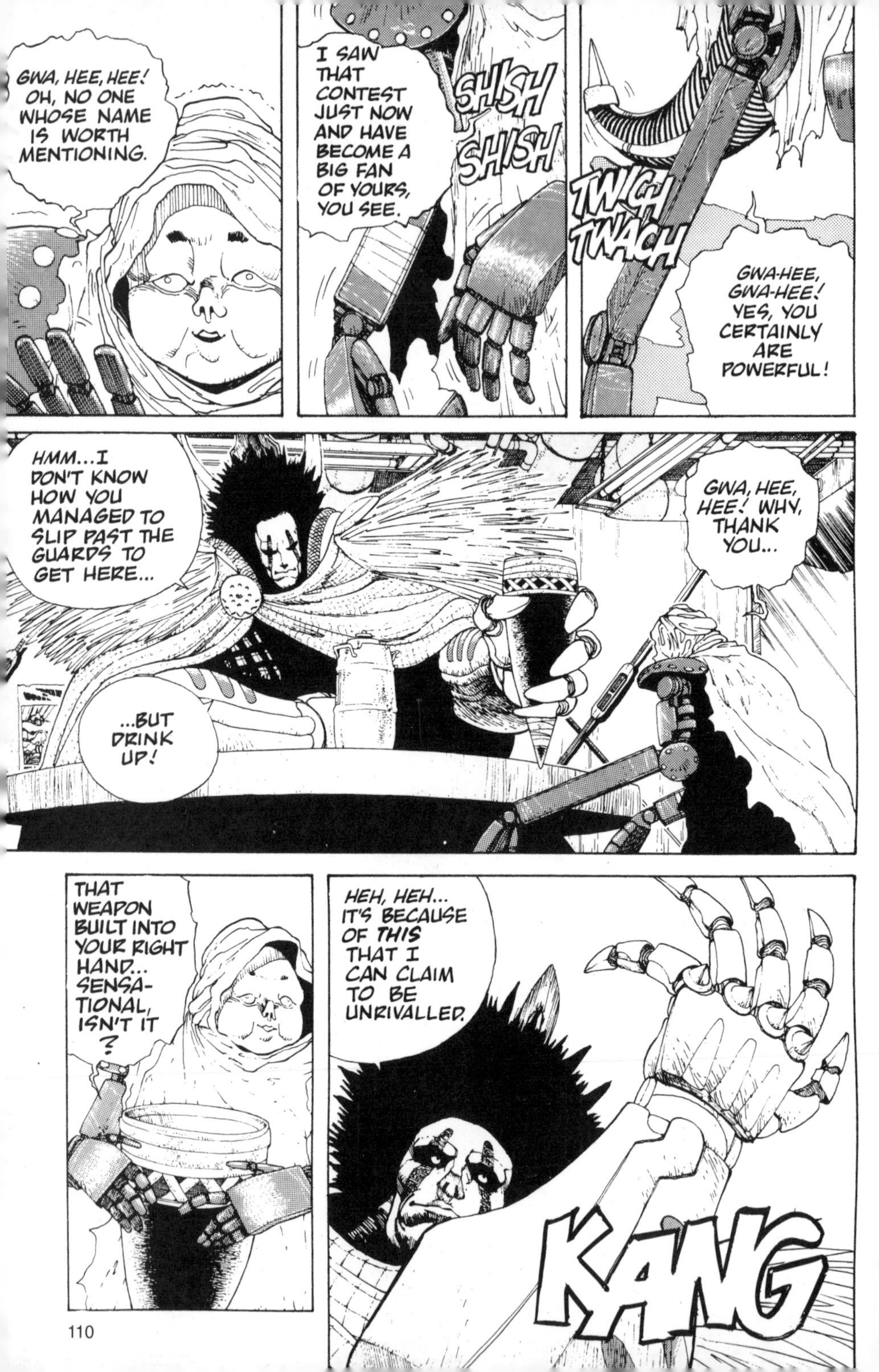
GWA, HEE, HEE! OH, NO ONE WHOSE NAME IS WORTH MENTIONING.
I SAW THAT CONTEST JUST NOW AND HAVE BECOME A BIG FAN OF YOURS, YOU SEE.
SHISH
SHISH
TWICH
TWACH
GWA-HEE, GWA-HEE! YES, YOU CERTAINLY ARE POWERFUL!
HMM...I DON'T KNOW HOW YOU MANAGED TO SLIP PAST THE GUARDS TO GET HERE...
GWA, HEE, HEE! WHY, THANK YOU...
...BUT DRINK UP!
THAT WEAPON BUILT INTO YOUR RIGHT HAND... SENSATIONAL, ISN'T IT?
HEH, HEH... IT'S BECAUSE OF THIS THAT I CAN CLAIM TO BE UNRIVALLED.
KANG

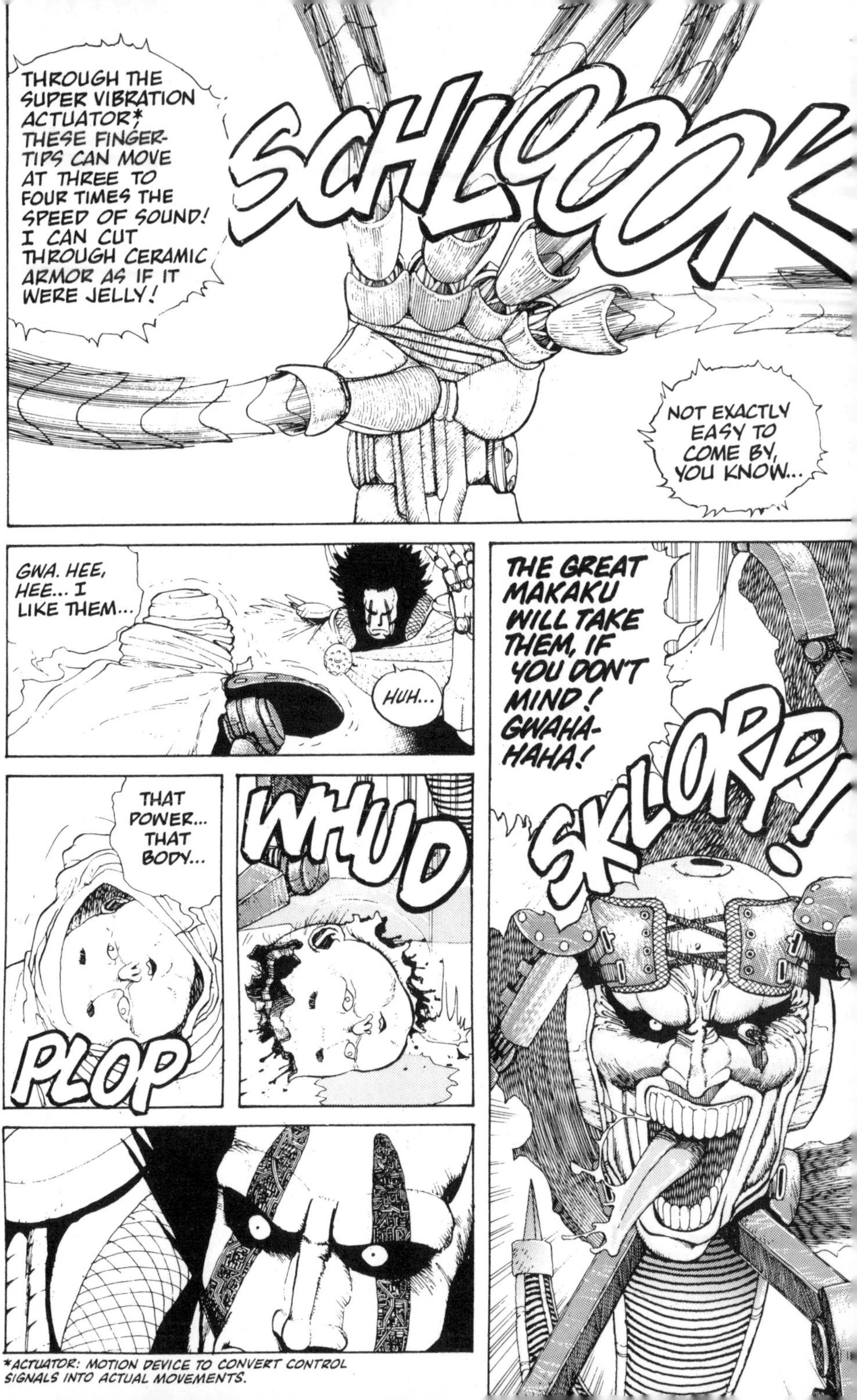
THROUGH THE SUPER VIBRATION ACTUATOR* THESE FINGER-TIPS CAN MOVE AT THREE TO FOUR TIMES THE SPEED OF SOUND! I CAN CUT THROUGH CERAMIC ARMOR AS IF IT WERE JELLY!
SCHLOOOK!
NOT EXACTLY EASY TO COME BY, YOU KNOW...
GWA. HEE, HEE... I LIKE THEM...
HUH...
THAT POWER... THAT BODY...
PLOP
WHUD
THE GREAT MAKAKU WILL TAKE THEM, IF YOU DON'T MIND! GWAHA-HAHA!
SKLORP!

*ACTUATOR: MOTION DEVICE TO CONVERT CONTROL SIGNALS INTO ACTUAL MOVEMENTS.

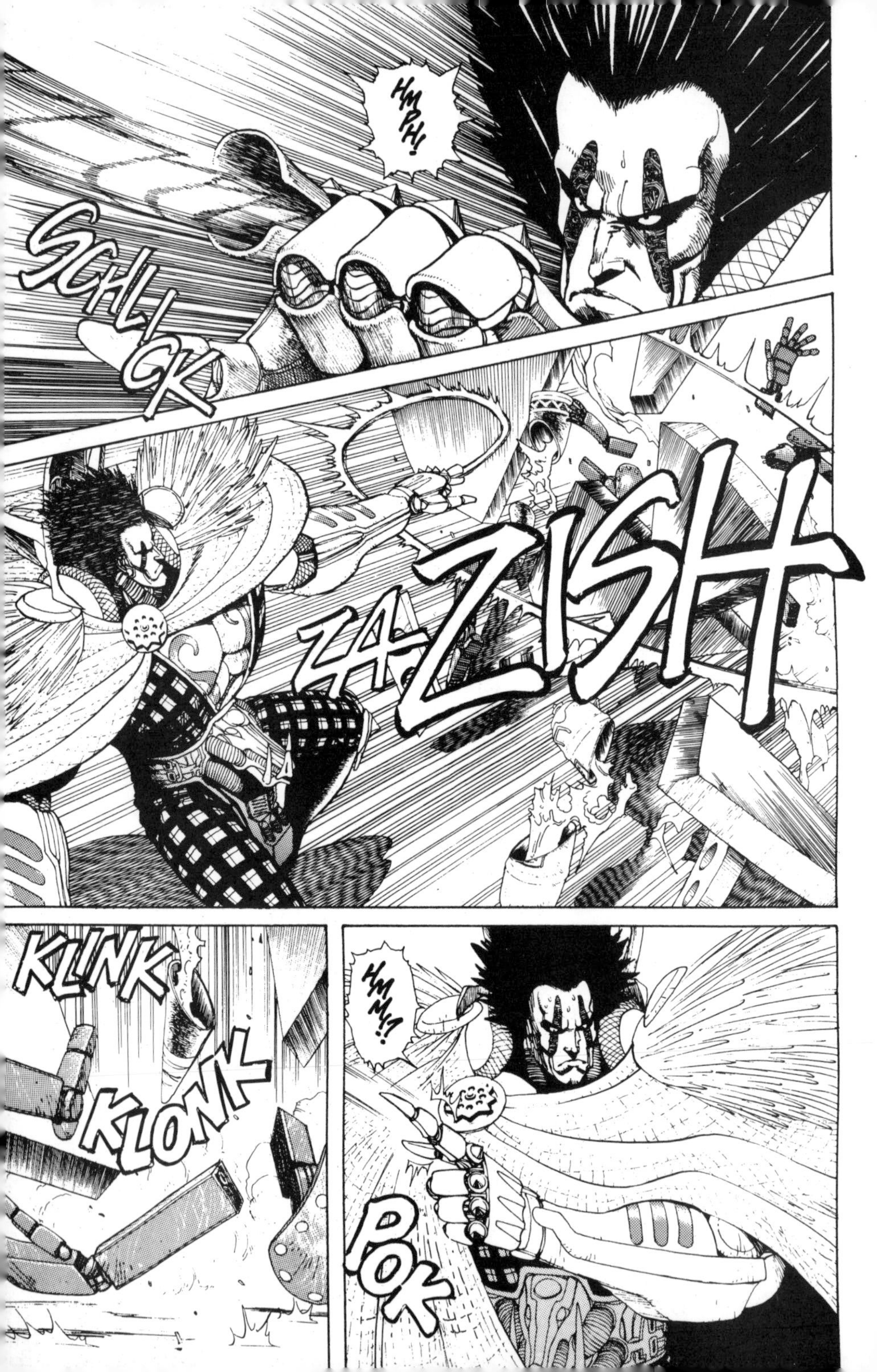
HMPH!
SCHLICK
ZA-ZISH
KLINK
KLONK
HMM?!
POK

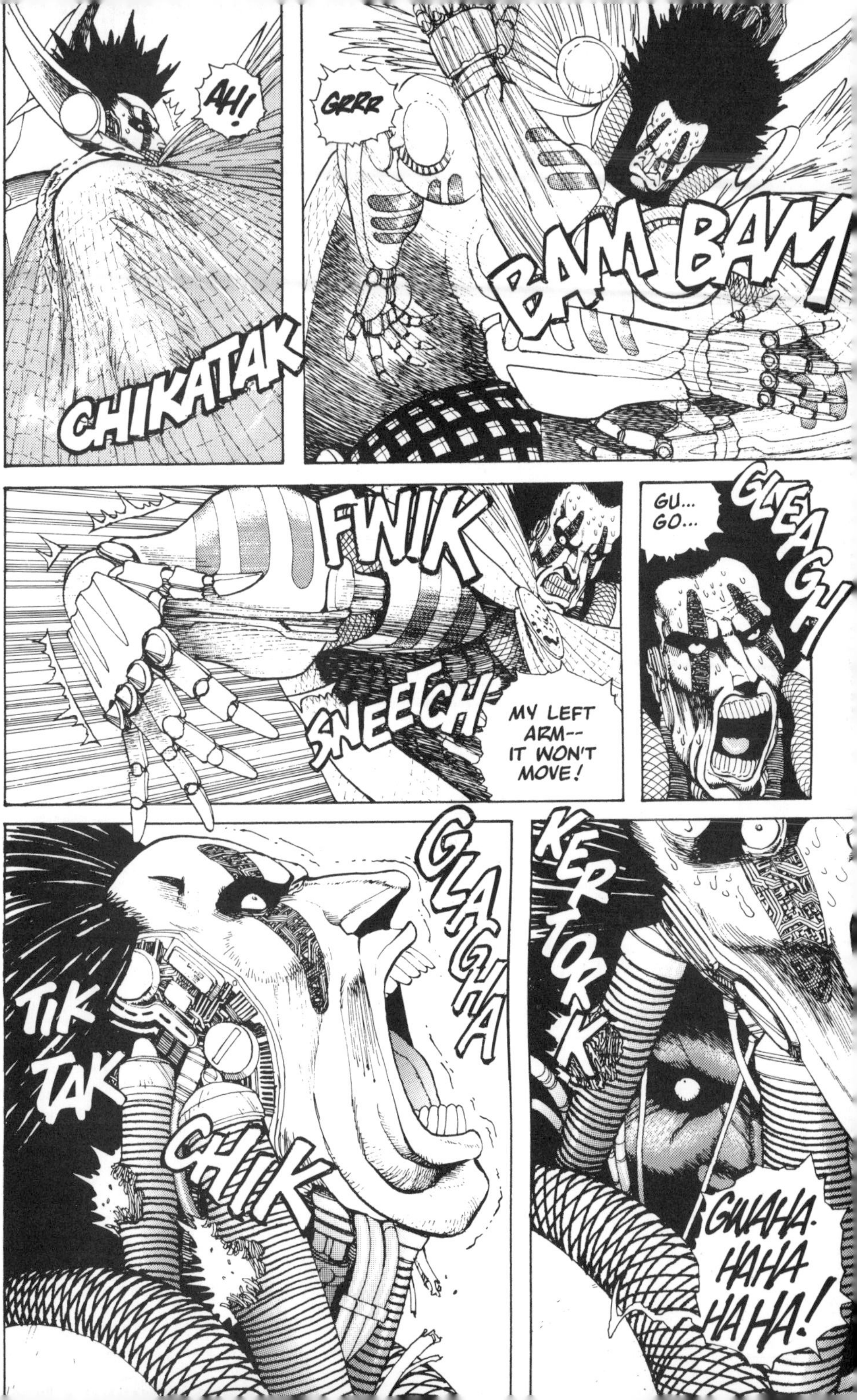
AH!
CHIKATAK
GRRR
BAM BAM
FWIK
SNEETCH
MY LEFT ARM-- IT WON'T MOVE!
GU... GO...
GLEAGH
TIK TAK
CHIK
GLAGHA
KERTORK
GWAHA-HAHA HAHA!

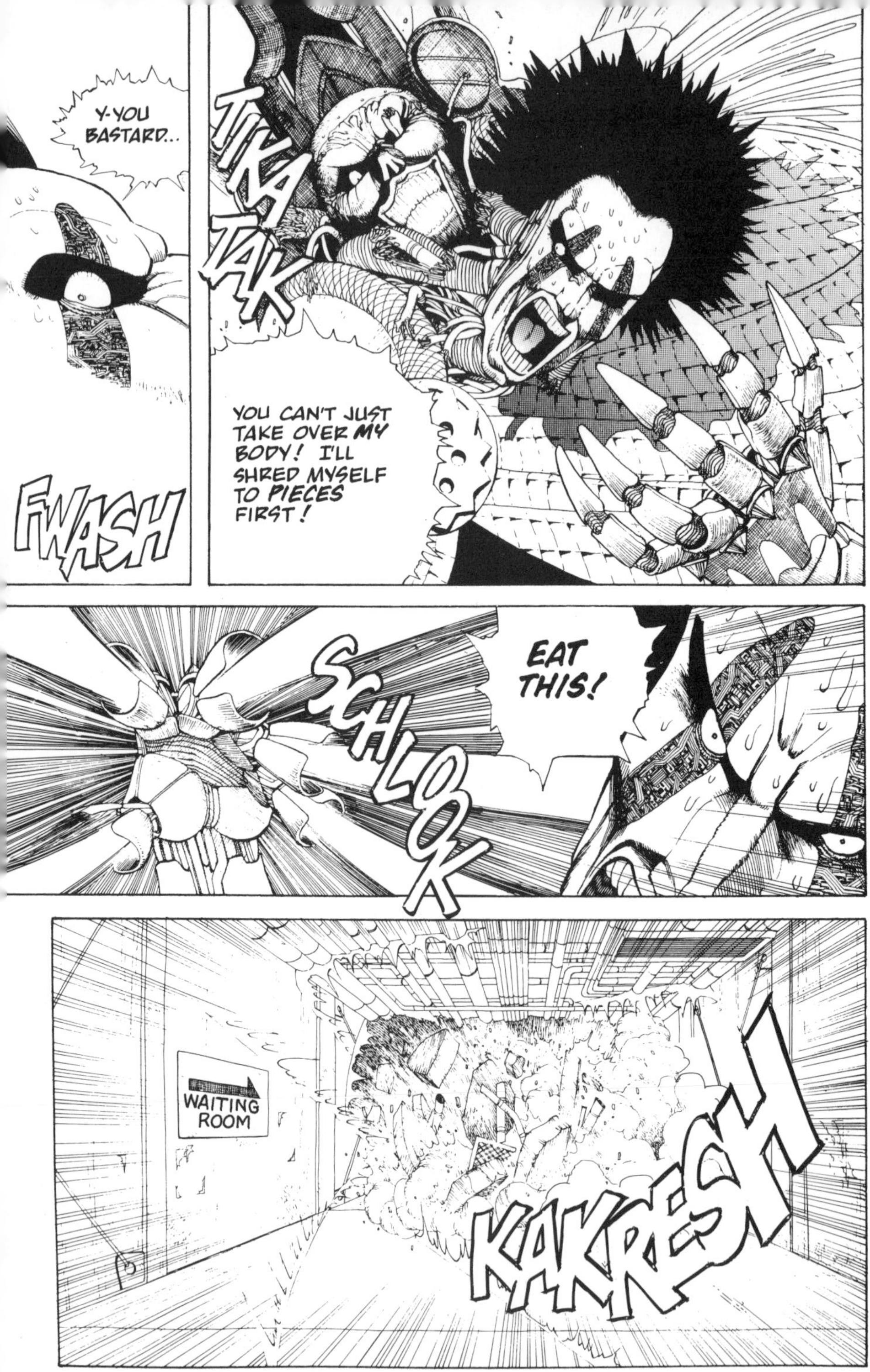
Y-YOU BASTARD...
FWASH
TIKA TAK
YOU CAN'T JUST TAKE OVER MY BODY! I'LL SHRED MYSELF TO PIECES FIRST!
SCHLOOK
EAT THIS!
WAITING ROOM
KAKRESH

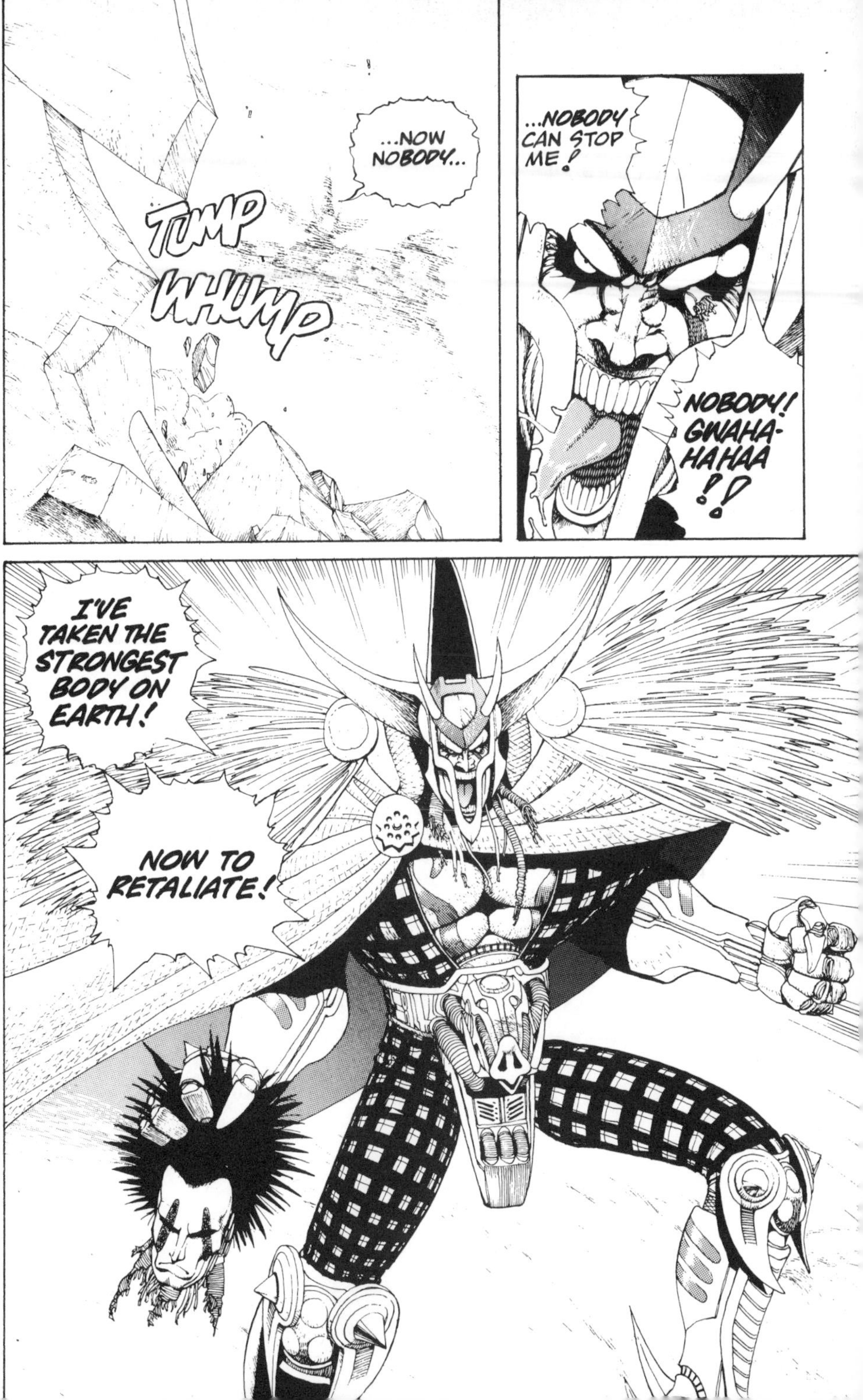
...NOW NOBODY...
TUMP
WHUMP
...NOBODY CAN STOP ME!
NOBODY! GWAHA-HAHAA!!
I'VE TAKEN THE STRONGEST BODY ON EARTH!
NOW TO RETALIATE!

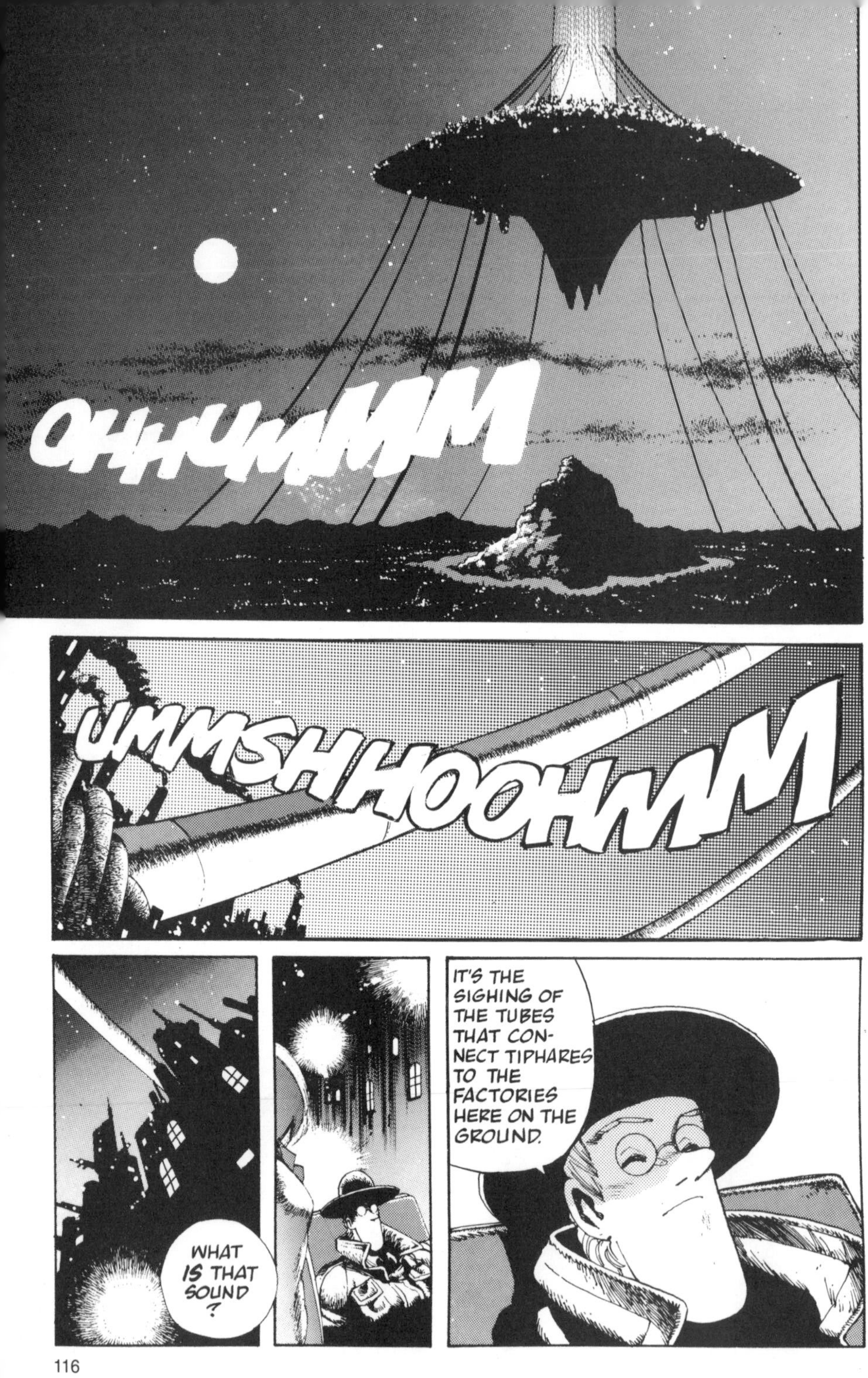

OHHMMMM
UMMSHHOOHMM
WHAT IS THAT SOUND ?
IT'S THE SIGHING OF THE TUBES THAT CONNECT TIPHARES TO THE FACTORIES HERE ON THE GROUND.

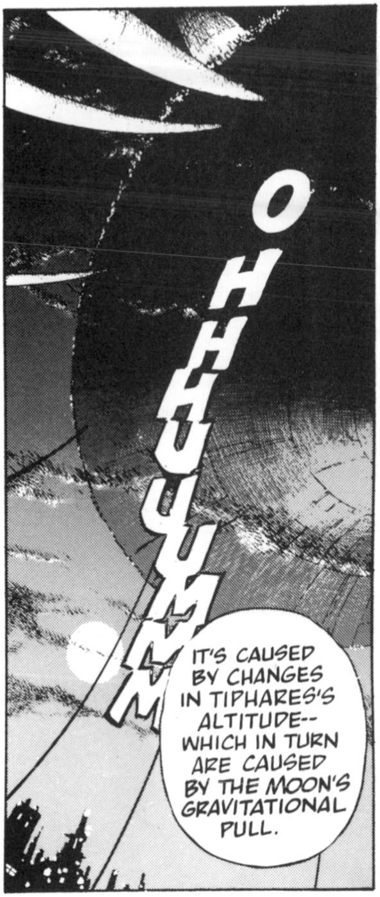
OHHUUUMMM
IT'S CAUSED BY CHANGES IN TIPHARES'S ALTITUDE-- WHICH IN TURN ARE CAUSED BY THE MOON'S GRAVITATIONAL PULL.
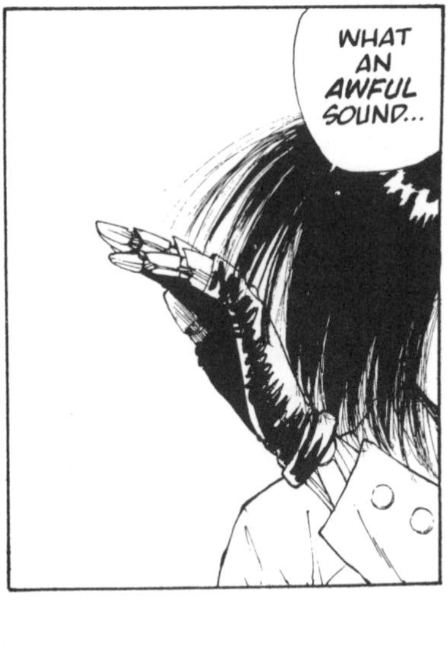
WHAT AN AWFUL SOUND...
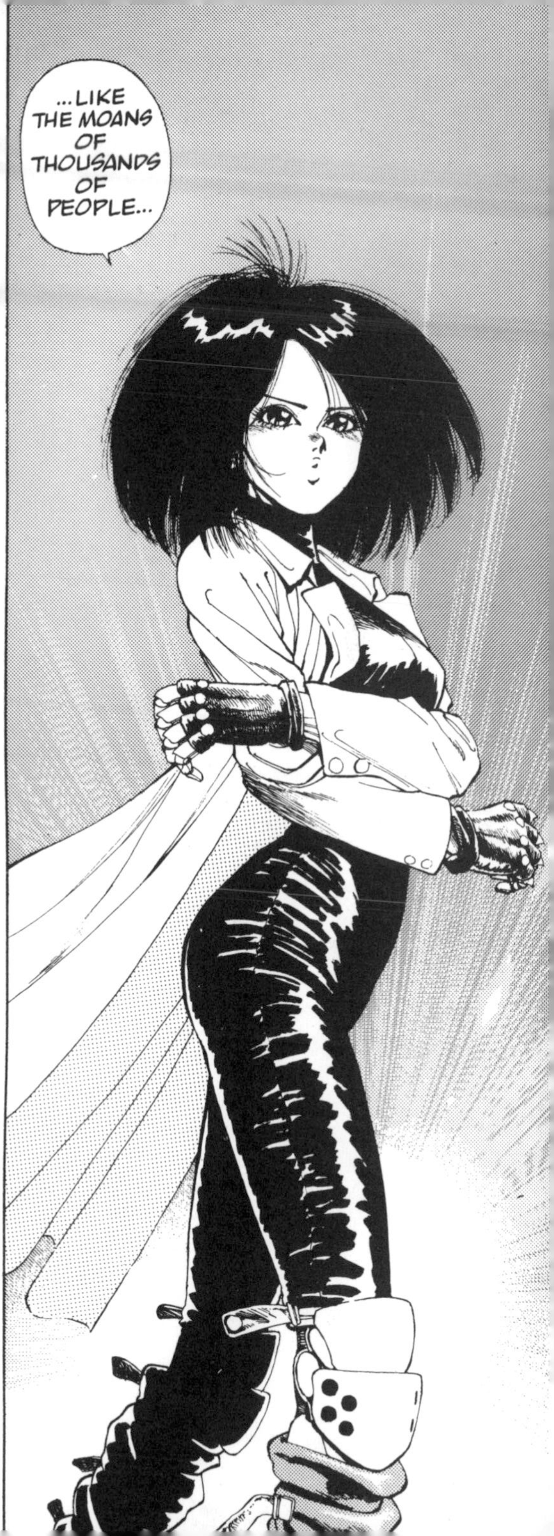
...LIKE THE MOANS OF THOUSANDS OF PEOPLE...

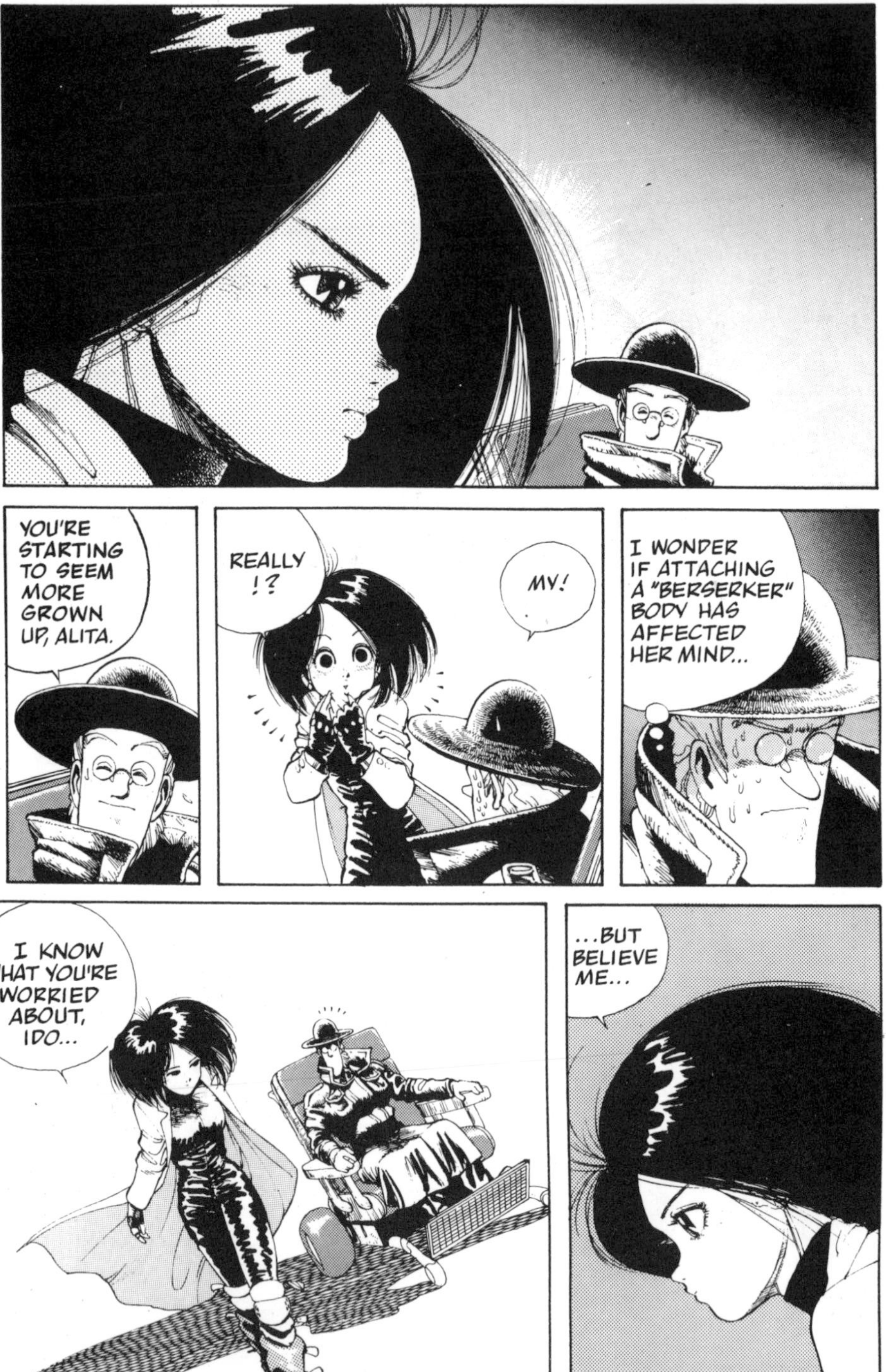
YOU'RE STARTING TO SEEM MORE GROWN UP, ALITA.
REALLY !?
MY!
I WONDER IF ATTACHING A "BERSERKER" BODY HAS AFFECTED HER MIND...
I KNOW WHAT YOU'RE WORRIED ABOUT, IDO...
...BUT BELIEVE ME...

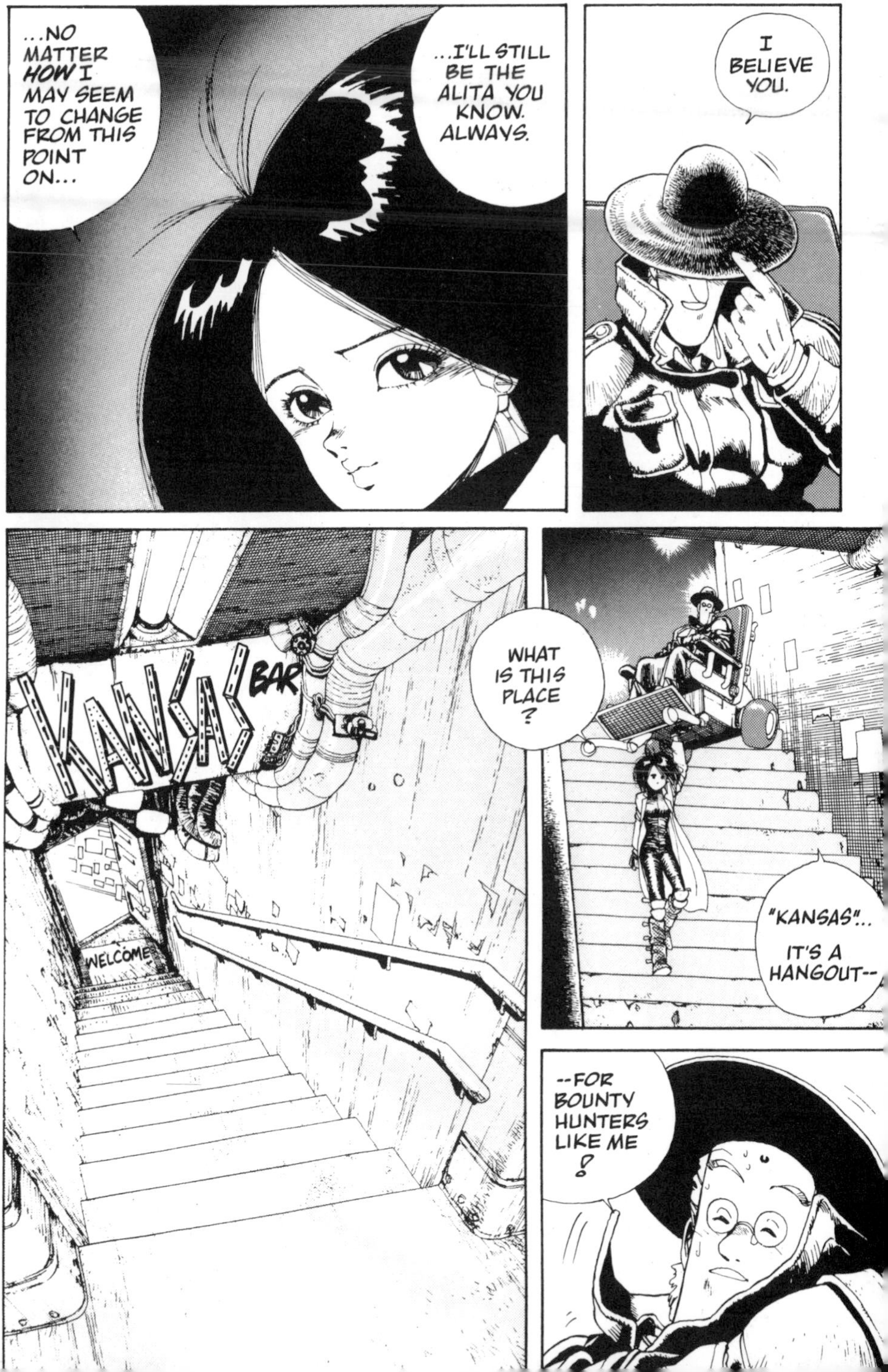
...NO MATTER HOW I MAY SEEM TO CHANGE FROM THIS POINT ON...
...I'LL STILL BE THE ALITA YOU KNOW. ALWAYS.
I BELIEVE YOU.
KANSAS
BAR
WELCOME
WHAT IS THIS PLACE ?
"KANSAS"...
IT'S A HANGOUT--
--FOR BOUNTY HUNTERS LIKE ME !

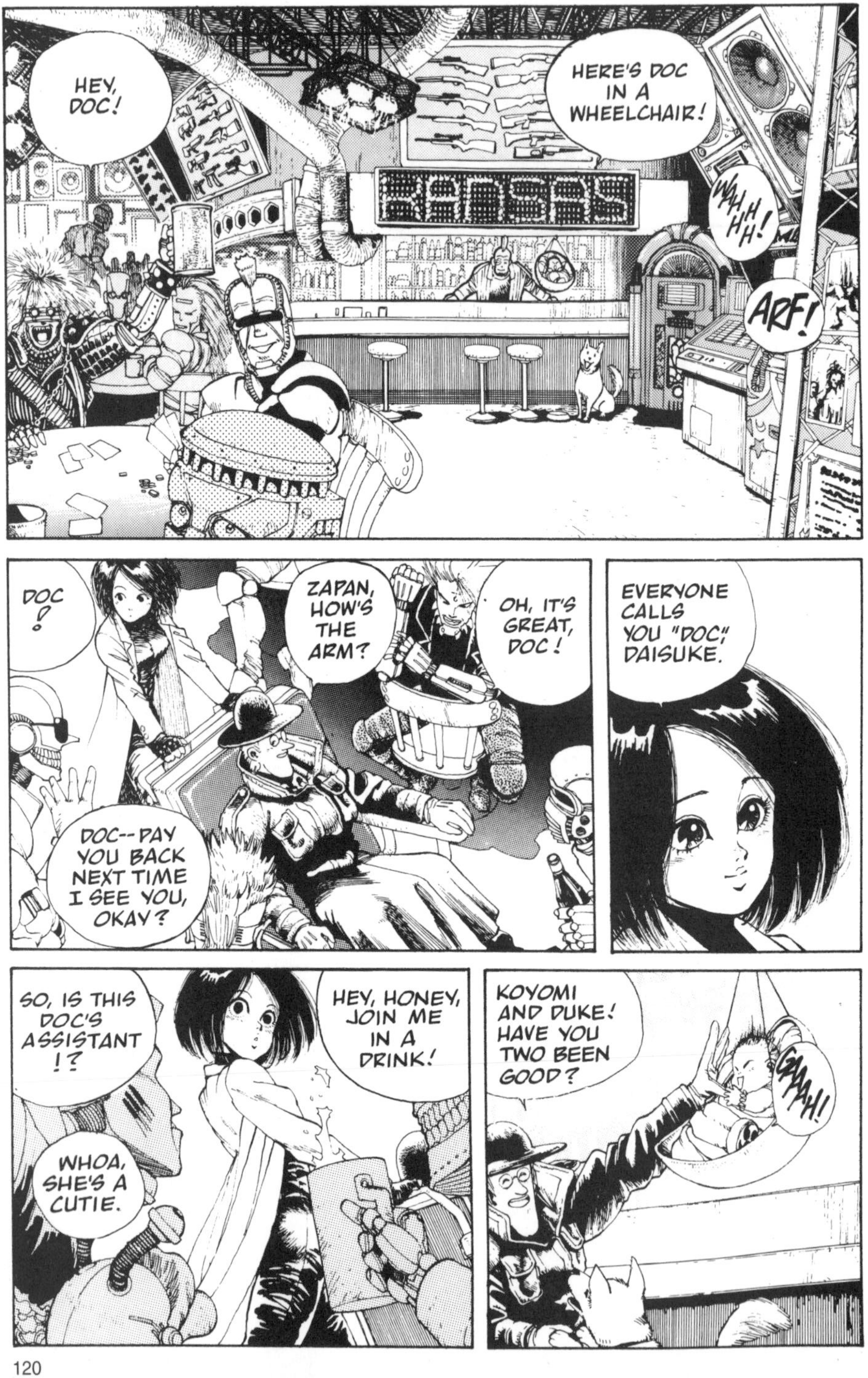
HEY, DOC!
HERE'S DOC IN A WHEELCHAIR!
WAHHHH!
ARF!
DOC?
ZAPAN, HOW'S THE ARM?
OH, IT'S GREAT, DOC!
DOC--PAY YOU BACK NEXT TIME I SEE YOU, OKAY?
EVERYONE CALLS YOU "DOC," DAISUKE.
SO, IS THIS DOC'S ASSISTANT!?
HEY, HONEY, JOIN ME IN A DRINK!
WHOA, SHE'S A CUTIE.
KOYOMI AND DUKE! HAVE YOU TWO BEEN GOOD?
GAAAH!

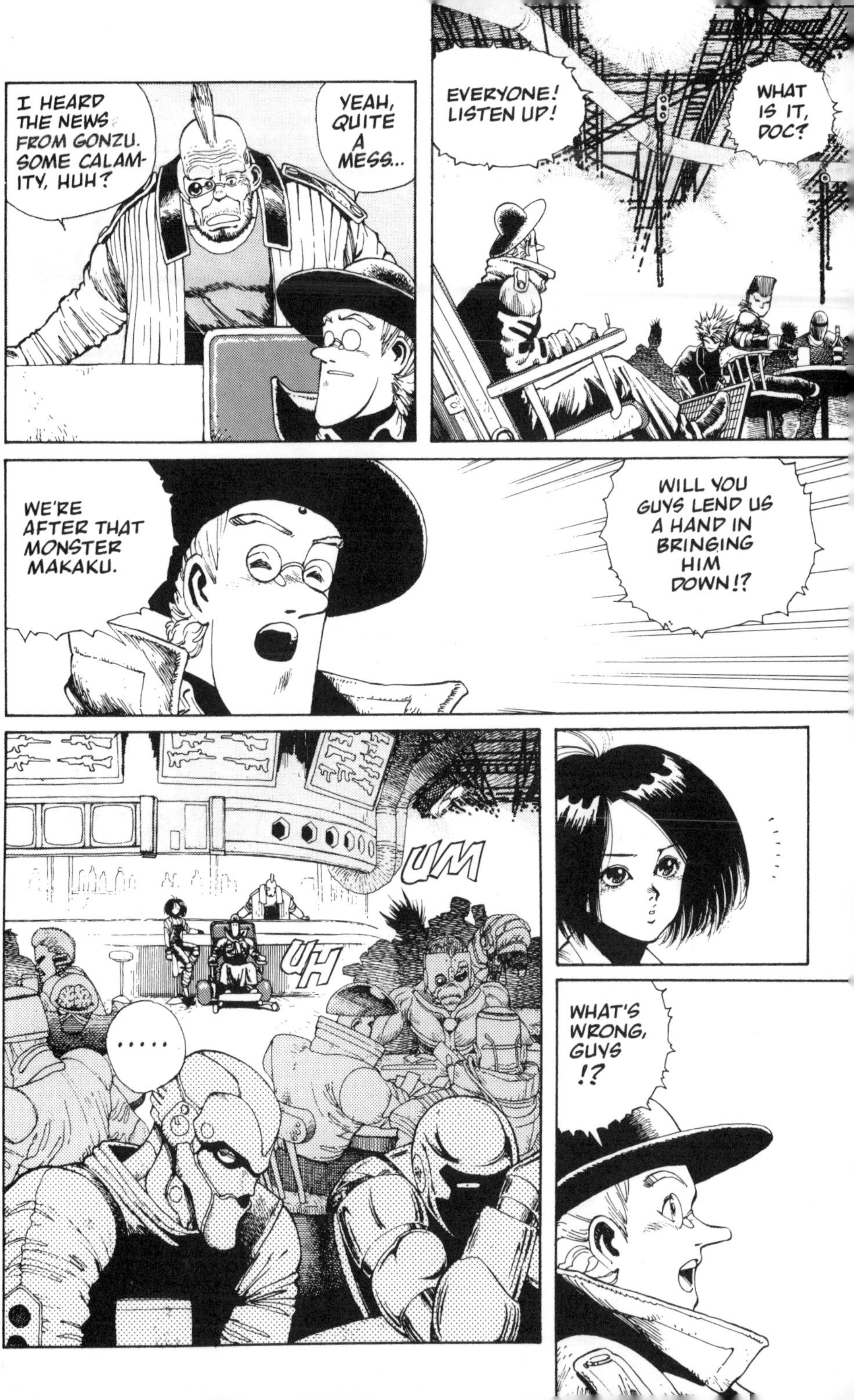
I HEARD THE NEWS FROM GONZU. SOME CALAMITY, HUH?
YEAH, QUITE A MESS...
EVERYONE! LISTEN UP!
WHAT IS IT, DOC?
WE'RE AFTER THAT MONSTER MAKAKU.
WILL YOU GUYS LEND US A HAND IN BRINGING HIM DOWN!?
UM
UH
.....
WHAT'S WRONG, GUYS !?

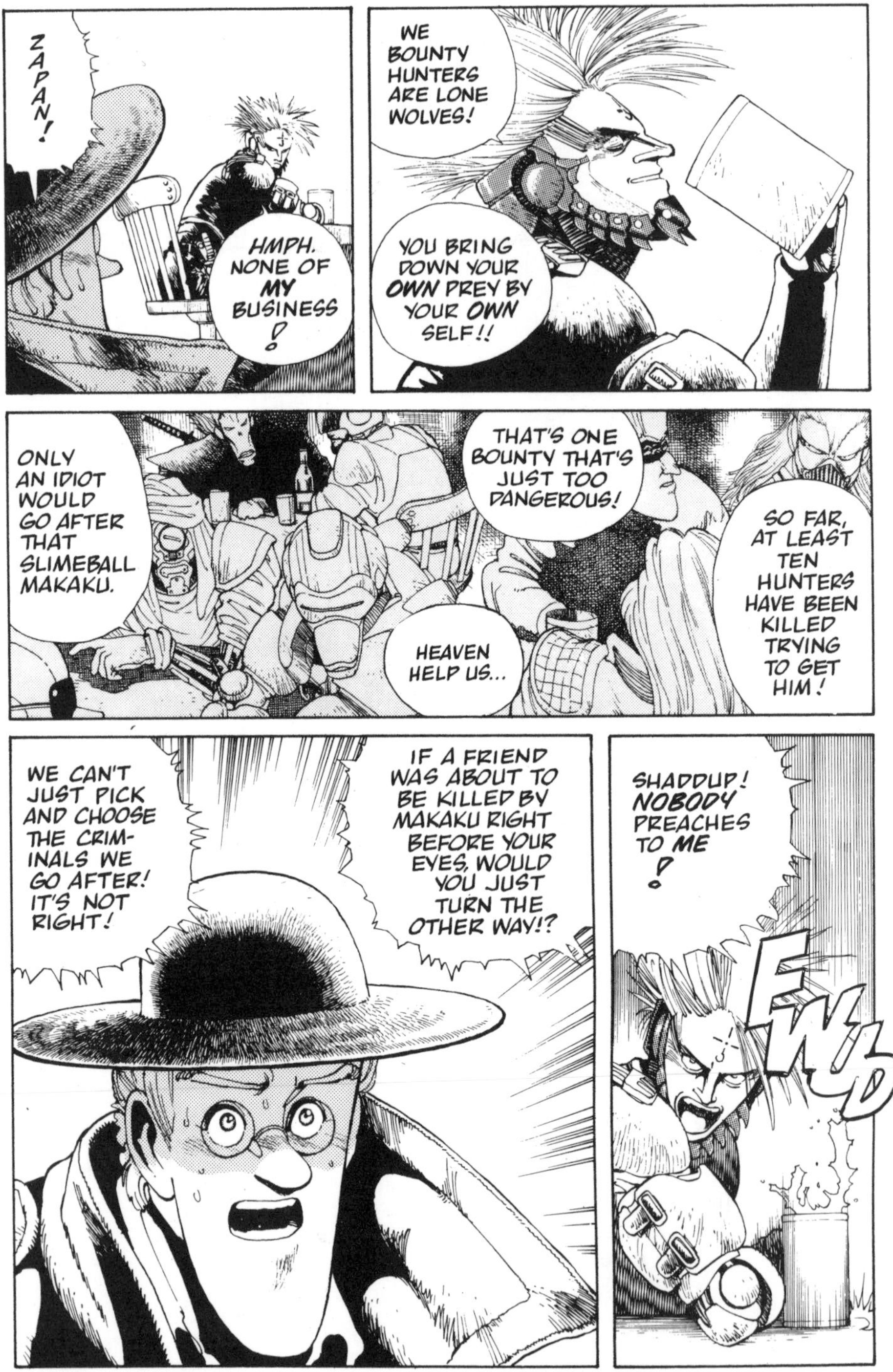
ZAPAN!
HMPH. NONE OF MY BUSINESS!
WE BOUNTY HUNTERS ARE LONE WOLVES!
YOU BRING DOWN YOUR OWN PREY BY YOUR OWN SELF!!
ONLY AN IDIOT WOULD GO AFTER THAT SLIMEBALL MAKAKU.
THAT'S ONE BOUNTY THAT'S JUST TOO DANGEROUS!
HEAVEN HELP US...
SO FAR, AT LEAST TEN HUNTERS HAVE BEEN KILLED TRYING TO GET HIM!
WE CAN'T JUST PICK AND CHOOSE THE CRIM-INALS WE GO AFTER! IT'S NOT RIGHT!
IF A FRIEND WAS ABOUT TO BE KILLED BY MAKAKU RIGHT BEFORE YOUR EYES, WOULD YOU JUST TURN THE OTHER WAY!?
SHADDUP! NOBODY PREACHES TO ME!
FWUD

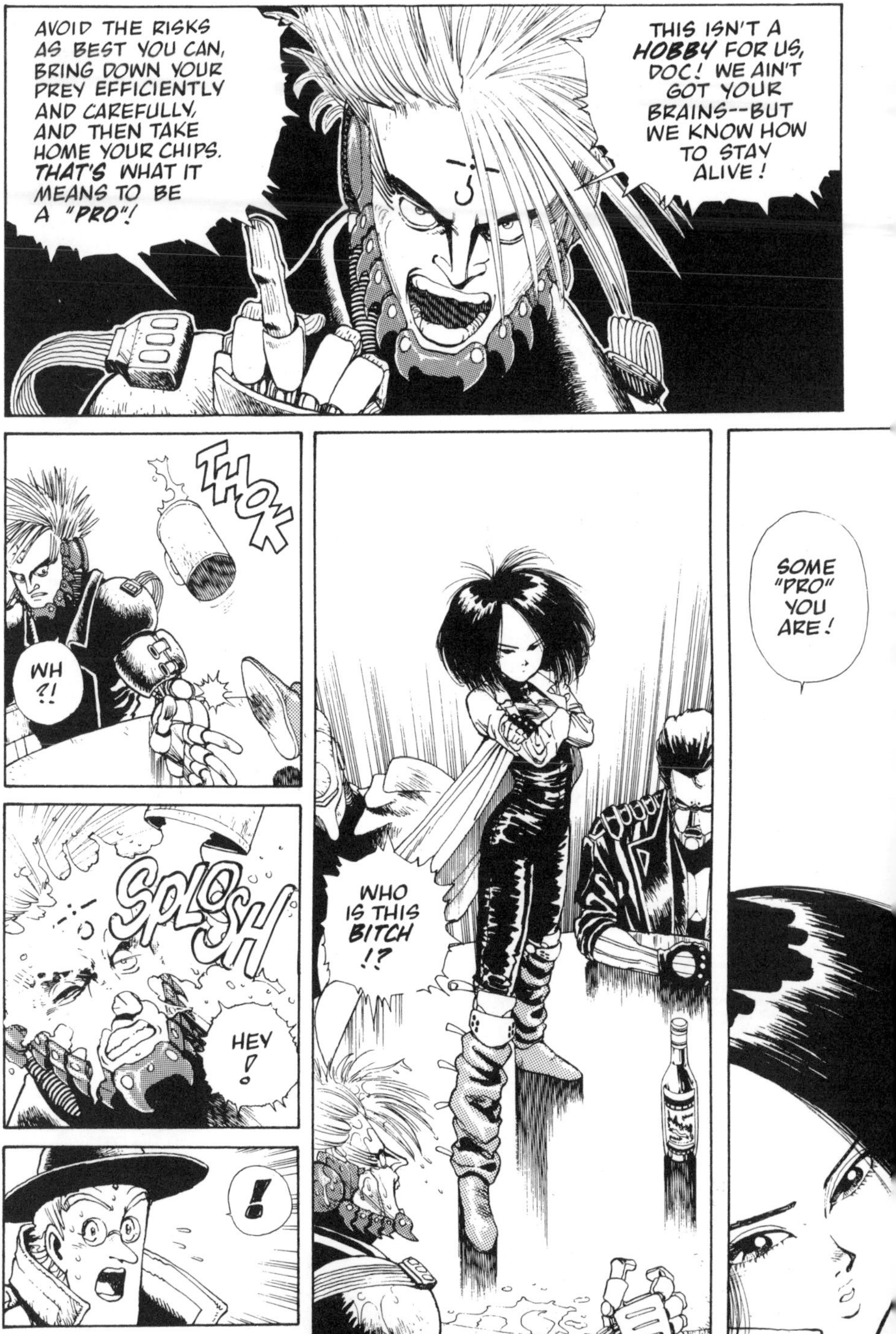
AVOID THE RISKS AS BEST YOU CAN, BRING DOWN YOUR PREY EFFICIENTLY AND CAREFULLY, AND THEN TAKE HOME YOUR CHIPS. *THAT'S* WHAT IT MEANS TO BE A "*PRO*"!
THIS ISN'T A *HOBBY* FOR US, DOC! WE AIN'T GOT YOUR BRAINS--BUT WE KNOW HOW TO STAY ALIVE!
THOK
WH?!
SPLOSH
HEY!
!
WHO IS THIS *BITCH*!?
SOME "PRO" YOU ARE!

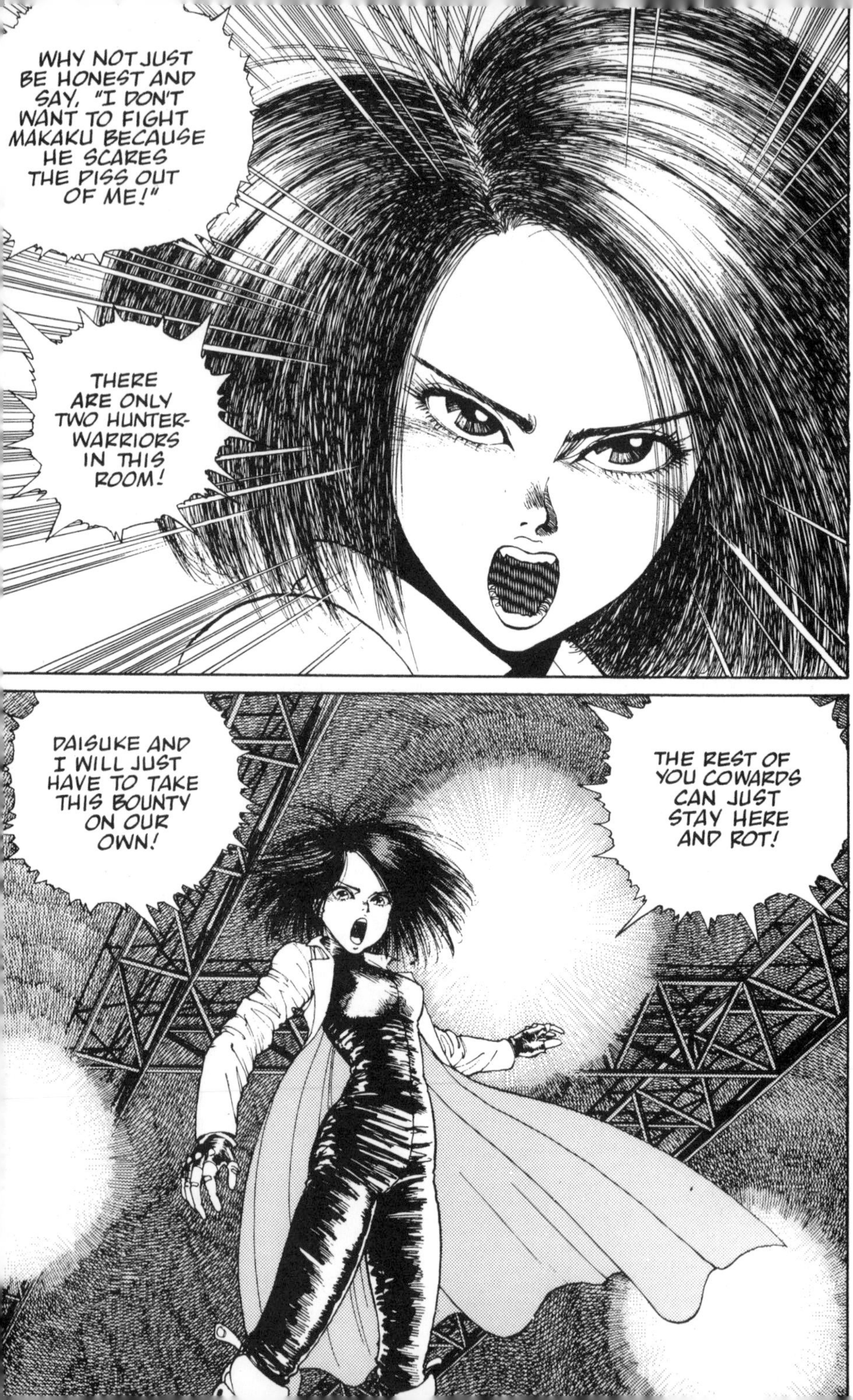
WHY NOT JUST BE HONEST AND SAY, "I DON'T WANT TO FIGHT MAKAKU BECAUSE HE SCARES THE PISS OUT OF ME!"
THERE ARE ONLY TWO HUNTER-WARRIORS IN THIS ROOM!
DAISUKE AND I WILL JUST HAVE TO TAKE THIS BOUNTY ON OUR OWN!
THE REST OF YOU COWARDS CAN JUST STAY HERE AND ROT!

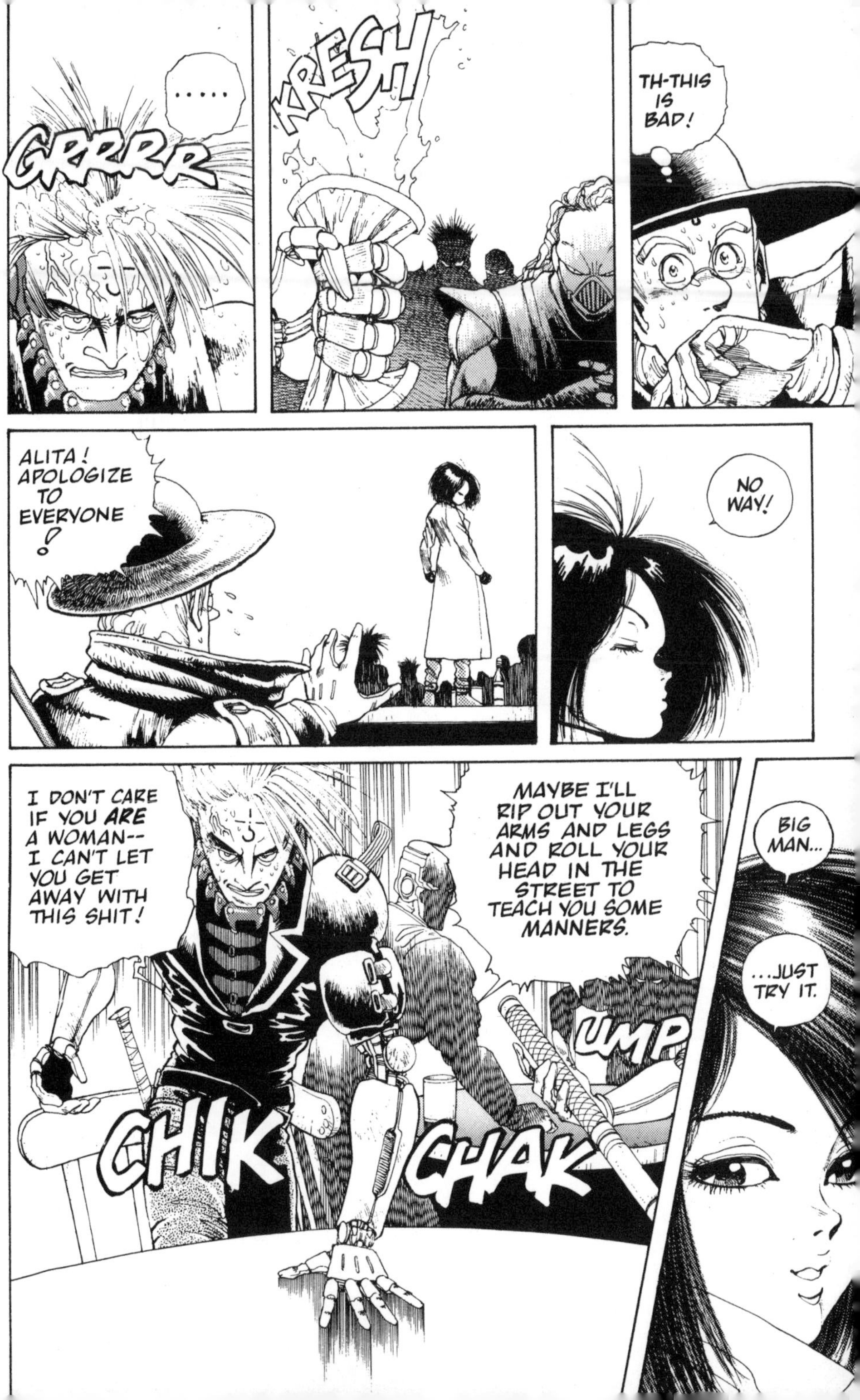

GRRRR
.....
KRESH
TH-THIS IS BAD!
ALITA! APOLOGIZE TO EVERYONE!
NO WAY!
I DON'T CARE IF YOU ARE A WOMAN-- I CAN'T LET YOU GET AWAY WITH THIS SHIT!
MAYBE I'LL RIP OUT YOUR ARMS AND LEGS AND ROLL YOUR HEAD IN THE STREET TO TEACH YOU SOME MANNERS.
UMP
CHIK
CHAK
BIG MAN...
...JUST TRY IT.

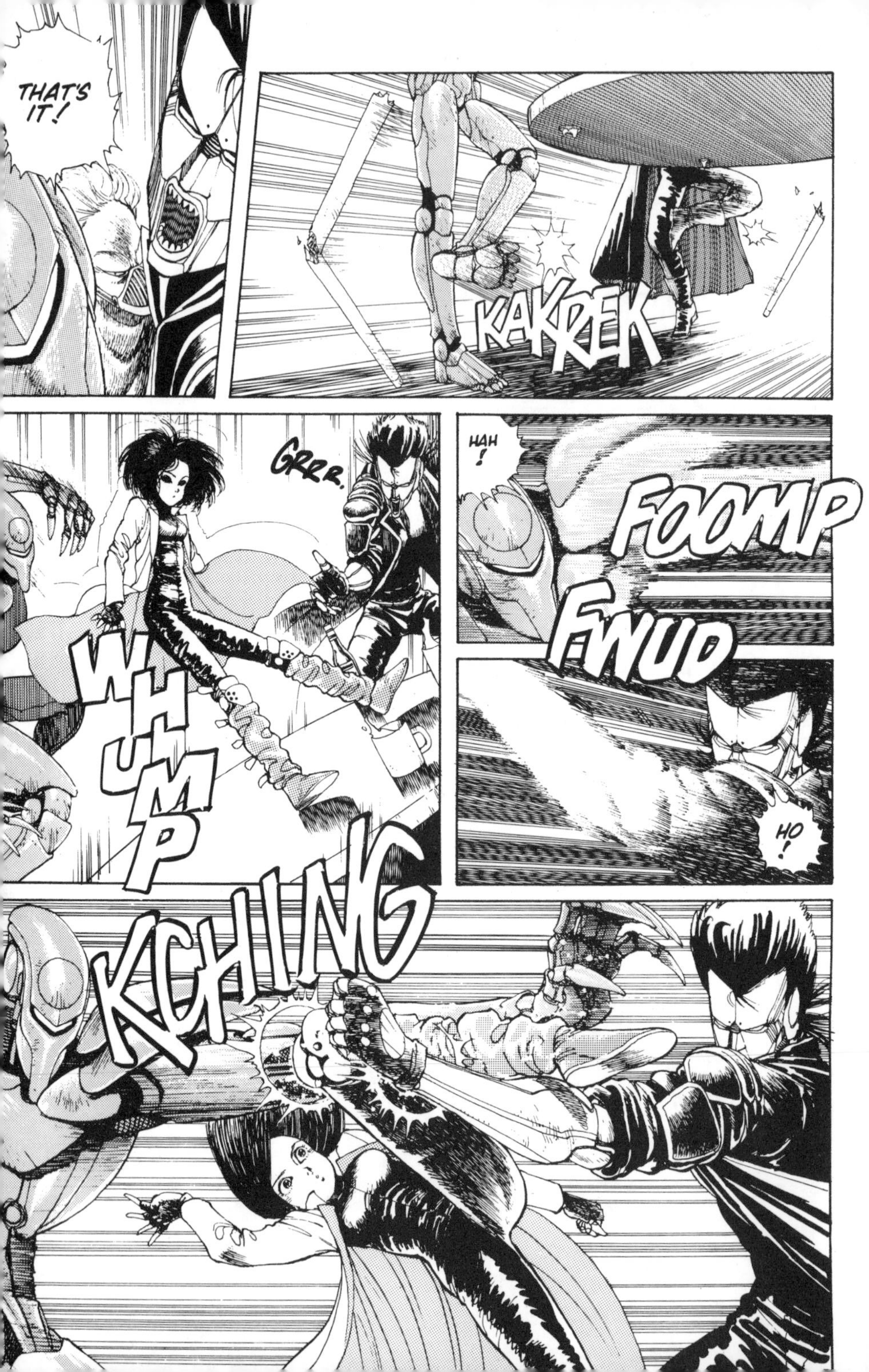
THAT'S IT!
KAKREK
GRRR.
WHUMP
HAH!
FOOMP
FWUD
HO!
KCHING

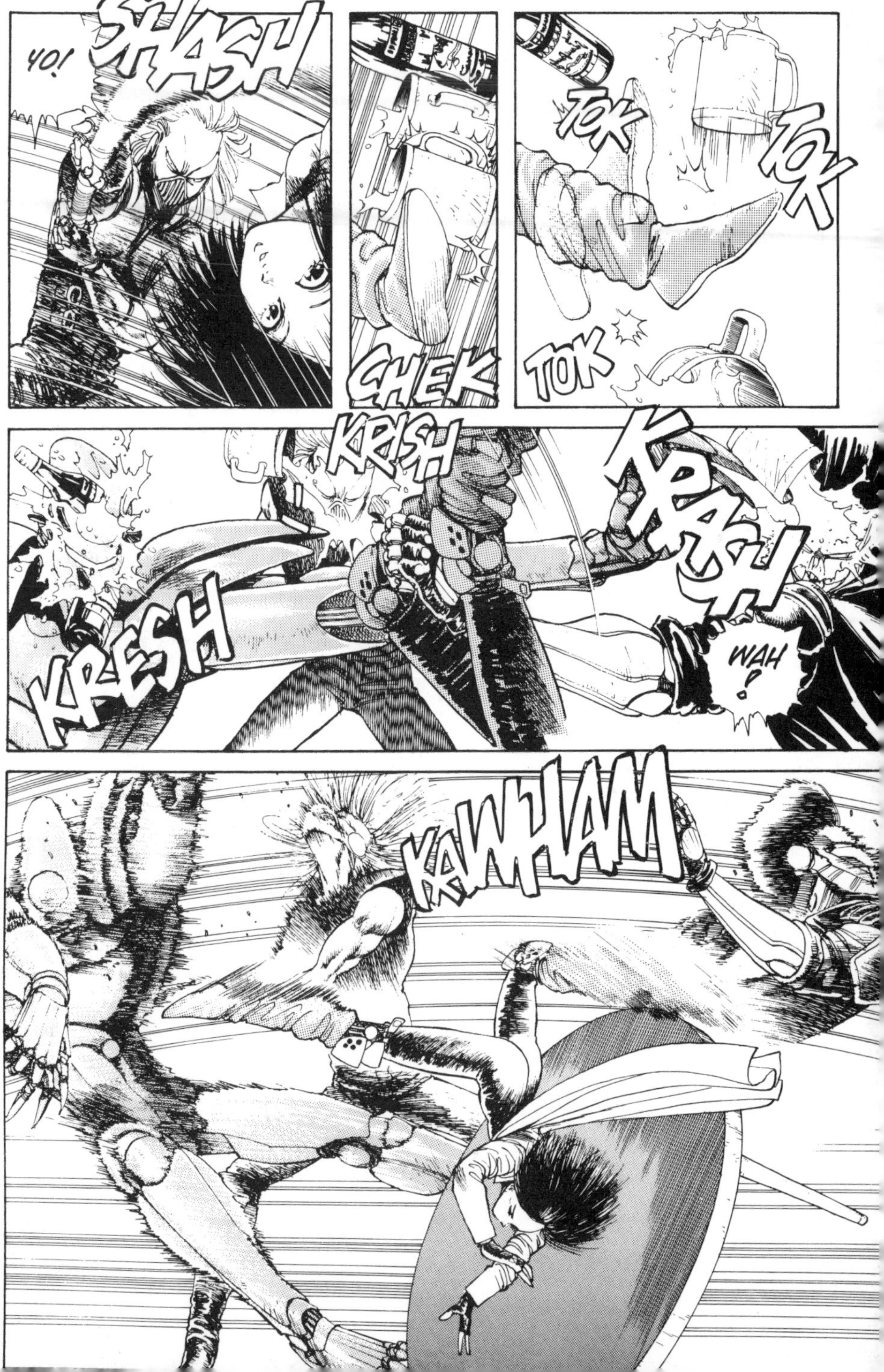
YO!
SHASH
CHEK
TOK
TOK
TOK
KRISH
KRESH
KRASH
WAH!?
KAWHAM

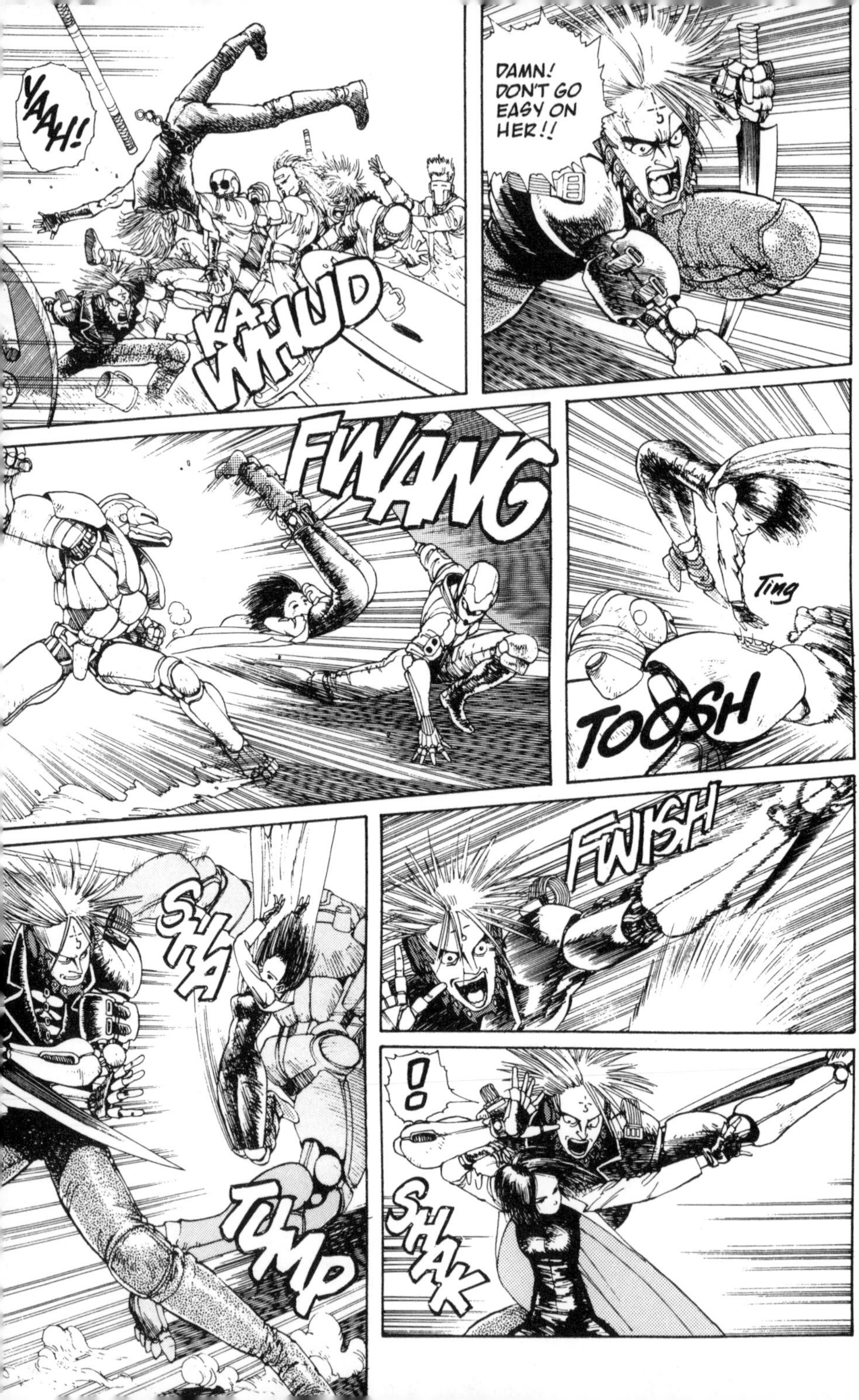
YAAAH!
KA WHUD
DAMN! DON'T GO EASY ON HER!!
FWANG
Ting
TOOSH
SHA
TUMP
FWISH
!
SHAK

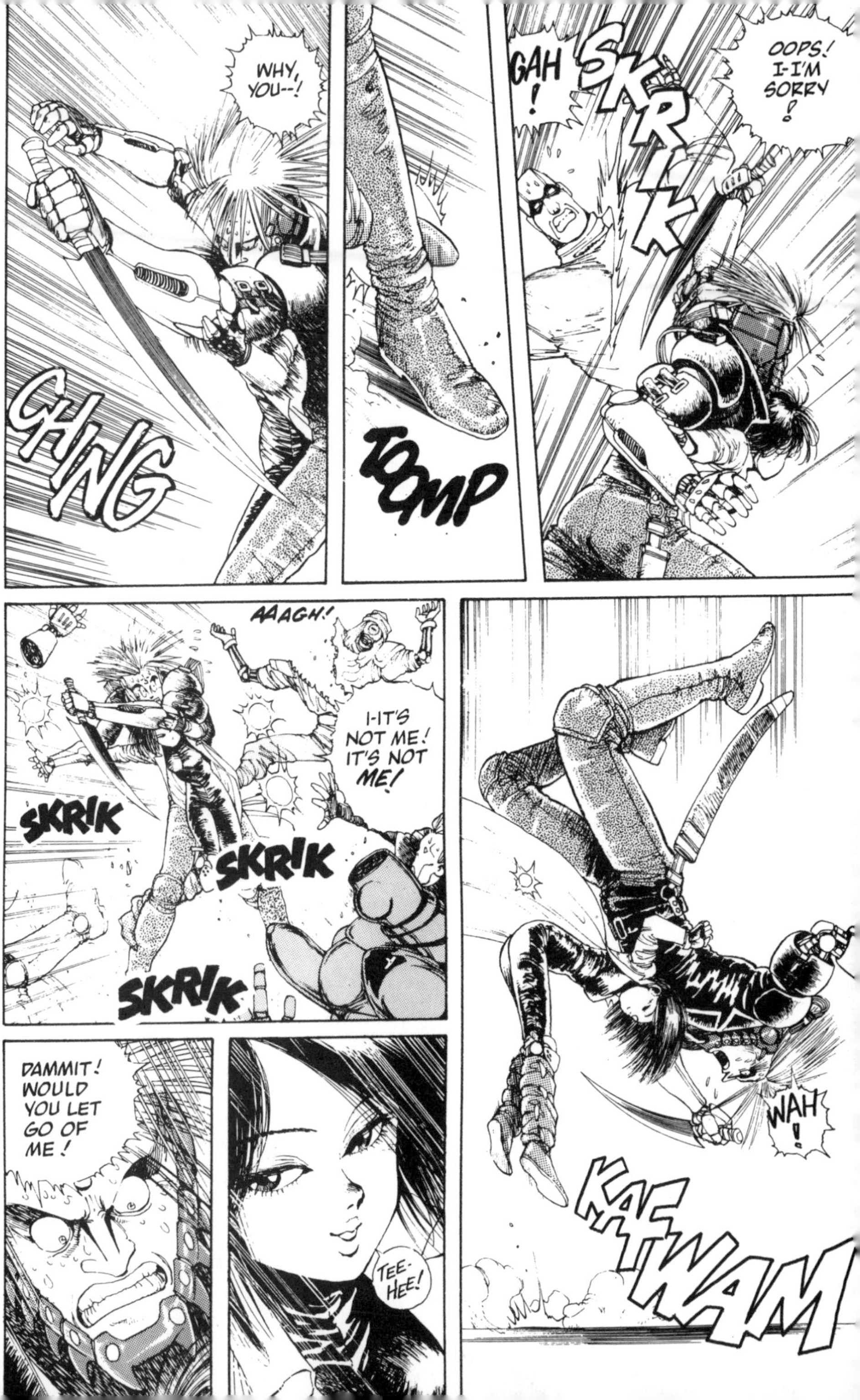
WHY, YOU--!
CHING
TOOMP
GAH!
SKRIK
OOPS! I-I'M SORRY!
AAAGH!
I-IT'S NOT ME! IT'S NOT ME!
SKRIK
SKRIK
SKRIK
WAH!
KA-TWAM
DAMMIT! WOULD YOU LET GO OF ME!
TEE-HEE!

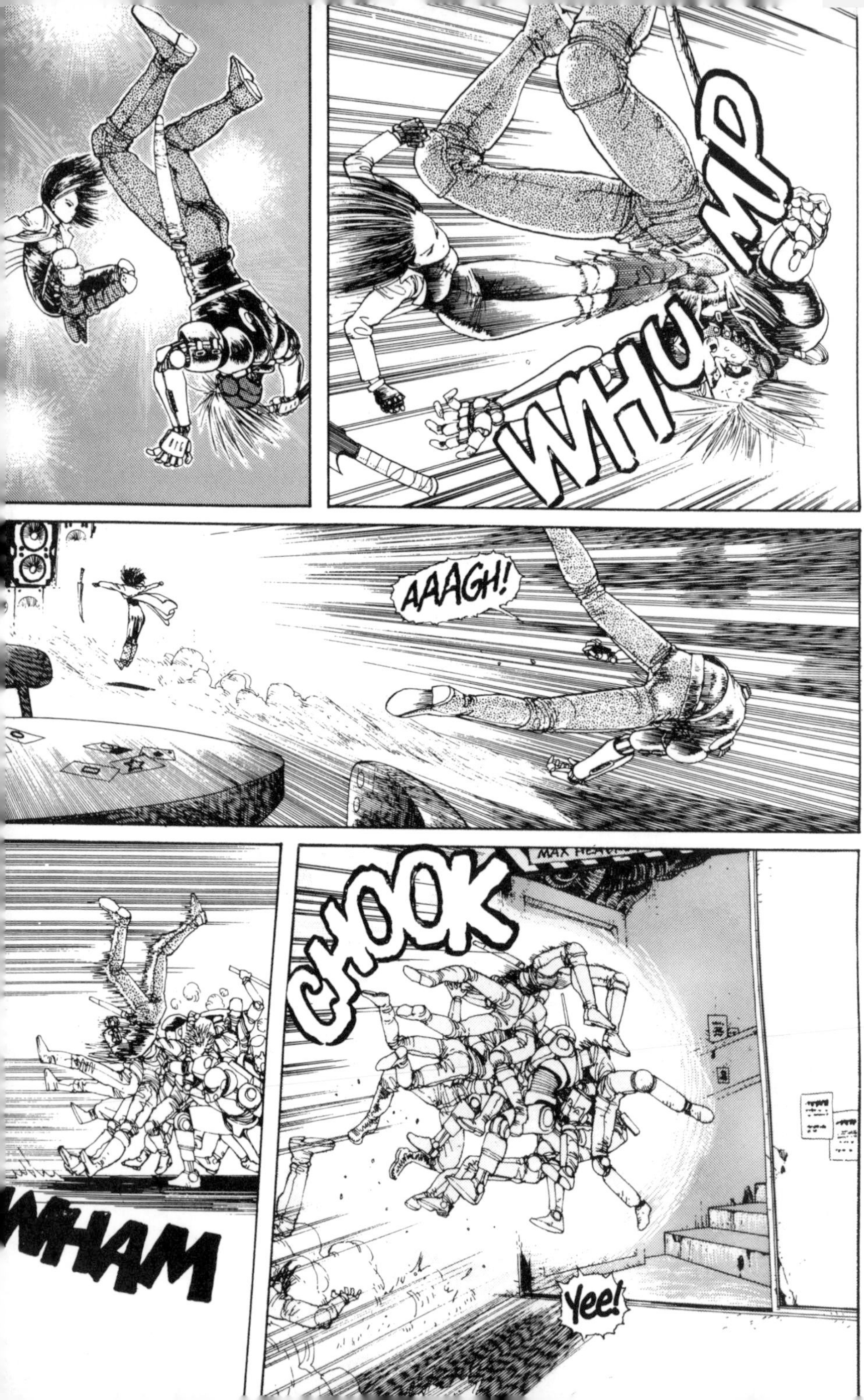
WHUMP
AAAGH!
WHAM
CHOOK
Yee!

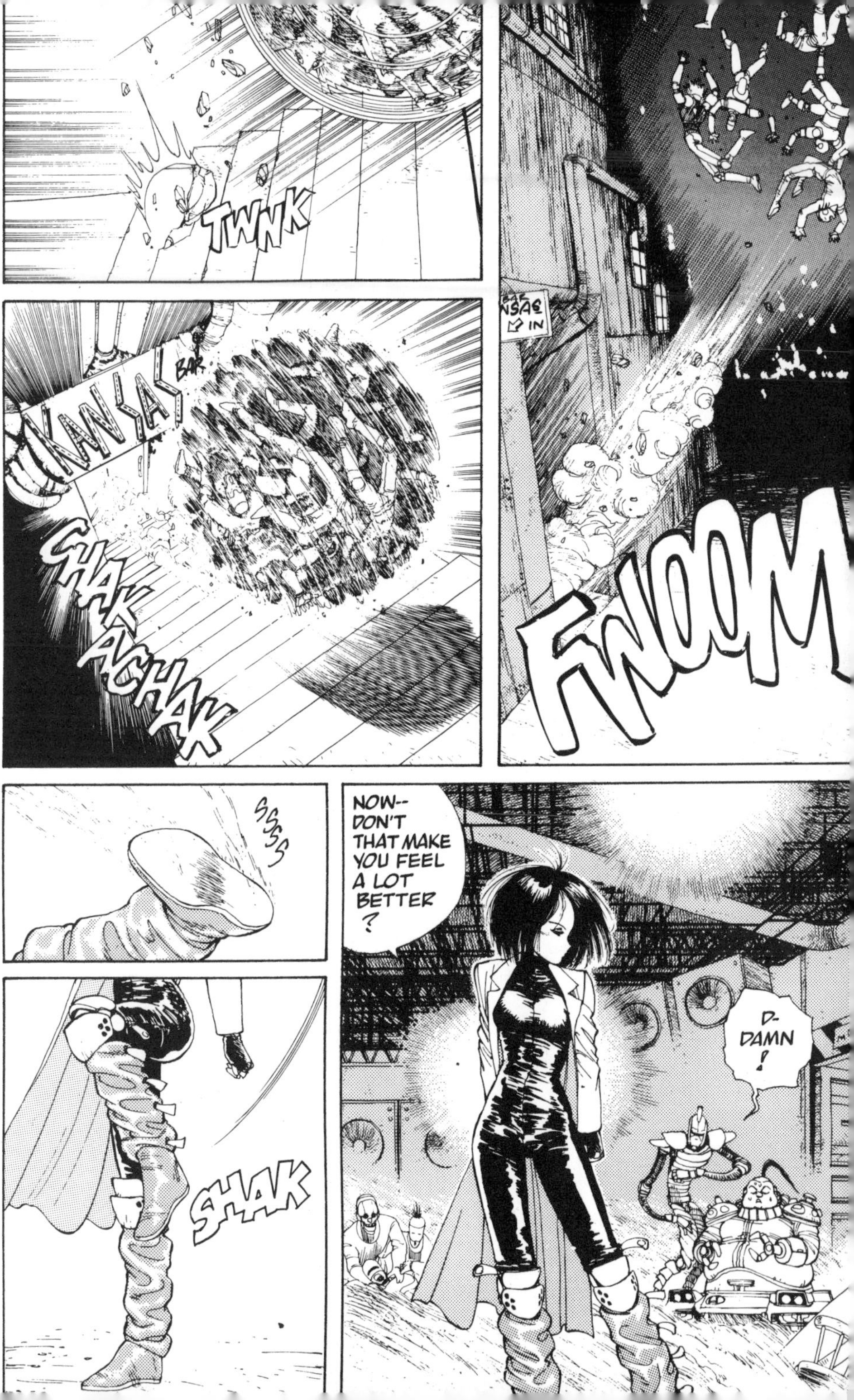
TWNK
KANSAS
BAR
CHAKACHAK
FWOOM
SSSS
SHAK
NOW-- DON'T THAT MAKE YOU FEEL A LOT BETTER ?
D-DAMN !

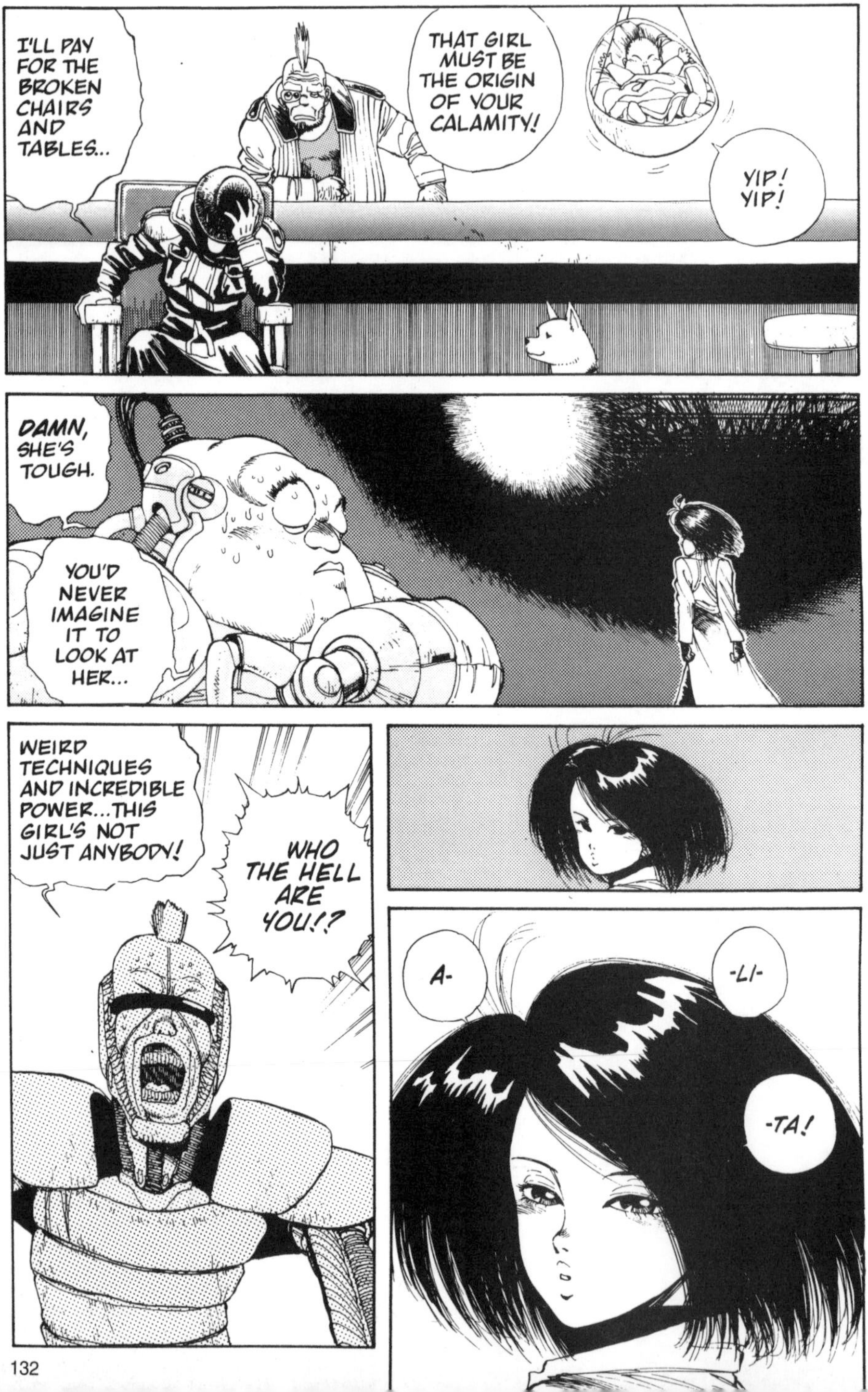

I'LL PAY FOR THE BROKEN CHAIRS AND TABLES...
THAT GIRL MUST BE THE ORIGIN OF YOUR CALAMITY!
YIP! YIP!
DAMN, SHE'S TOUGH.
YOU'D NEVER IMAGINE IT TO LOOK AT HER...
WEIRD TECHNIQUES AND INCREDIBLE POWER...THIS GIRL'S NOT JUST ANYBODY!
WHO THE HELL ARE YOU!?
A-
-LI-
-TA!

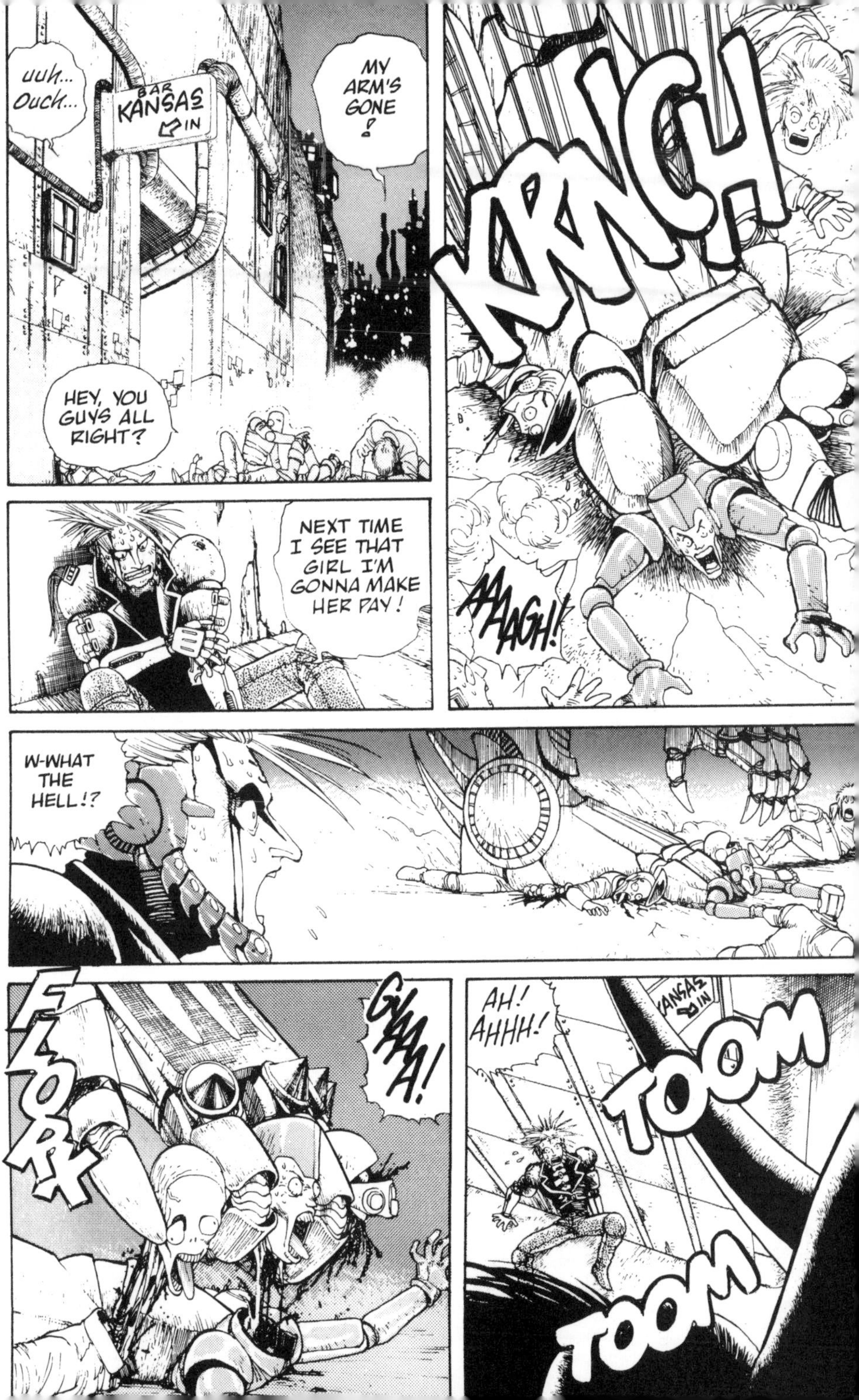
uuh... ouch...
BAR KANSAS IN
MY ARM'S GONE!
HEY, YOU GUYS ALL RIGHT?
NEXT TIME I SEE THAT GIRL I'M GONNA MAKE HER PAY!
KRANCH!
AAAAGH!
W-WHAT THE HELL!?
FLORK
GWAAA!
AH! AHHH!
KANSAS IN
TOOM
TOOM

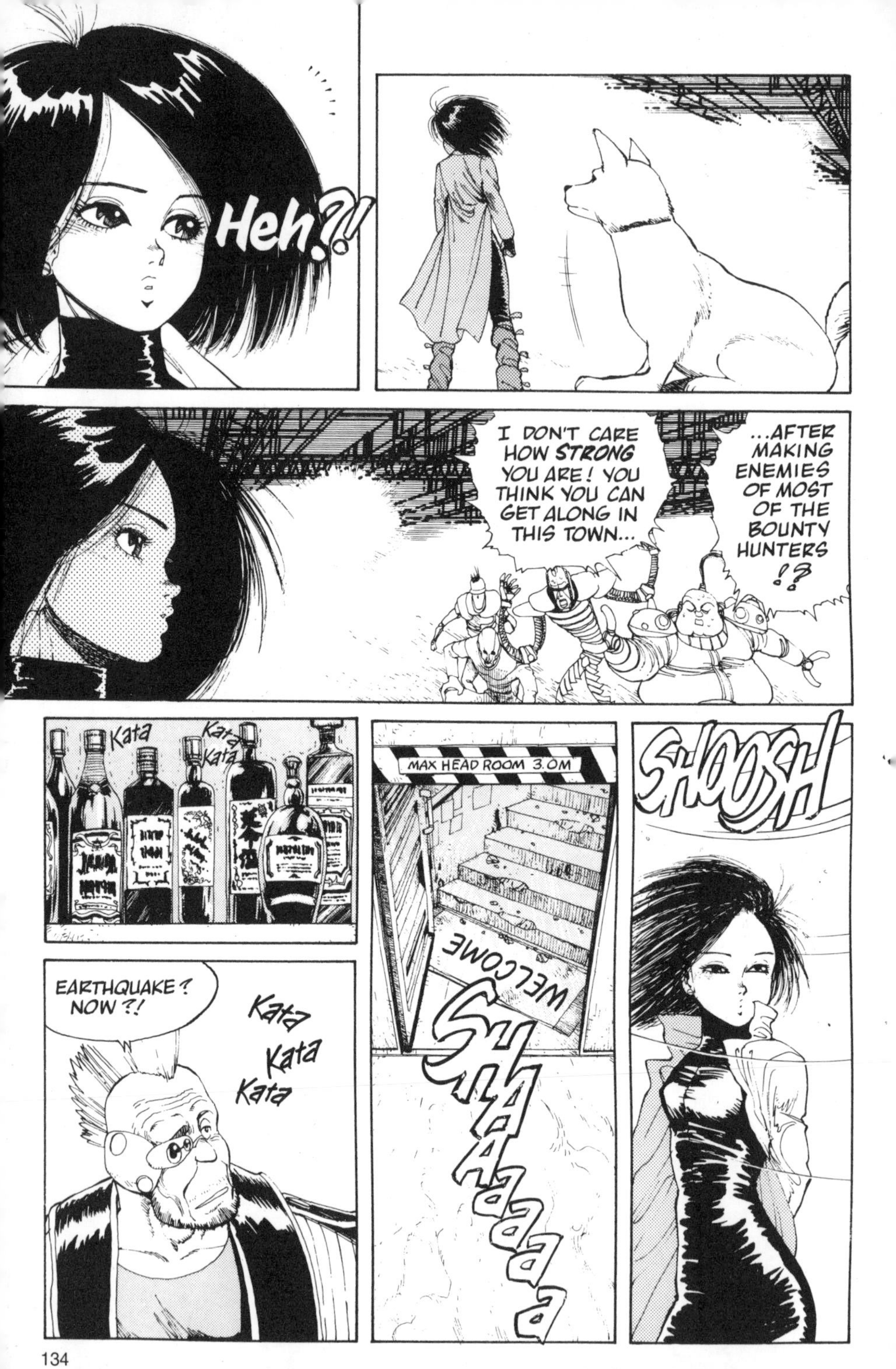

Heh?!
I DON'T CARE HOW STRONG YOU ARE! YOU THINK YOU CAN GET ALONG IN THIS TOWN...
...AFTER MAKING ENEMIES OF MOST OF THE BOUNTY HUNTERS !?
Kata
Kata
Kata
MAX HEAD ROOM 3.0M
WELCOME
SHOOSH
EARTHQUAKE? NOW?!
Kata
Kata
Kata
Shaaaaaaaa

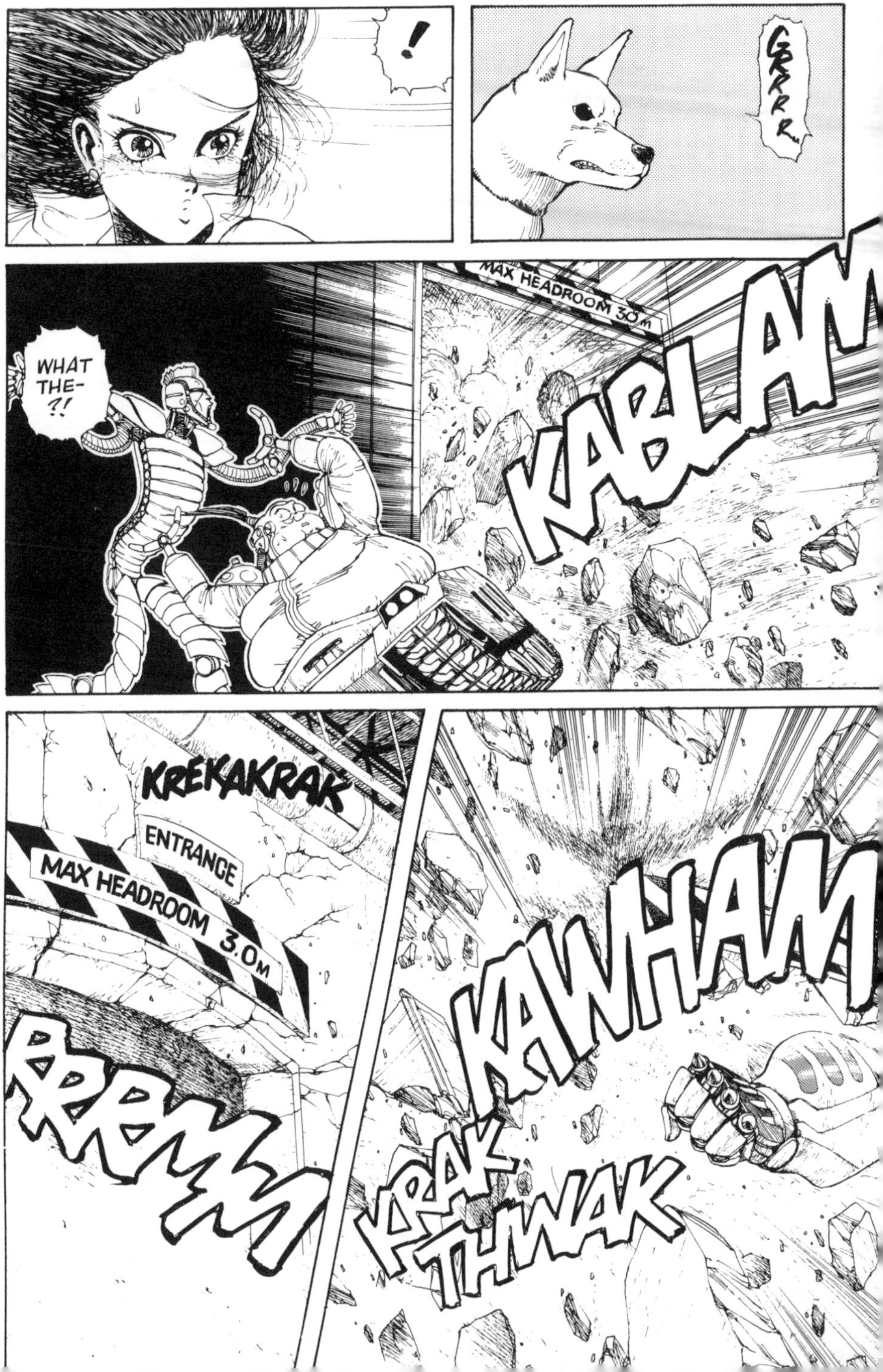

!
GRRRR
WHAT THE-?!
MAX HEADROOM 3.0m
KABLAM
KREKAKRAK
ENTRANCE
MAX HEADROOM 3.0m
KAWHAM
KRAK
THWAK

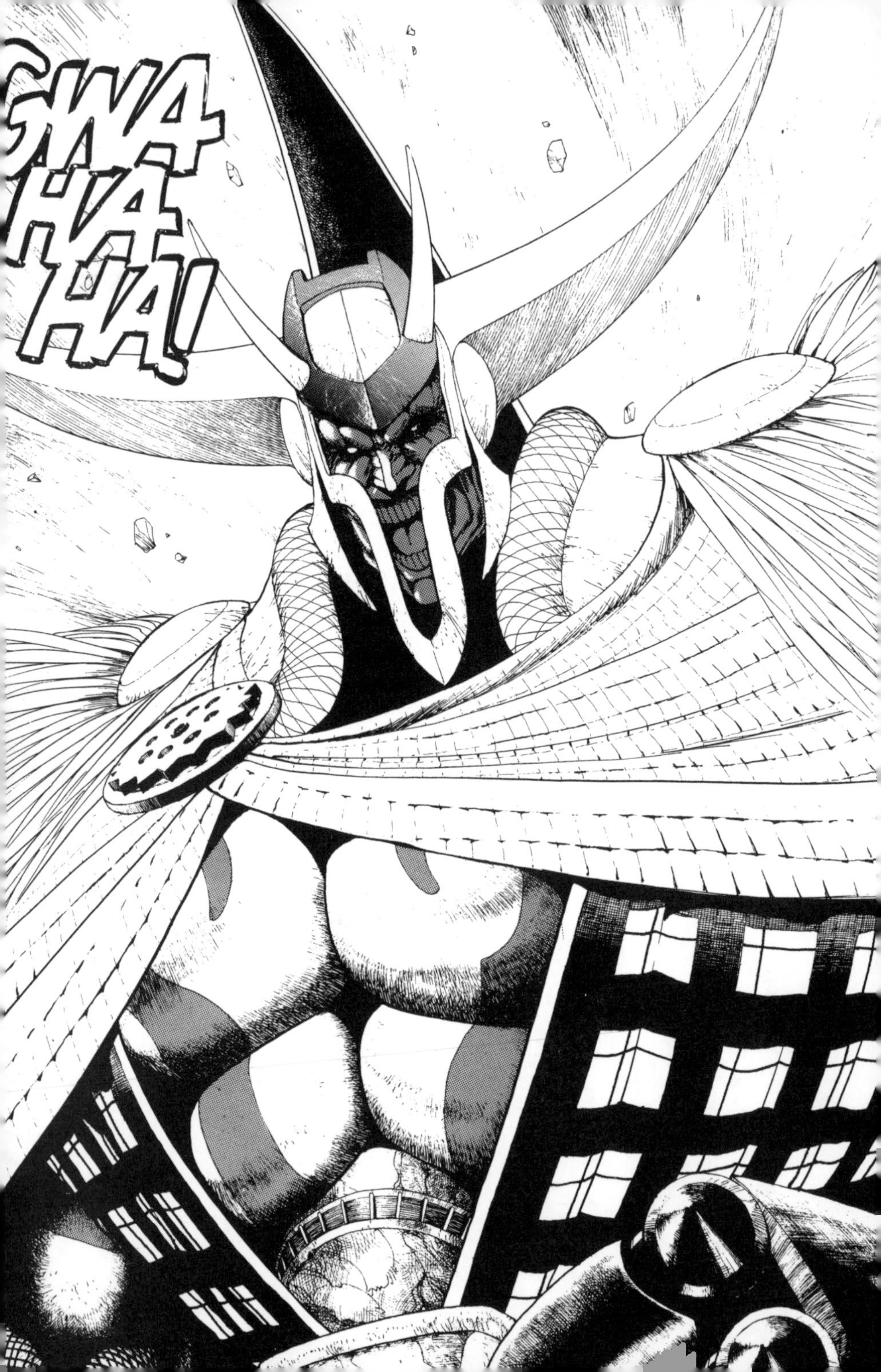
GWA HA HA HA!

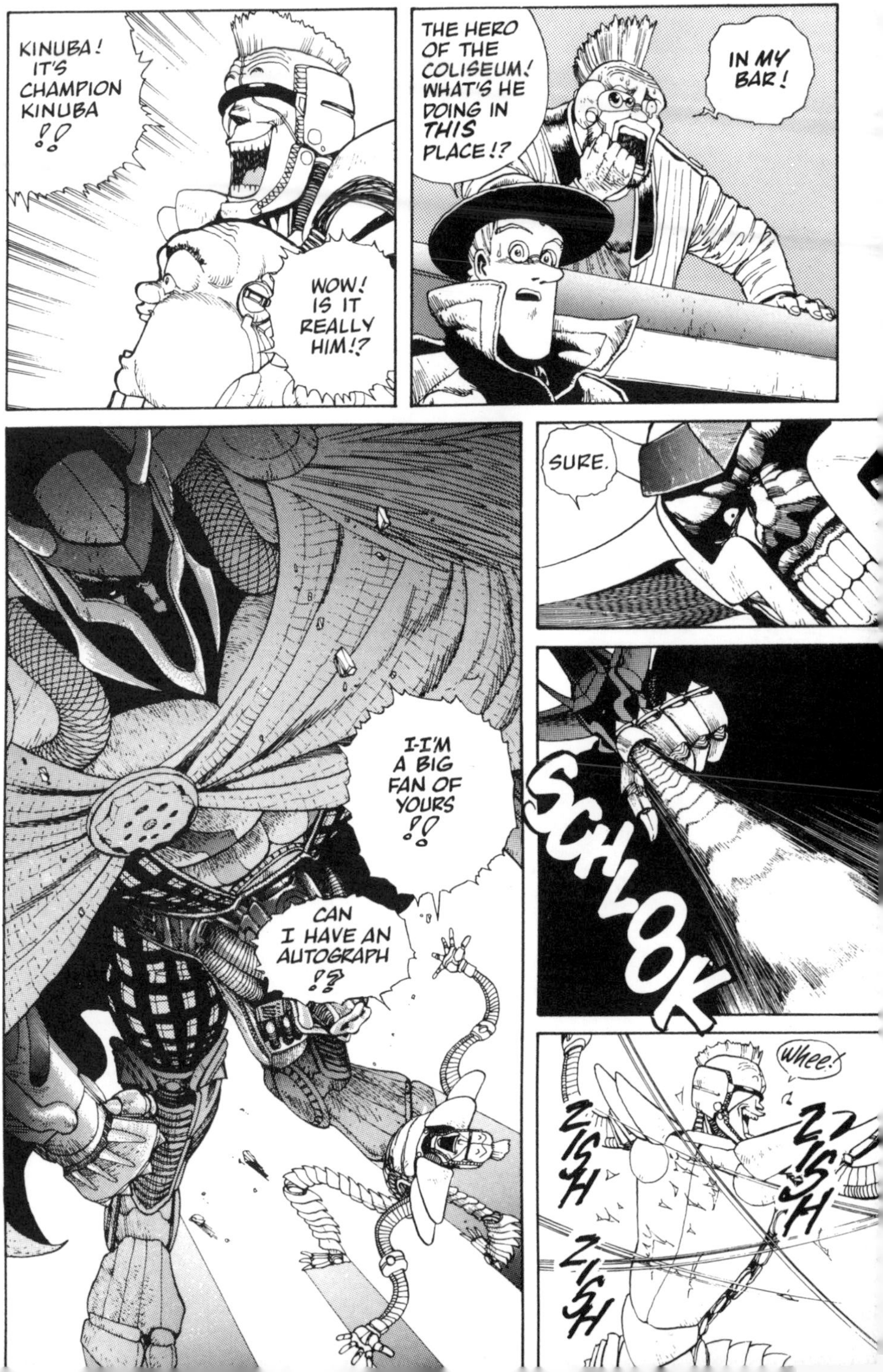
KINUBA! IT'S CHAMPION KINUBA !!
WOW! IS IT REALLY HIM!?
THE HERO OF THE COLISEUM! WHAT'S HE DOING IN THIS PLACE!?
IN MY BAR!
I-I'M A BIG FAN OF YOURS !!
CAN I HAVE AN AUTOGRAPH !?
SURE.
SCHLOOK
whee!
ZISH
ZISH
ZISH

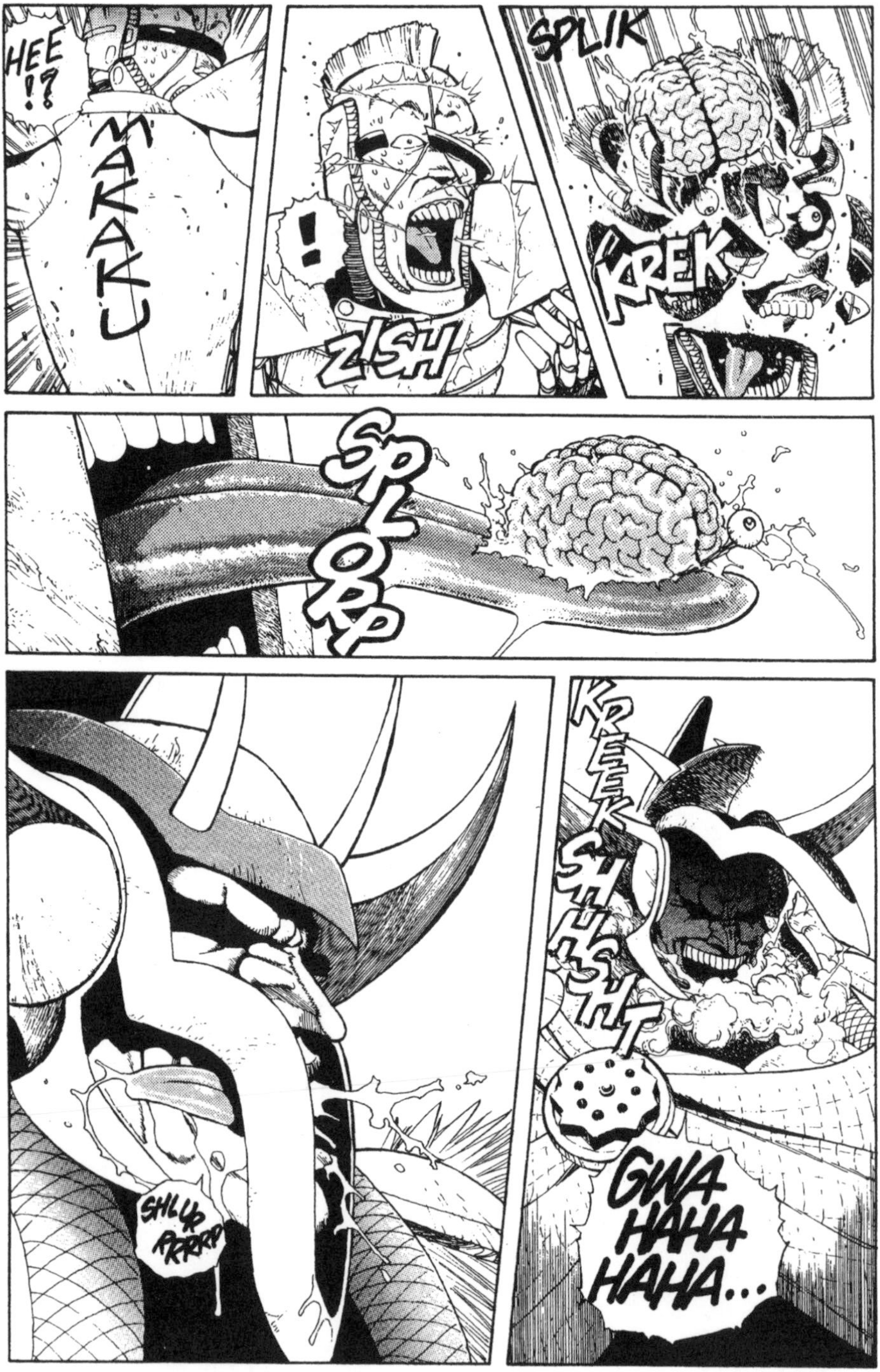
HEE!?
MAKAKU
!
ZISH
SPLIK
KREK
SPLORP
SHLURRRRRP
KREEK
SHUHSHT
GWA HAHA HAHA...

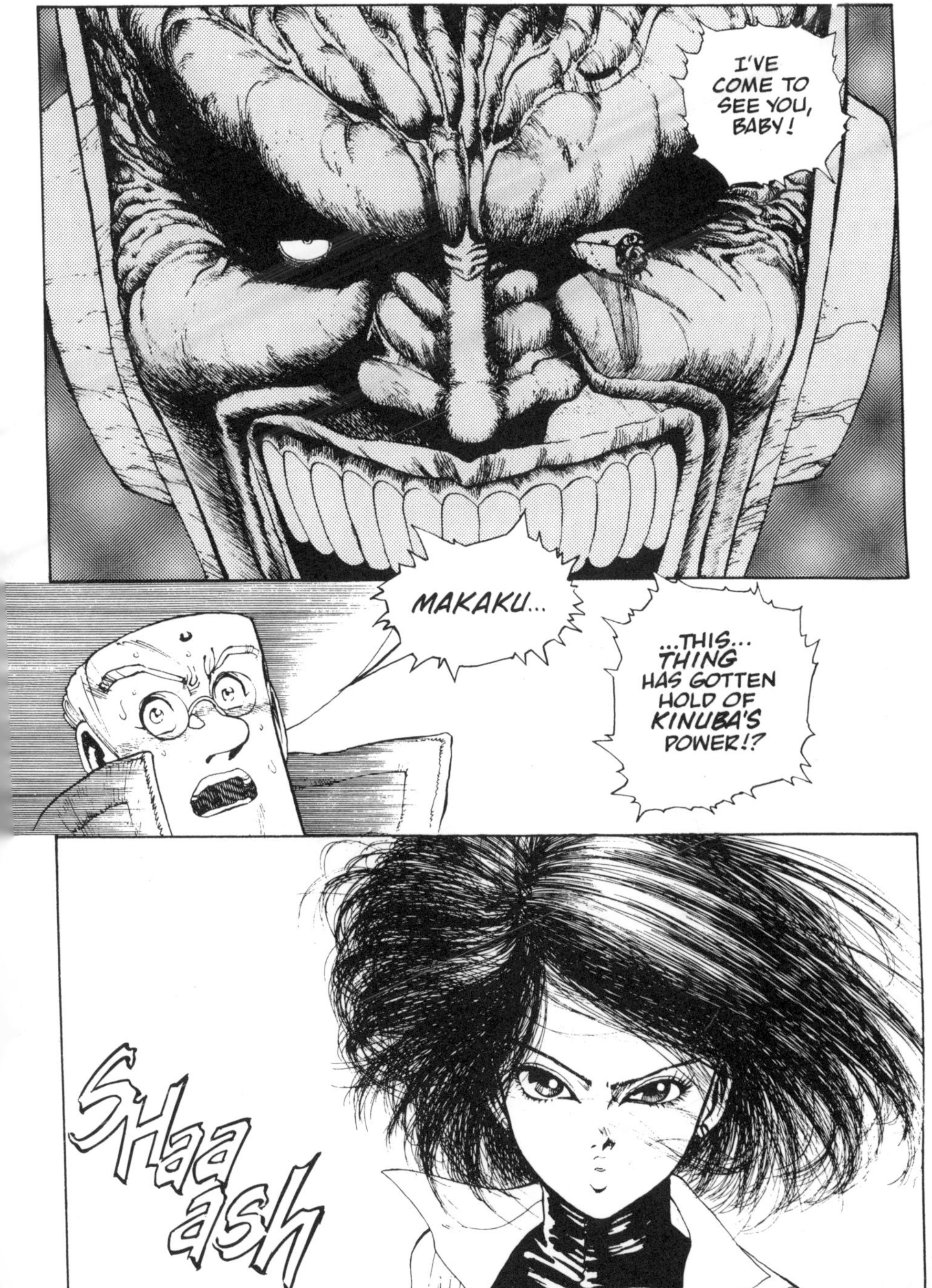
I'VE COME TO SEE YOU, BABY!
MAKAKU...
...THIS... THING HAS GOTTEN HOLD OF KINUBA'S POWER!?
SHaaash

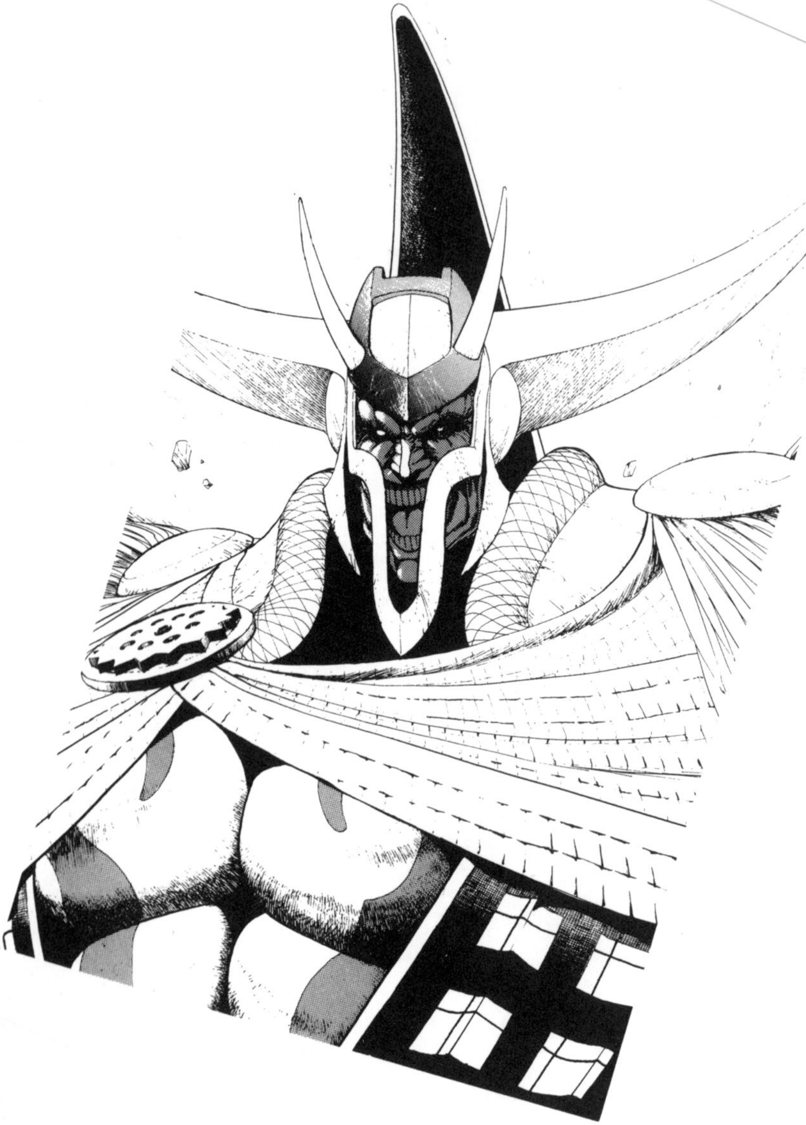

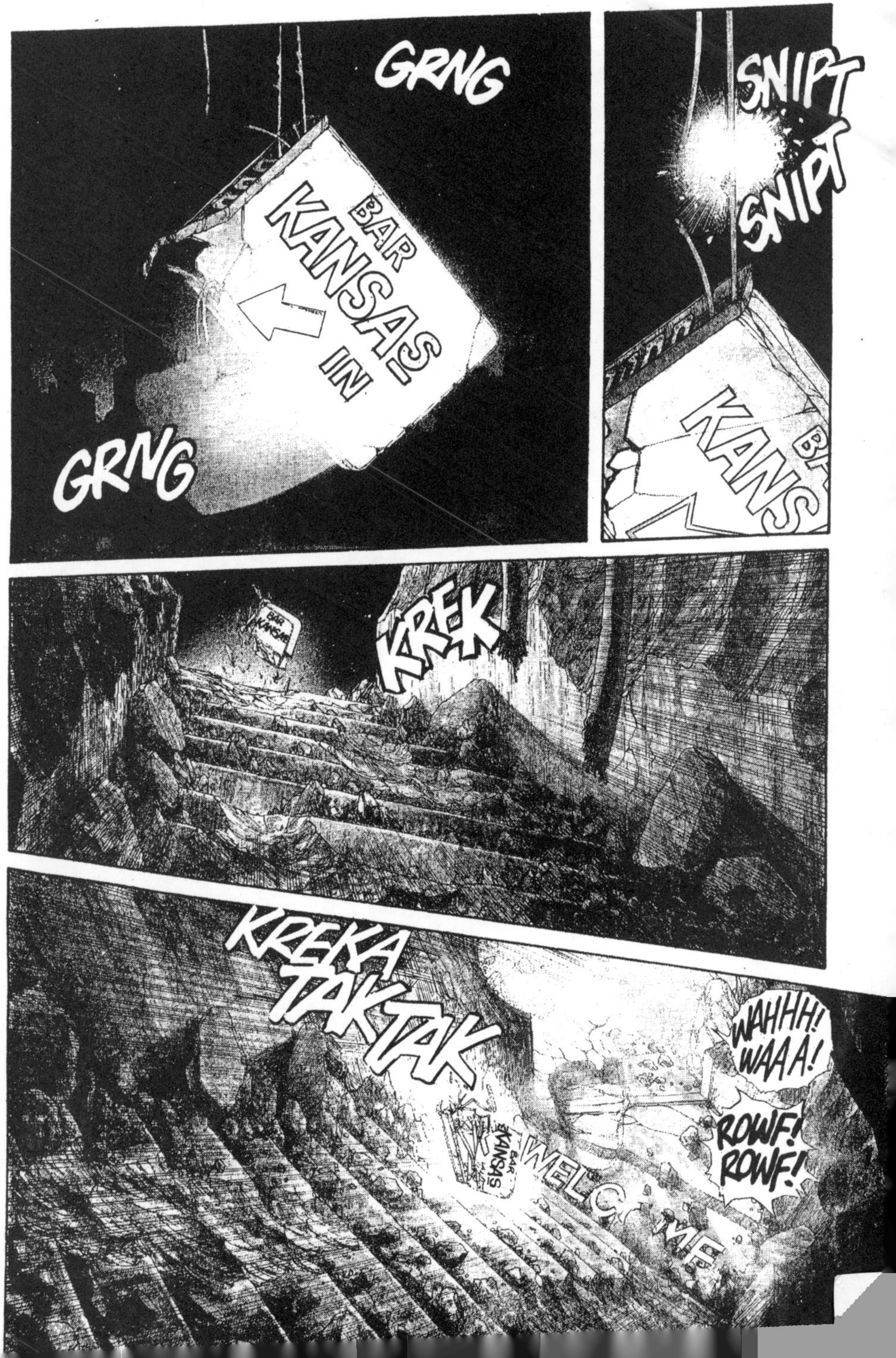
GRNG
BAR
KANSAS!
IN
GRNG
SNIPT
SNIPT
BAR KANSAS!
KREK
KREKA TAKTAK
BAR KANSAS!
WELC ME
WAHHH! WAAA!
ROWF! ROWF!

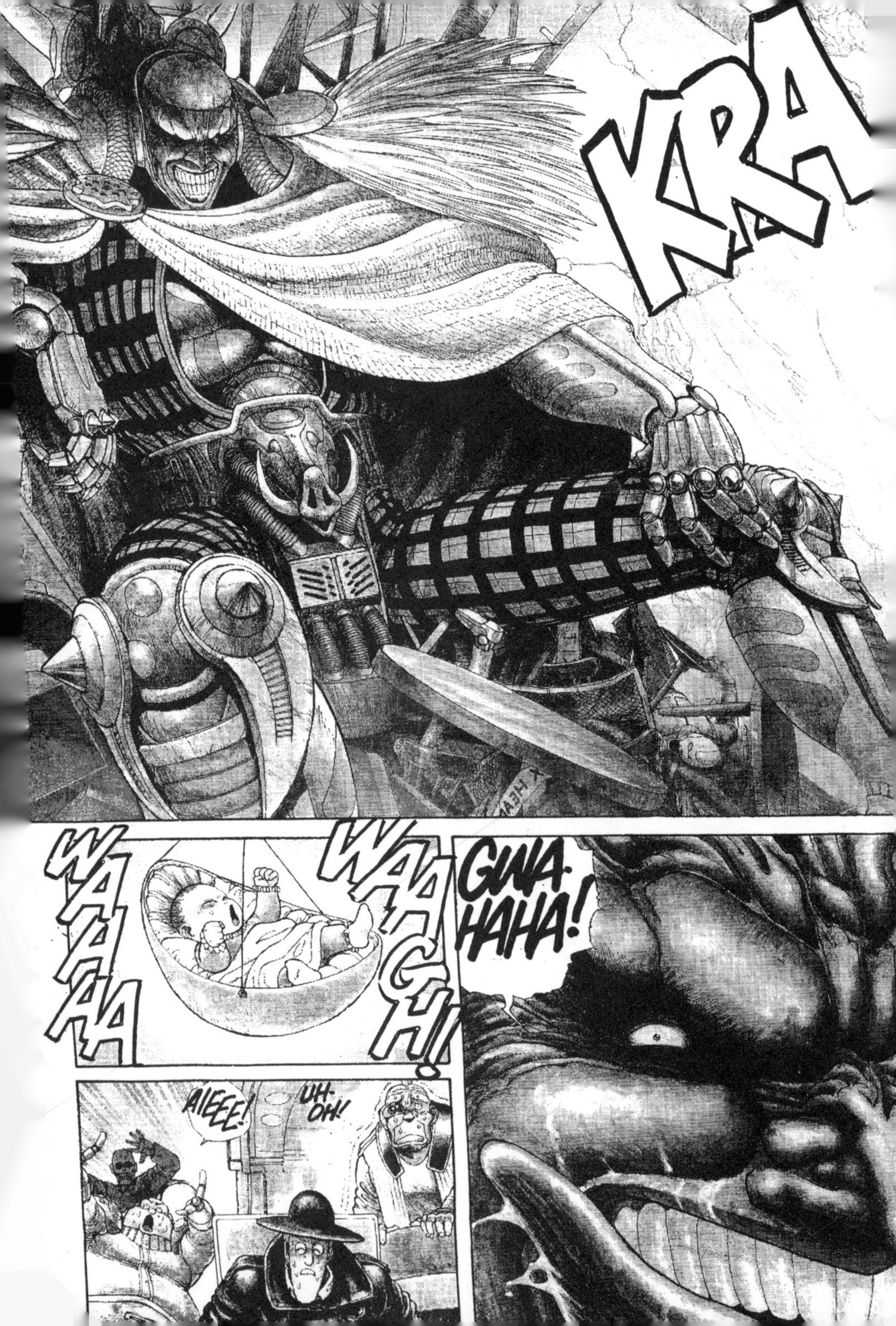
KRA
WAAAAA
WAAAGH!
AIEEE!
UH-OH!
GWAHAHA!

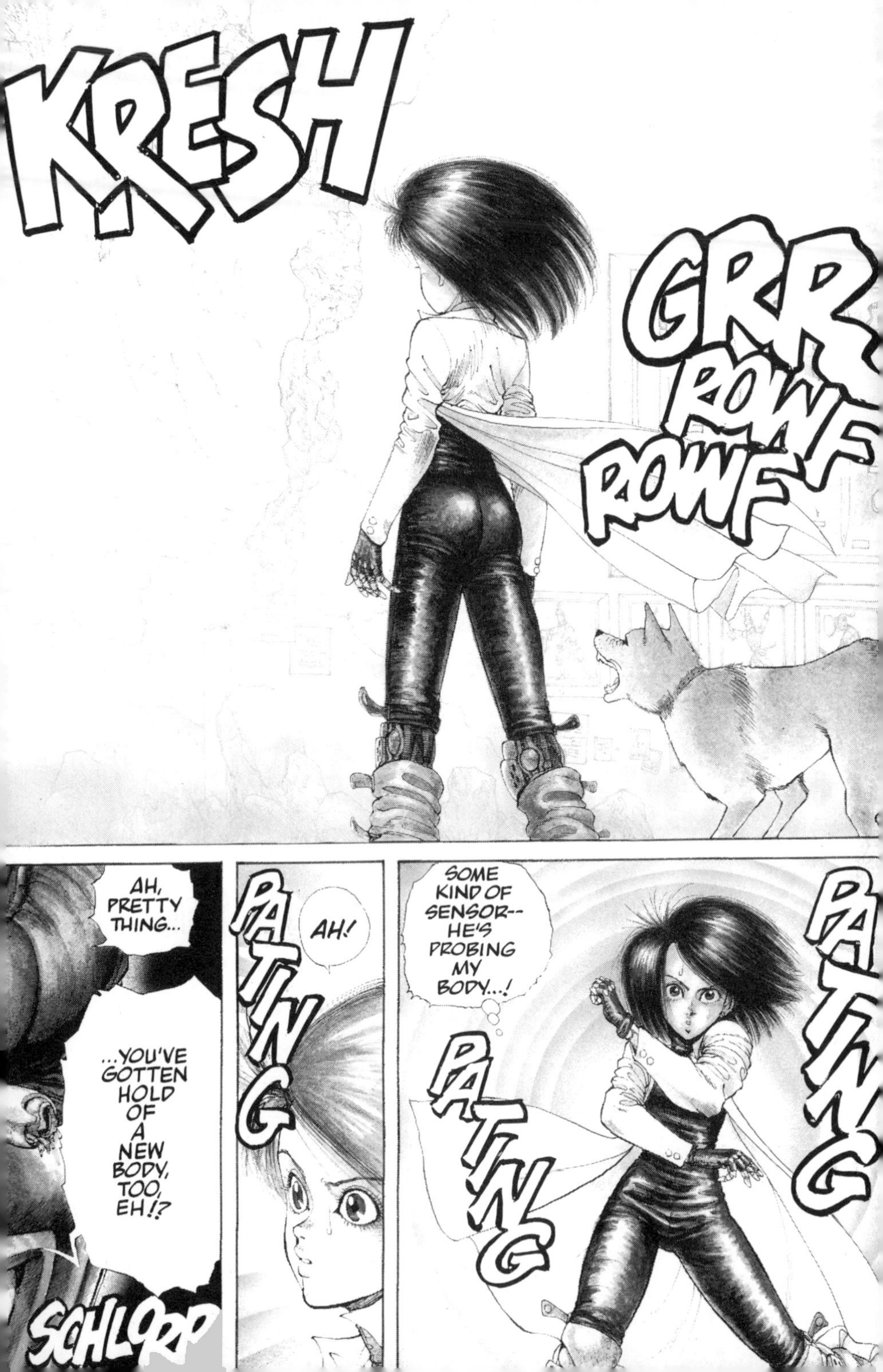
KRESH
GRR ROWF ROWF
AH, PRETTY THING...
...YOU'VE GOTTEN HOLD OF A NEW BODY, TOO, EH!?
SCHLORP
PATING
AH!
SOME KIND OF SENSOR-- HE'S PROBING MY BODY...!
PATING
PATING

HELL TRAP
Battle 5: Responsibility

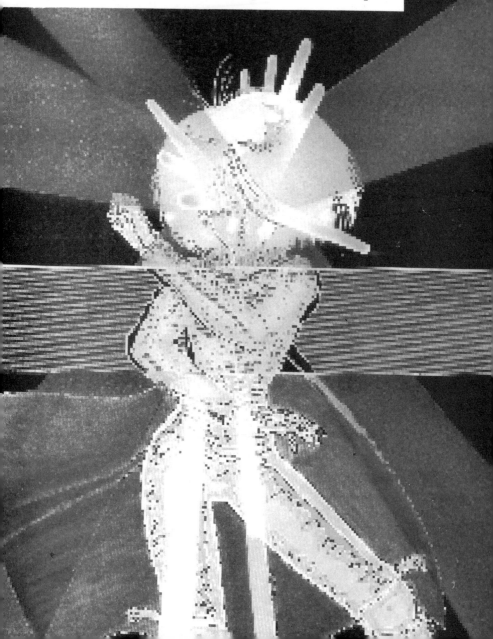

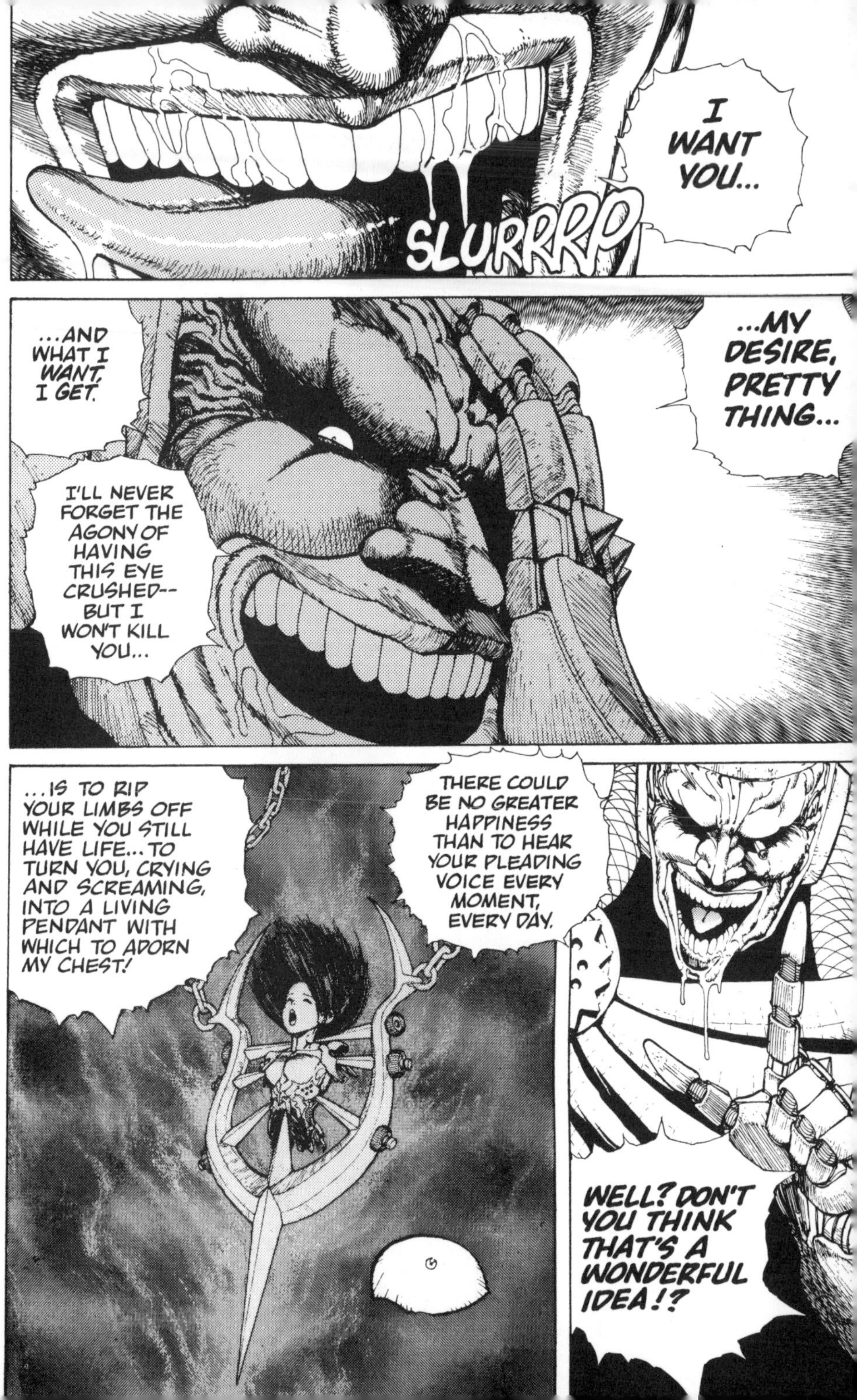
I WANT YOU...
SLURRRP
...AND WHAT I WANT, I GET.
...MY DESIRE, PRETTY THING...
I'LL NEVER FORGET THE AGONY OF HAVING THIS EYE CRUSHED-- BUT I WON'T KILL YOU...
...IS TO RIP YOUR LIMBS OFF WHILE YOU STILL HAVE LIFE...TO TURN YOU, CRYING AND SCREAMING, INTO A LIVING PENDANT WITH WHICH TO ADORN MY CHEST!
THERE COULD BE NO GREATER HAPPINESS THAN TO HEAR YOUR PLEADING VOICE EVERY MOMENT, EVERY DAY.
WELL? DON'T YOU THINK THAT'S A WONDERFUL IDEA!?

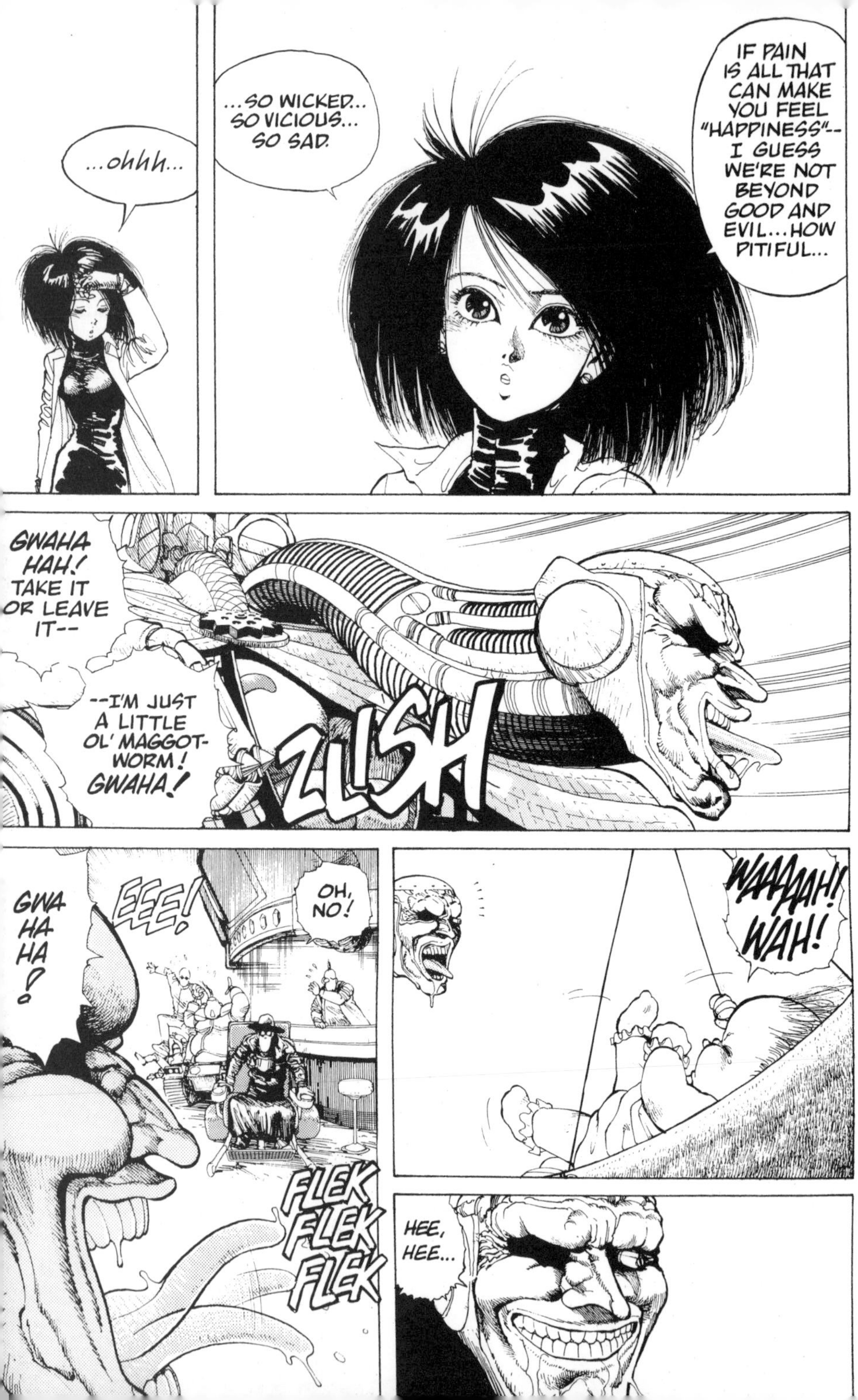
...ohhh...
...SO WICKED... SO VICIOUS... SO SAD.
IF PAIN IS ALL THAT CAN MAKE YOU FEEL "HAPPINESS"-- I GUESS WE'RE NOT BEYOND GOOD AND EVIL...HOW PITIFUL...
GWAHA HAH! TAKE IT OR LEAVE IT--
--I'M JUST A LITTLE OL' MAGGOT-WORM! GWAHA!
ZLISH
GWA HA HA HA!
EEEE!
OH, NO!
FLEK FLEK FLEK
WAAAAAH! WAH!
HEE, HEE...

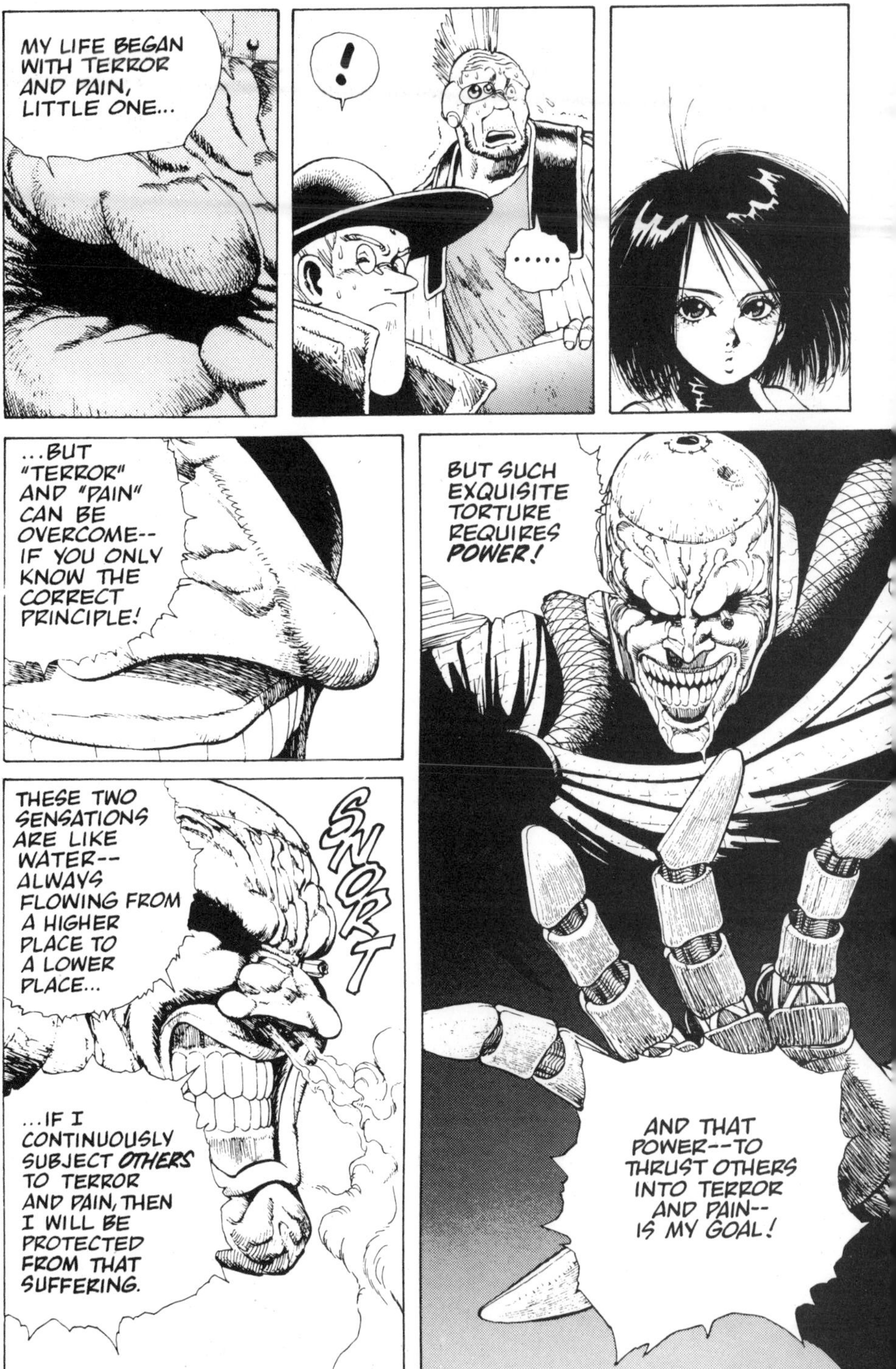
MY LIFE BEGAN WITH TERROR AND PAIN, LITTLE ONE...
!
.....
...BUT "TERROR" AND "PAIN" CAN BE OVERCOME-- IF YOU ONLY KNOW THE CORRECT PRINCIPLE!
BUT SUCH EXQUISITE TORTURE REQUIRES POWER!
THESE TWO SENSATIONS ARE LIKE WATER-- ALWAYS FLOWING FROM A HIGHER PLACE TO A LOWER PLACE...
SNORT
...IF I CONTINUOUSLY SUBJECT OTHERS TO TERROR AND PAIN, THEN I WILL BE PROTECTED FROM THAT SUFFERING.
AND THAT POWER--TO THRUST OTHERS INTO TERROR AND PAIN-- IS MY GOAL!

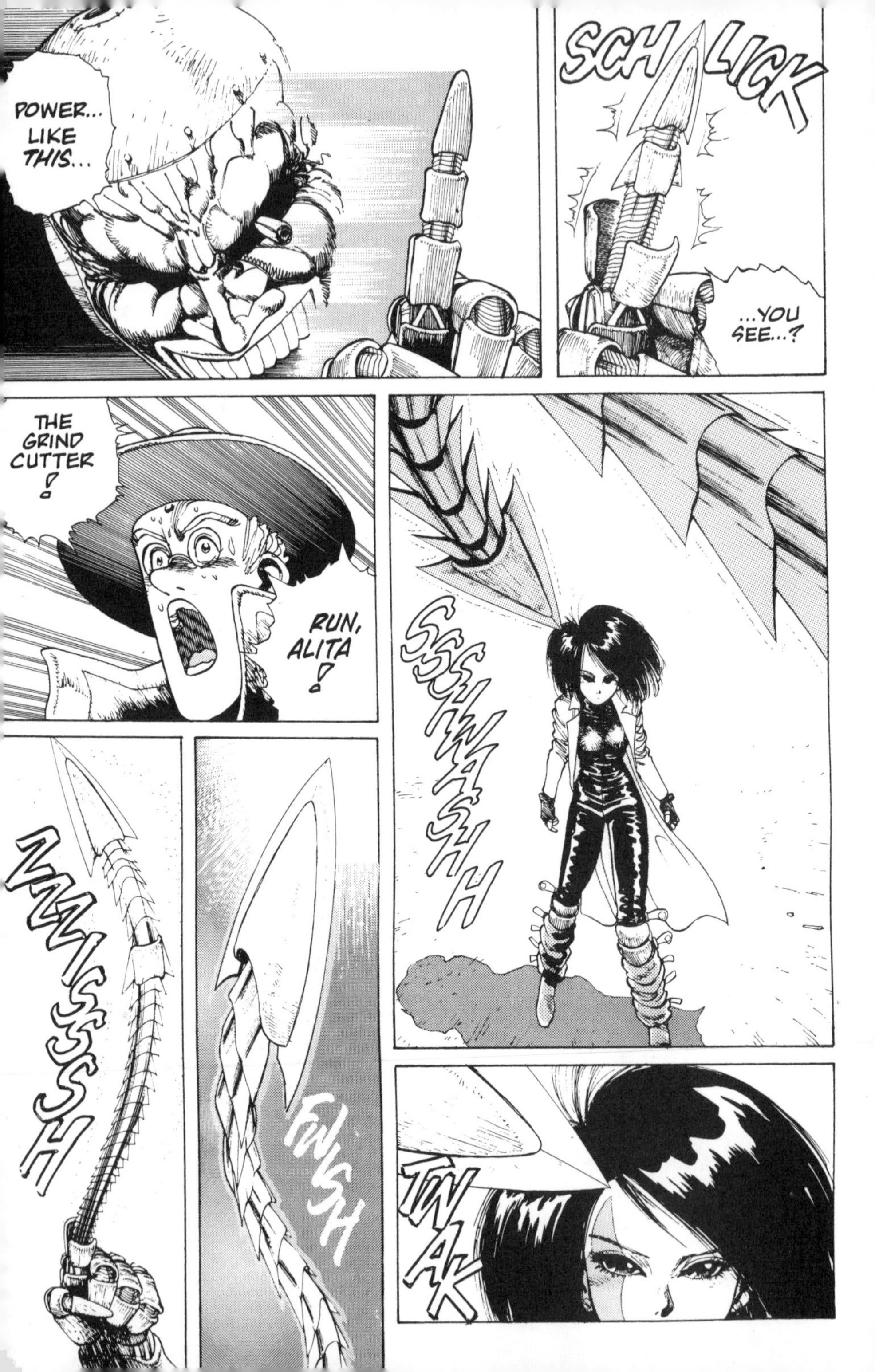
POWER... LIKE THIS...
SCHLICK
...YOU SEE...?
THE GRIND CUTTER!
RUN, ALITA!
SSSHWASHHH
NNNNISSSSH
FWISH
TINAK

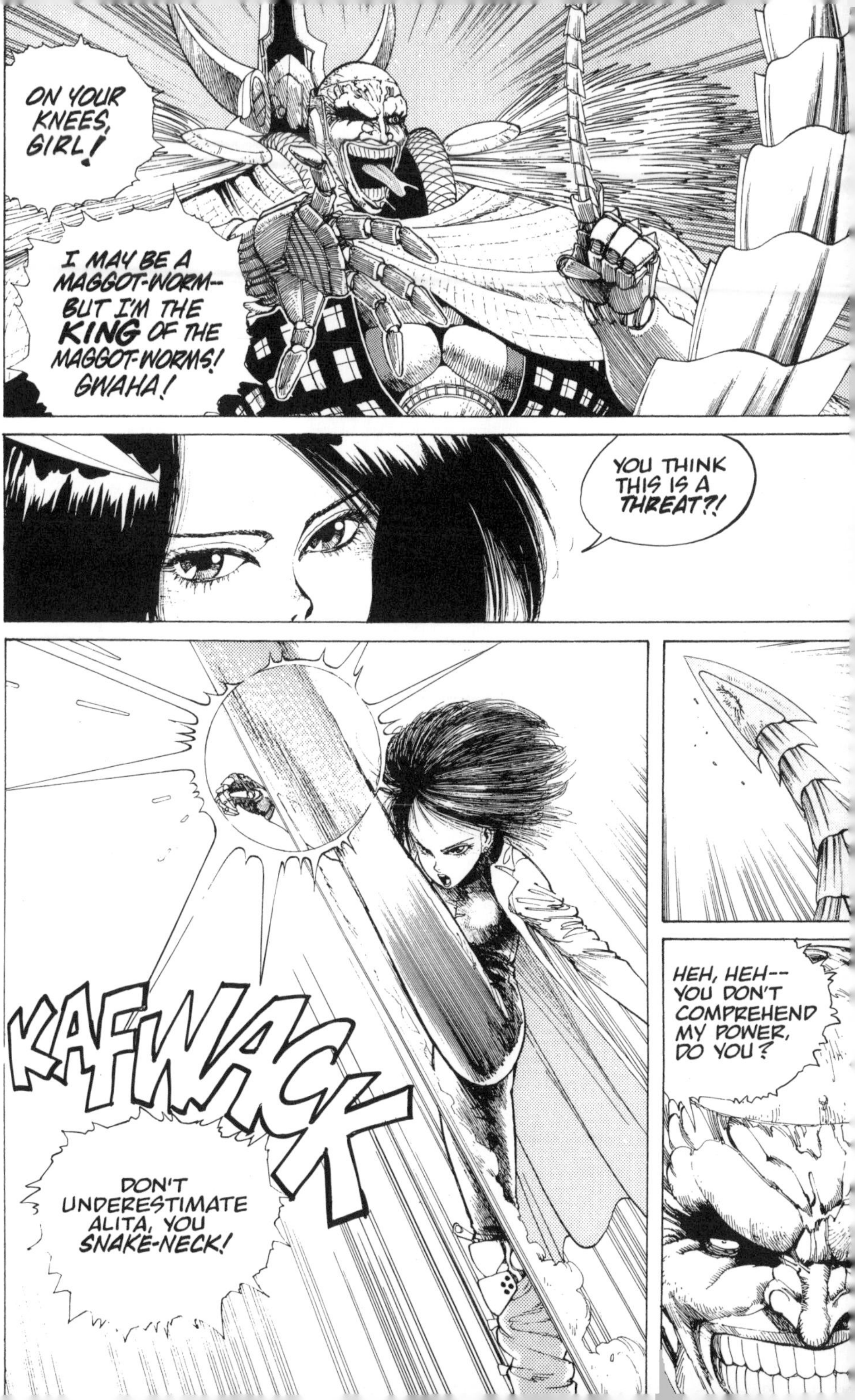
ON YOUR KNEES, GIRL!
I MAY BE A MAGGOT-WORM-- BUT I'M THE KING OF THE MAGGOT-WORMS! GWAHA!
YOU THINK THIS IS A THREAT?!
KAFWACK
DON'T UNDERESTIMATE ALITA, YOU SNAKE-NECK!
HEH, HEH-- YOU DON'T COMPREHEND MY POWER, DO YOU?

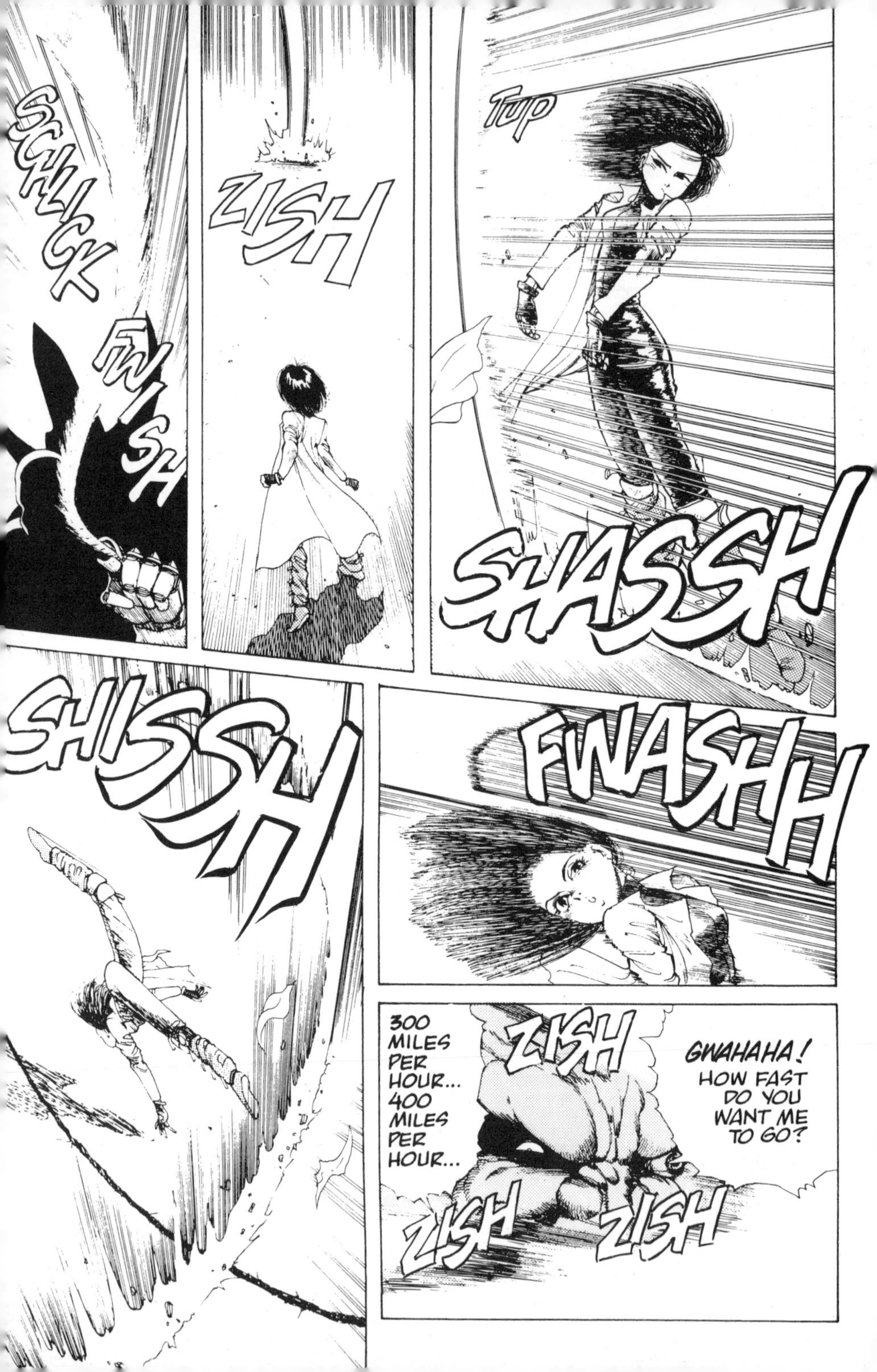
SCHLICK
FWISH
ZISH
TUP
SWASSH
SHISSSH
FWASHH
300 MILES PER HOUR... 400 MILES PER HOUR...
ZISH
GWAHAHA! HOW FAST DO YOU WANT ME TO GO?
ZISH
ZISH

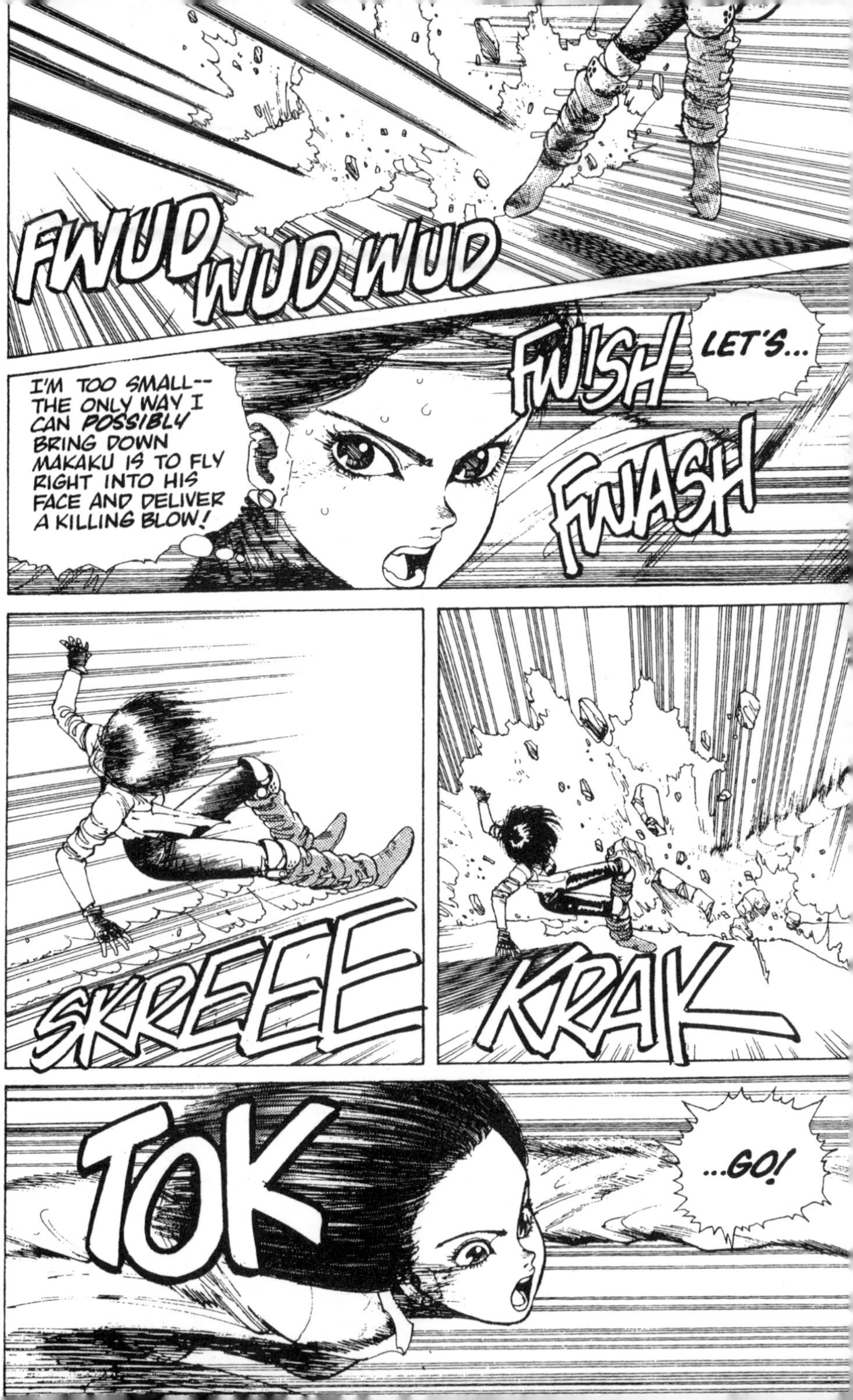
FWUD WUD WUD
I'M TOO SMALL--
THE ONLY WAY I
CAN POSSIBLY
BRING DOWN
MAKAKU IS TO FLY
RIGHT INTO HIS
FACE AND DELIVER
A KILLING BLOW!
FWISH
LET'S...
FWASH
SKREEE
KRAK
TOK
...GO!

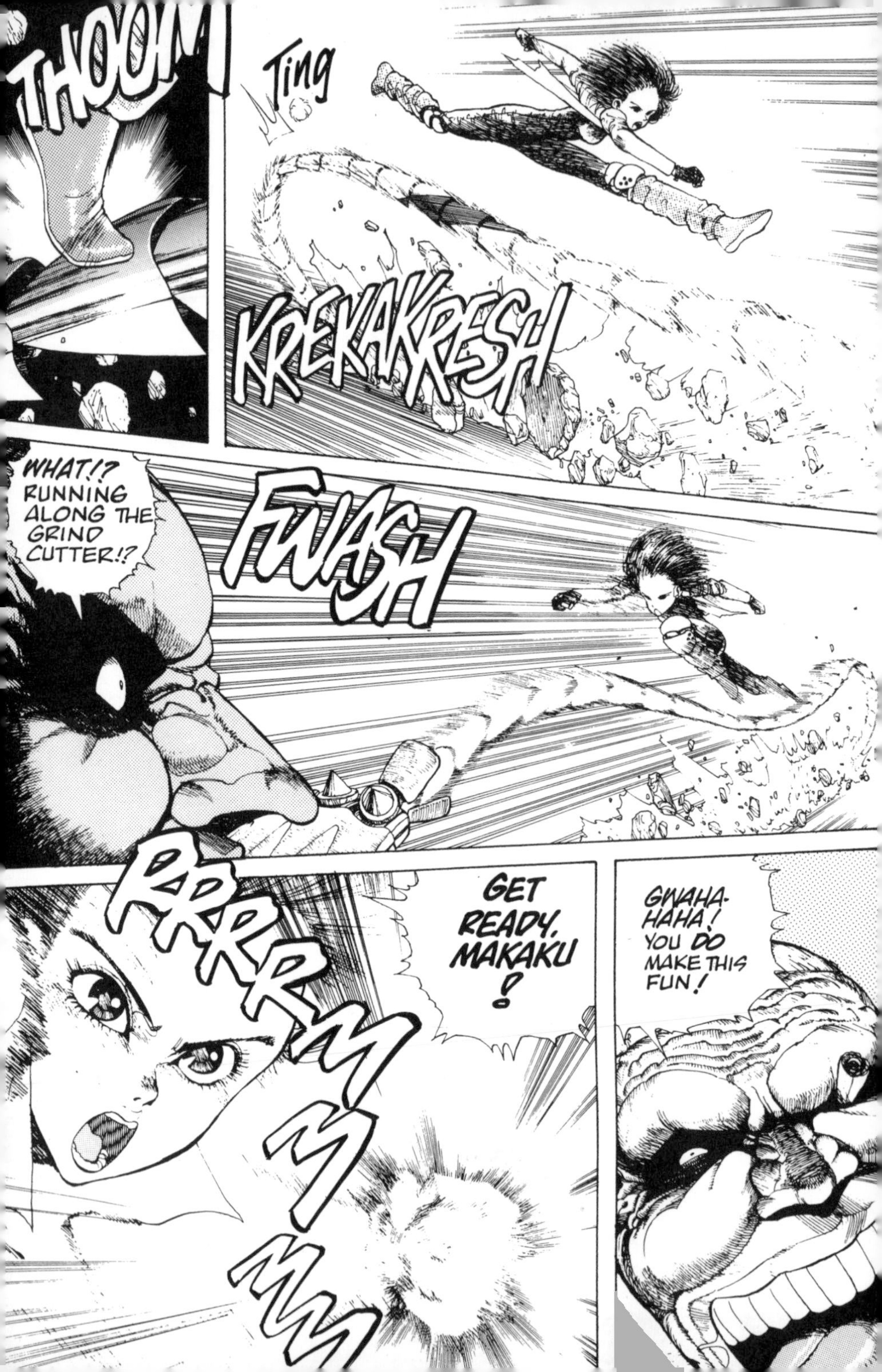
THOOM
Ting
KREKAKRESH
WHAT!? RUNNING ALONG THE GRIND CUTTER!?
FWASH
RRRRMMMM
GET READY, MAKAKU!
GWAHAHAHA! YOU DO MAKE THIS FUN!

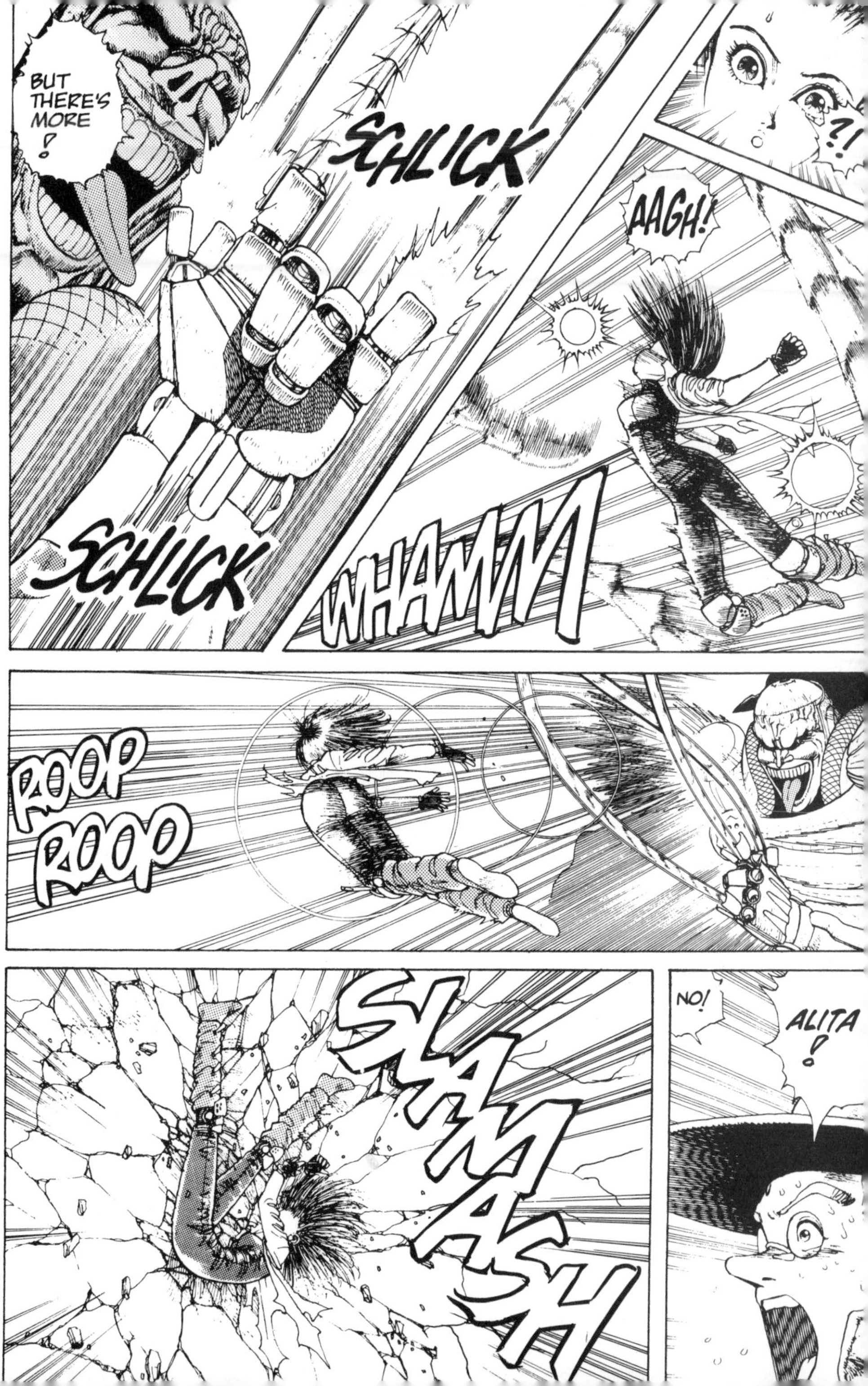
BUT THERE'S MORE!
SCHLICK
SCHLICK
?!
AAGH!
WHAMM
ROOP ROOP
SLAMASH
NO!
ALITA!

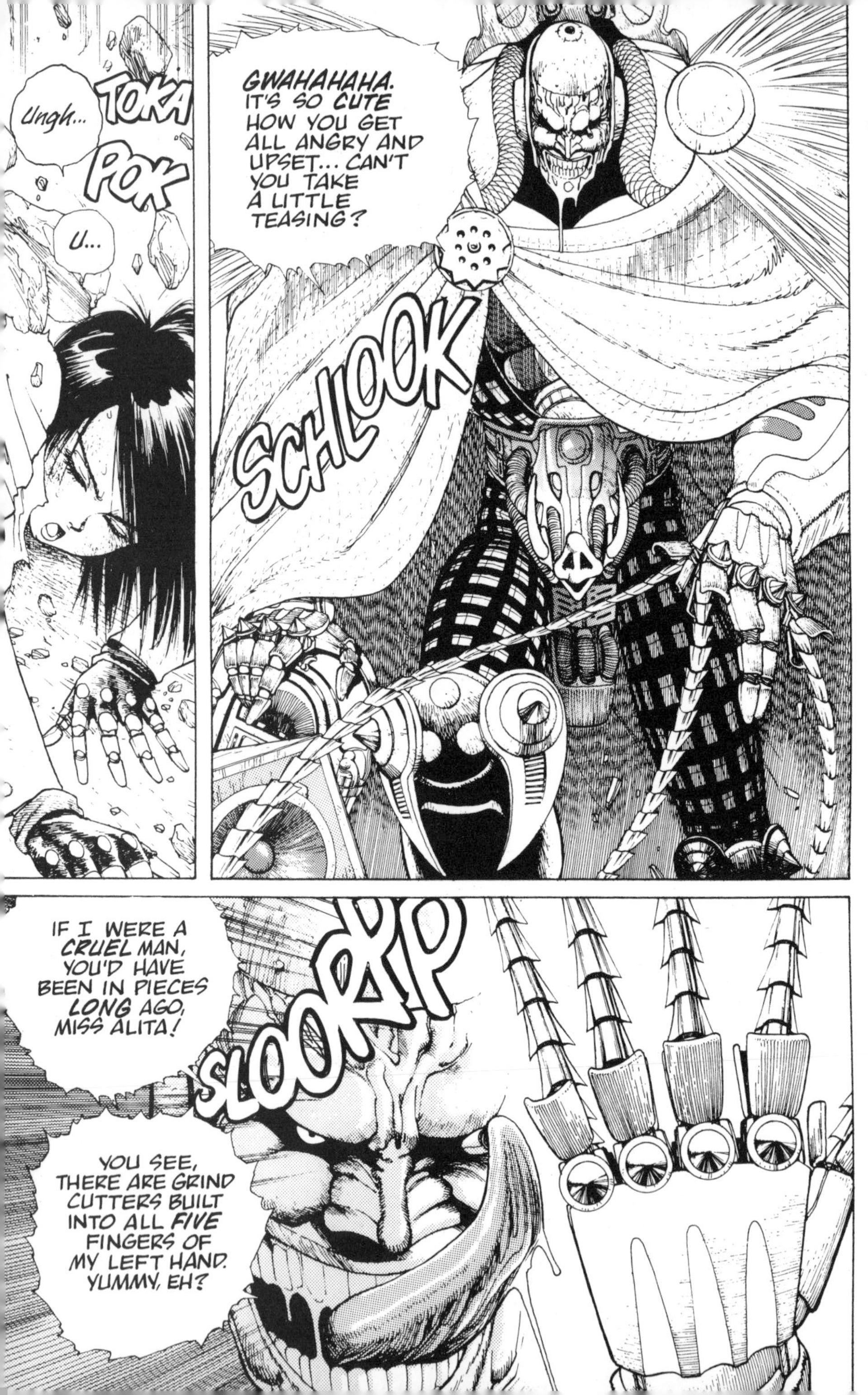
Ungh...
TOKA
POK
U...
GWAHAHAHA. IT'S SO CUTE HOW YOU GET ALL ANGRY AND UPSET... CAN'T YOU TAKE A LITTLE TEASING?
SCHLOOK
IF I WERE A CRUEL MAN, YOU'D HAVE BEEN IN PIECES LONG AGO, MISS ALITA!
SLOOORP
YOU SEE, THERE ARE GRIND CUTTERS BUILT INTO ALL FIVE FINGERS OF MY LEFT HAND. YUMMY, EH?

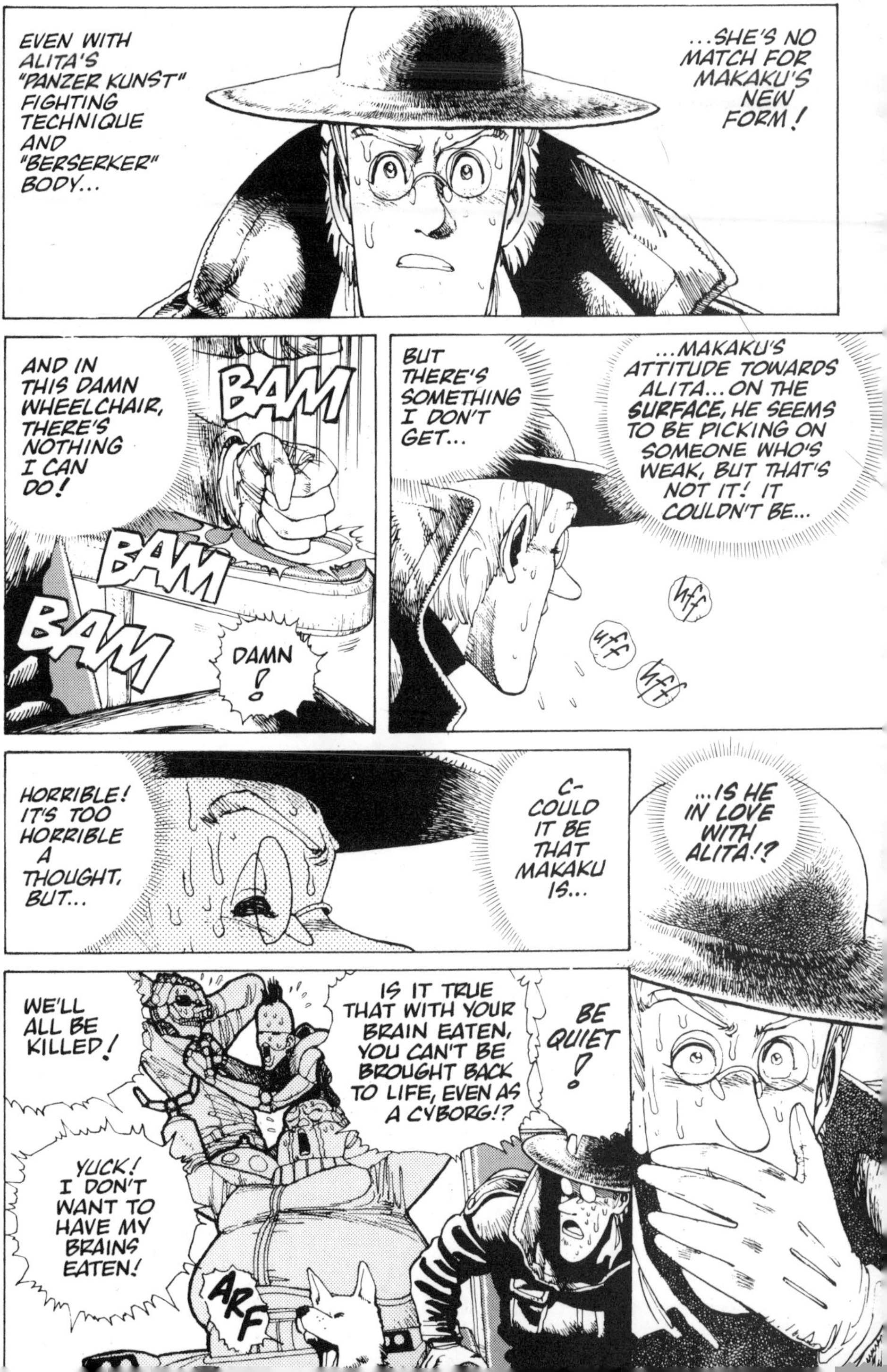
EVEN WITH ALITA'S "PANZER KUNST" FIGHTING TECHNIQUE AND "BERSERKER" BODY...
...SHE'S NO MATCH FOR MAKAKU'S NEW FORM!
AND IN THIS DAMN WHEELCHAIR, THERE'S NOTHING I CAN DO!
BAM
BAM
BAM
DAMN!
BUT THERE'S SOMETHING I DON'T GET...
...MAKAKU'S ATTITUDE TOWARDS ALITA... ON THE SURFACE, HE SEEMS TO BE PICKING ON SOMEONE WHO'S WEAK, BUT THAT'S NOT IT! IT COULDN'T BE...
HFF
HFF
HFF
HORRIBLE! IT'S TOO HORRIBLE A THOUGHT, BUT...
C- COULD IT BE THAT MAKAKU IS...
...IS HE IN LOVE WITH ALITA!?
WE'LL ALL BE KILLED!
IS IT TRUE THAT WITH YOUR BRAIN EATEN, YOU CAN'T BE BROUGHT BACK TO LIFE, EVEN AS A CYBORG!?
BE QUIET!
YUCK! I DON'T WANT TO HAVE MY BRAINS EATEN!
ARF

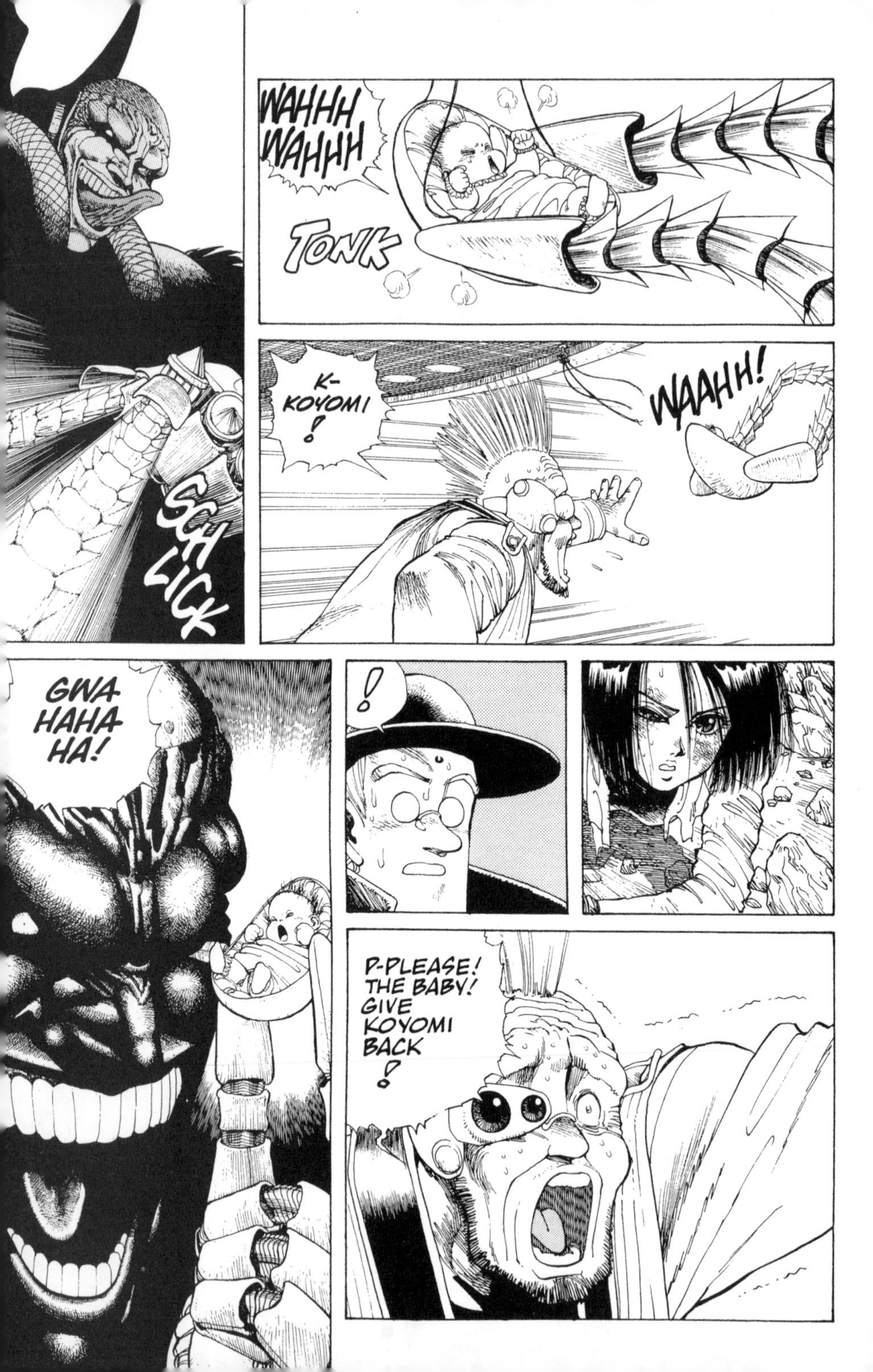
SCHLICK
WAHHH WAHHH
TONK
K-KOYOMI!
WAAHH!
GWAHAHAHA!
!
P-PLEASE! THE BABY! GIVE KOYOMI BACK!

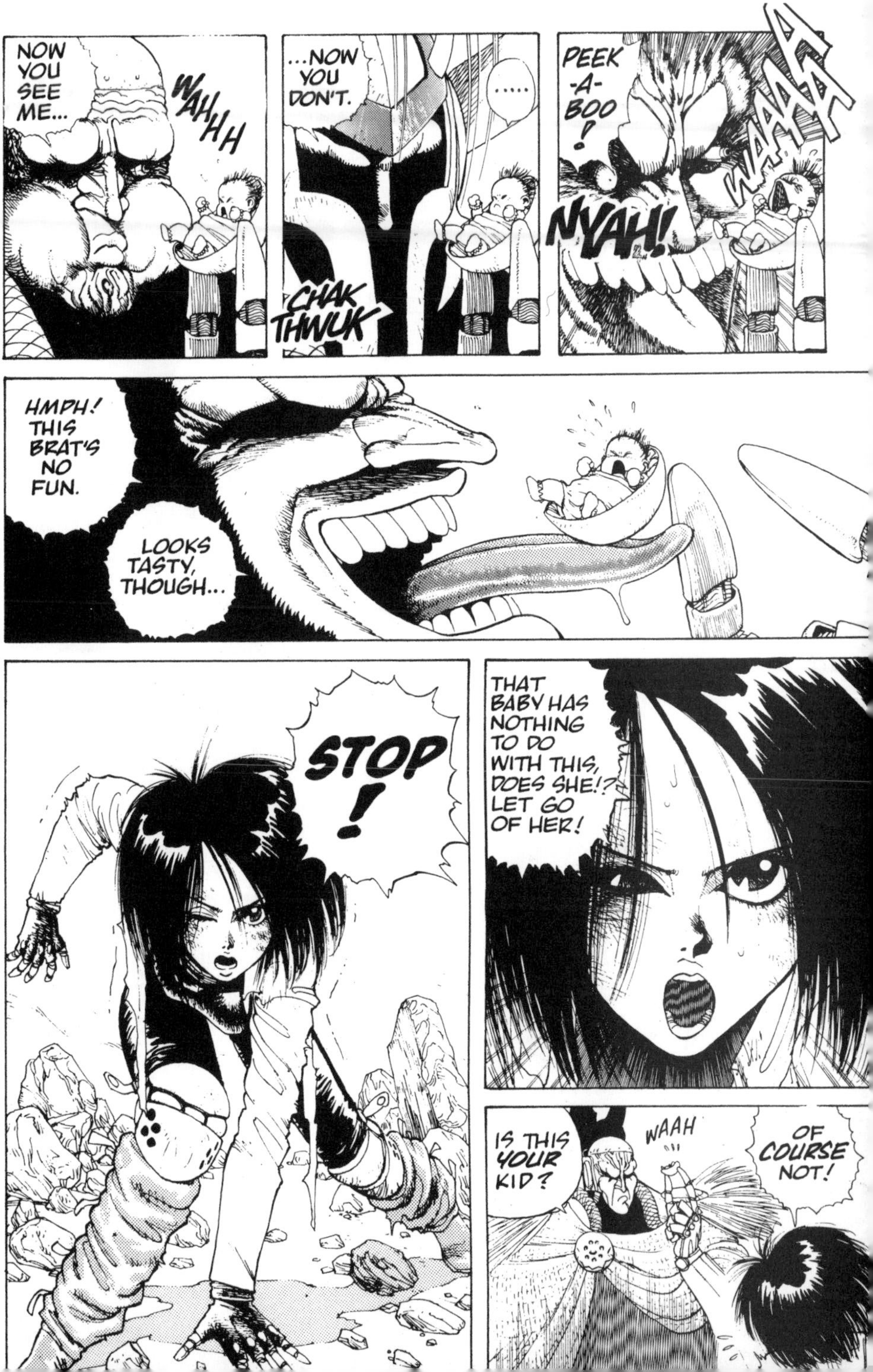
NOW YOU SEE ME...
WAHHH
...NOW YOU DON'T.
.....
CHAK THWUK
PEEK -A- BOO!
NYAH!
WAAAAA
HMPH! THIS BRAT'S NO FUN.
LOOKS TASTY, THOUGH...
STOP!
THAT BABY HAS NOTHING TO DO WITH THIS, DOES SHE!? LET GO OF HER!
IS THIS YOUR KID?
WAAH
OF COURSE NOT!

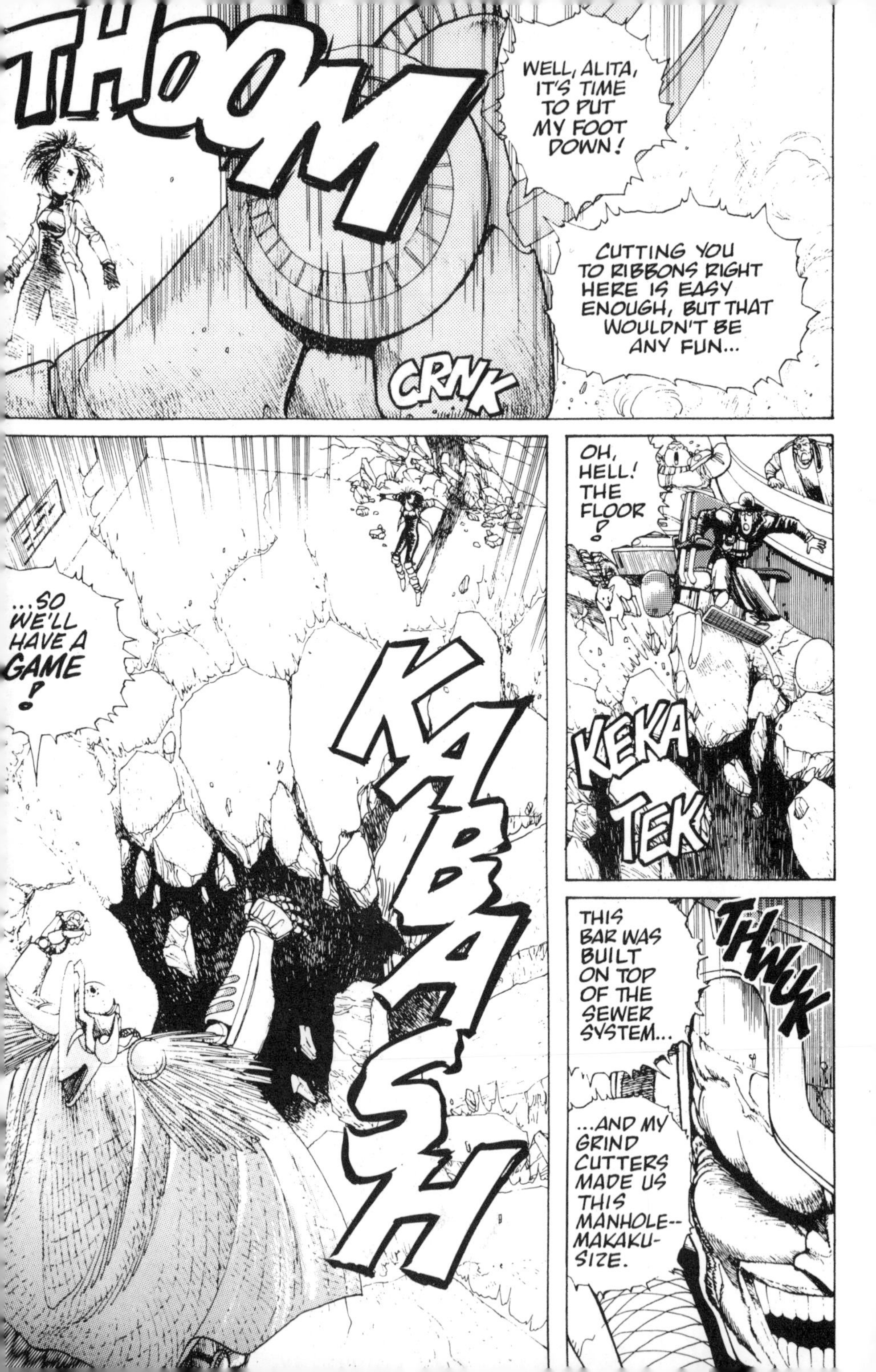
THOOM
WELL, ALITA, IT'S TIME TO PUT MY FOOT DOWN!
CUTTING YOU TO RIBBONS RIGHT HERE IS EASY ENOUGH, BUT THAT WOULDN'T BE ANY FUN...
CRNK
...SO WE'LL HAVE A GAME!
KABASH
OH, HELL! THE FLOOR!
KEKA TEK
THIS BAR WAS BUILT ON TOP OF THE SEWER SYSTEM...
THWUK
...AND MY GRIND CUTTERS MADE US THIS MANHOLE--MAKAKU-SIZE.

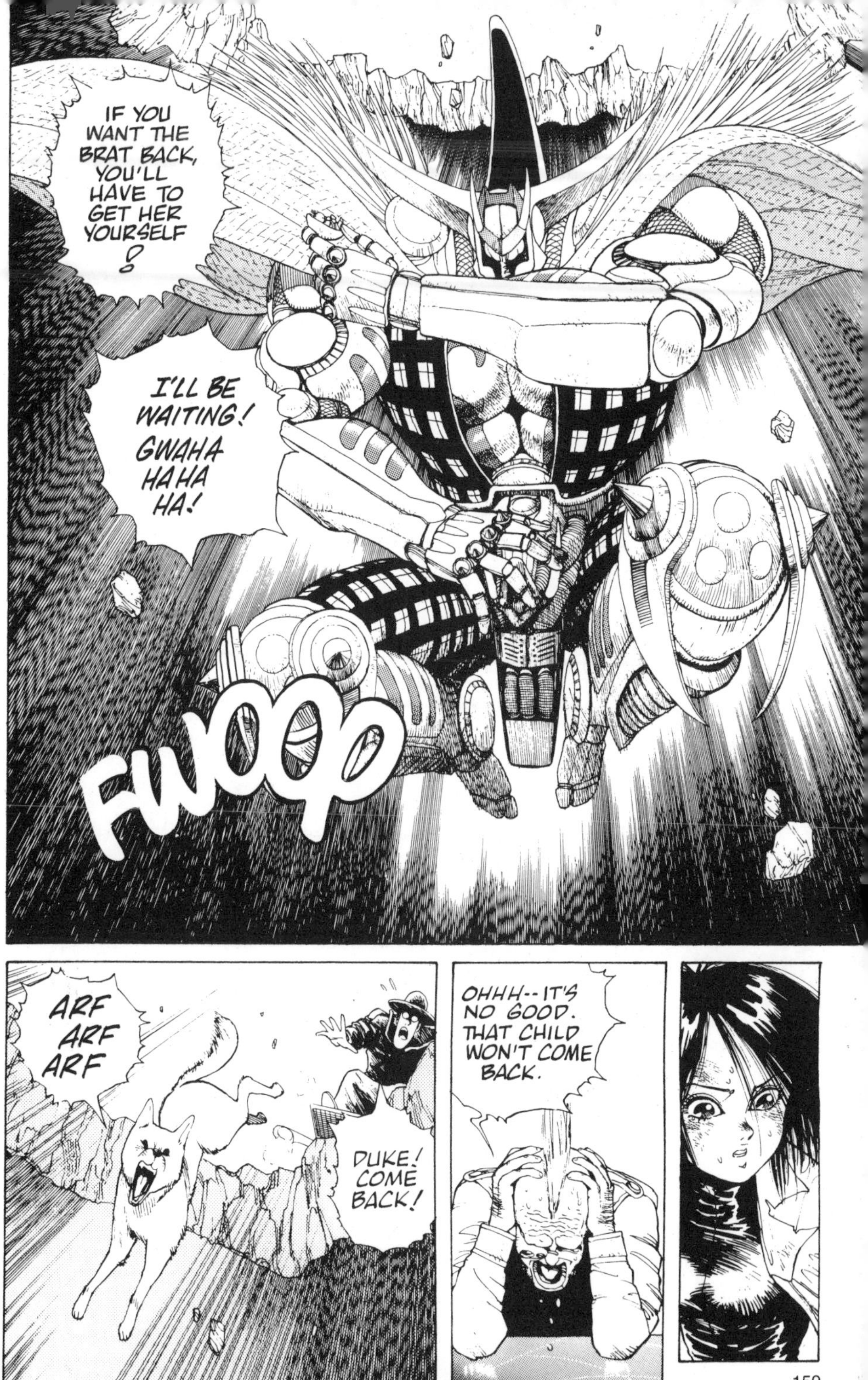
IF YOU WANT THE BRAT BACK, YOU'LL HAVE TO GET HER YOURSELF!
I'LL BE WAITING! GWAHA HAHA HA!
FWOOP
ARF ARF ARF
DUKE! COME BACK!
OHHH--IT'S NO GOOD. THAT CHILD WON'T COME BACK.

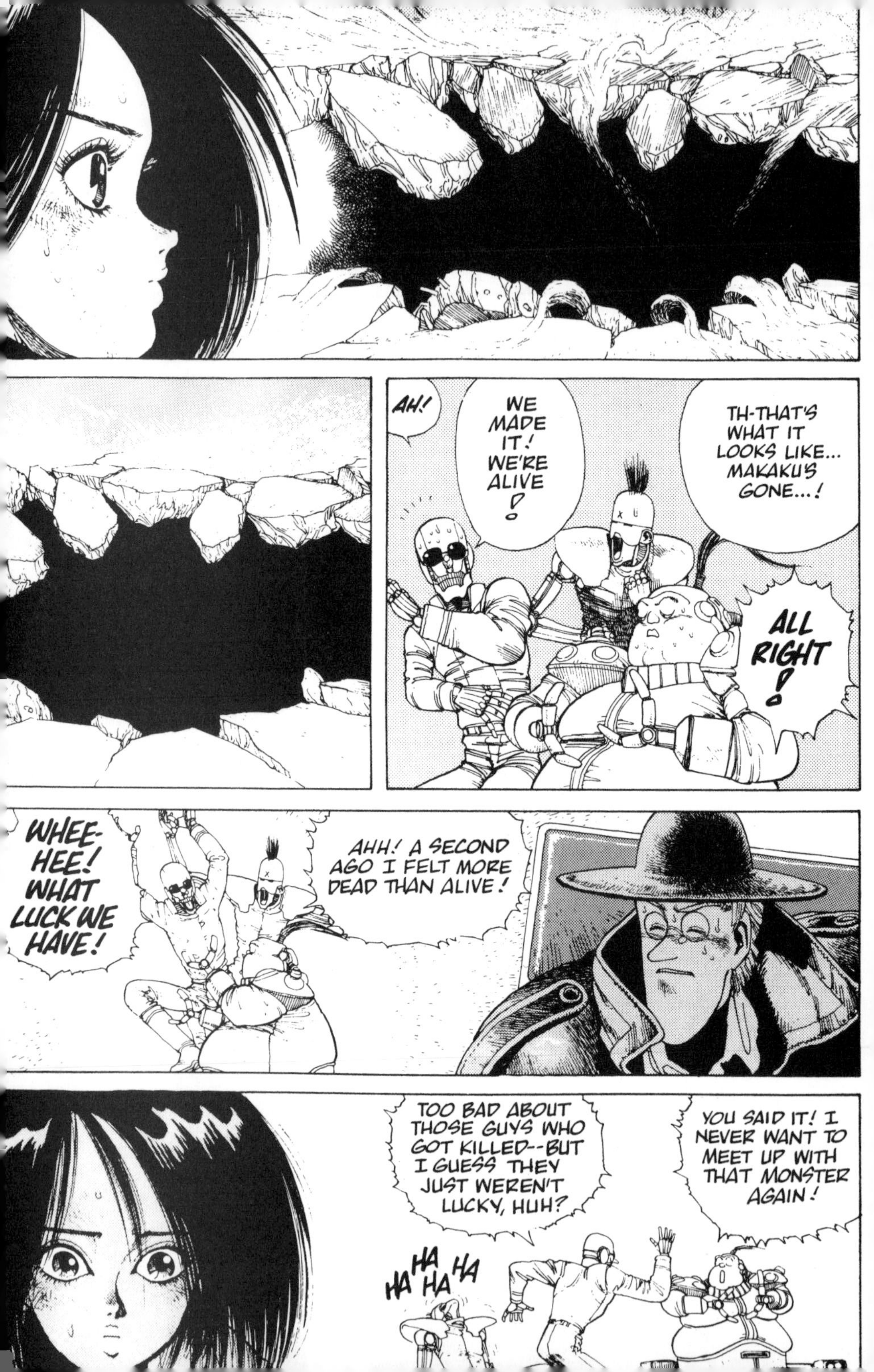
AH!
WE MADE IT! WE'RE ALIVE!
TH-THAT'S WHAT IT LOOKS LIKE... MAKAKU'S GONE...!
ALL RIGHT!
WHEE-HEE! WHAT LUCK WE HAVE!
AHH! A SECOND AGO I FELT MORE DEAD THAN ALIVE!
TOO BAD ABOUT THOSE GUYS WHO GOT KILLED--BUT I GUESS THEY JUST WEREN'T LUCKY, HUH?
YOU SAID IT! I NEVER WANT TO MEET UP WITH THAT MONSTER AGAIN!
HA HA HA HA HA

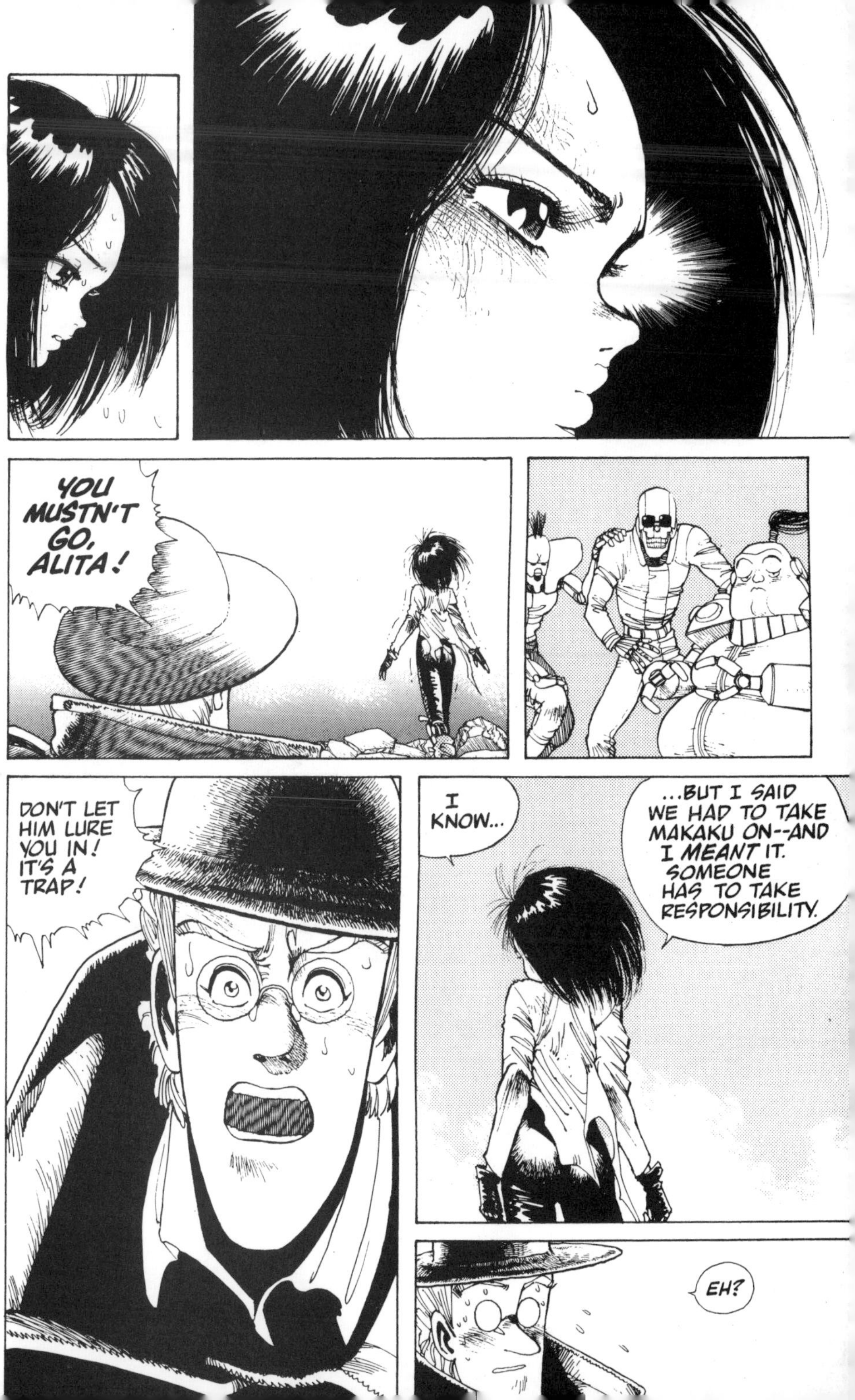
YOU MUSTN'T GO, ALITA!
DON'T LET HIM LURE YOU IN! IT'S A TRAP!
I KNOW...
...BUT I SAID WE HAD TO TAKE MAKAKU ON--AND I MEANT IT. SOMEONE HAS TO TAKE RESPONSIBILITY.
EH?

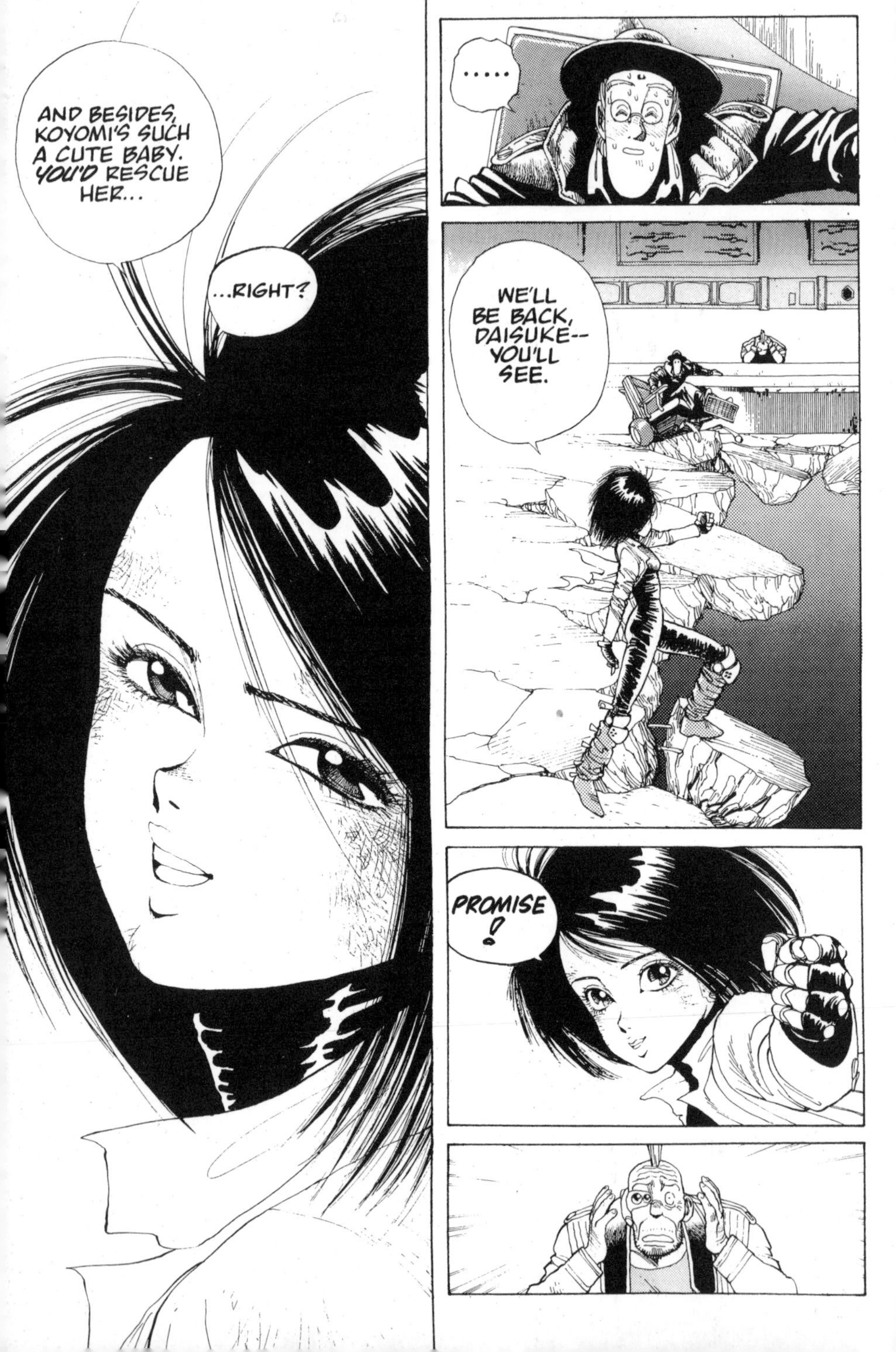
AND BESIDES, KOYOMI'S SUCH A CUTE BABY. YOU'D RESCUE HER...
...RIGHT?
.....
WE'LL BE BACK, DAISUKE-- YOU'LL SEE.
PROMISE!

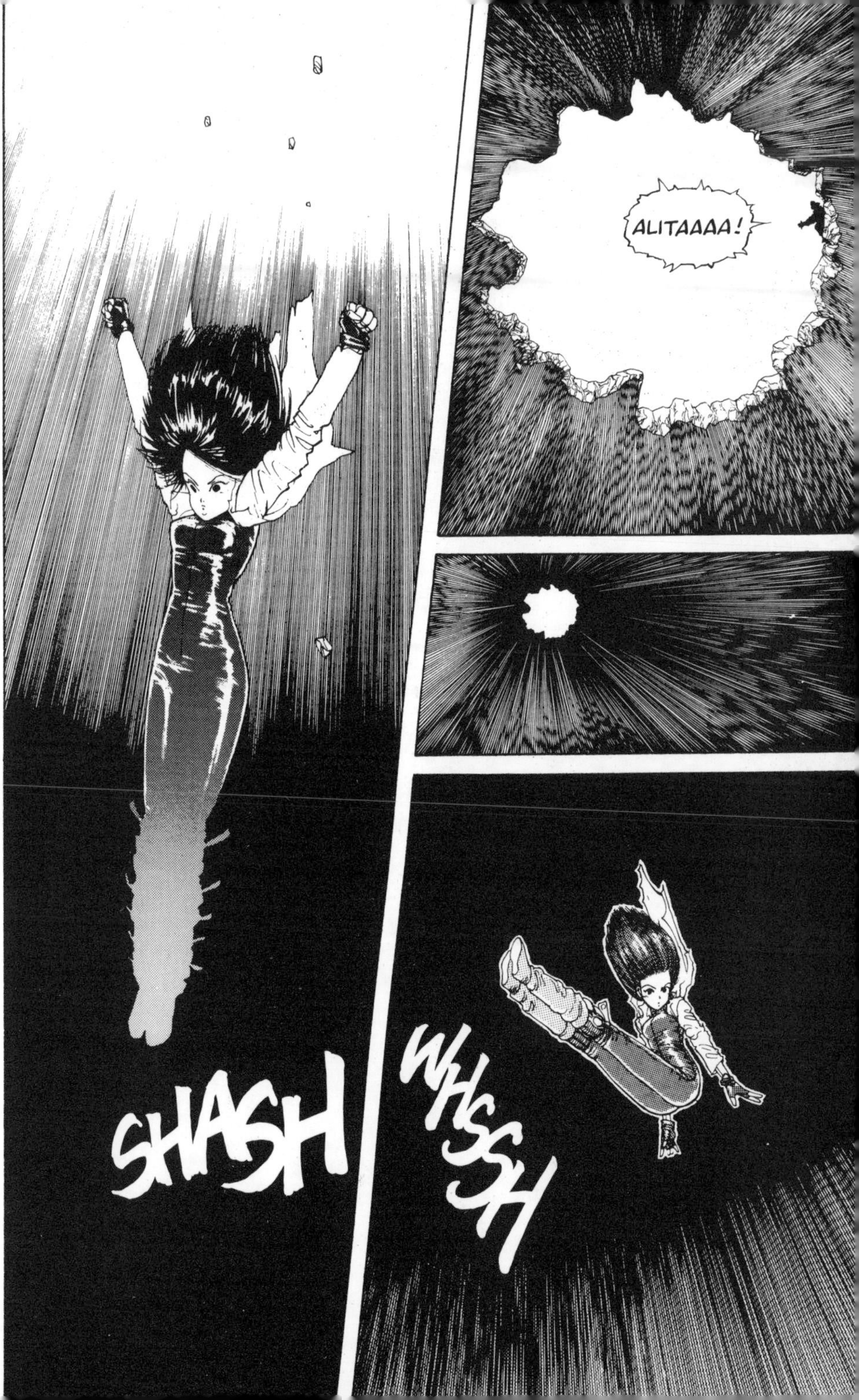
SHASH
ALITAAAA!
WHSSH

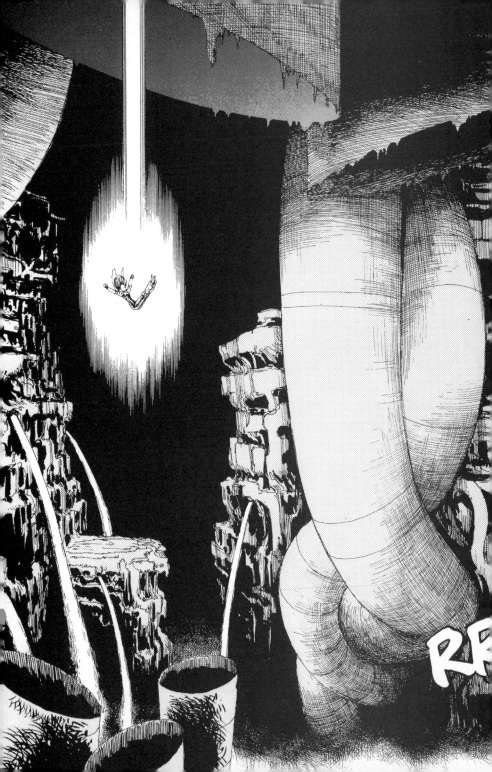

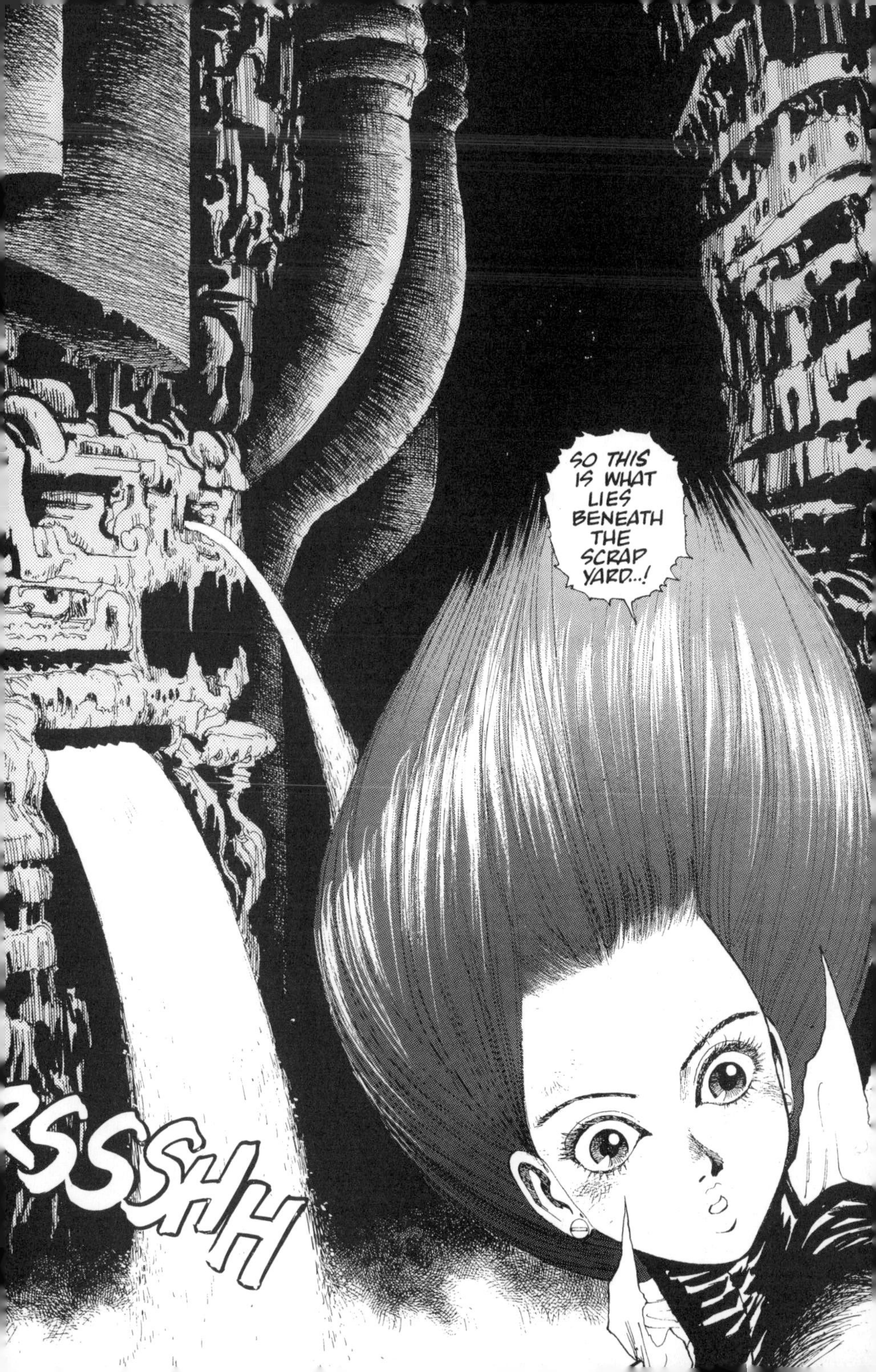
SO THIS IS WHAT LIES BENEATH THE SCRAP YARD...!
SSSHH

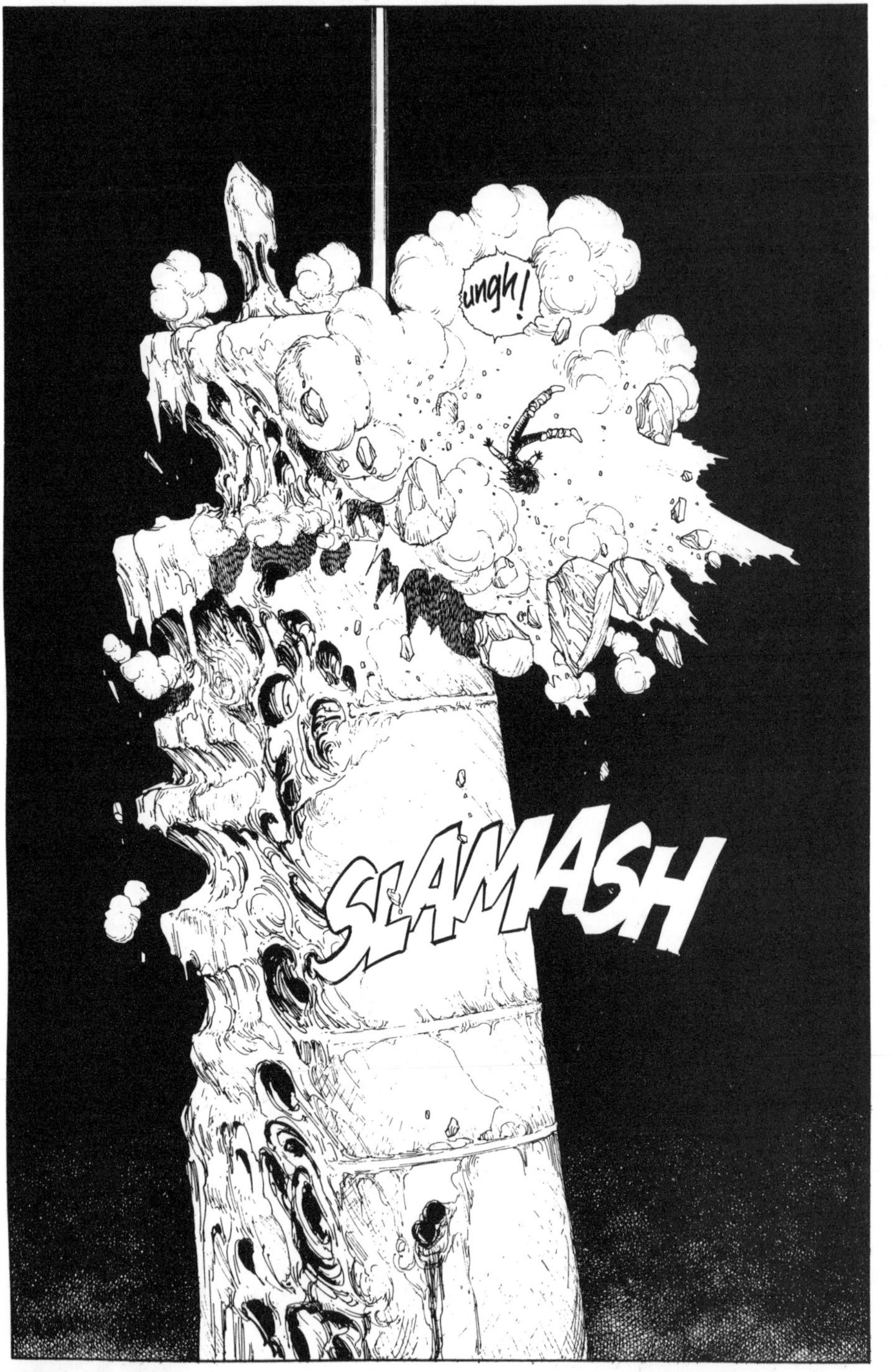
ungh!
SLAMASH

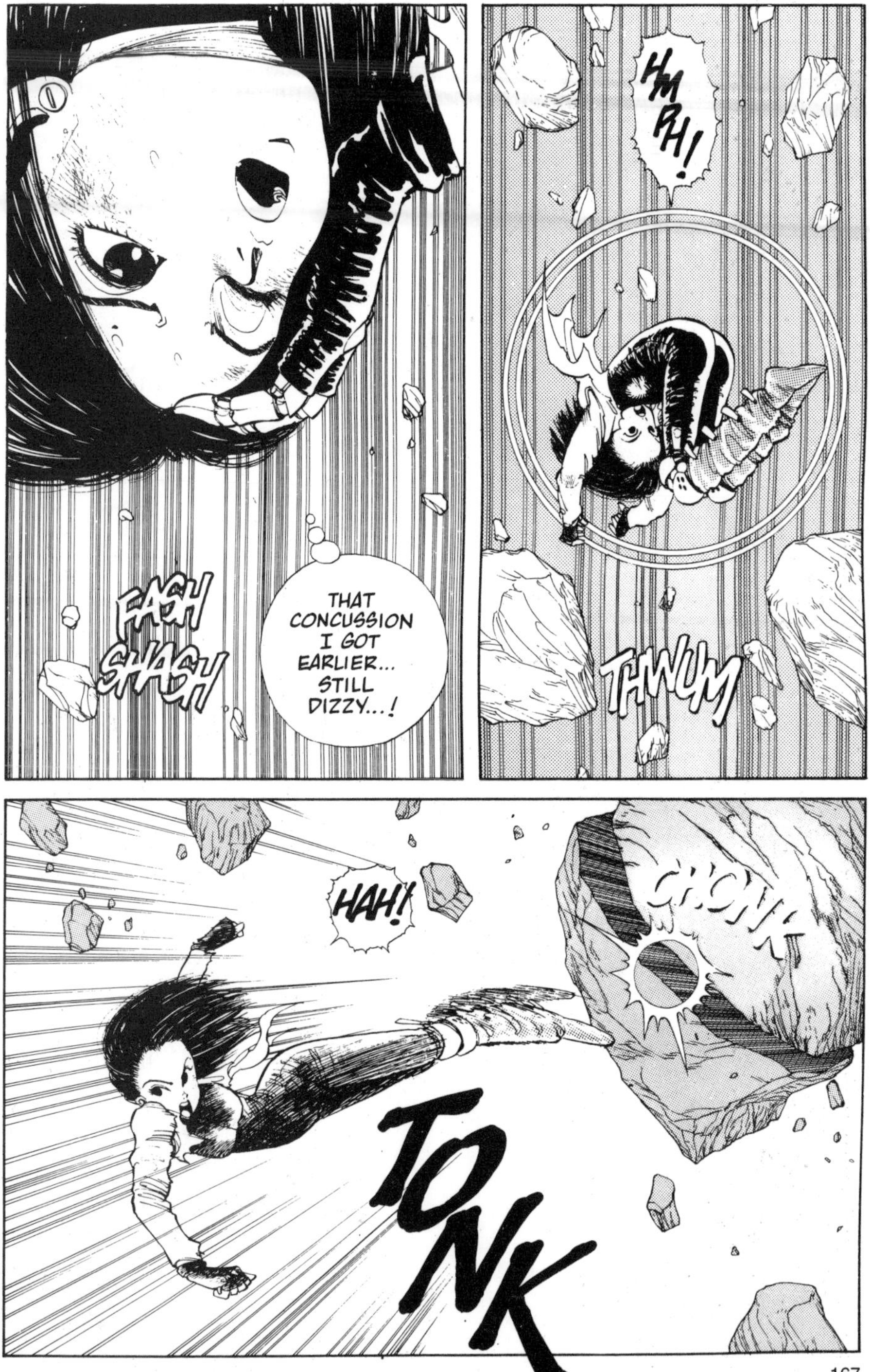
FASH SHASH
THAT CONCUSSION I GOT EARLIER... STILL DIZZY...!
HMPH!
THWUM
HAH!
GRONK
TONK

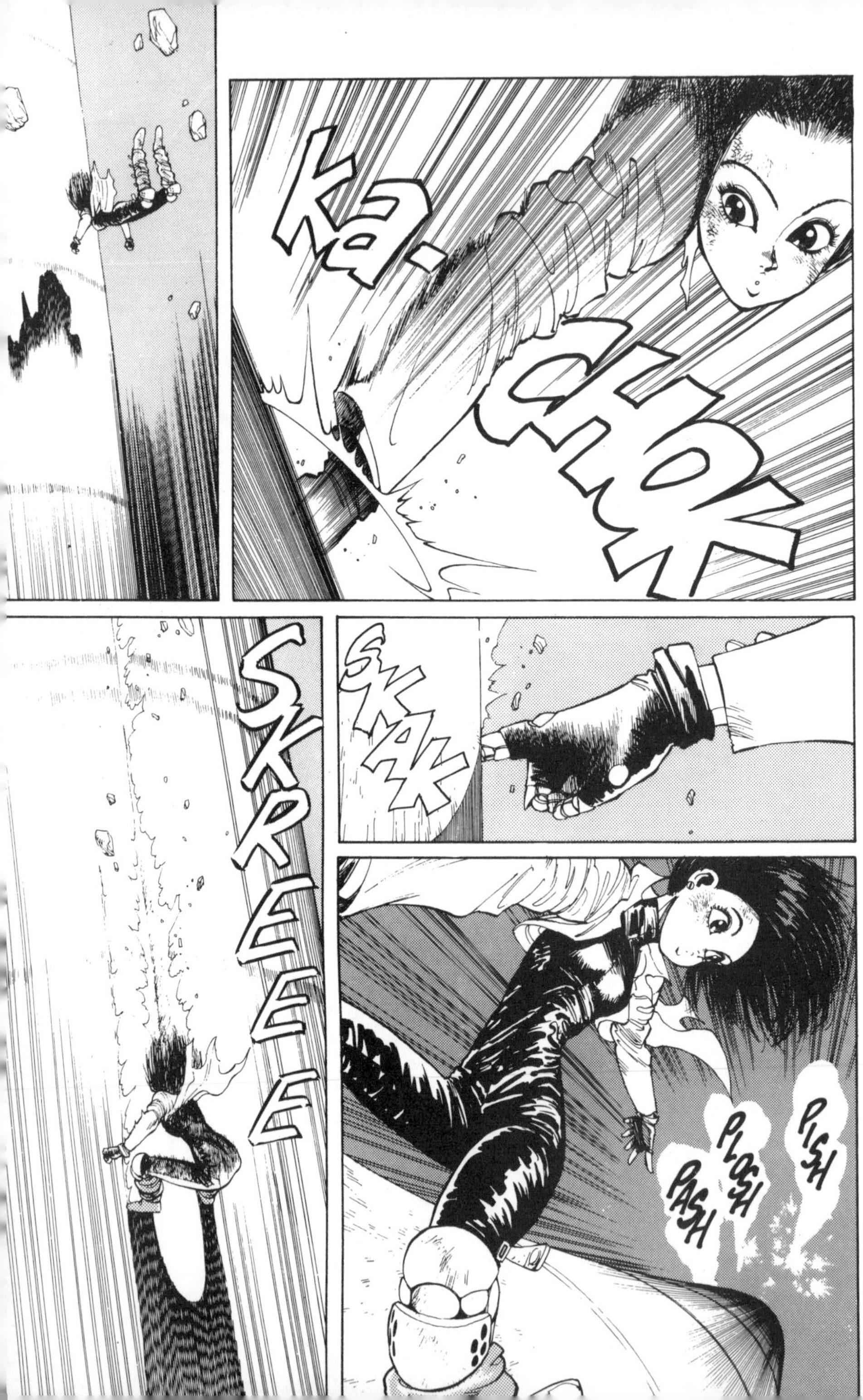
ka-CHOK
SKREEEE
SKRAK
PISH
PLOSH
PASH

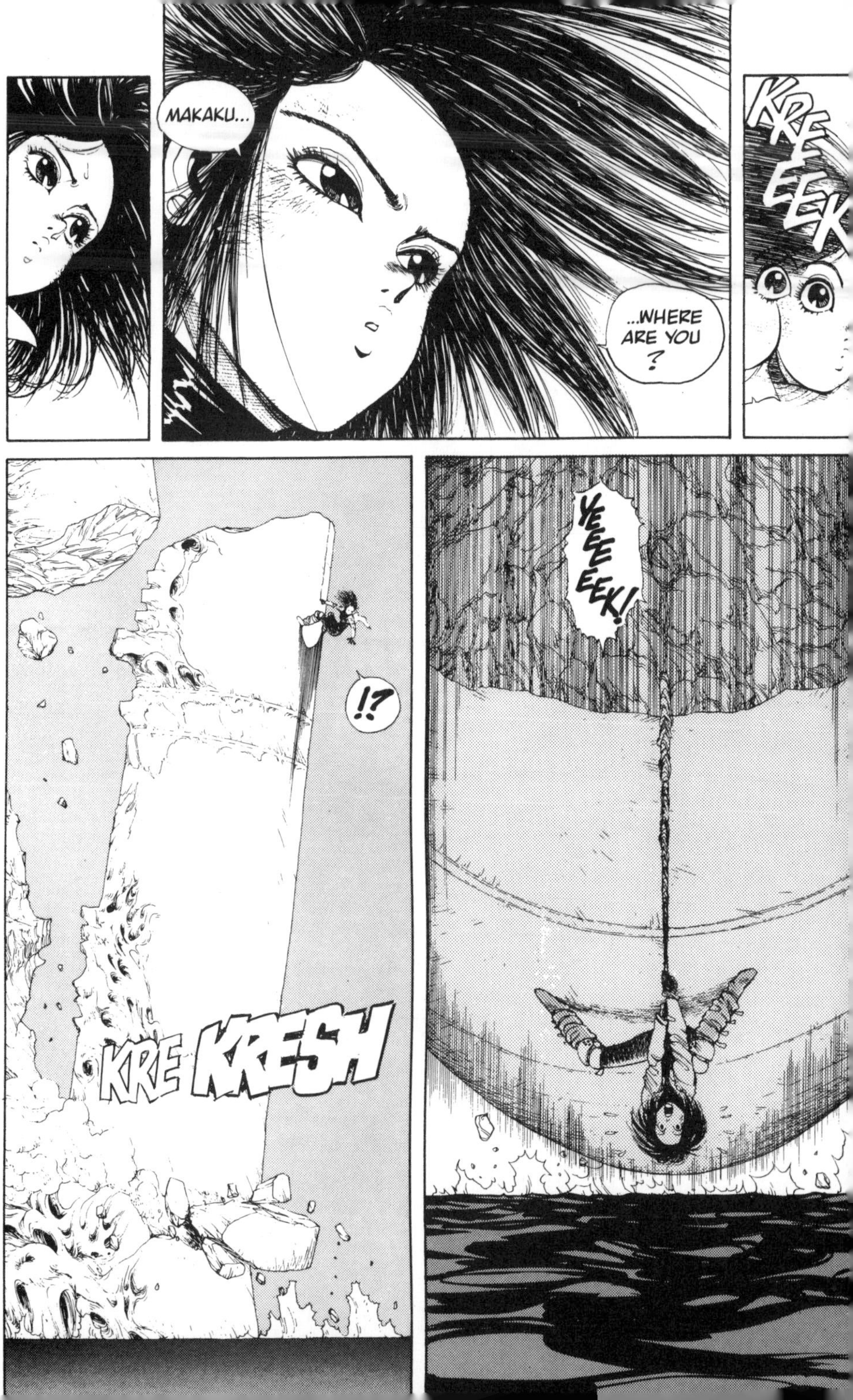
MAKAKU...
...WHERE ARE YOU ?
KREEEEK
!?
KRE KRESH
YEEEEEK!

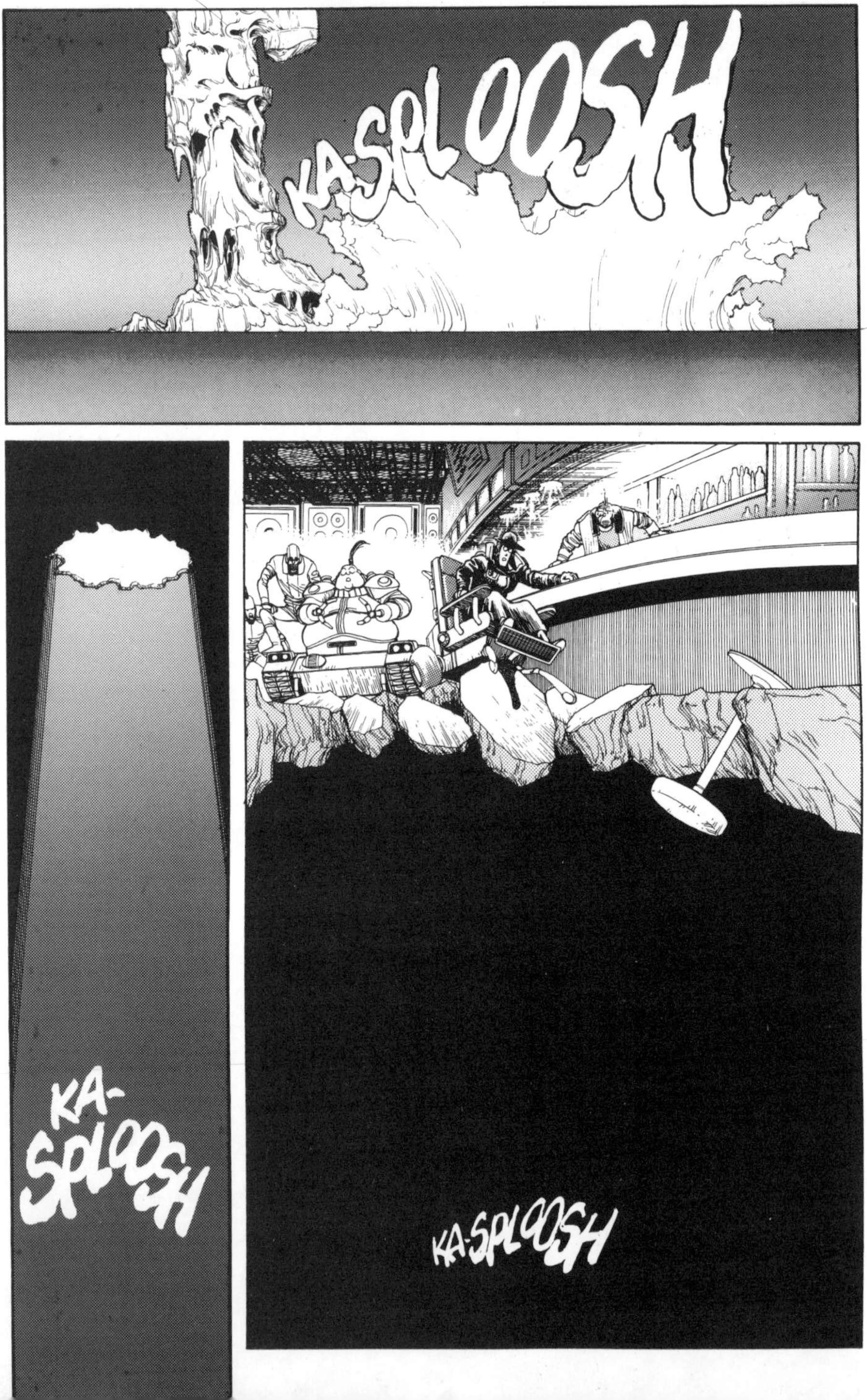
KA-SPLOOOSH
KA-SPLOOSH
KA-SPLOOSH

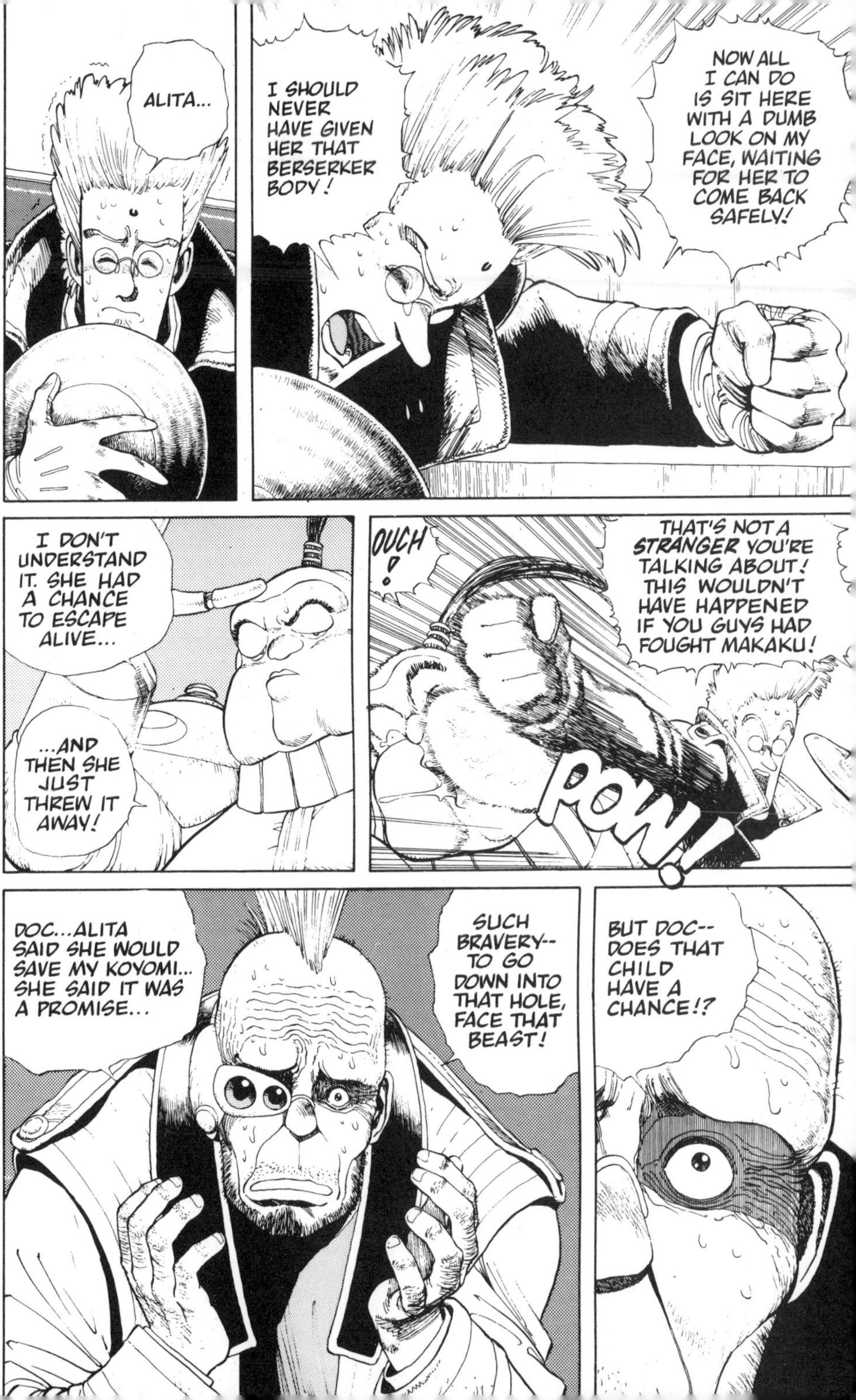
ALITA...
I SHOULD NEVER HAVE GIVEN HER THAT BERSERKER BODY!
NOW ALL I CAN DO IS SIT HERE WITH A DUMB LOOK ON MY FACE, WAITING FOR HER TO COME BACK SAFELY!
I DON'T UNDERSTAND IT. SHE HAD A CHANCE TO ESCAPE ALIVE...
...AND THEN SHE JUST THREW IT AWAY!
OUCH!
THAT'S NOT A STRANGER YOU'RE TALKING ABOUT! THIS WOULDN'T HAVE HAPPENED IF YOU GUYS HAD FOUGHT MAKAKU!
POW!
DOC...ALITA SAID SHE WOULD SAVE MY KOYOMI... SHE SAID IT WAS A PROMISE...
SUCH BRAVERY--TO GO DOWN INTO THAT HOLE, FACE THAT BEAST!
BUT DOC--DOES THAT CHILD HAVE A CHANCE!?

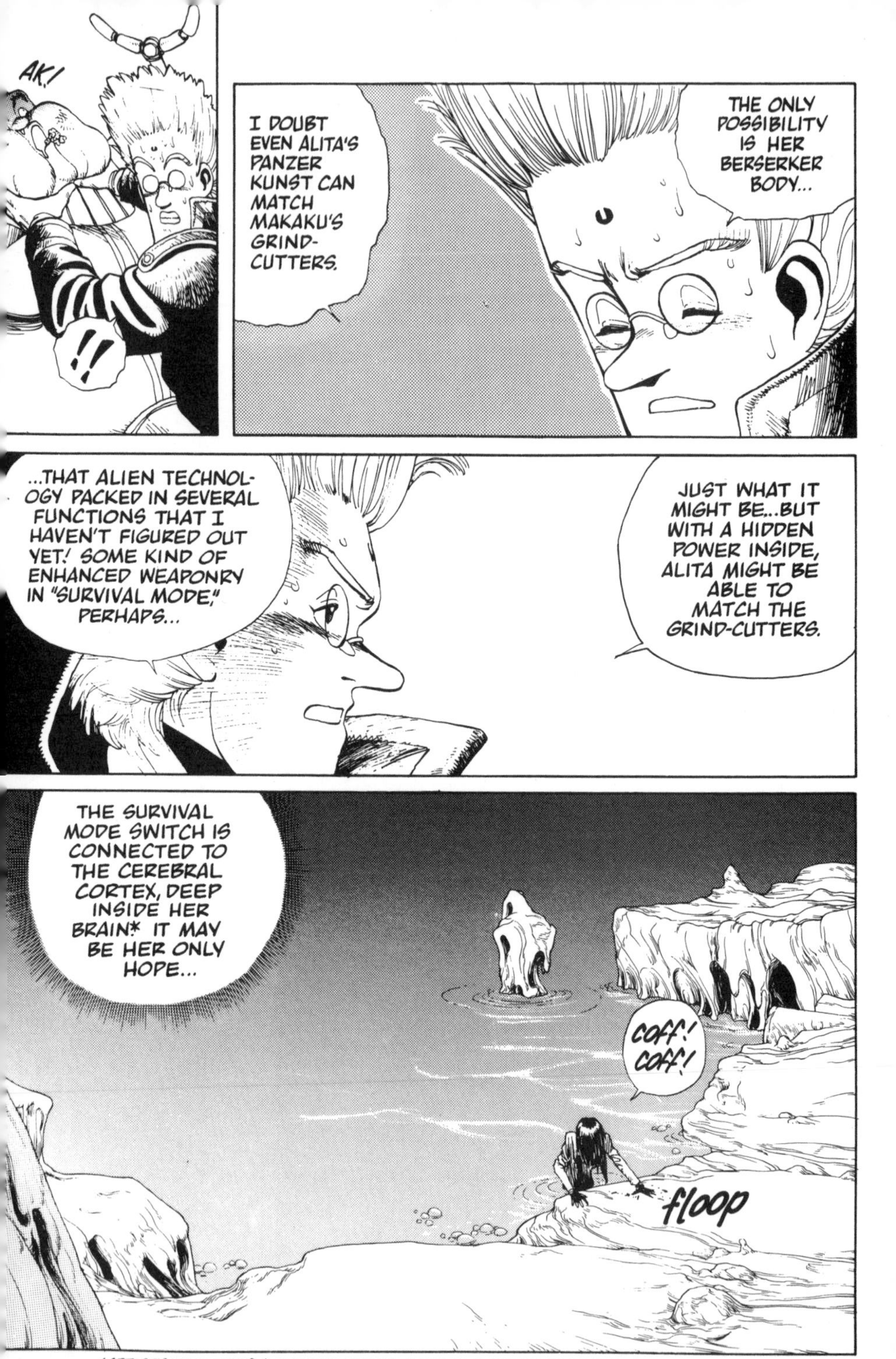

AK!
!!
I DOUBT EVEN ALITA'S PANZER KUNST CAN MATCH MAKAKU'S GRIND-CUTTERS.
THE ONLY POSSIBILITY IS HER BERSERKER BODY...
...THAT ALIEN TECHNOLOGY PACKED IN SEVERAL FUNCTIONS THAT I HAVEN'T FIGURED OUT YET! SOME KIND OF ENHANCED WEAPONRY IN "SURVIVAL MODE," PERHAPS...
JUST WHAT IT MIGHT BE...BUT WITH A HIDDEN POWER INSIDE, ALITA MIGHT BE ABLE TO MATCH THE GRIND-CUTTERS.
THE SURVIVAL MODE SWITCH IS CONNECTED TO THE CEREBRAL CORTEX, DEEP INSIDE HER BRAIN.* IT MAY BE HER ONLY HOPE...
coff! coff!
floop

(ARTIST'S FOOTNOTE) *CEREBRAL CORTEX: THE REGION OF THE BRAIN THAT CONTROLS LARGE-SCALE MOVEMENTS OF THE MUSCLES, THIS "CROCODILE BRAIN" MANAGES THE PRIMITIVE/REPTILIAN INSTINCTIVE ACTIONS.

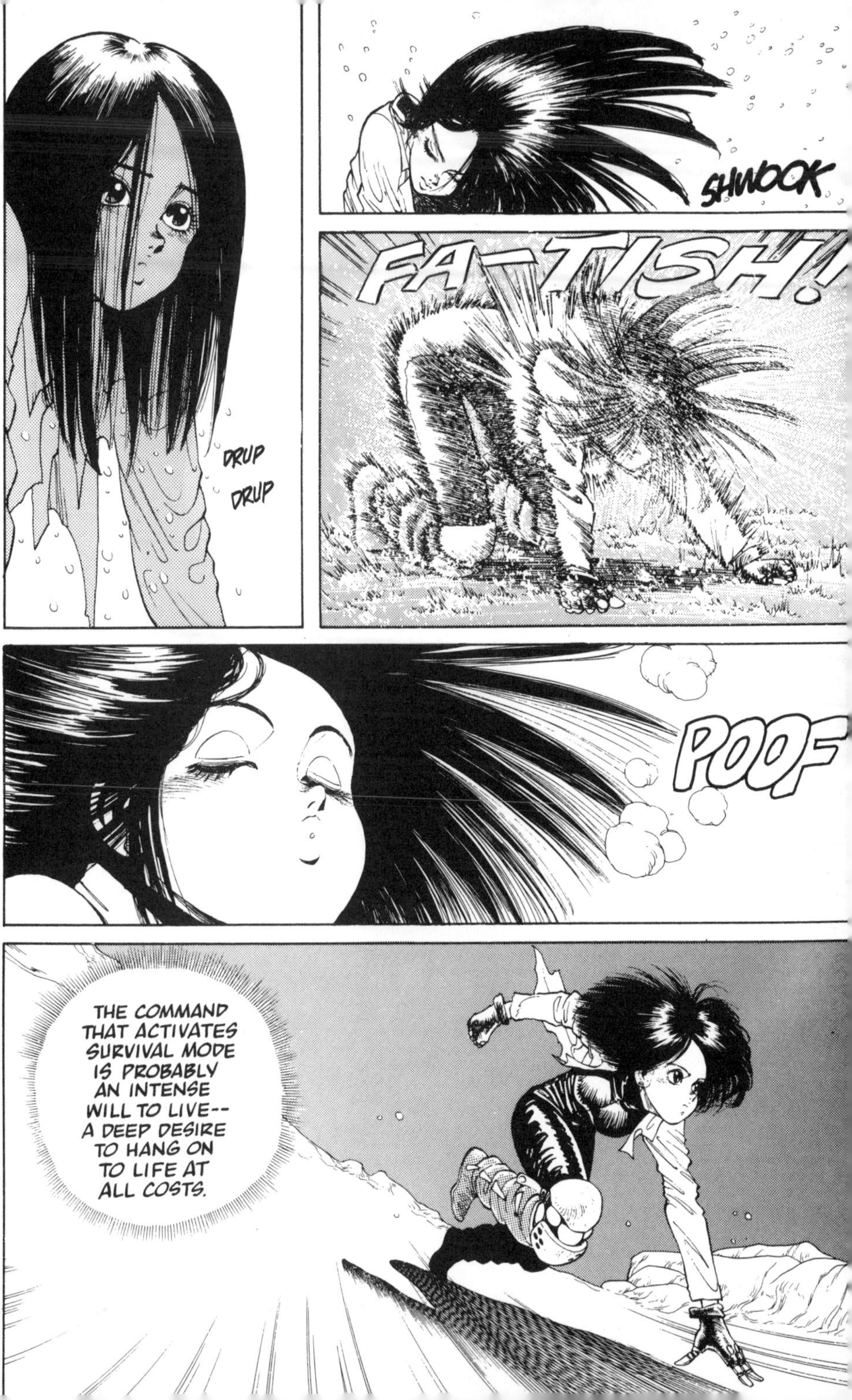
DRUP
DRUP
SHWOOK
FA-TISH!
POOF
THE COMMAND THAT ACTIVATES SURVIVAL MODE IS PROBABLY AN INTENSE WILL TO LIVE-- A DEEP DESIRE TO HANG ON TO LIFE AT ALL COSTS.

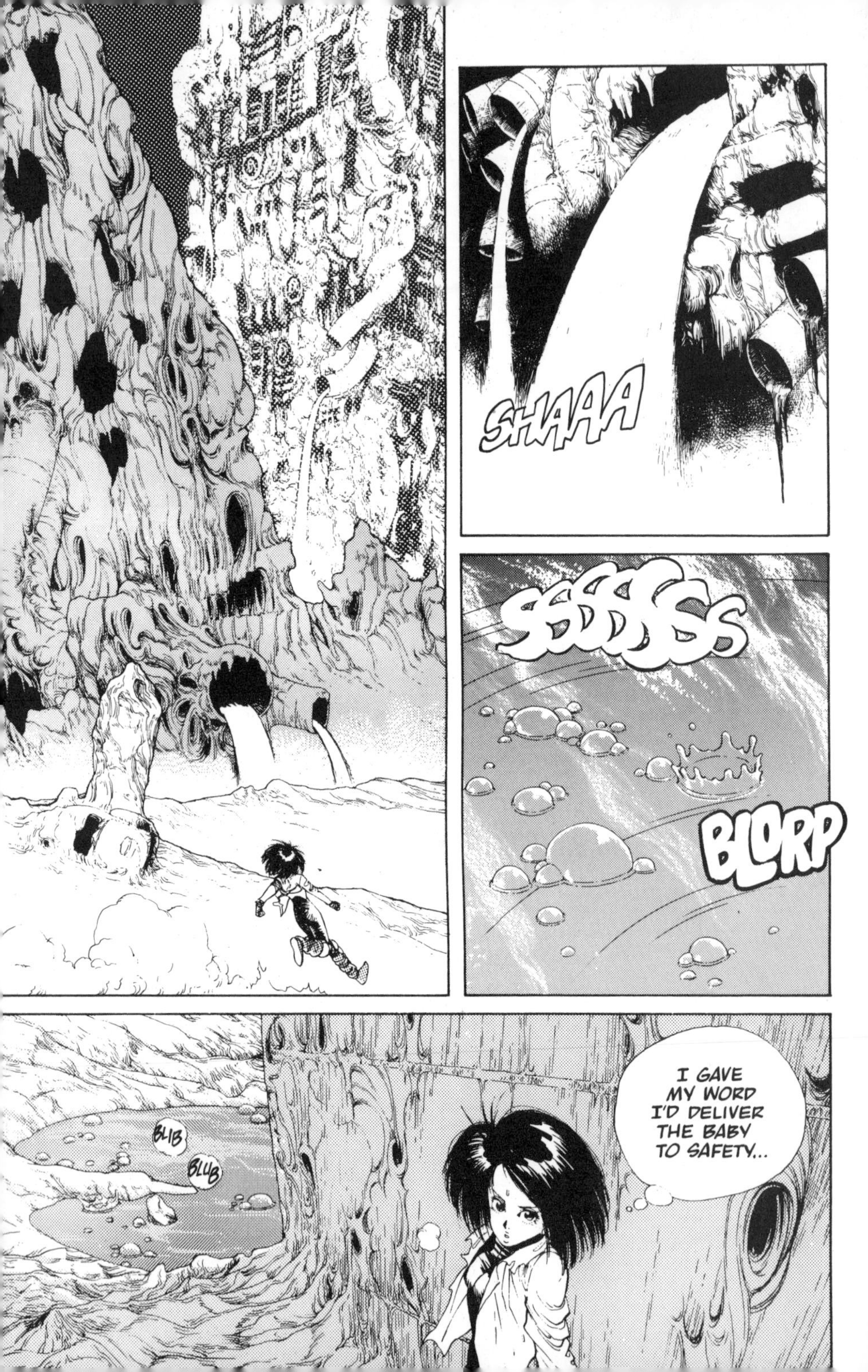
SHAAA
SSSSSSSs
BLORP
BLIB
BLUB
I GAVE MY WORD I'D DELIVER THE BABY TO SAFETY...

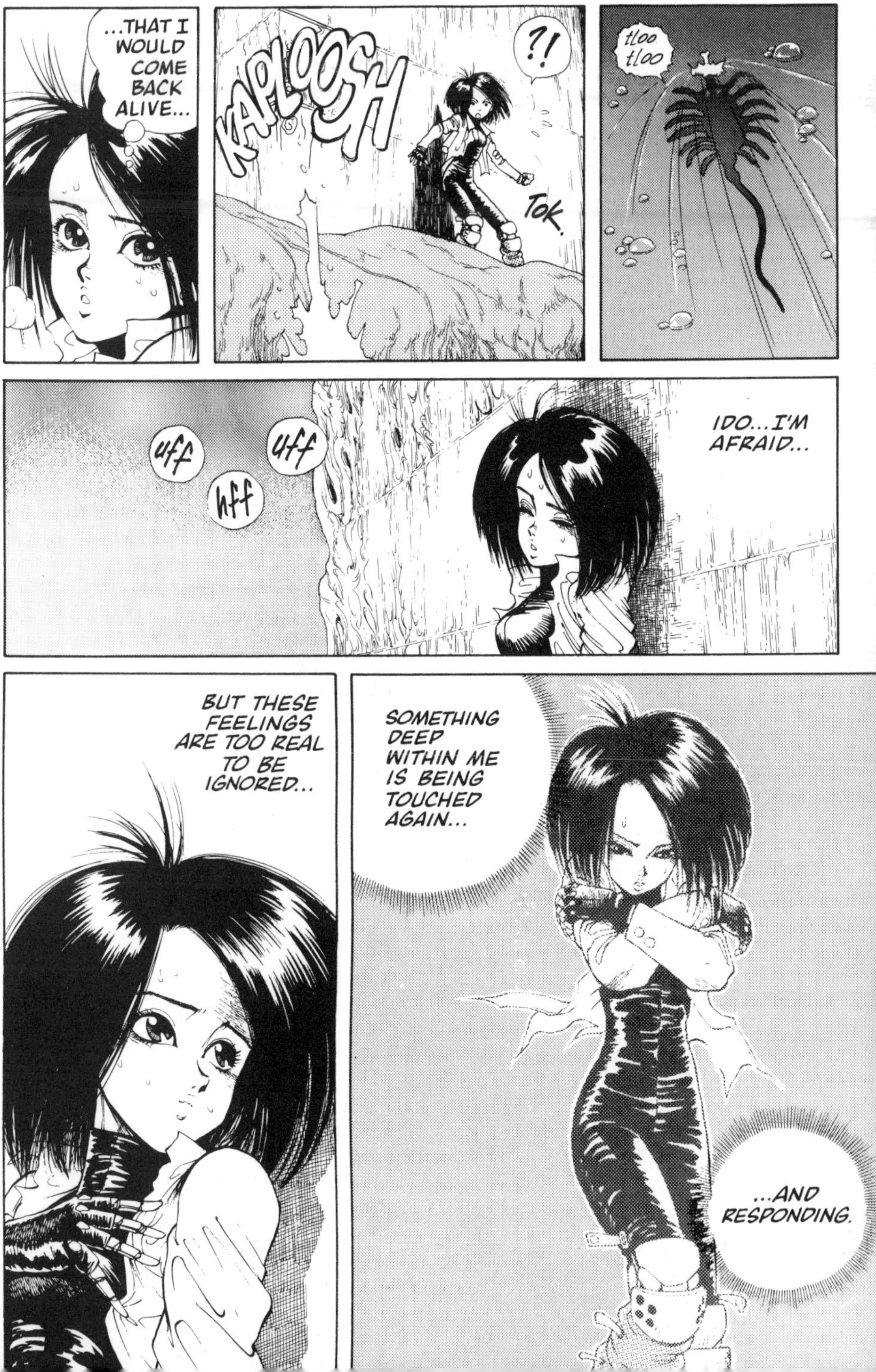
...THAT I WOULD COME BACK ALIVE...
KAPLOOSH
?!
TOK
tloo tloo
uff
uff
hff
IDO...I'M AFRAID...
BUT THESE FEELINGS ARE TOO REAL TO BE IGNORED...
SOMETHING DEEP WITHIN ME IS BEING TOUCHED AGAIN...
...AND RESPONDING.

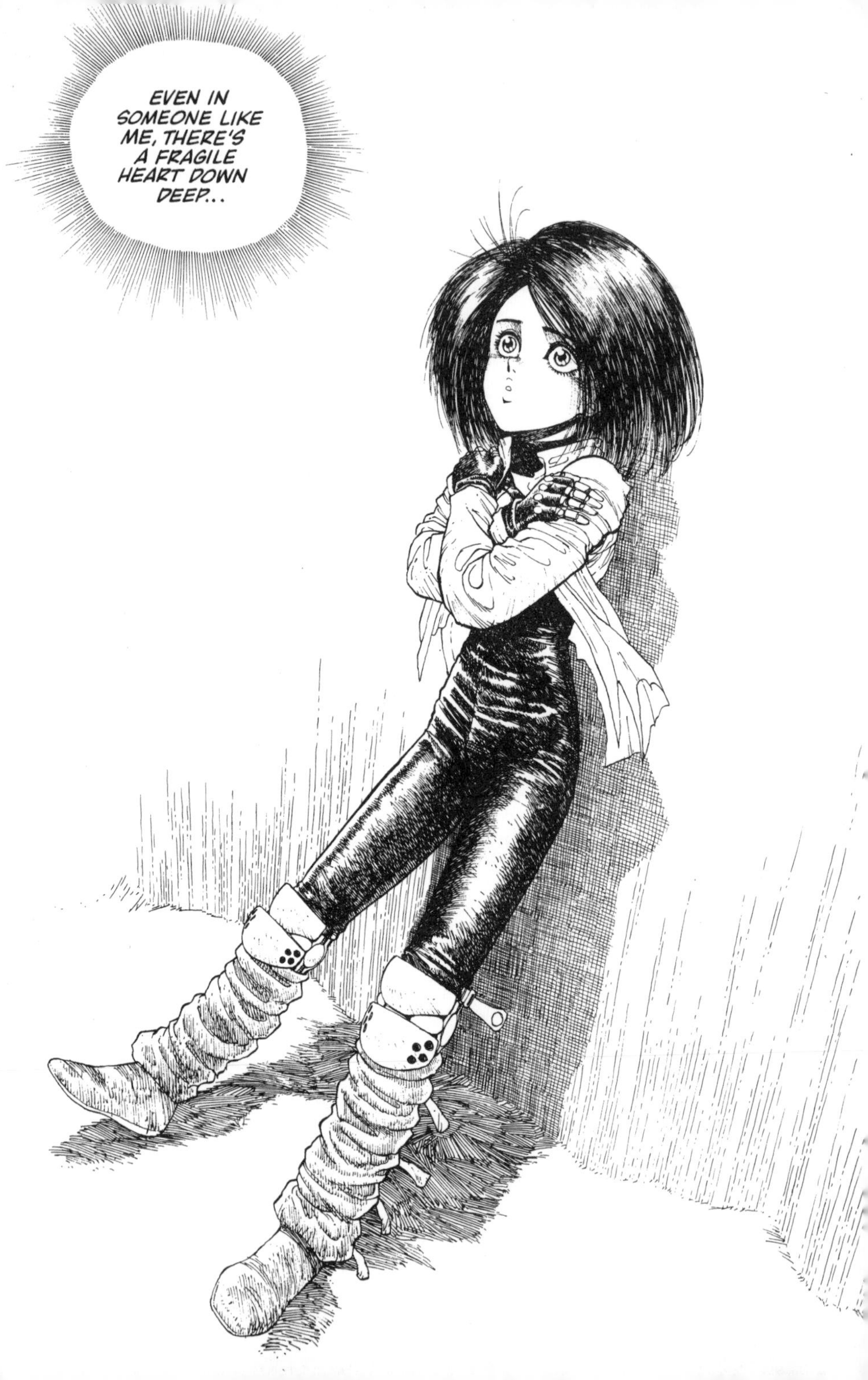
EVEN IN SOMEONE LIKE ME, THERE'S A FRAGILE HEART DOWN DEEP...

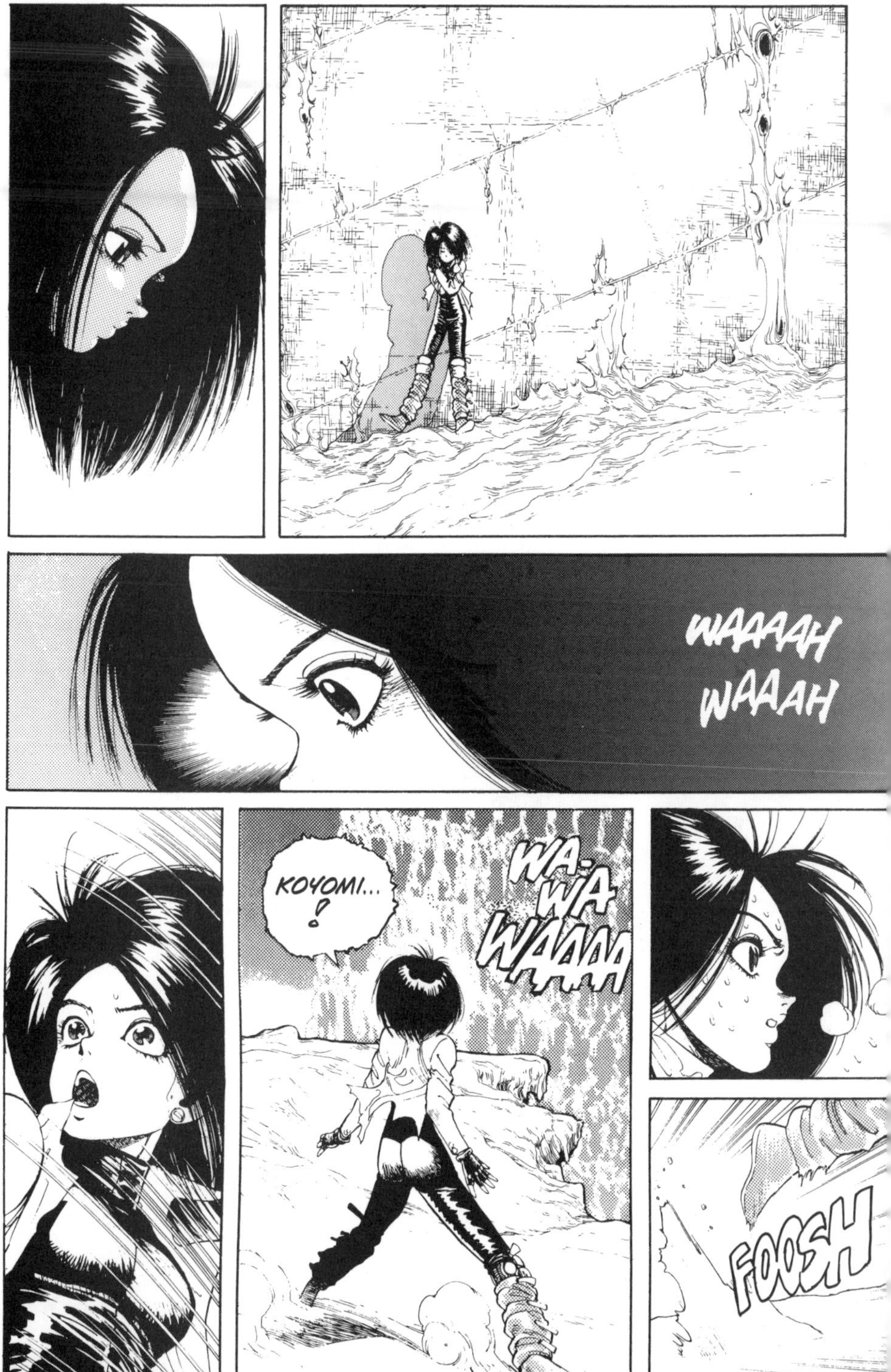
WAAAAH
WAAAH
KOYOMI... !
WA-WA WAAAA
FOOSH

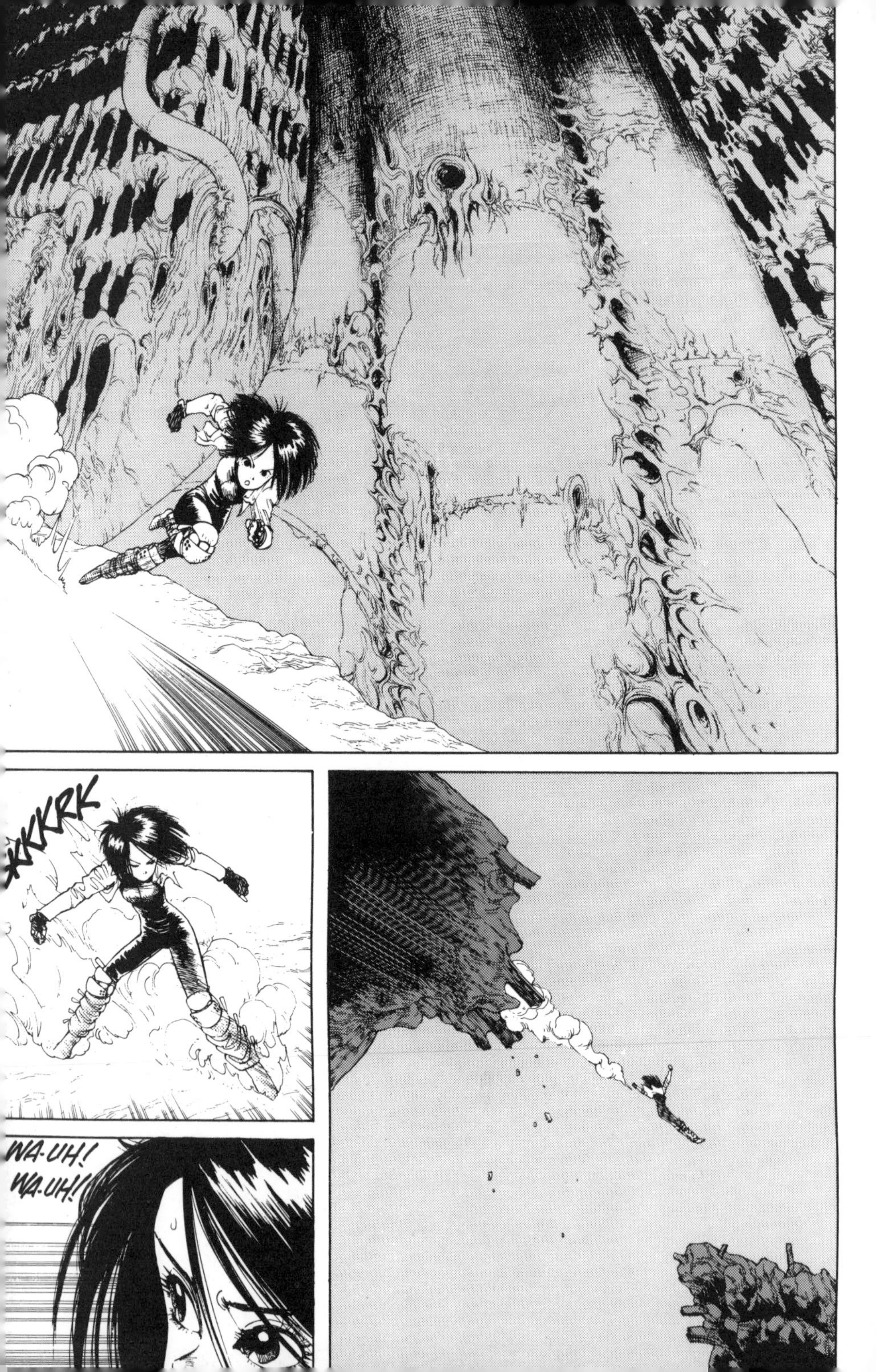
KKKRK
WA-UH!
WA-UH!

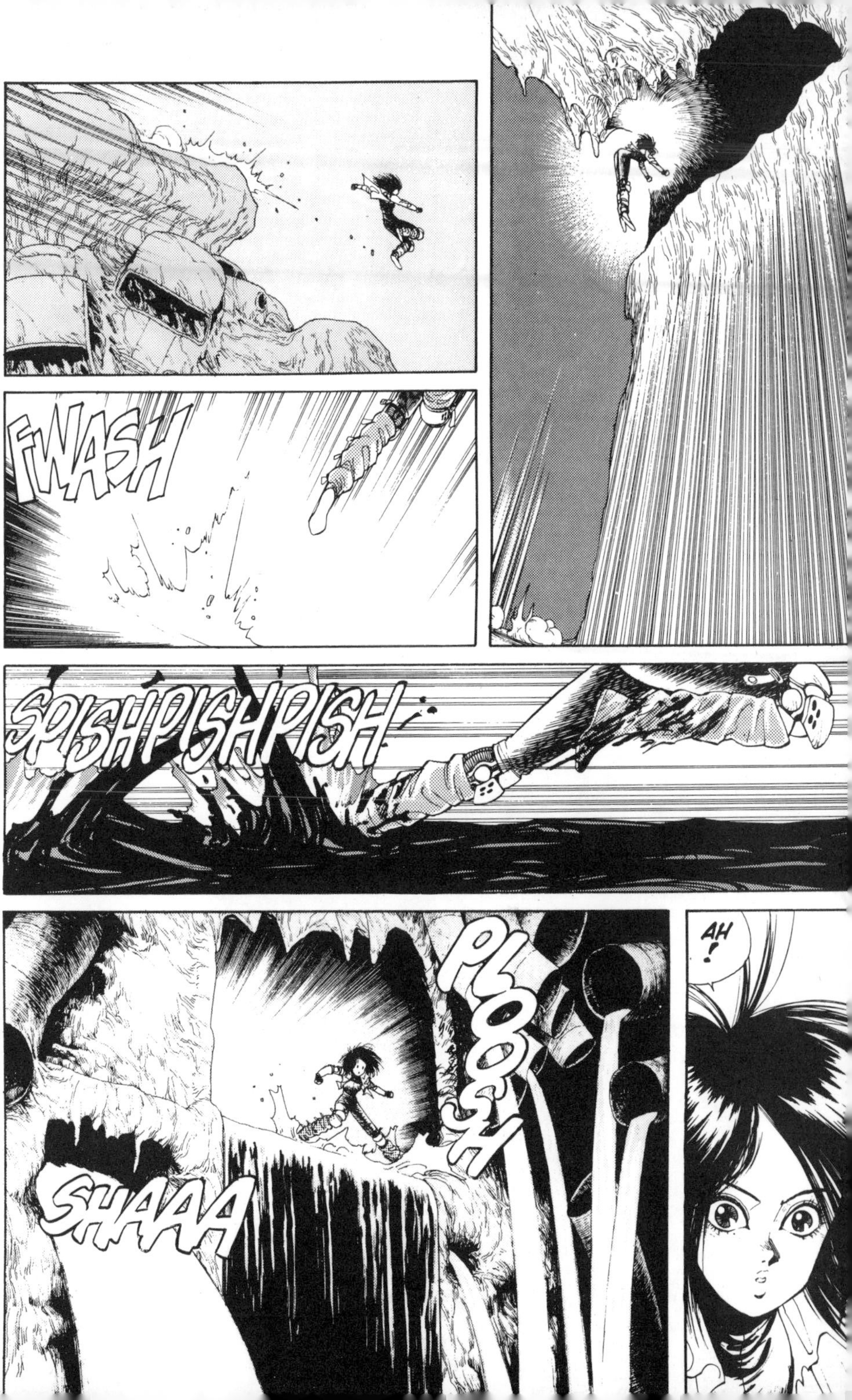
FWASH
SPISHPISHPISH
PLOOSH
SHAAA
AH!

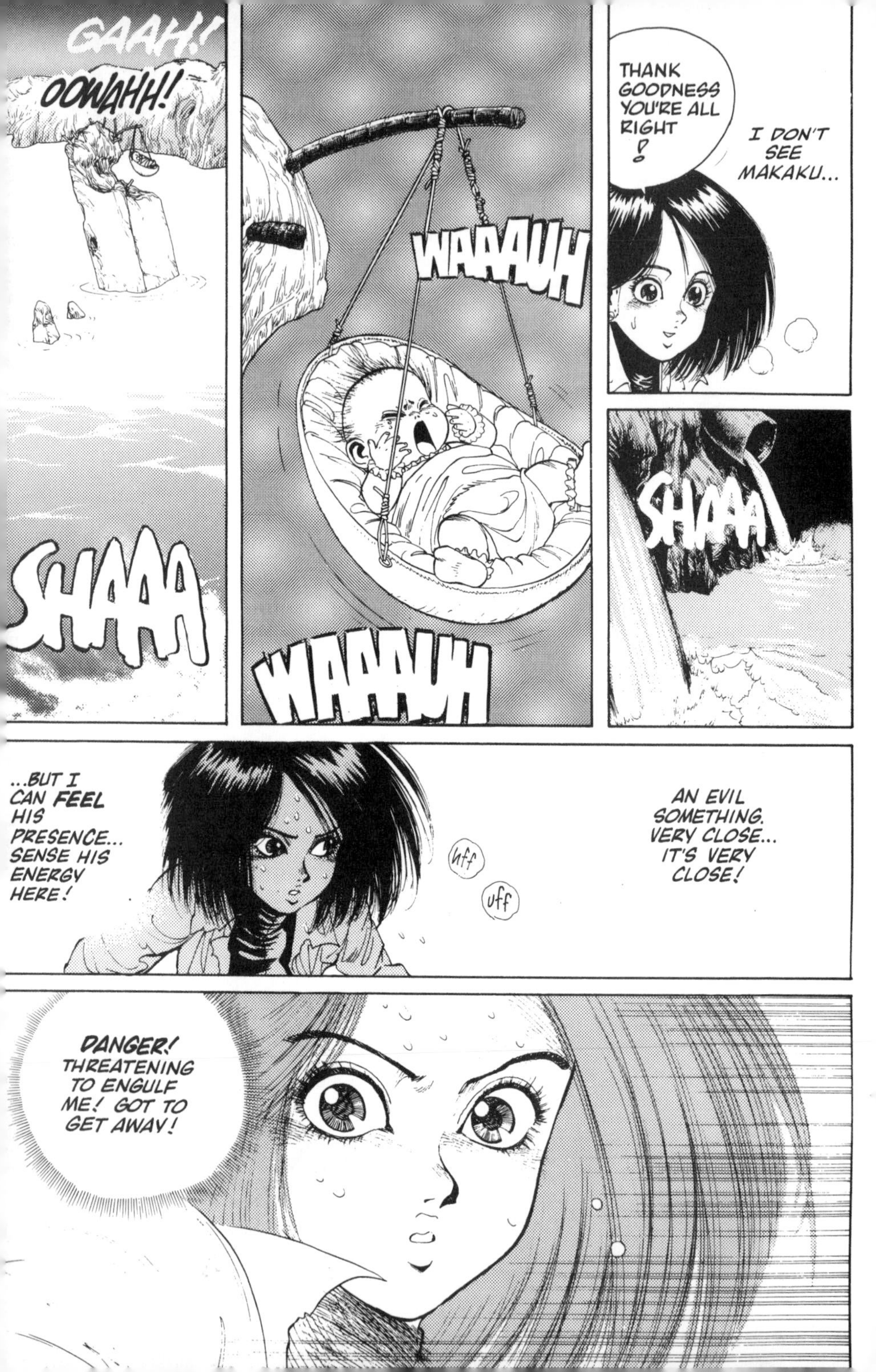
GAAH!
OOWAHH!
SHAAA
WAAAUH
WAAAUH
THANK GOODNESS YOU'RE ALL RIGHT!
I DON'T SEE MAKAKU...
SHAAA
...BUT I CAN FEEL HIS PRESENCE... SENSE HIS ENERGY HERE!
uff
uff
AN EVIL SOMETHING. VERY CLOSE... IT'S VERY CLOSE!
DANGER! THREATENING TO ENGULF ME! GOT TO GET AWAY!

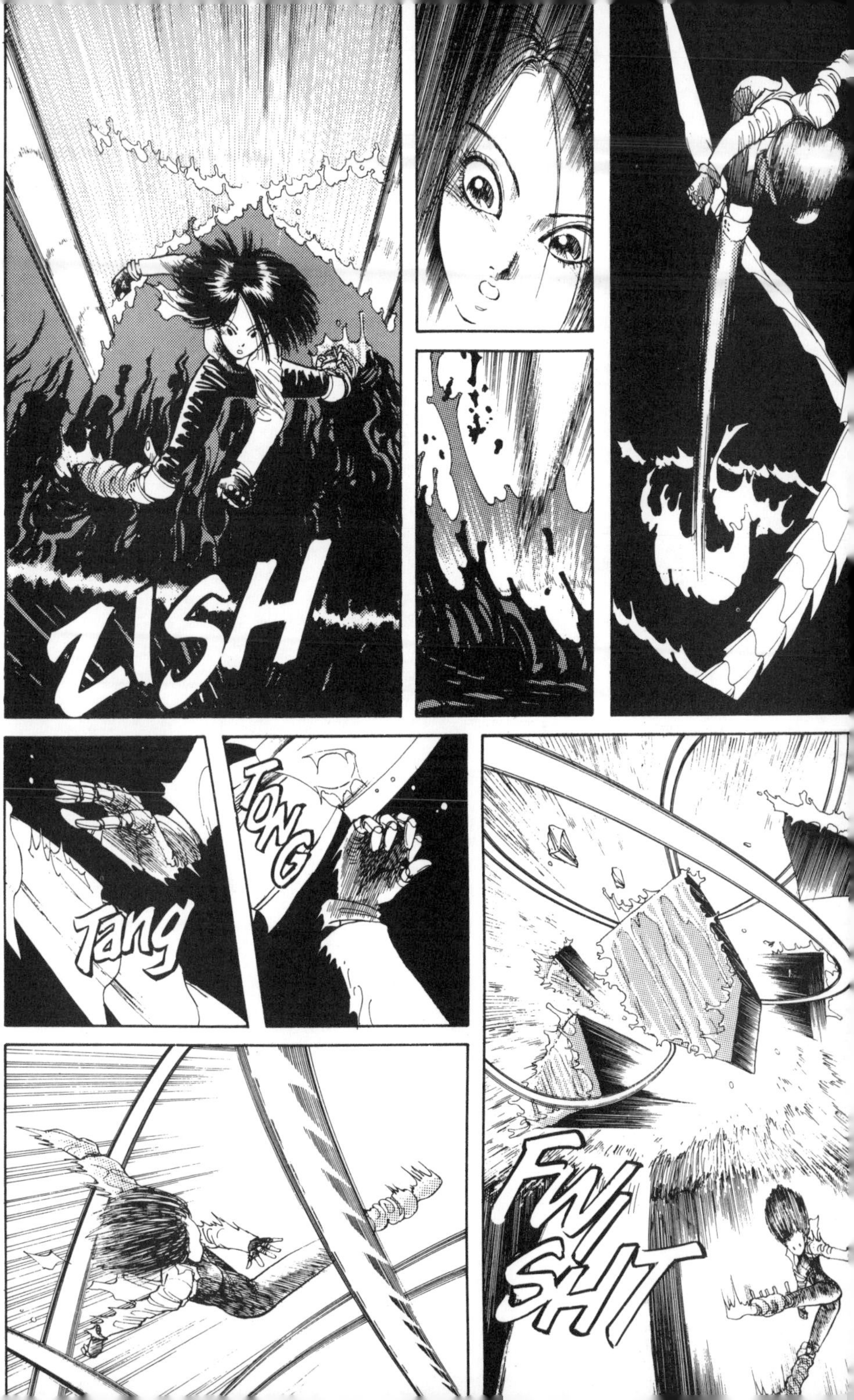
ZISH
Tang
TONG
FWISHT

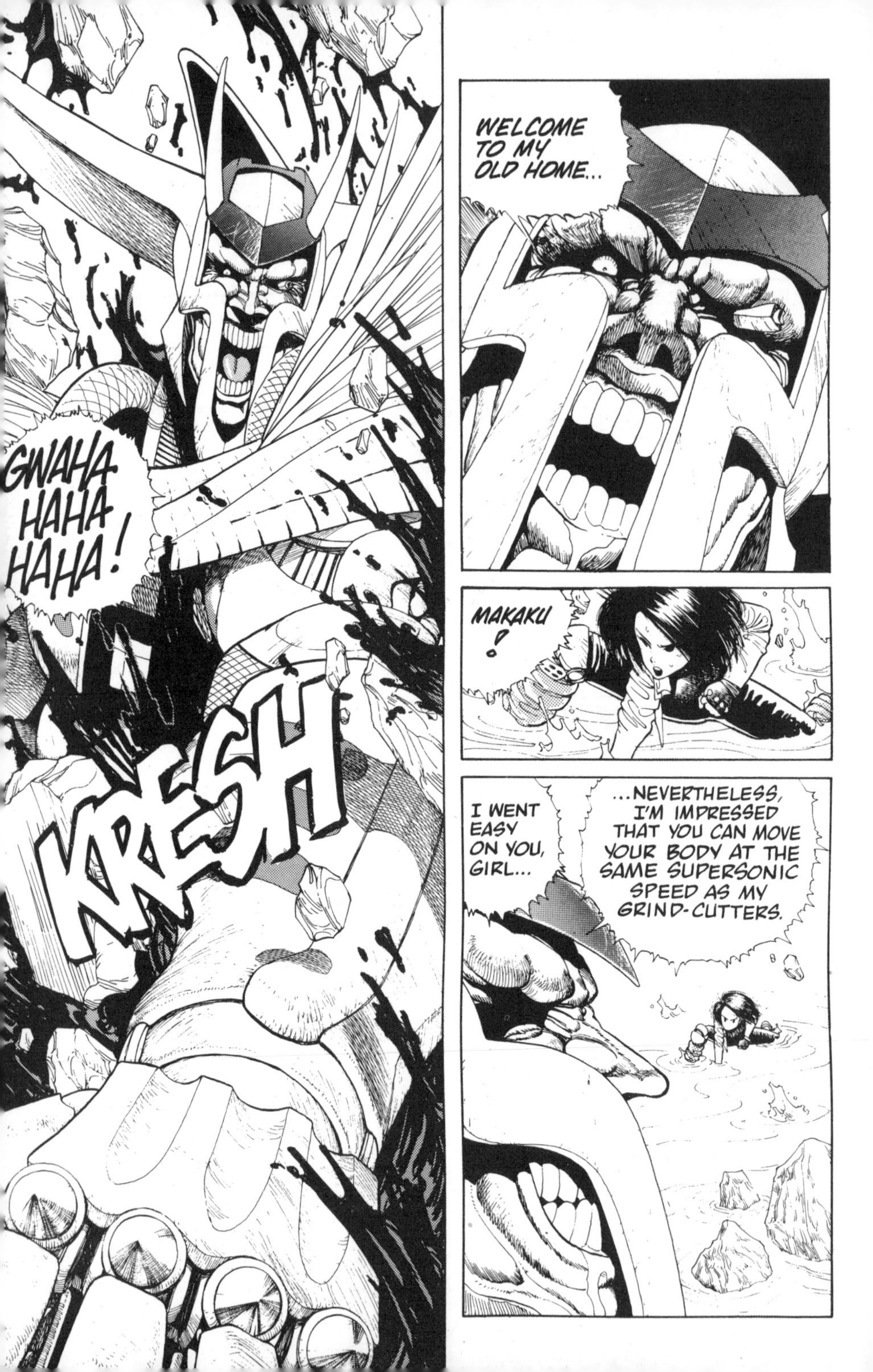
GWAHA HAHA HAHA!
KRESH
WELCOME TO MY OLD HOME...
MAKAKU!
I WENT EASY ON YOU, GIRL...
...NEVERTHELESS, I'M IMPRESSED THAT YOU CAN MOVE YOUR BODY AT THE SAME SUPERSONIC SPEED AS MY GRIND-CUTTERS.

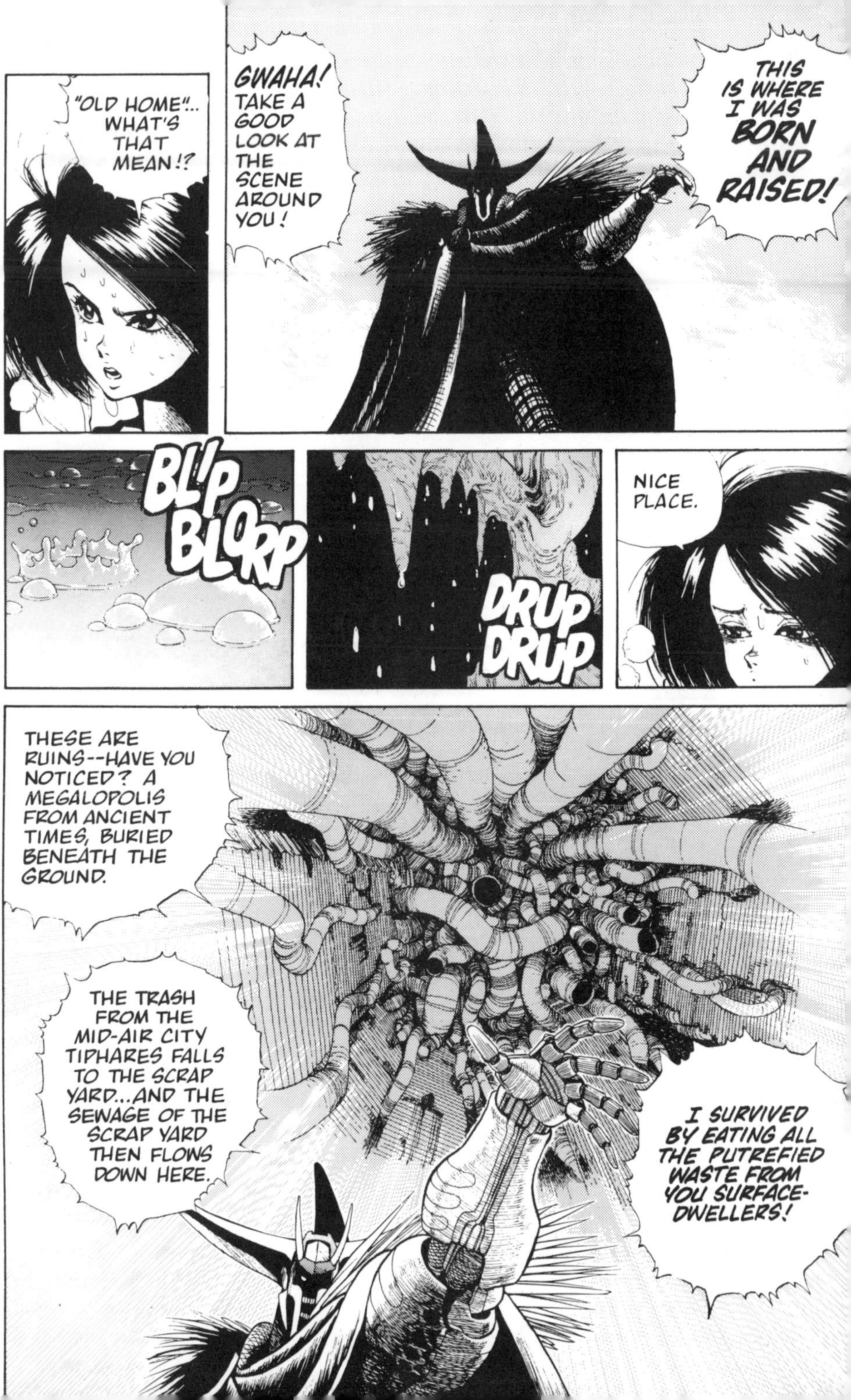
"OLD HOME"... WHAT'S THAT MEAN!?
GWAHA! TAKE A GOOD LOOK AT THE SCENE AROUND YOU!
THIS IS WHERE I WAS BORN AND RAISED!
BLIP BLORP
DRUP DRUP
NICE PLACE.
THESE ARE RUINS--HAVE YOU NOTICED? A MEGALOPOLIS FROM ANCIENT TIMES, BURIED BENEATH THE GROUND.
THE TRASH FROM THE MID-AIR CITY TIPHARES FALLS TO THE SCRAP YARD...AND THE SEWAGE OF THE SCRAP YARD THEN FLOWS DOWN HERE.
I SURVIVED BY EATING ALL THE PUTREFIED WASTE FROM YOU SURFACE-DWELLERS!

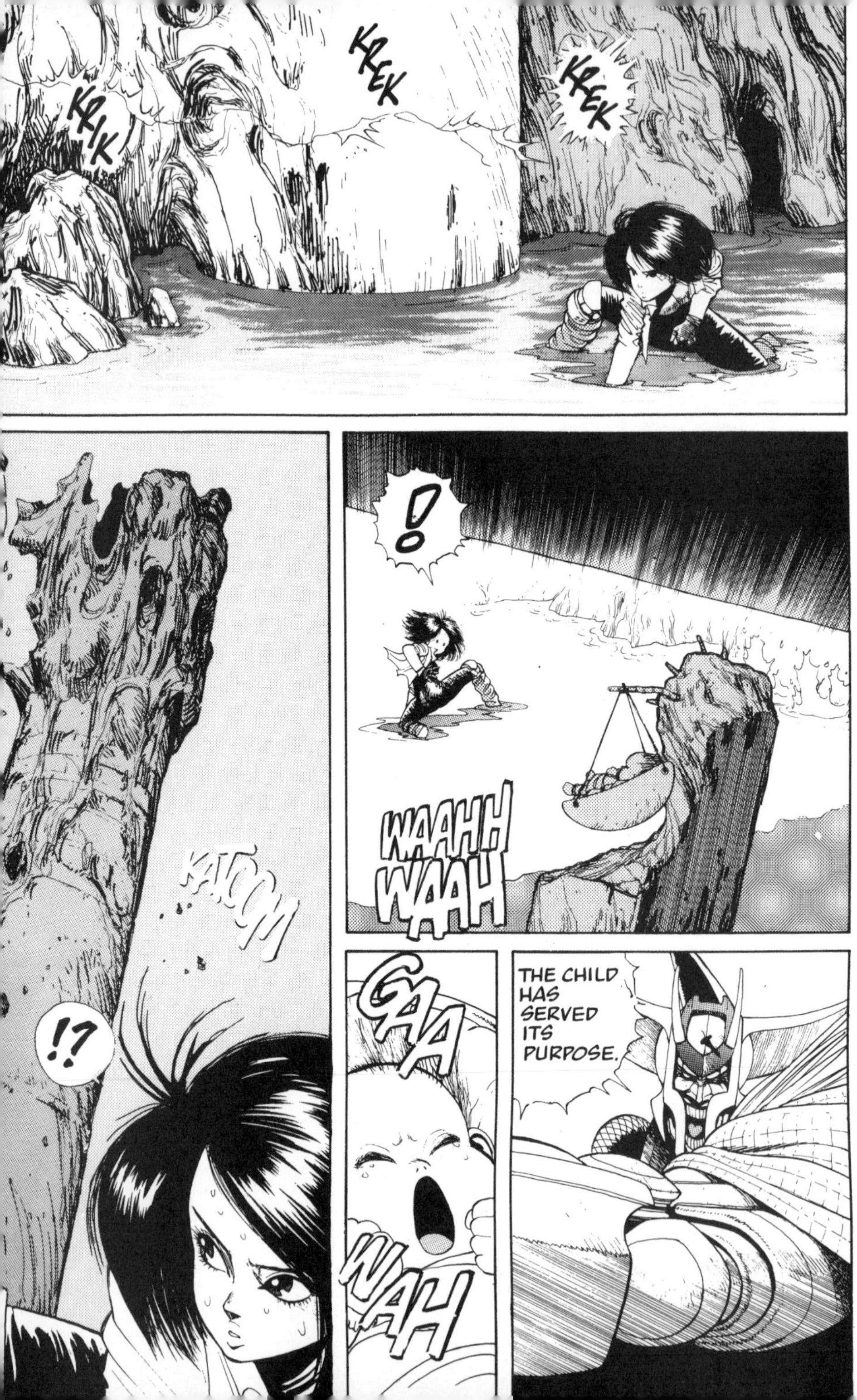
KRIK
KREK
KREK
KATOOM
!?
!
WAAHH
WAAH
GAA
WAH
THE CHILD HAS SERVED ITS PURPOSE.

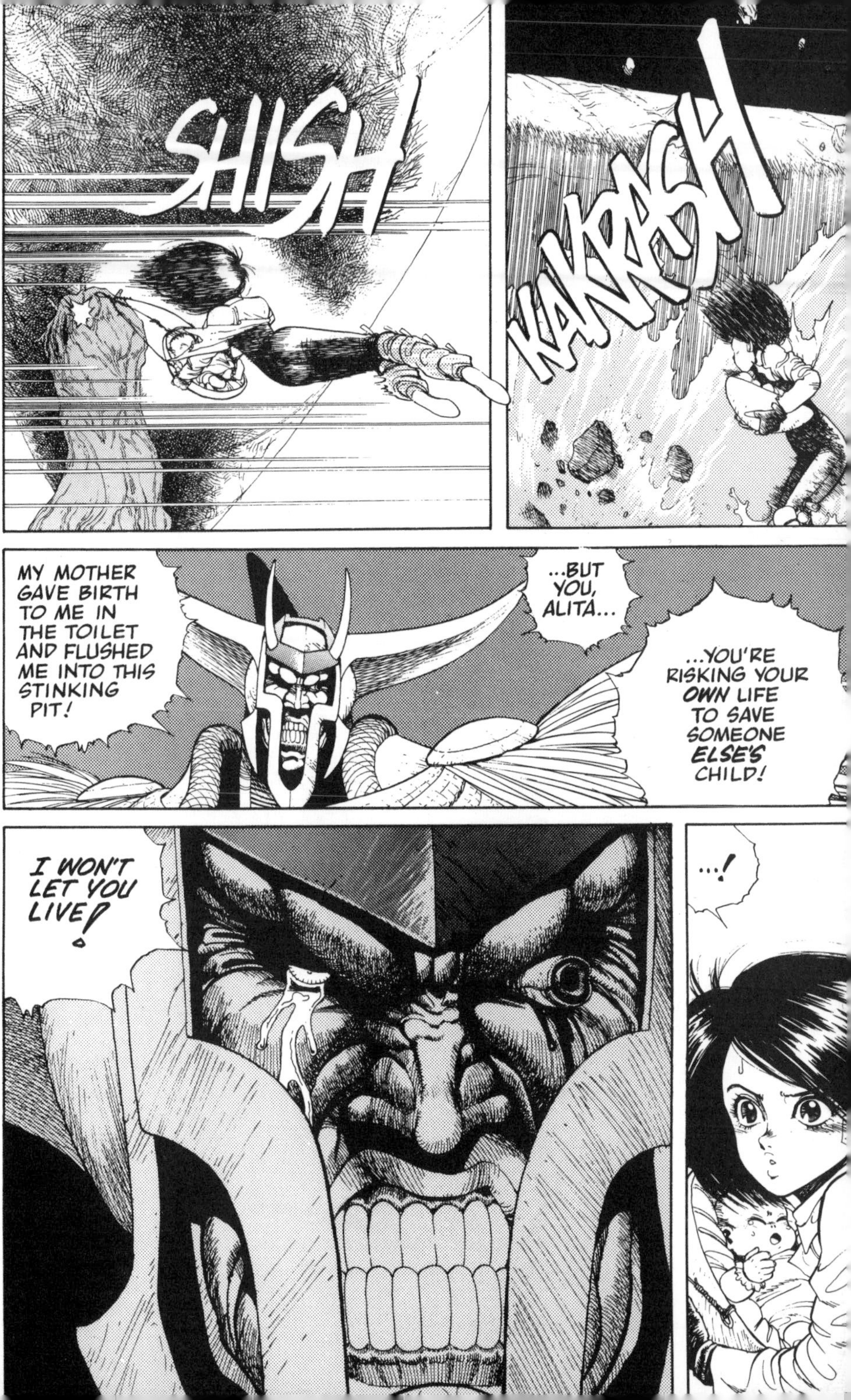
SHISH
KAKRASH
MY MOTHER GAVE BIRTH TO ME IN THE TOILET AND FLUSHED ME INTO THIS STINKING PIT!
...BUT YOU, ALITA...
...YOU'RE RISKING YOUR OWN LIFE TO SAVE SOMEONE ELSE'S CHILD!
I WON'T LET YOU LIVE!
...!

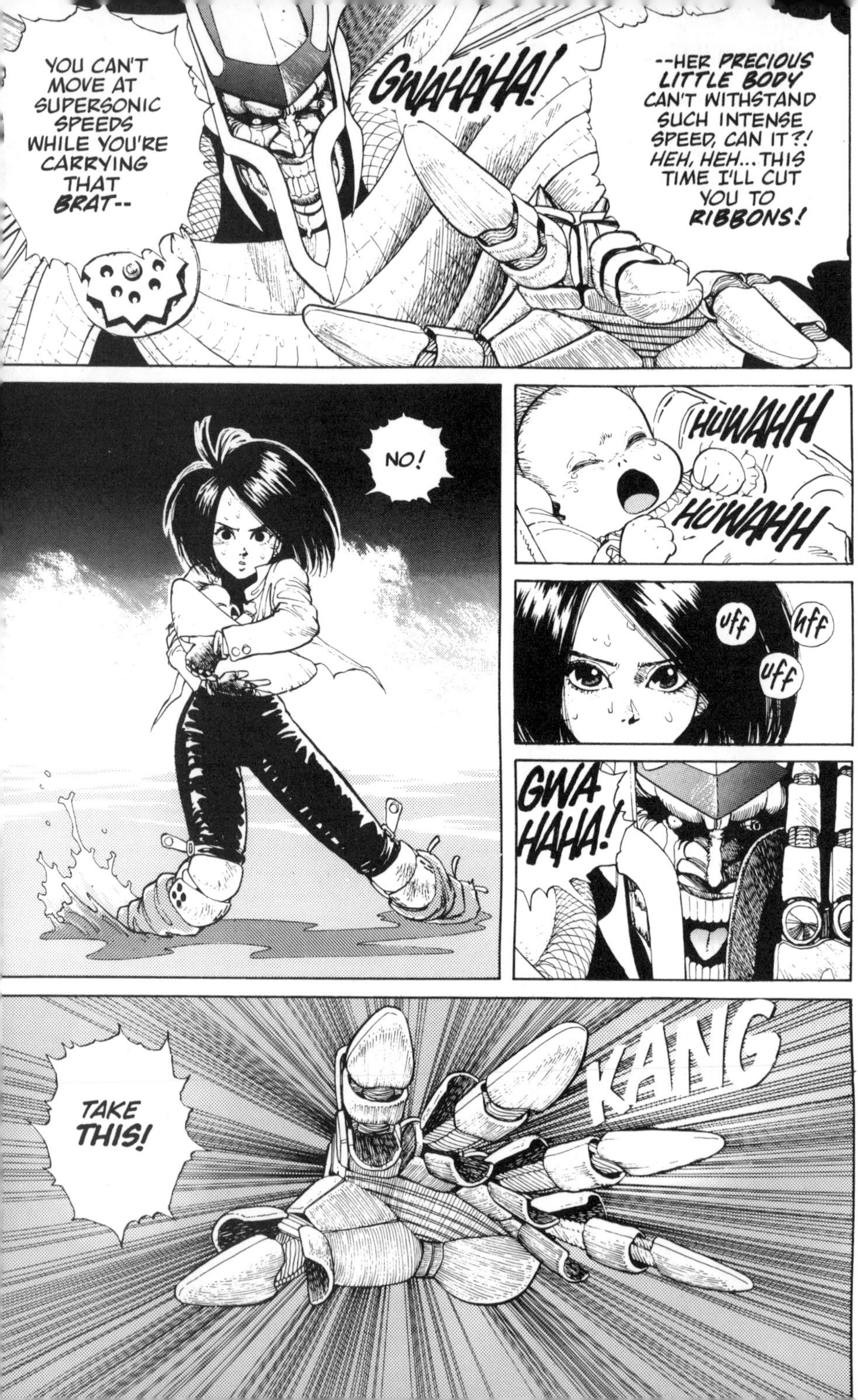
YOU CAN'T MOVE AT SUPERSONIC SPEEDS WHILE YOU'RE CARRYING THAT BRAT--
GWAHAHA!
--HER PRECIOUS LITTLE BODY CAN'T WITHSTAND SUCH INTENSE SPEED, CAN IT?! HEH, HEH... THIS TIME I'LL CUT YOU TO RIBBONS!
NO!
HUWAHH
HUWAHH
uff
hff
uff
GWA HAHA!
TAKE THIS!
KANG

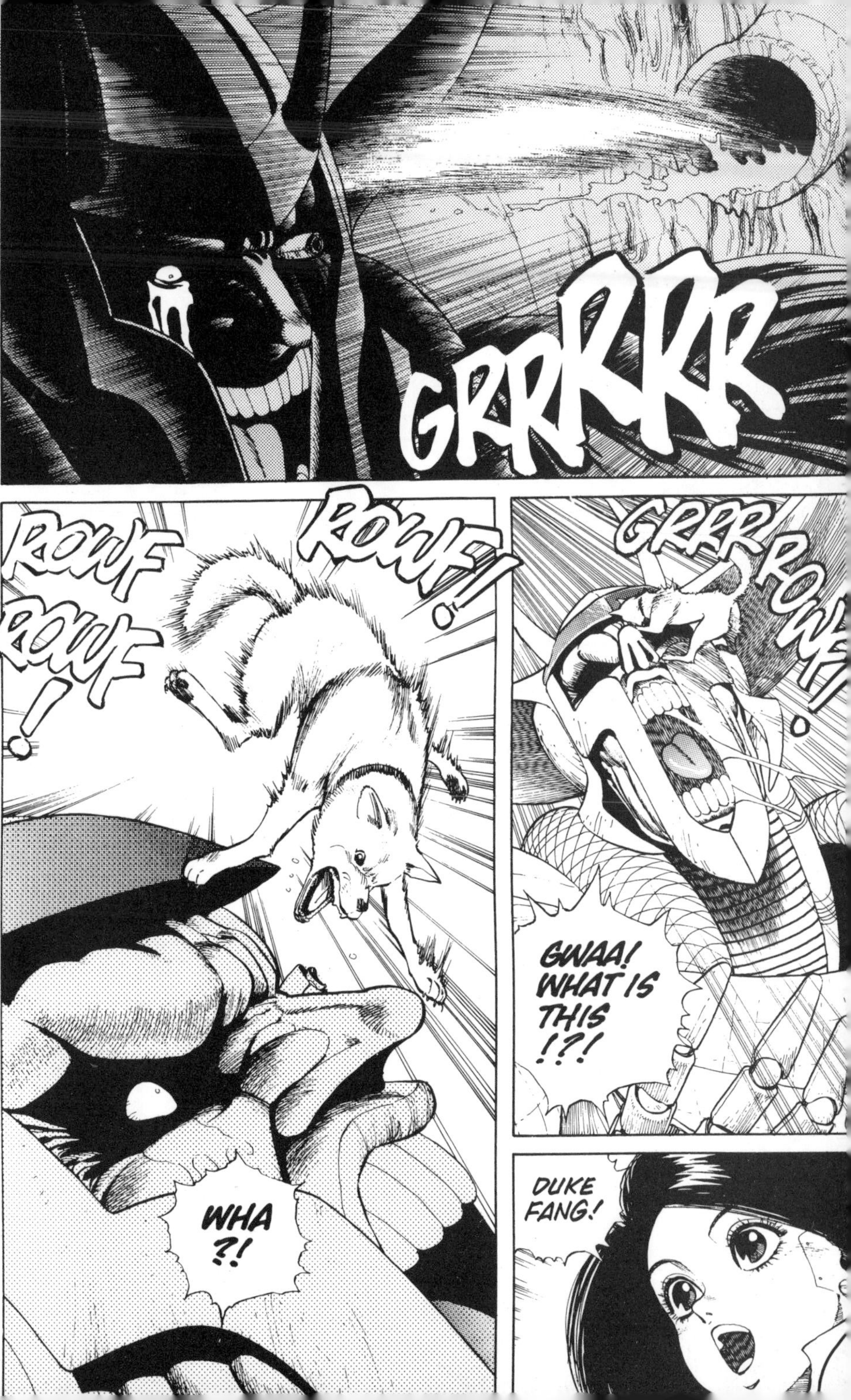
GRRRRR
ROWF ROWF!
ROWF!!
WHA ?!
GRRR
ROWF!!
GWAA! WHAT IS THIS !?!
DUKE FANG!

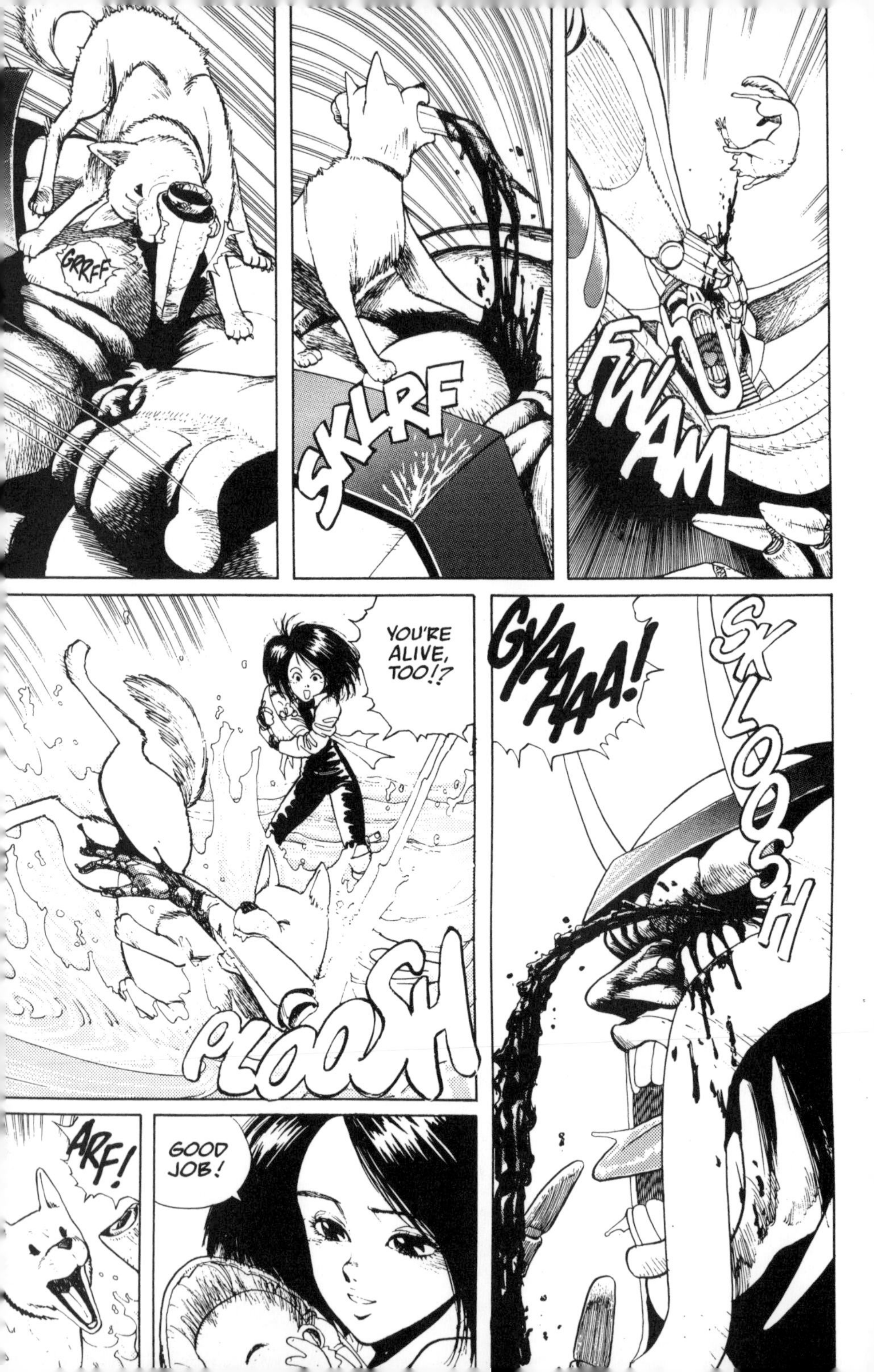
GRRFF
SKLRF
FWAM
YOU'RE ALIVE, TOO!?
PLOOSH
GYAAAAA!
SKLOOSH
ARF!
GOOD JOB!

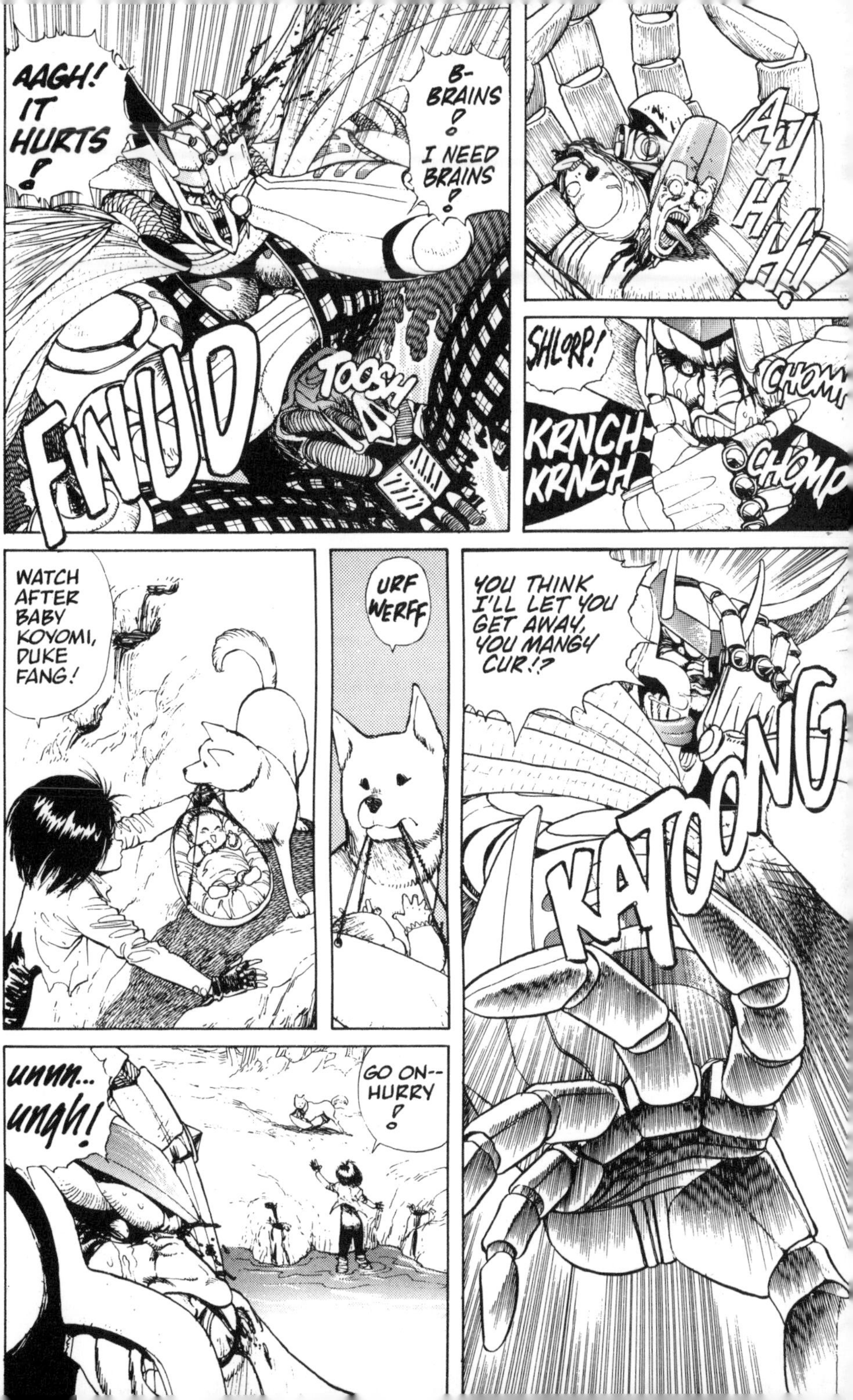
AAGH! IT HURTS!
B-BRAINS! I NEED BRAINS!
FWUD
TOOSH
AHHHH!
SHLORP!
CHOMP
KRNCH-KRNCH
CHOMP
WATCH AFTER BABY KOYOMI, DUKE FANG!
URF WERFF
unnn... unngh!
GO ON--HURRY!
YOU THINK I'LL LET YOU GET AWAY, YOU MANGY CUR!?
KATOONG

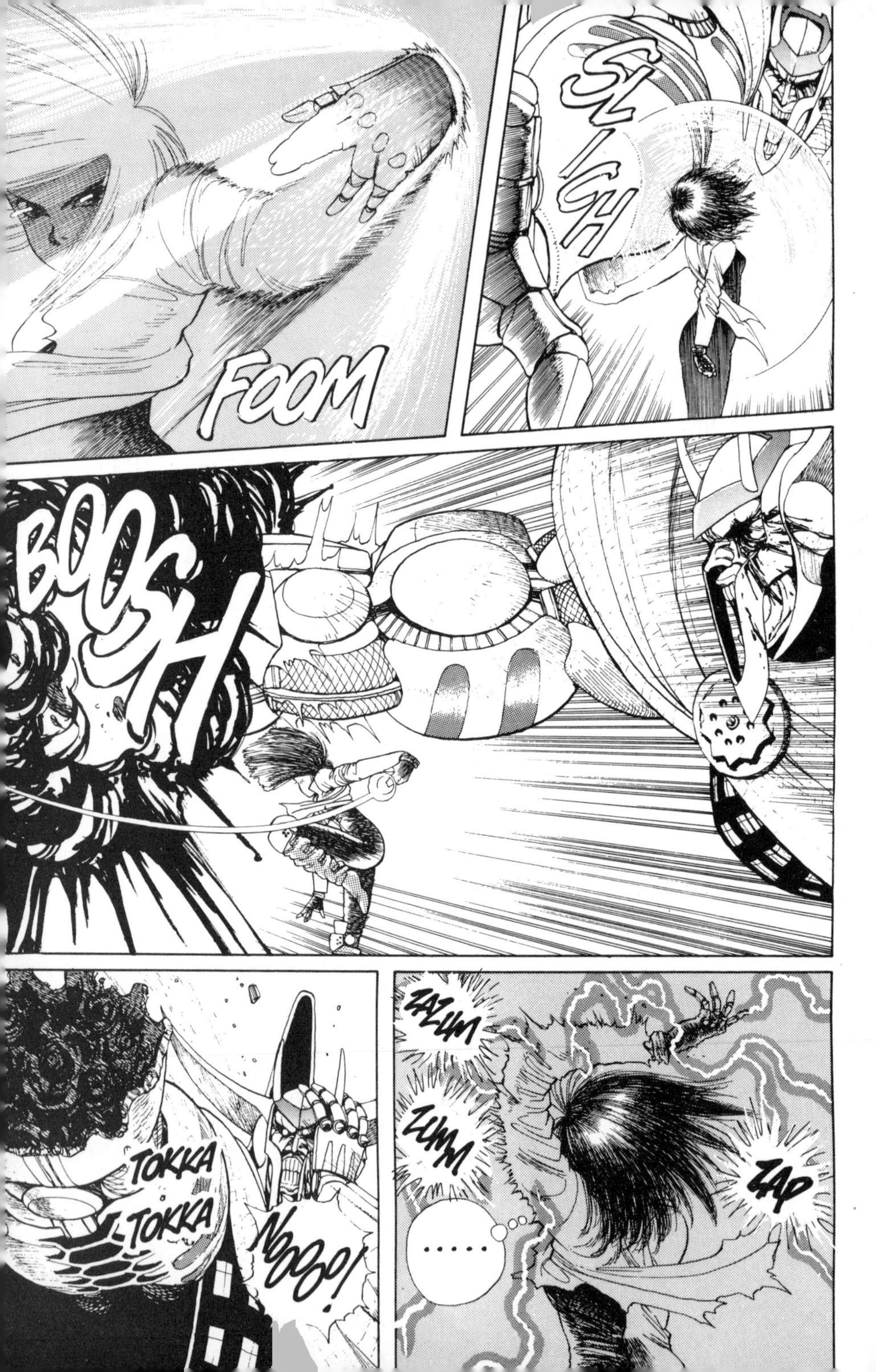
FOOM
SLICH
BOOSH
TOKKA
TOKKA
NOOOOO!
ZAZUM
ZUMM
ZAP
.....

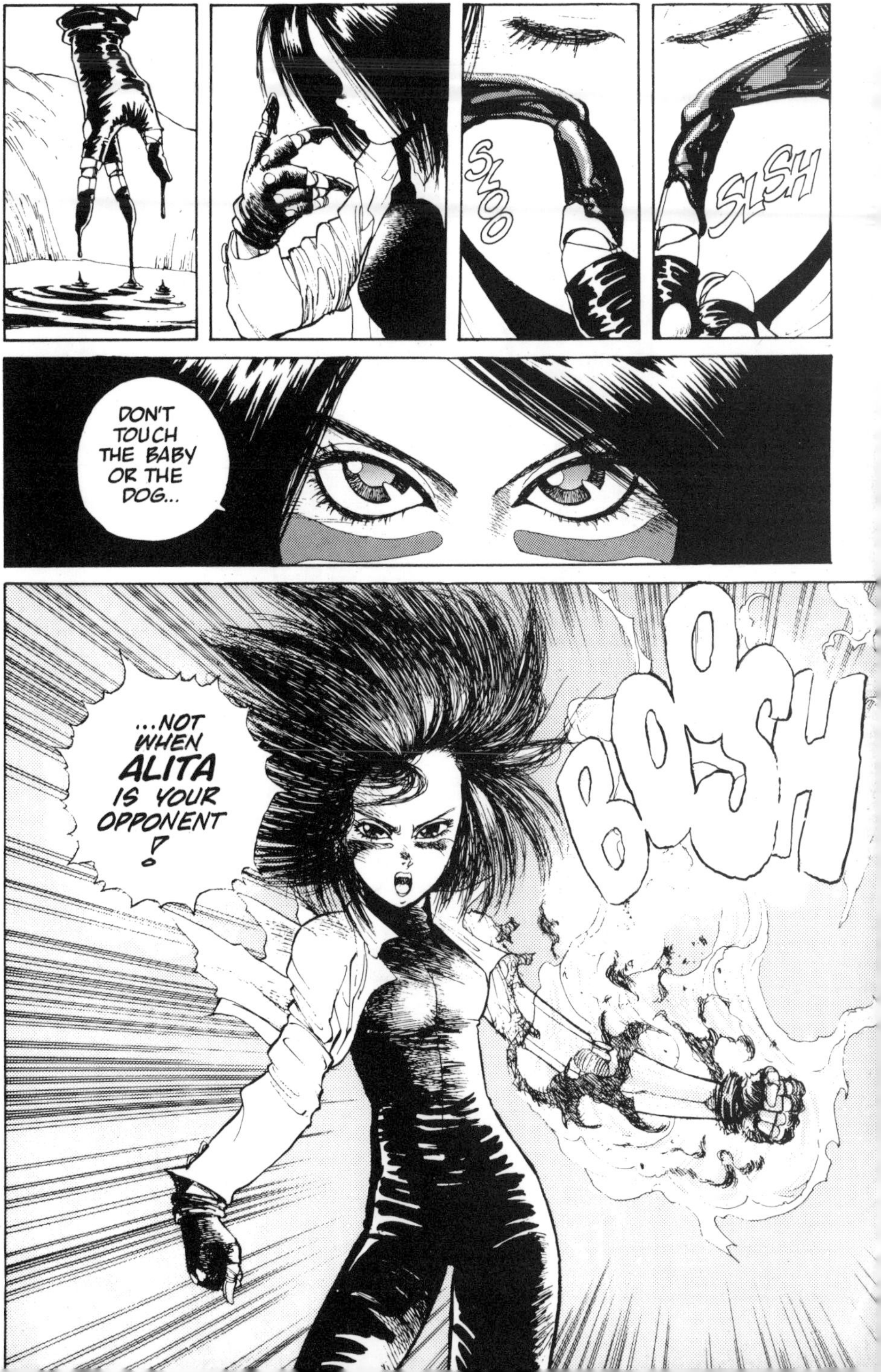
SLOO
SLSH
DON'T TOUCH THE BABY OR THE DOG...
...NOT WHEN ALITA IS YOUR OPPONENT!
BOOSH

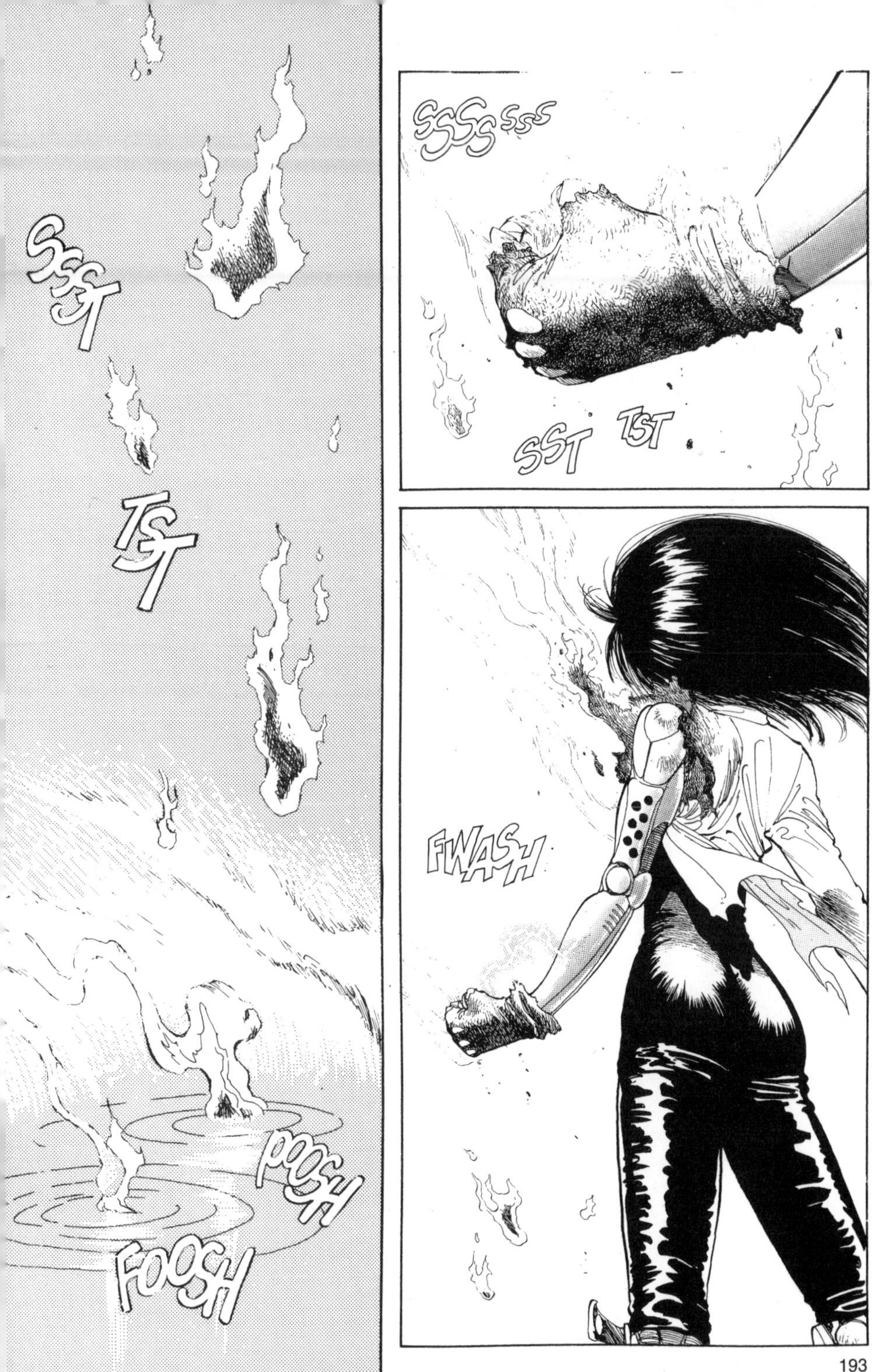
SSST
TST
POOSH
FOOSH
SSSSSSS
SST
TST
FWASH

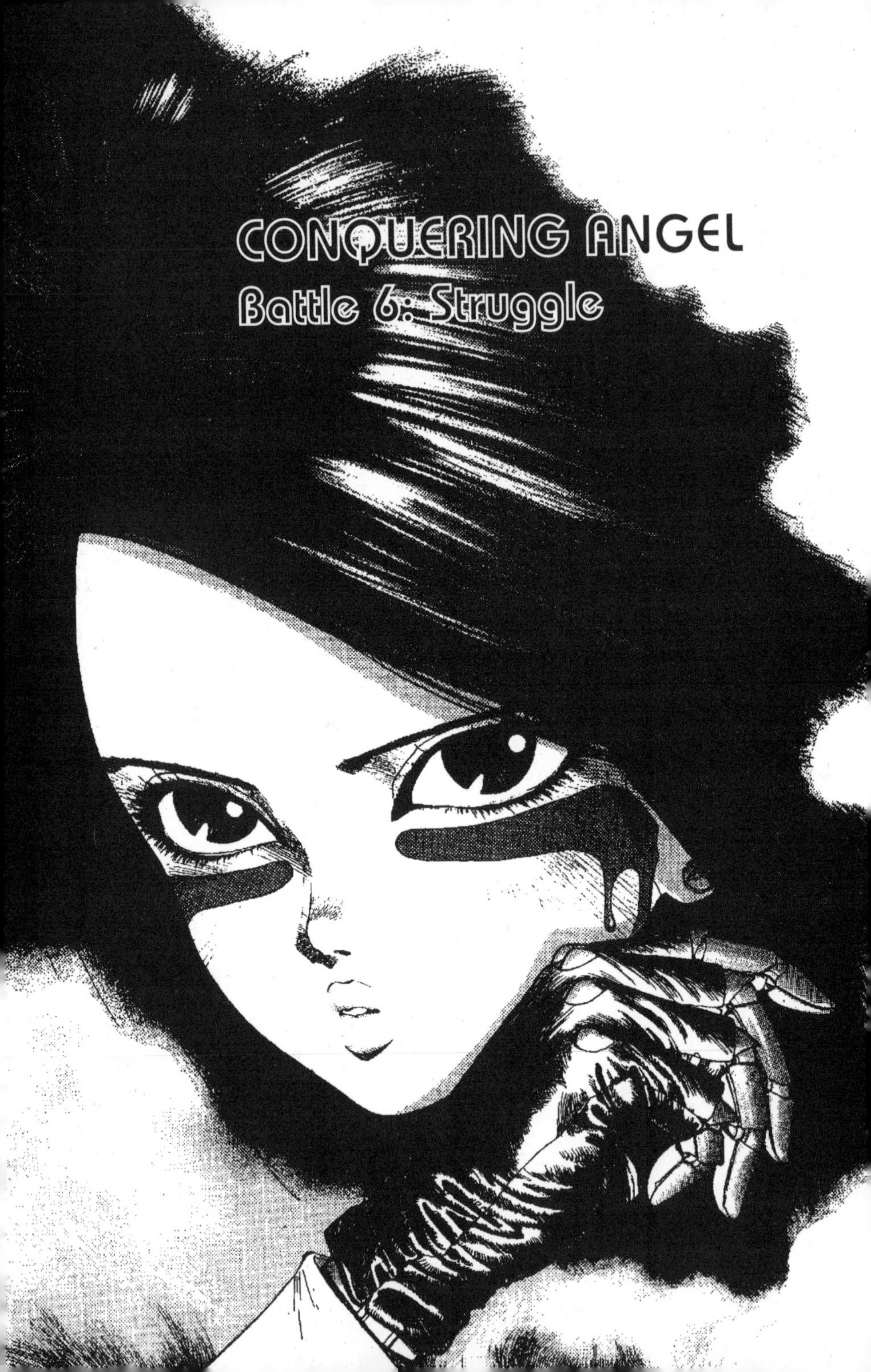
CONQUERING ANGEL
Battle 6: Struggle

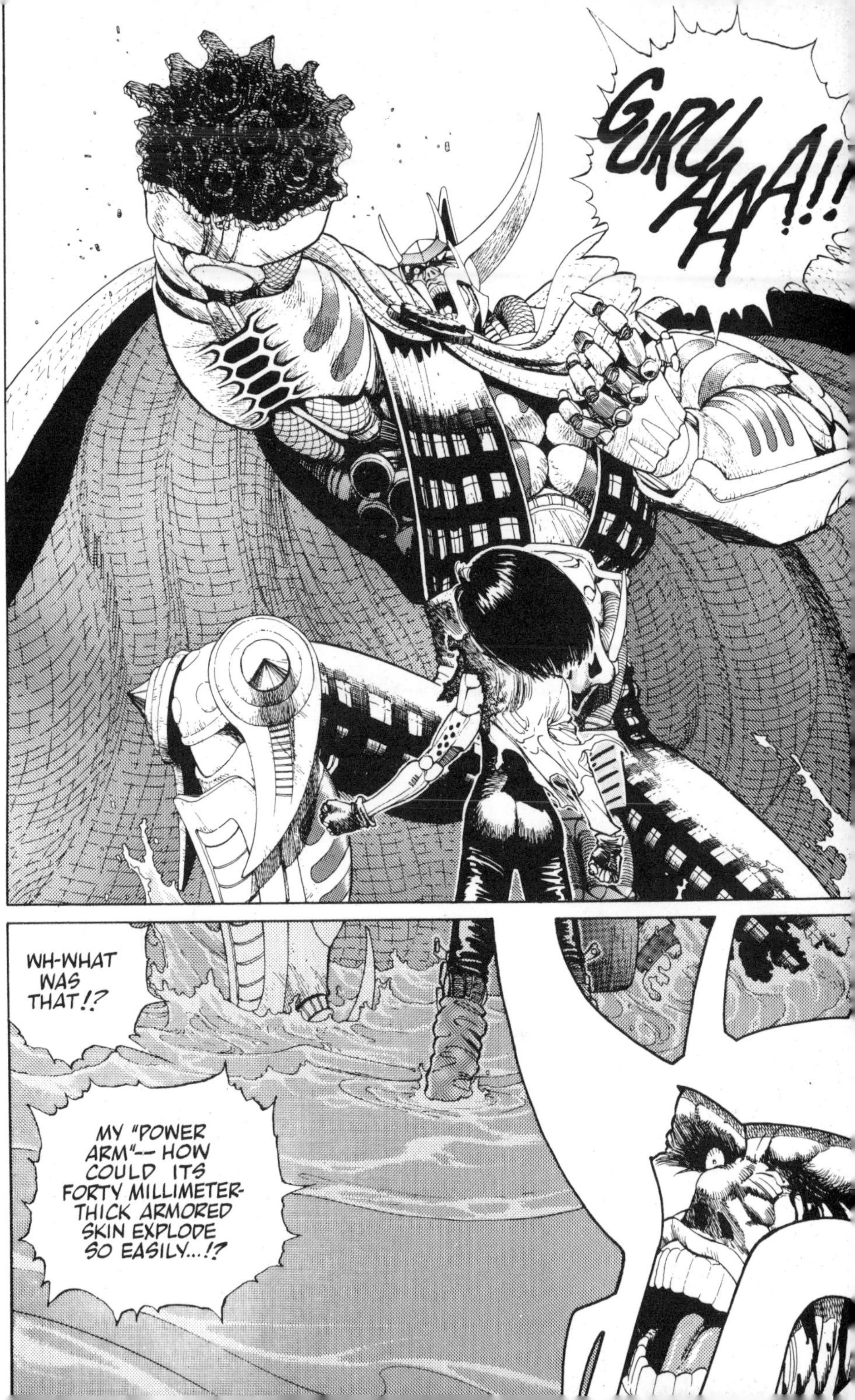
GURUAAA!!
WH-WHAT WAS THAT!?
MY "POWER ARM"-- HOW COULD ITS FORTY MILLIMETER-THICK ARMORED SKIN EXPLODE SO EASILY...!?

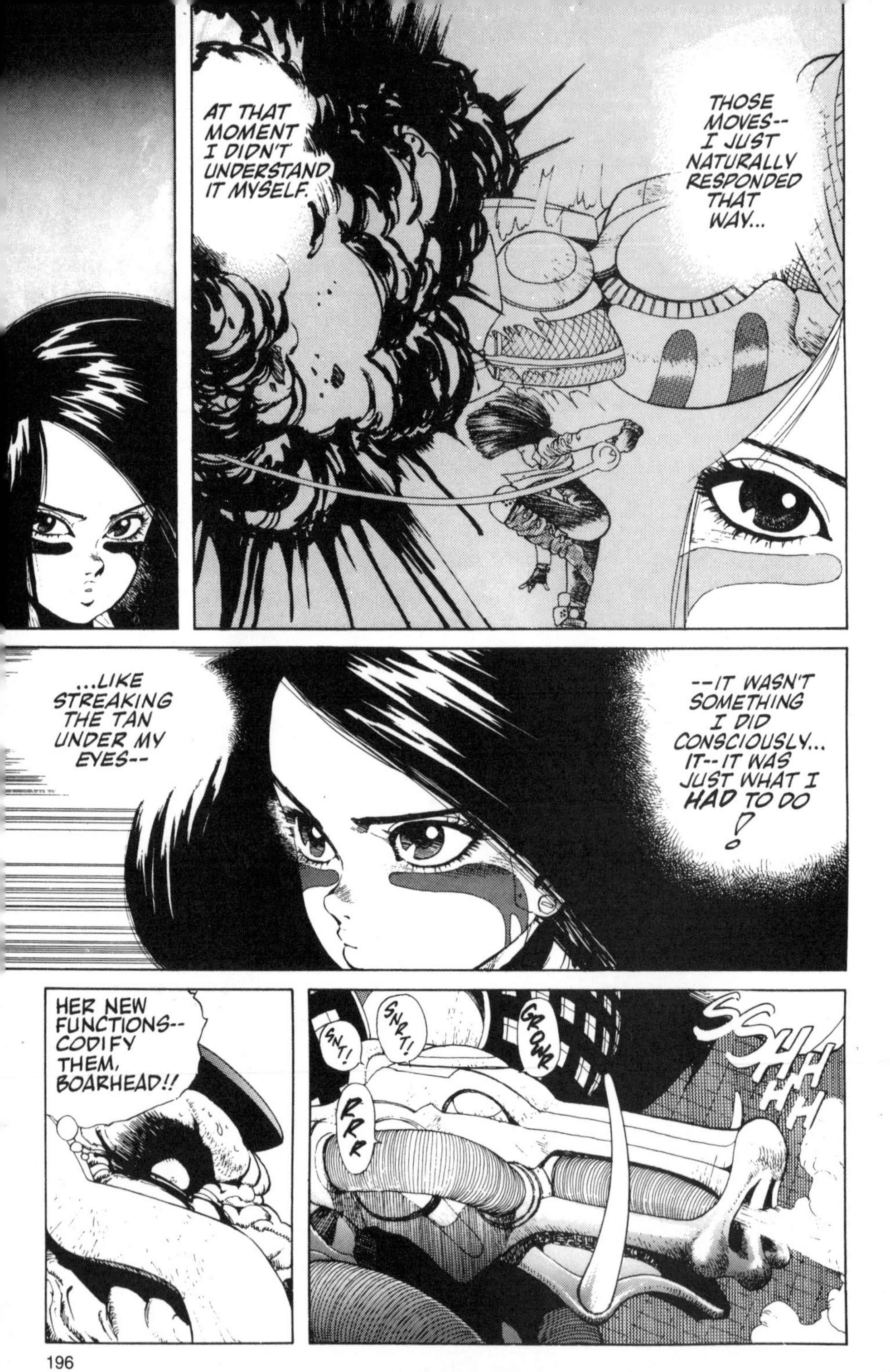
AT THAT MOMENT I DIDN'T UNDERSTAND IT MYSELF.
THOSE MOVES-- I JUST NATURALLY RESPONDED THAT WAY...
...LIKE STREAKING THE TAN UNDER MY EYES--
--IT WASN'T SOMETHING I DID CONSCIOUSLY... IT-- IT WAS JUST WHAT I HAD TO DO!
HER NEW FUNCTIONS-- CODIFY THEM, BOARHEAD!!
SNT!
SNRT!
GROWR
RRR
SSHHHH!

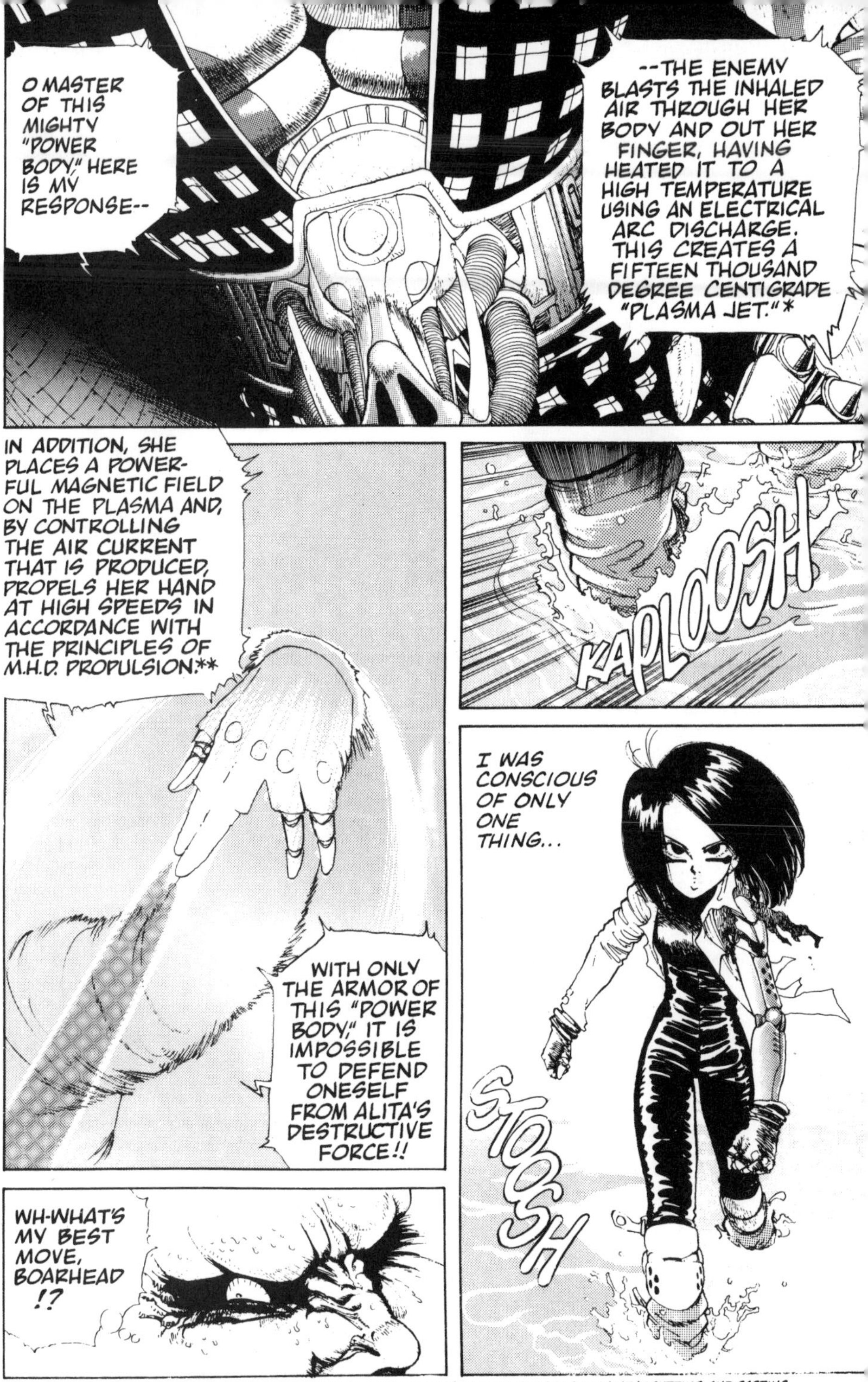
O MASTER OF THIS MIGHTY "POWER BODY," HERE IS MY RESPONSE--
--THE ENEMY BLASTS THE INHALED AIR THROUGH HER BODY AND OUT HER FINGER, HAVING HEATED IT TO A HIGH TEMPERATURE USING AN ELECTRICAL ARC DISCHARGE. THIS CREATES A FIFTEEN THOUSAND DEGREE CENTIGRADE "PLASMA JET."*
IN ADDITION, SHE PLACES A POWERFUL MAGNETIC FIELD ON THE PLASMA AND, BY CONTROLLING THE AIR CURRENT THAT IS PRODUCED, PROPELS HER HAND AT HIGH SPEEDS IN ACCORDANCE WITH THE PRINCIPLES OF M.H.D. PROPULSION.**
WITH ONLY THE ARMOR OF THIS "POWER BODY," IT IS IMPOSSIBLE TO DEFEND ONESELF FROM ALITA'S DESTRUCTIVE FORCE!!
KAPLOOSH
I WAS CONSCIOUS OF ONLY ONE THING...
STOOSH
WH-WHAT'S MY BEST MOVE, BOARHEAD !?

*PLASMA JET: A HIGH-SPEED JET OF HIGH-TEMPERATURE IONIZED GAS. A TECHNOLOGY USED IN HEAT-CUTTING AND CASTING.

**M.H.D. PROPULSION: A TYPE OF PROPULSION WHICH APPLIES MAGNETOHYDRODYNAMICS TO ELECTRICITY-CONDUCTING PLASMA.

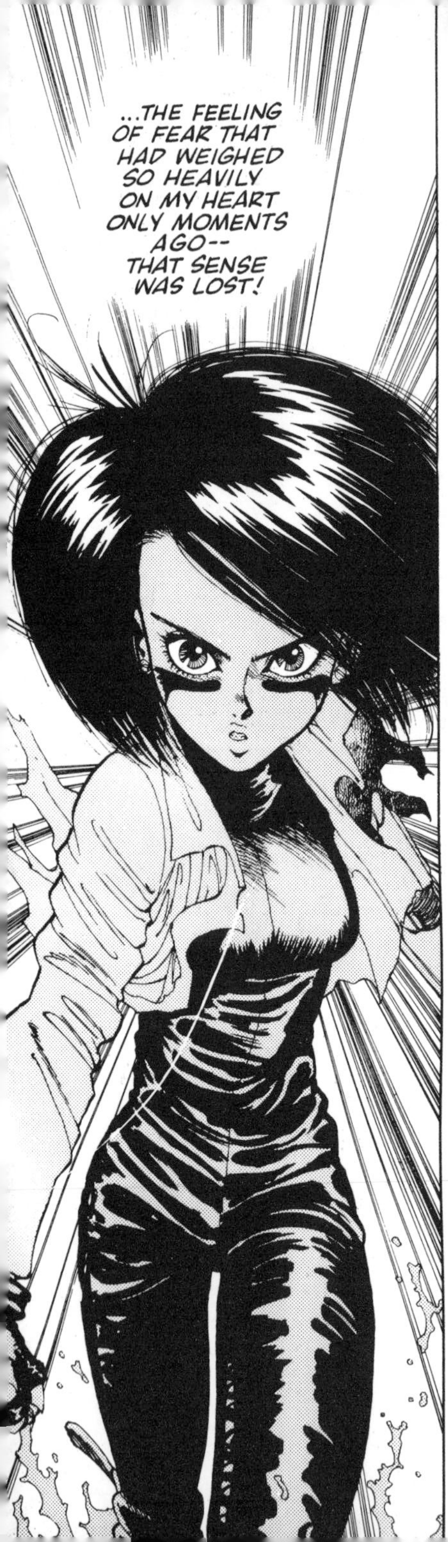
...THE FEELING OF FEAR THAT HAD WEIGHED SO HEAVILY ON MY HEART ONLY MOMENTS AGO-- THAT SENSE WAS LOST!
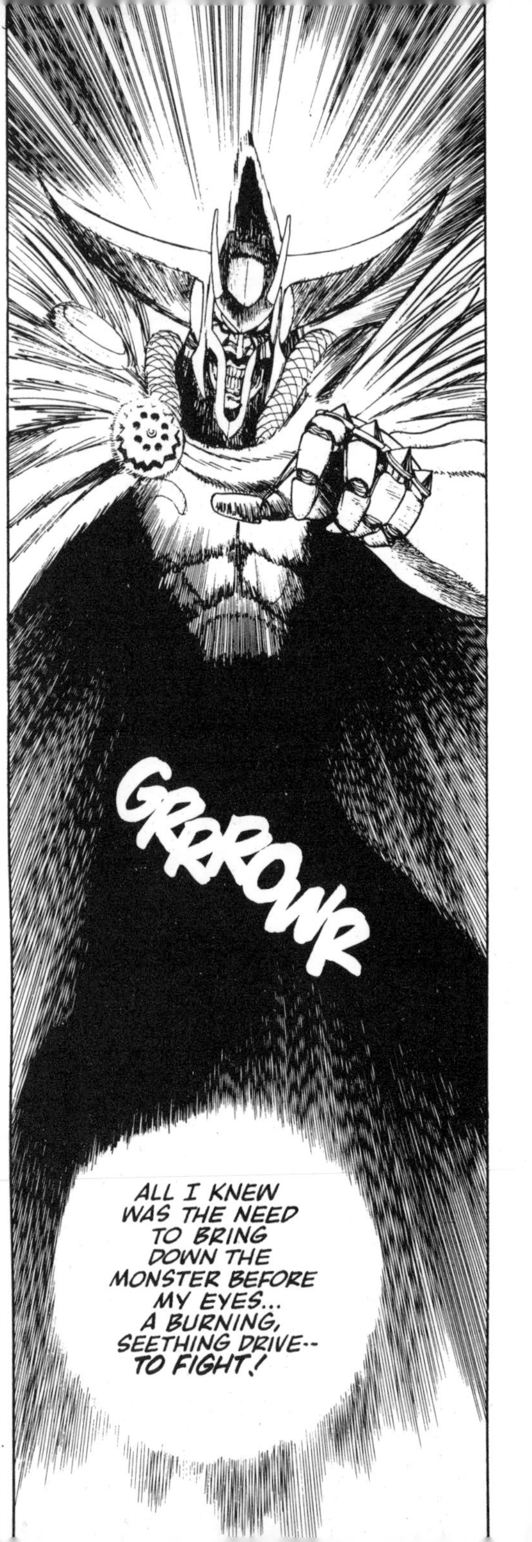
GRRROWR
ALL I KNEW WAS THE NEED TO BRING DOWN THE MONSTER BEFORE MY EYES... A BURNING, SEETHING DRIVE-- TO FIGHT!

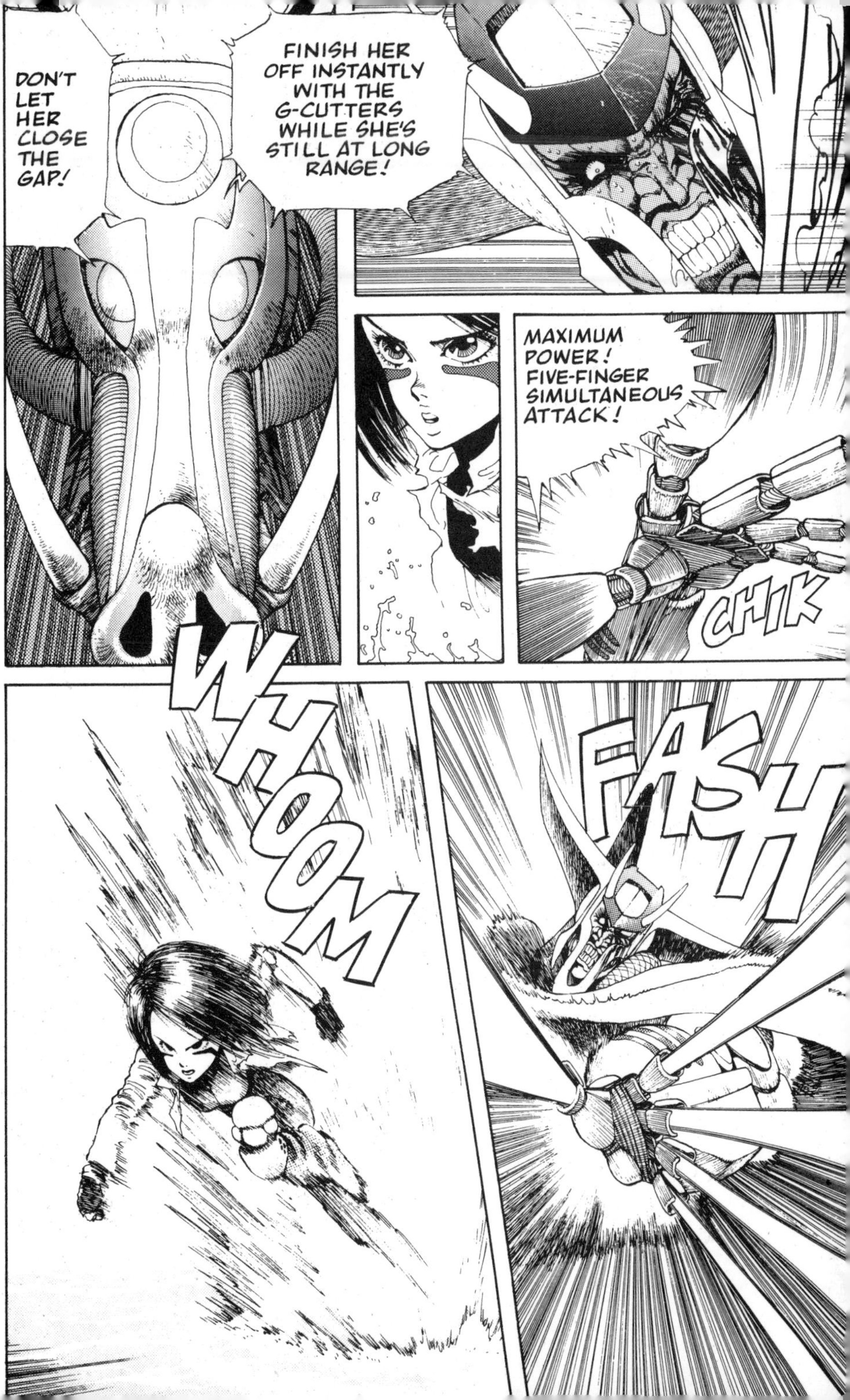
DON'T LET HER CLOSE THE GAP!
FINISH HER OFF INSTANTLY WITH THE G-CUTTERS WHILE SHE'S STILL AT LONG RANGE!
MAXIMUM POWER! FIVE-FINGER SIMULTANEOUS ATTACK!
CHIK
WHOOM
FASH

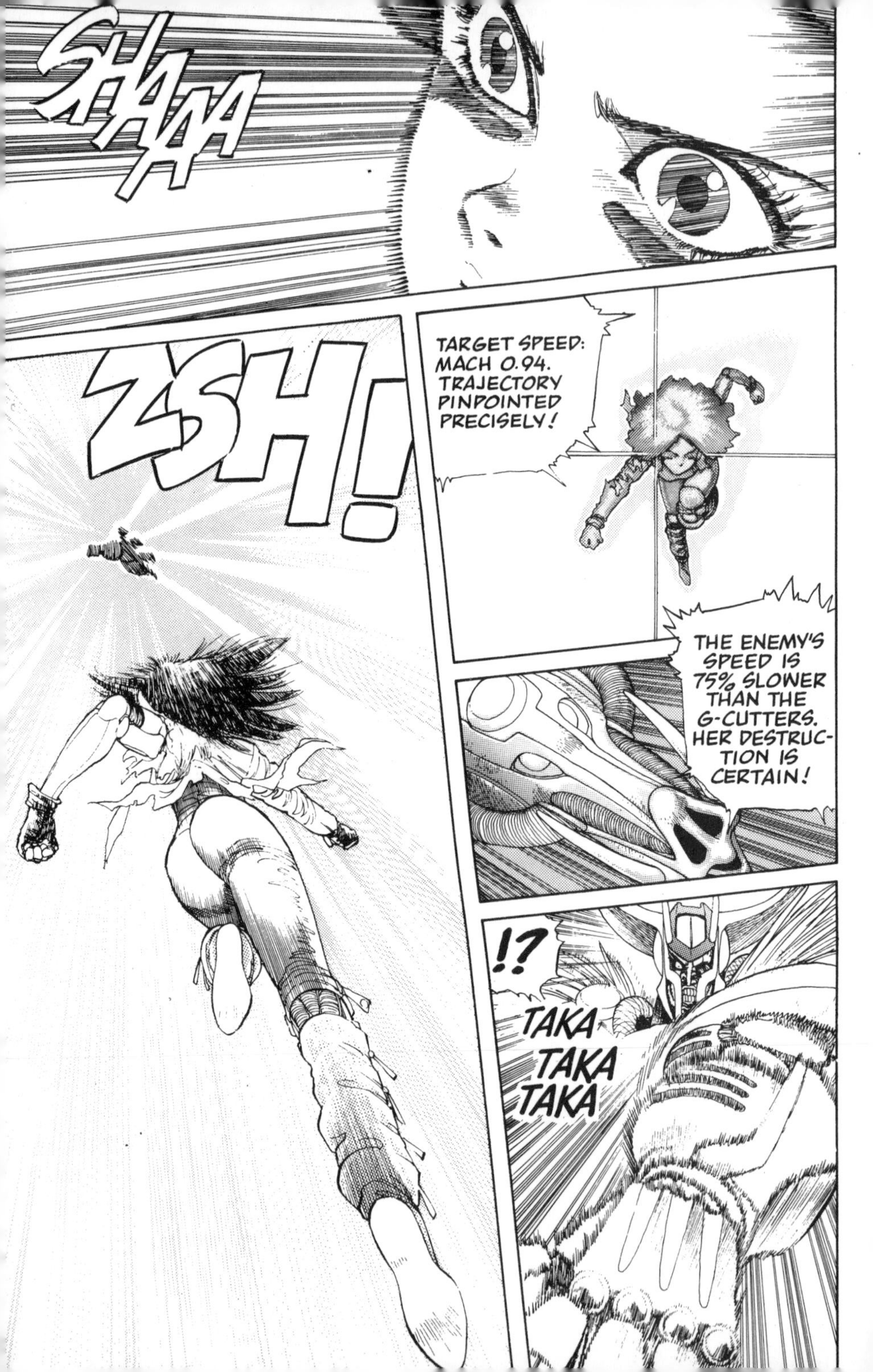
SHAAAA
ZSH!
TARGET SPEED: MACH 0.94. TRAJECTORY PINPOINTED PRECISELY!
THE ENEMY'S SPEED IS 75% SLOWER THAN THE G-CUTTERS. HER DESTRUCTION IS CERTAIN!
!?
TAKA TAKA TAKA

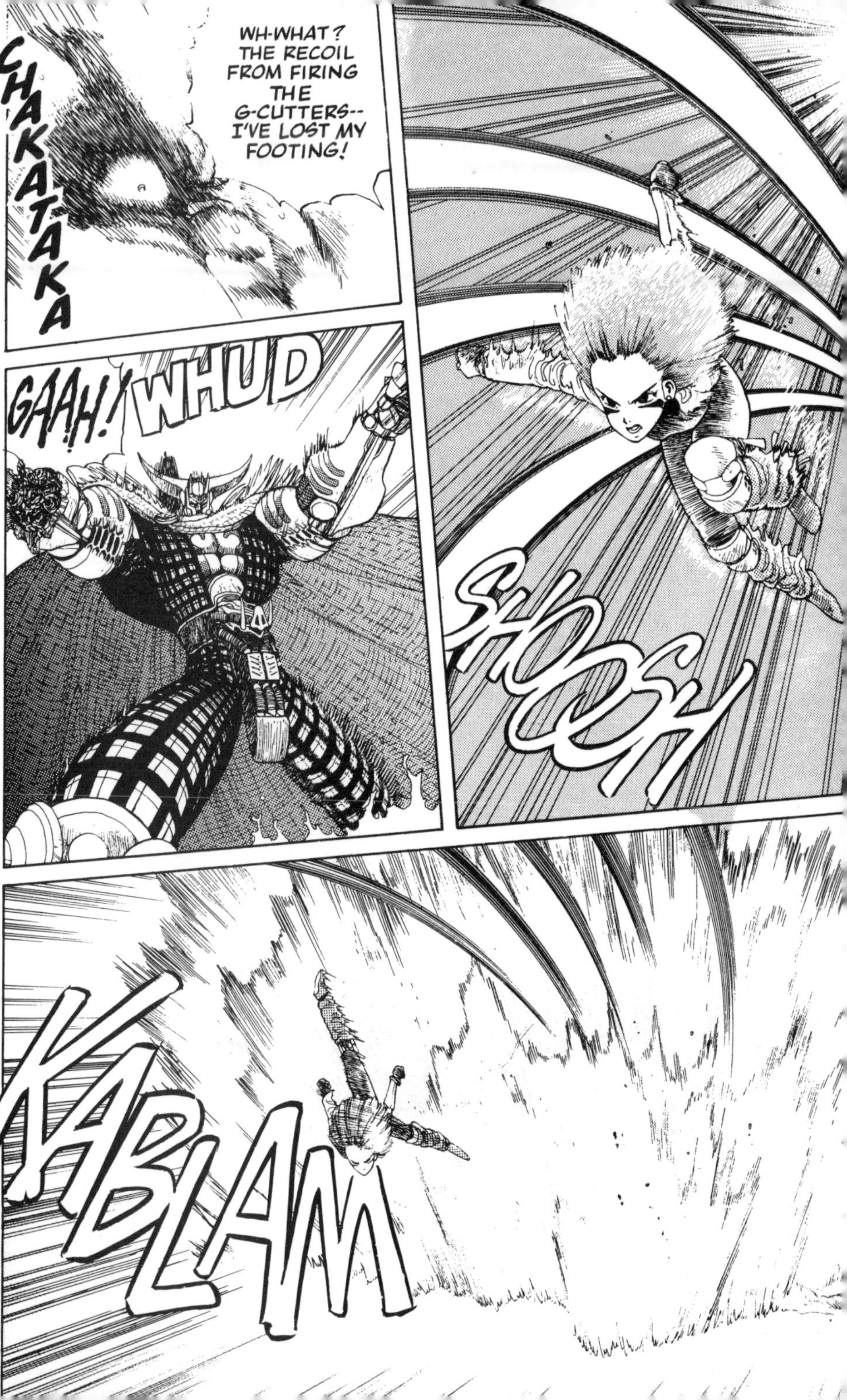
CHAKATAKA
WH-WHAT? THE RECOIL FROM FIRING THE G-CUTTERS-- I'VE LOST MY FOOTING!
GAAH!
WHUD
SHOOSH
KABLAM

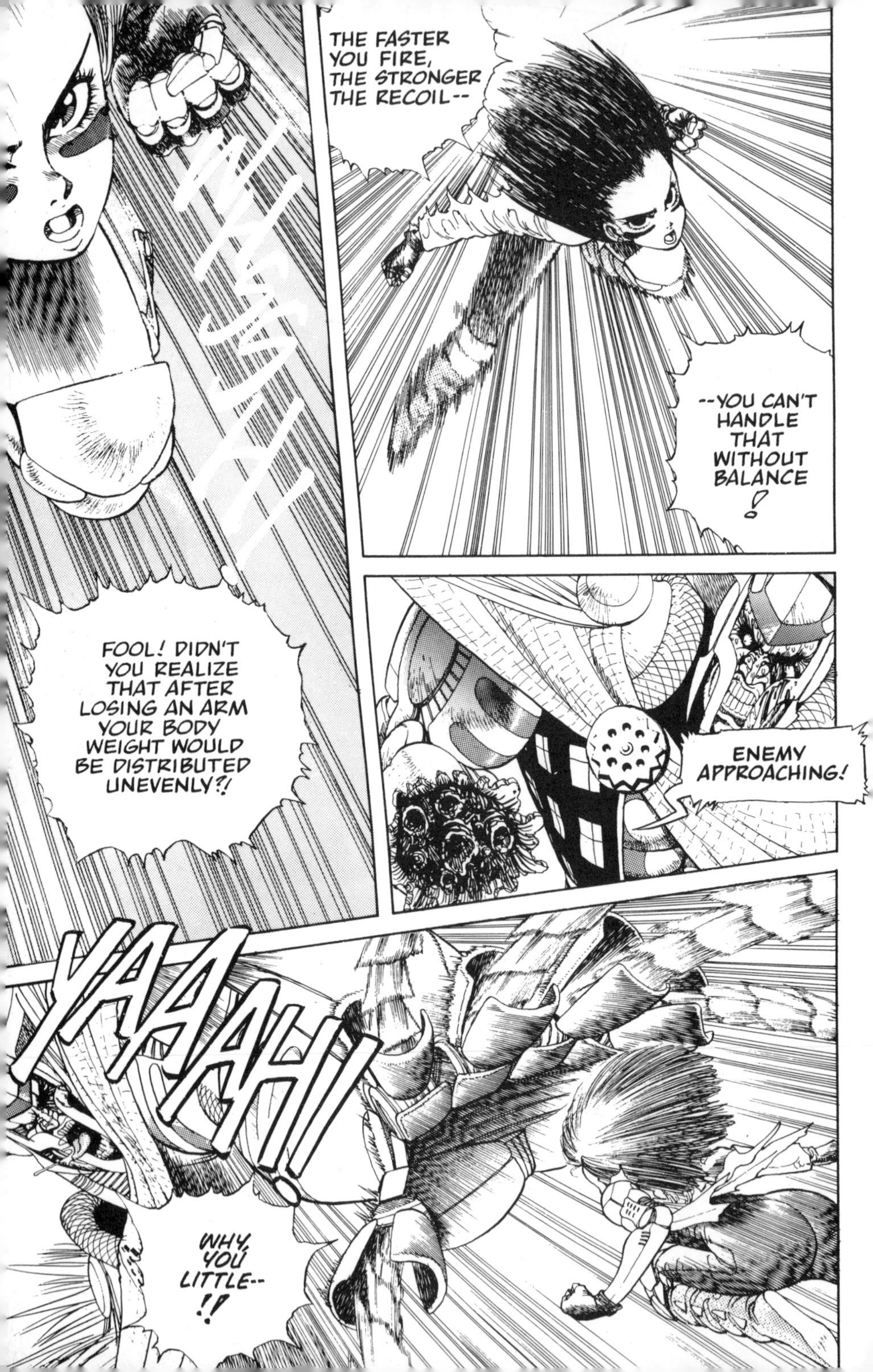
FOOL! DIDN'T YOU REALIZE THAT AFTER LOSING AN ARM YOUR BODY WEIGHT WOULD BE DISTRIBUTED UNEVENLY?!
THE FASTER YOU FIRE, THE STRONGER THE RECOIL--
--YOU CAN'T HANDLE THAT WITHOUT BALANCE!
ENEMY APPROACHING!
YAAAHH!
WHY, YOU LITTLE--!!

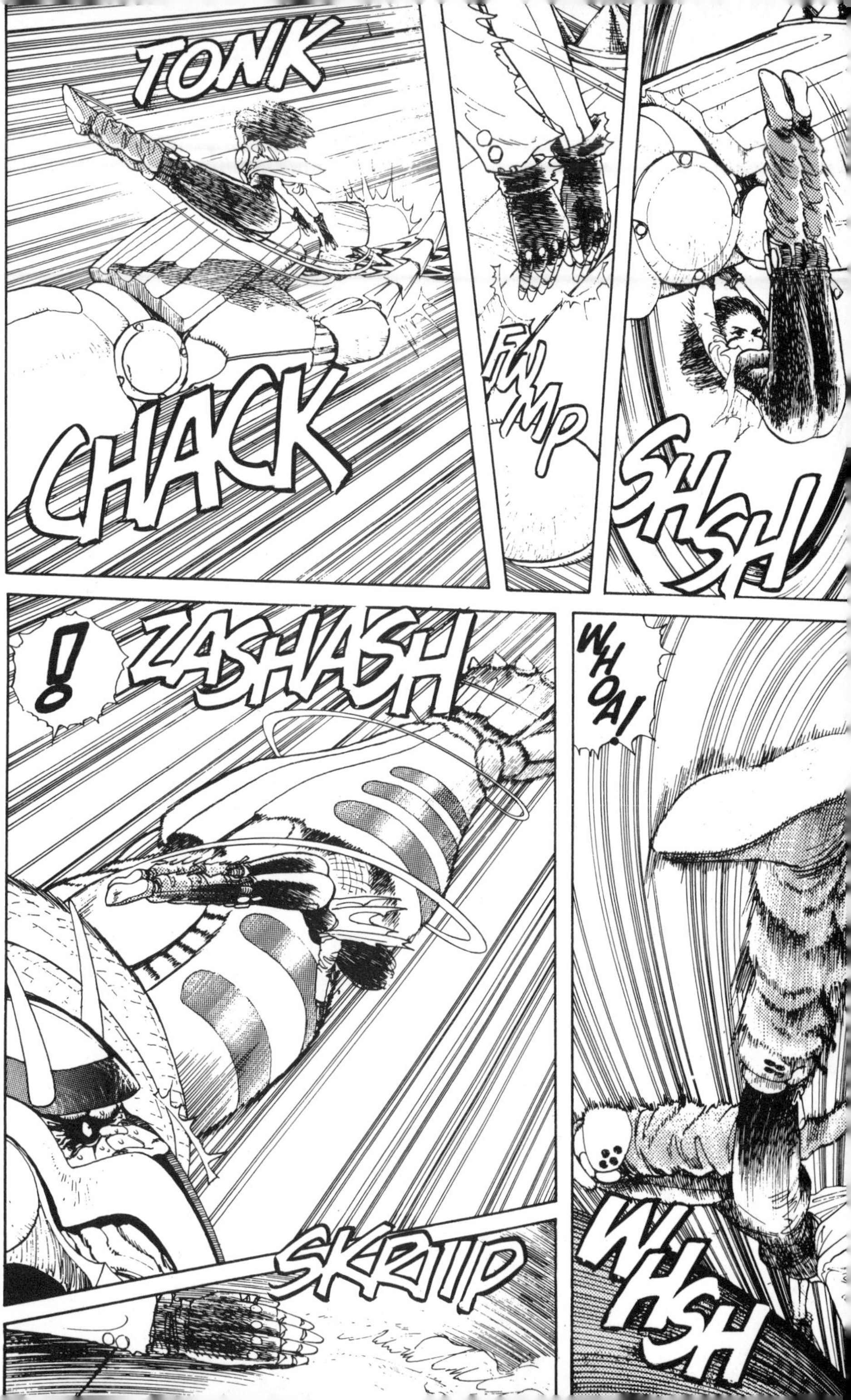
TONK
CHACK
FWUMP
SHSH
!
ZASHASH
SKRTTP
WHOA!
WHSH

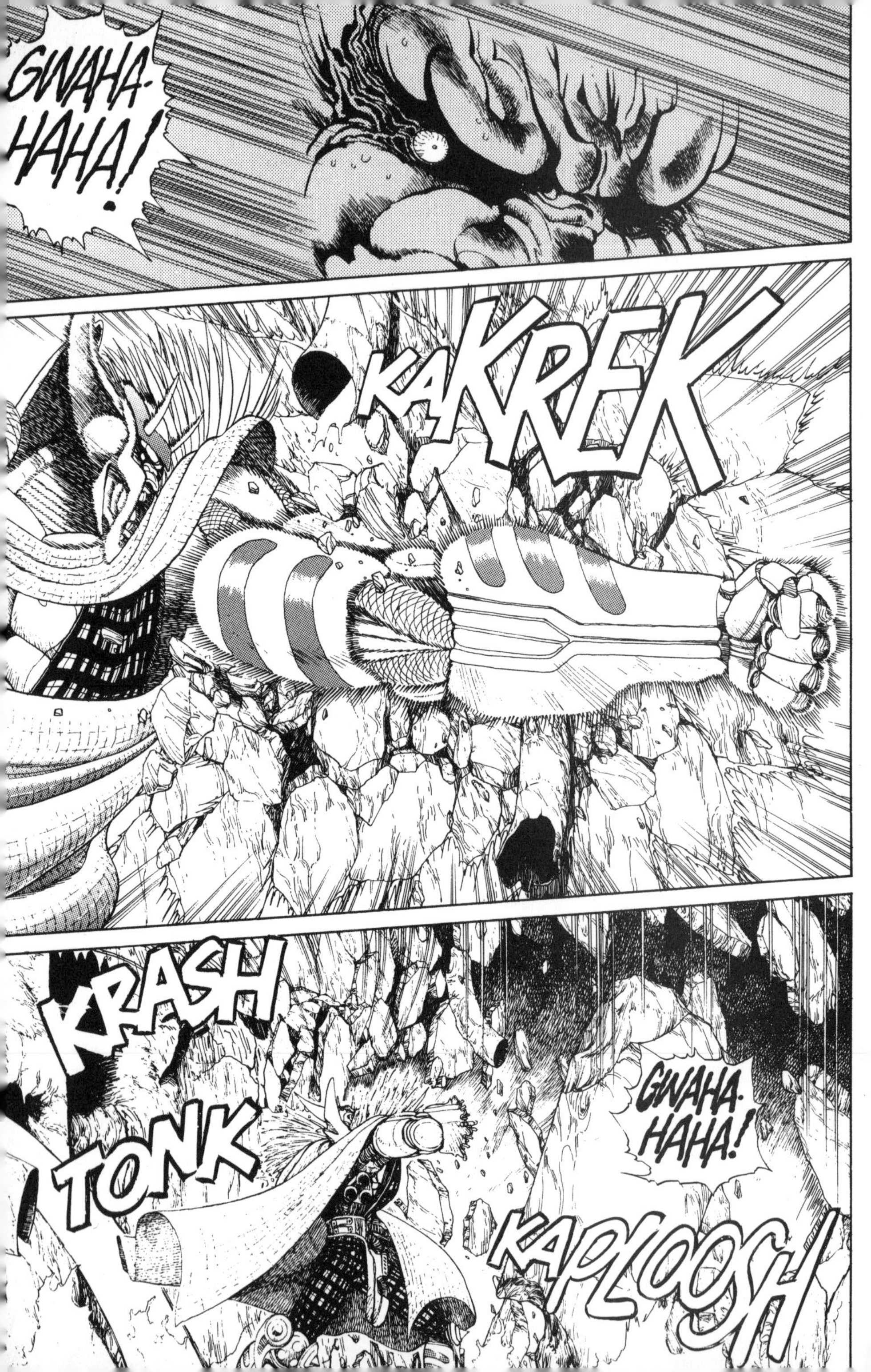
GWAHA-HAHA!
KAKREK
KRASH
TONK
GWAHA-HAHA!
KAPLOOSH

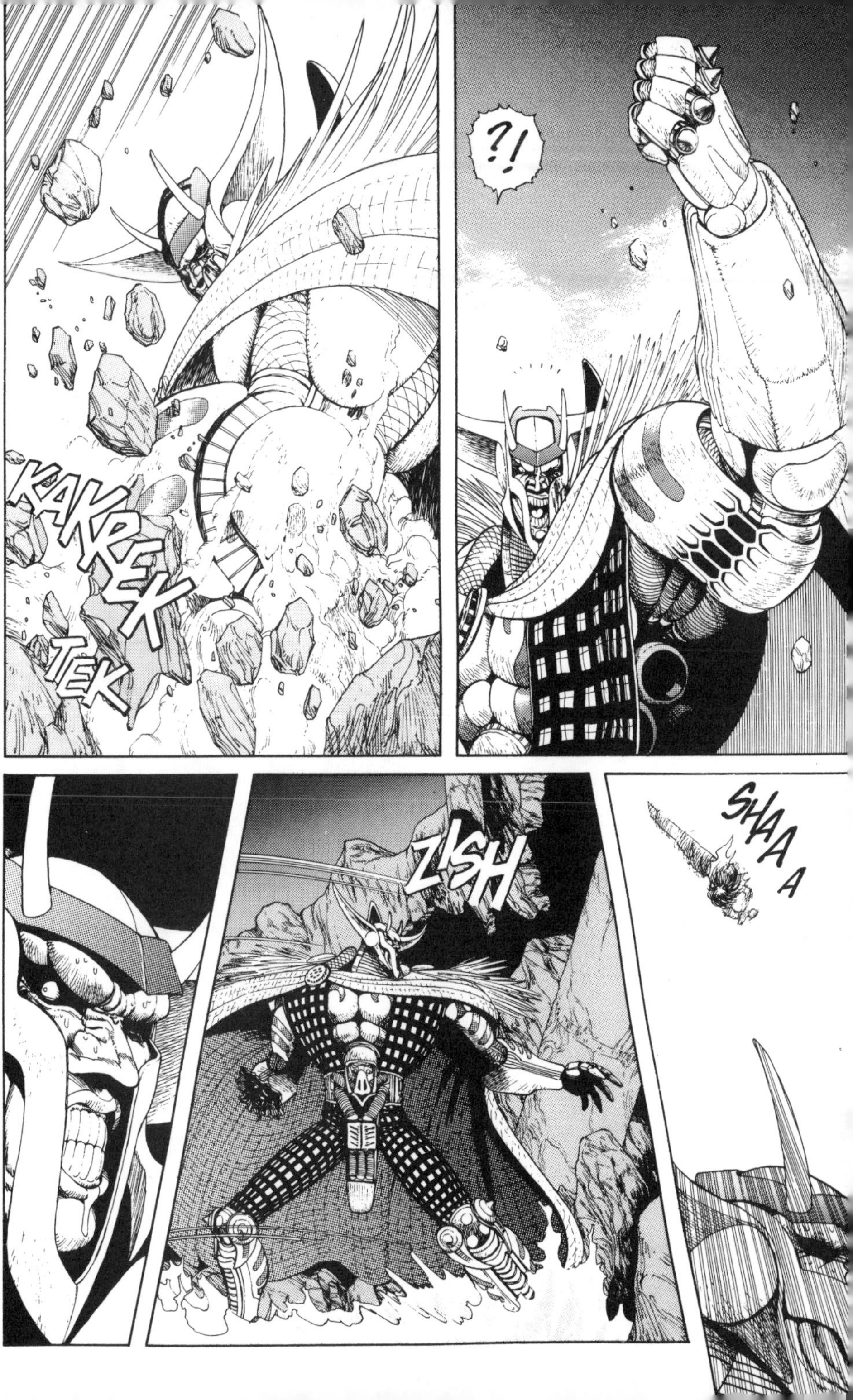
KAKREK
TEK
?!
ZISH
SHAAA
A

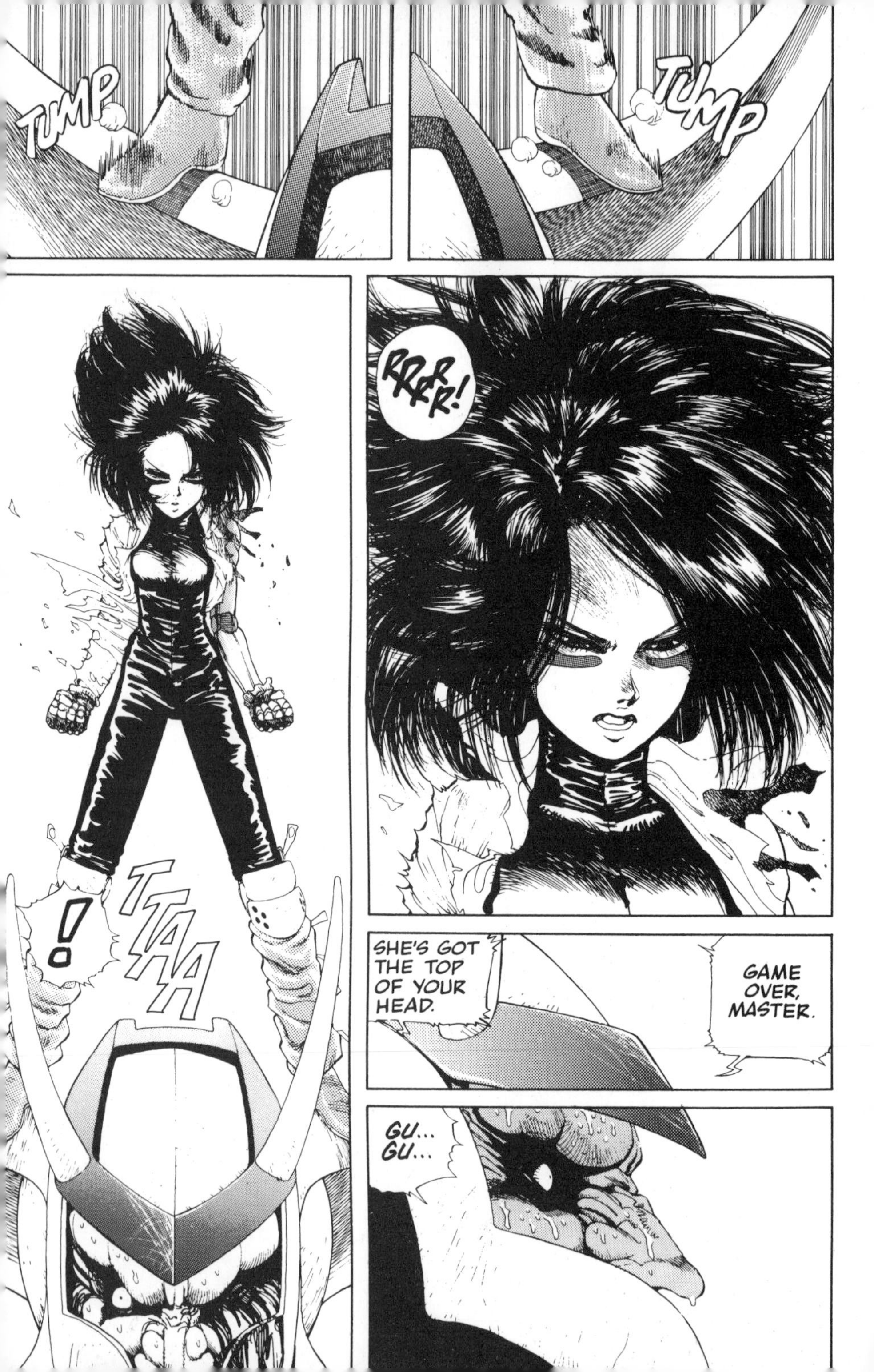
TUMP
TUMP
!
TTAAA
RRRRR!
SHE'S GOT THE TOP OF YOUR HEAD.
GAME OVER, MASTER.
GU... GU...

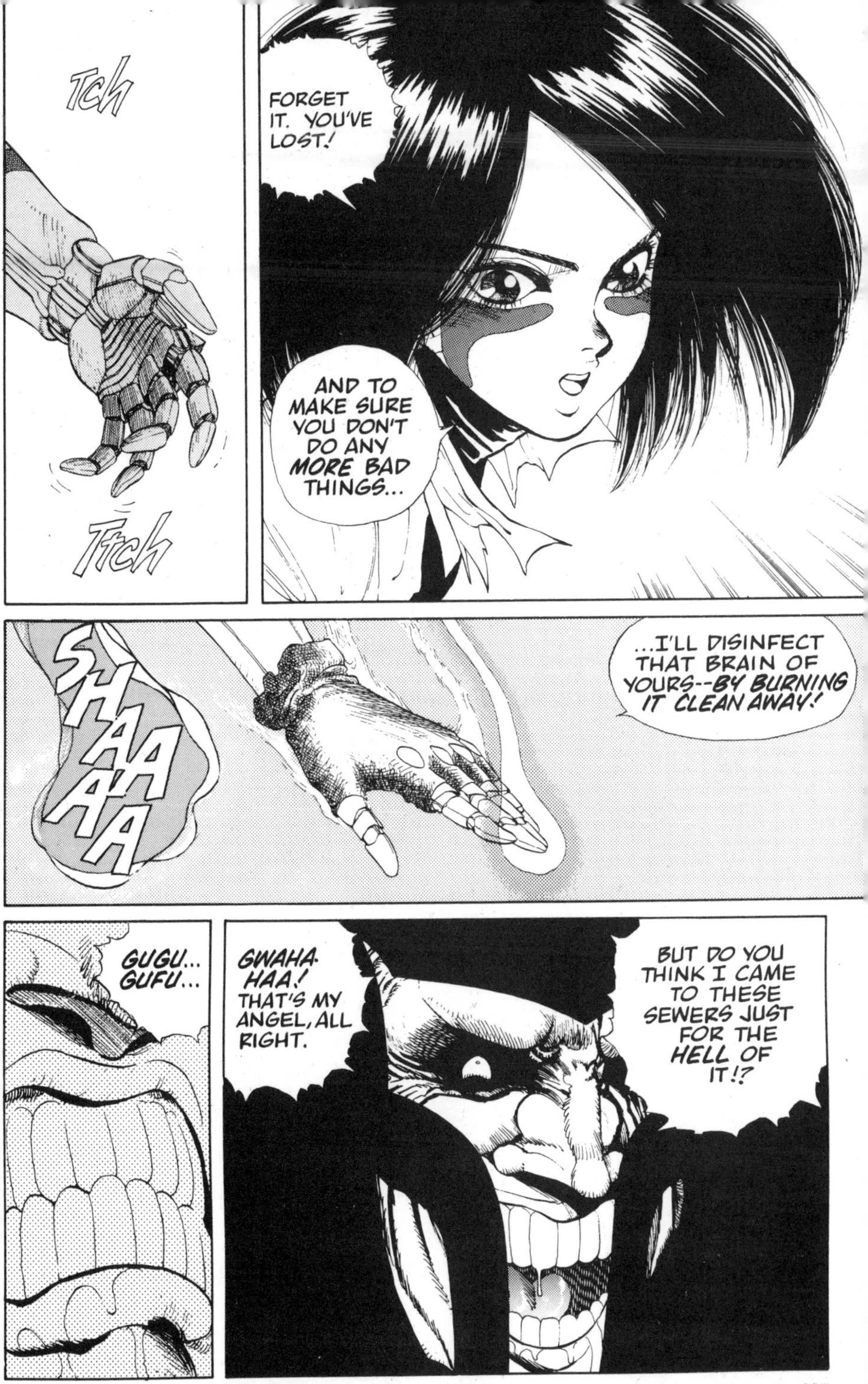
Tch
Ttch
FORGET IT. YOU'VE LOST!
AND TO MAKE SURE YOU DON'T DO ANY MORE BAD THINGS...
SHAAAAAA
...I'LL DISINFECT THAT BRAIN OF YOURS--BY BURNING IT CLEAN AWAY!
GUGU... GUFU...
GWAHA-HAA! THAT'S MY ANGEL, ALL RIGHT.
BUT DO YOU THINK I CAME TO THESE SEWERS JUST FOR THE HELL OF IT!?

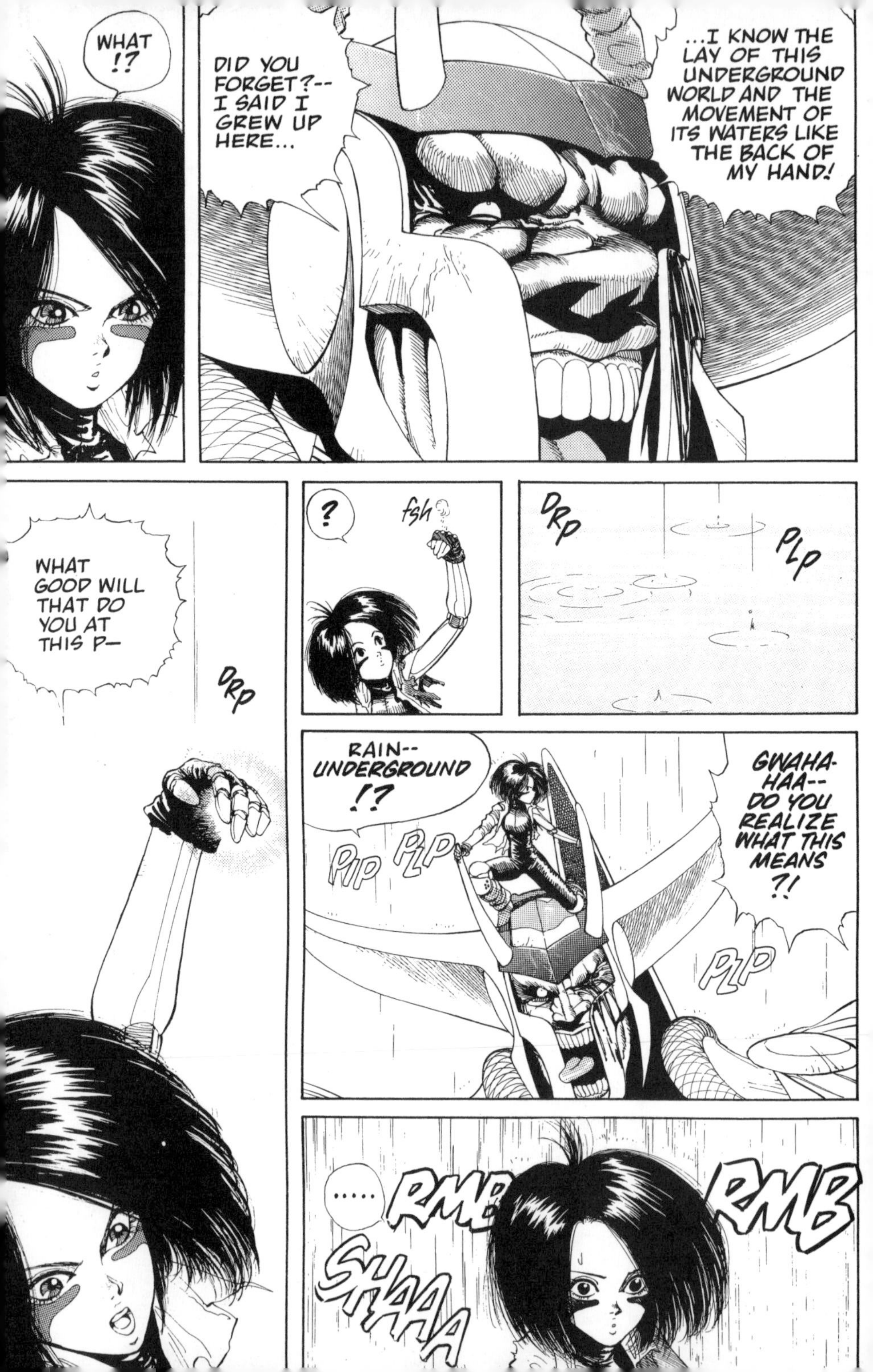
WHAT !?
DID YOU FORGET?-- I SAID I GREW UP HERE...
...I KNOW THE LAY OF THIS UNDERGROUND WORLD AND THE MOVEMENT OF ITS WATERS LIKE THE BACK OF MY HAND!
WHAT GOOD WILL THAT DO YOU AT THIS P—
DRP
?
fsh
DRP
PLP
RAIN-- UNDERGROUND !?
PLP
PLP
GWAHAHAA-- DO YOU REALIZE WHAT THIS MEANS ?!
PLP
.....
RMB
RMB
SHAAA

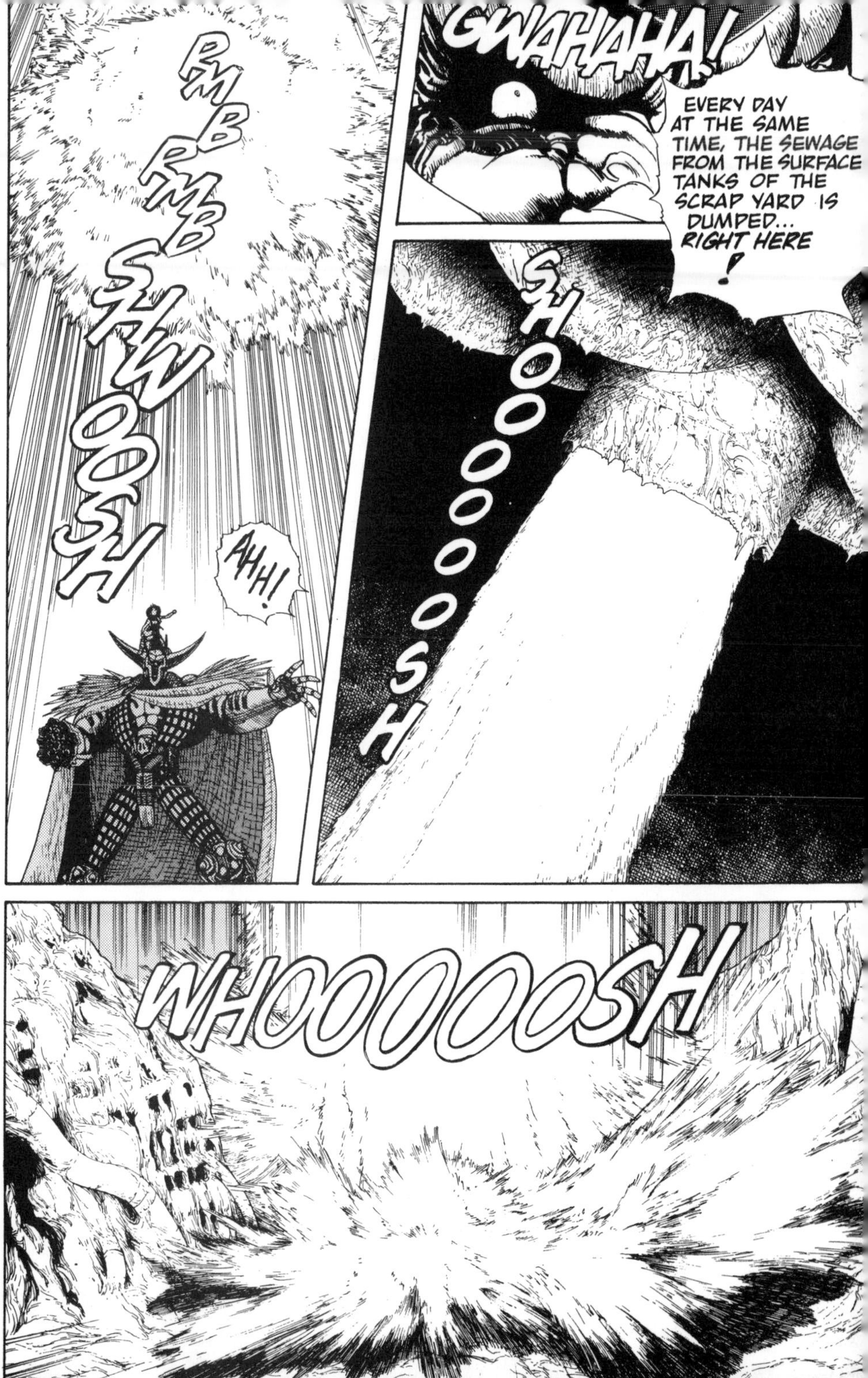
RMB
RMB
SHWOOOSH
AHH!
GWAHAHA!
EVERY DAY AT THE SAME TIME, THE SEWAGE FROM THE SURFACE TANKS OF THE SCRAP YARD IS DUMPED... RIGHT HERE!
SHOOOOOOOSH
WHOOOOOOSH

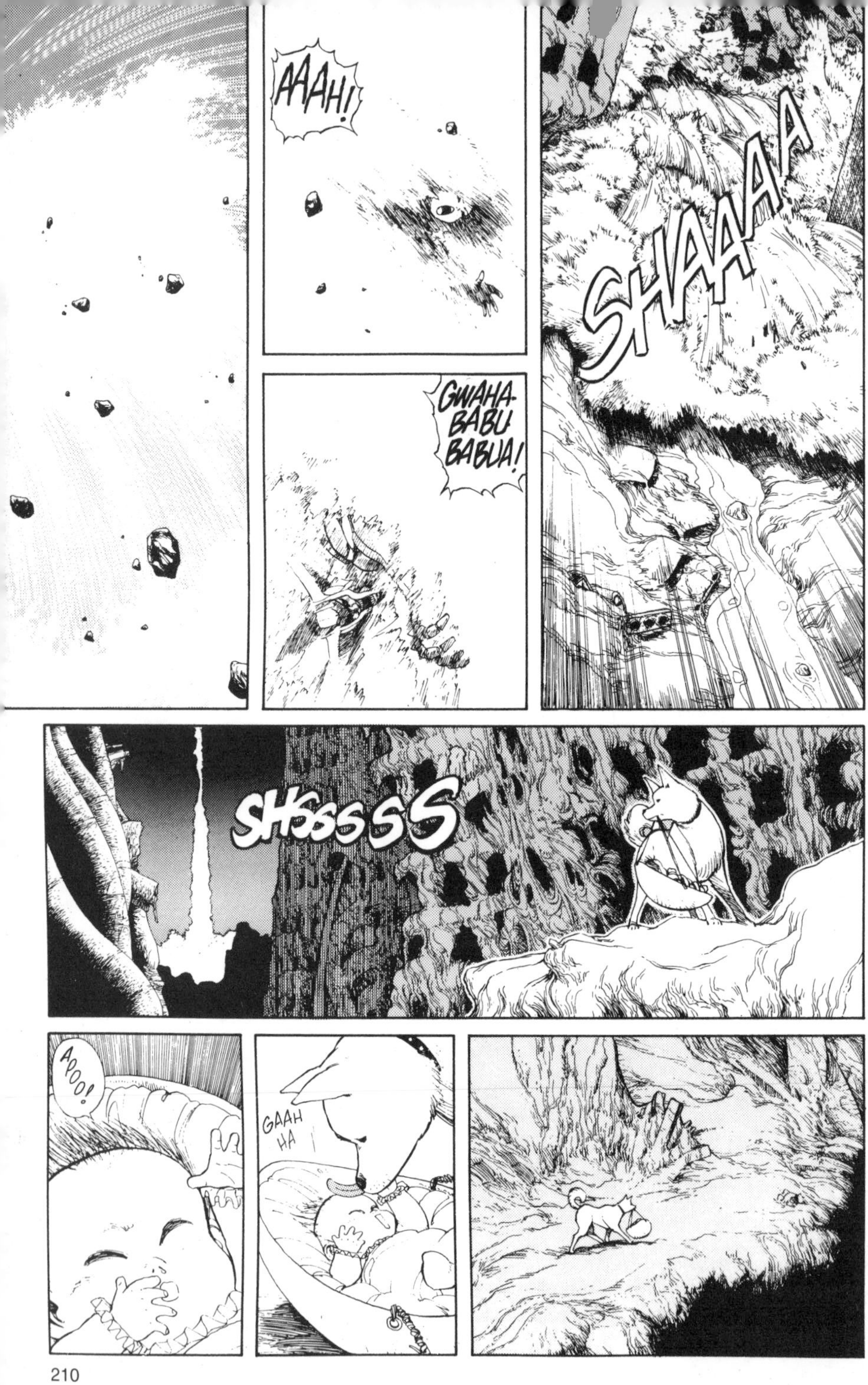
AAAH!
SHAAAA
GWAHA-BABU-BABUA!
SHSSSSS
APOO!
GAAH HA

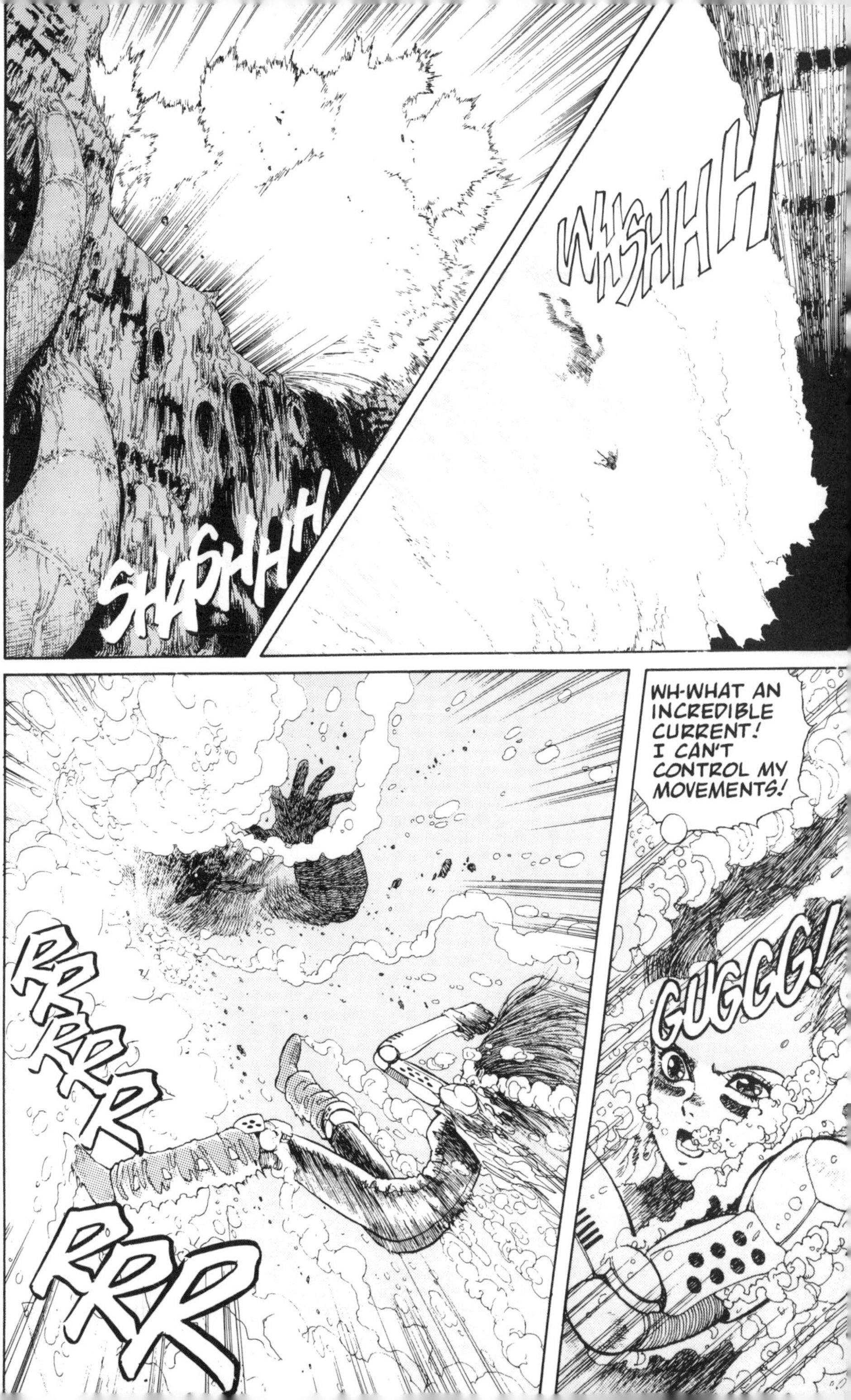
SHASHHH
WHSHHH
RRRRRRR
RRRR
WH-WHAT AN INCREDIBLE CURRENT! I CAN'T CONTROL MY MOVEMENTS!
GUGGG!

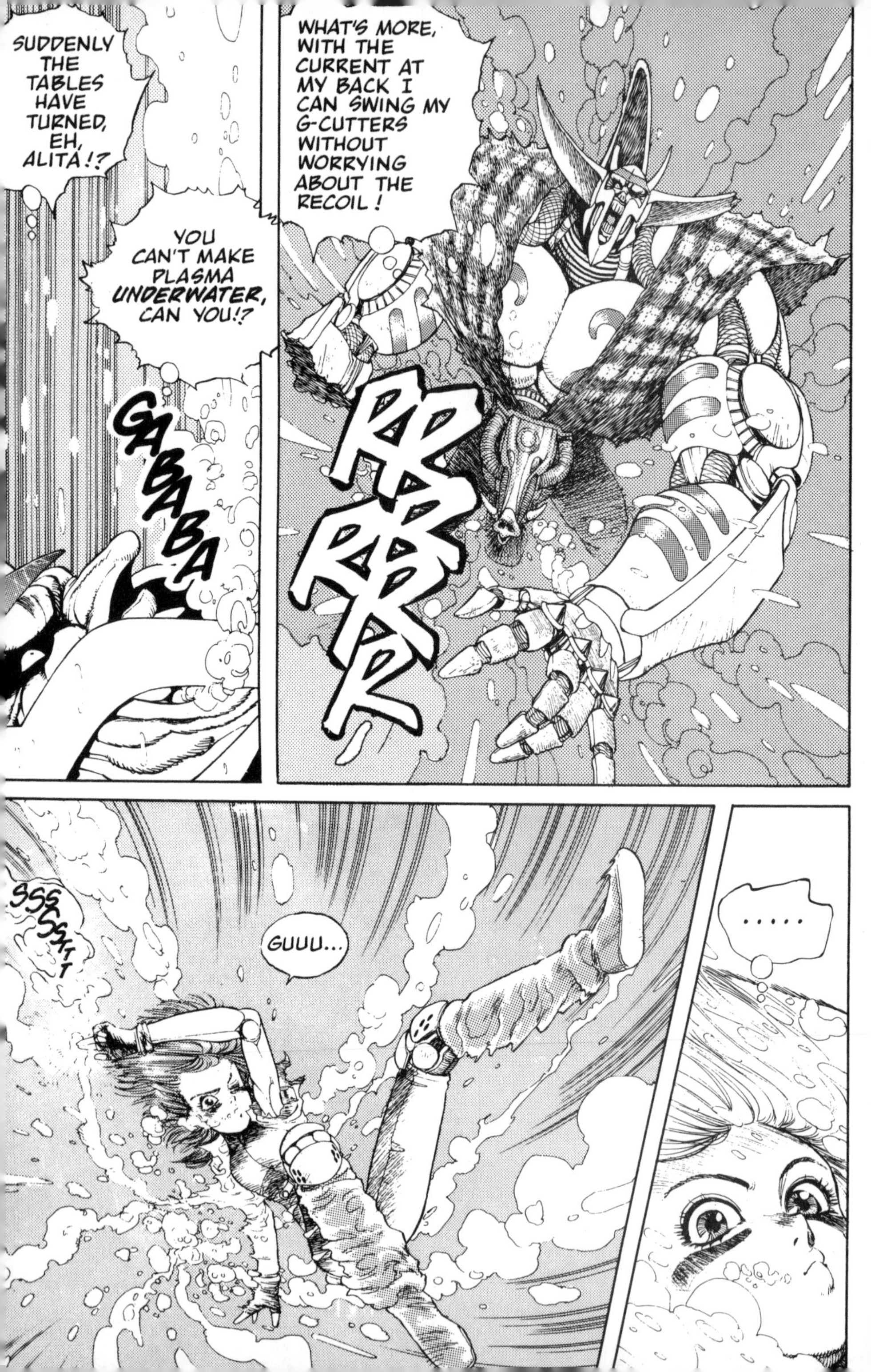
SUDDENLY THE TABLES HAVE TURNED, EH, ALITA!?
YOU CAN'T MAKE PLASMA UNDERWATER, CAN YOU!?
GABABA
WHAT'S MORE, WITH THE CURRENT AT MY BACK I CAN SWING MY G-CUTTERS WITHOUT WORRYING ABOUT THE RECOIL!
RRRRRR
SSSSSKTT
GUUU...
.....

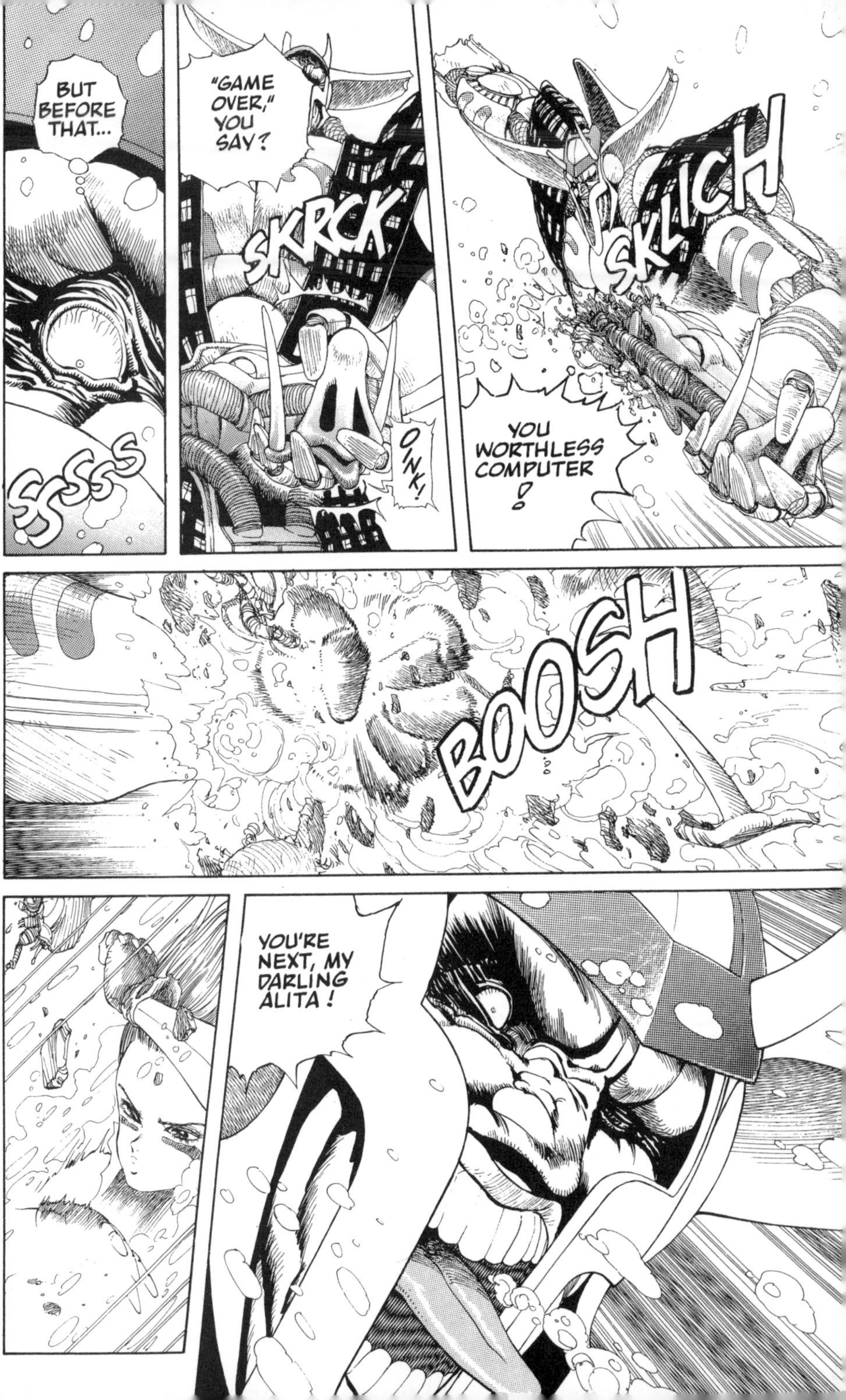
BUT BEFORE THAT...
SSSSS
"GAME OVER," YOU SAY?
SKRCK
OINK!
SKLICH
YOU WORTHLESS COMPUTER!
BOOSH
YOU'RE NEXT, MY DARLING ALITA!

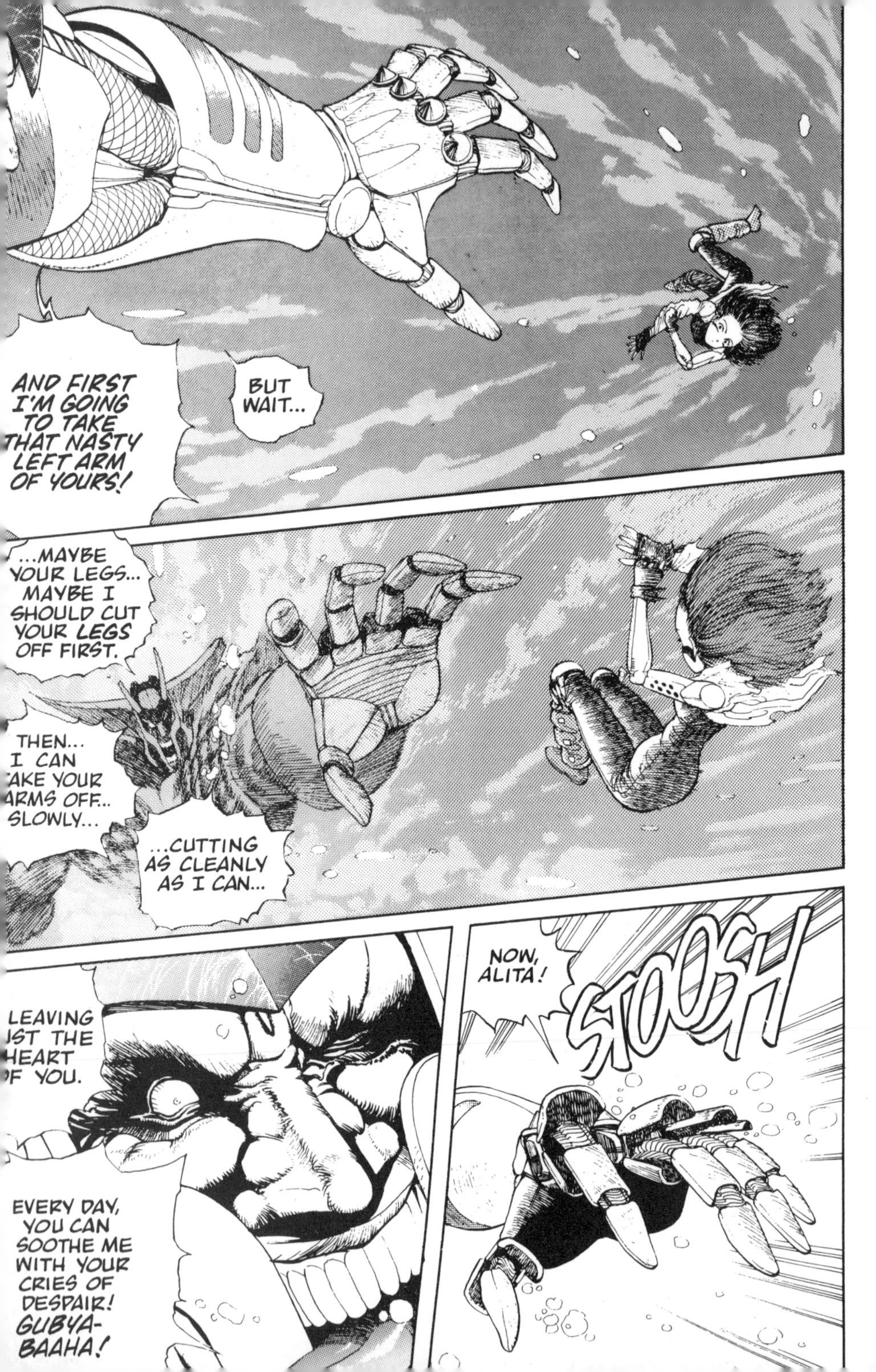
AND FIRST I'M GOING TO TAKE THAT NASTY LEFT ARM OF YOURS!
BUT WAIT...
...MAYBE YOUR LEGS... MAYBE I SHOULD CUT YOUR LEGS OFF FIRST.
THEN... I CAN TAKE YOUR ARMS OFF... SLOWLY...
...CUTTING AS CLEANLY AS I CAN...
LEAVING JUST THE HEART OF YOU.
EVERY DAY, YOU CAN SOOTHE ME WITH YOUR CRIES OF DESPAIR! GUBYA-BAAHA!
NOW, ALITA!
STOOSH

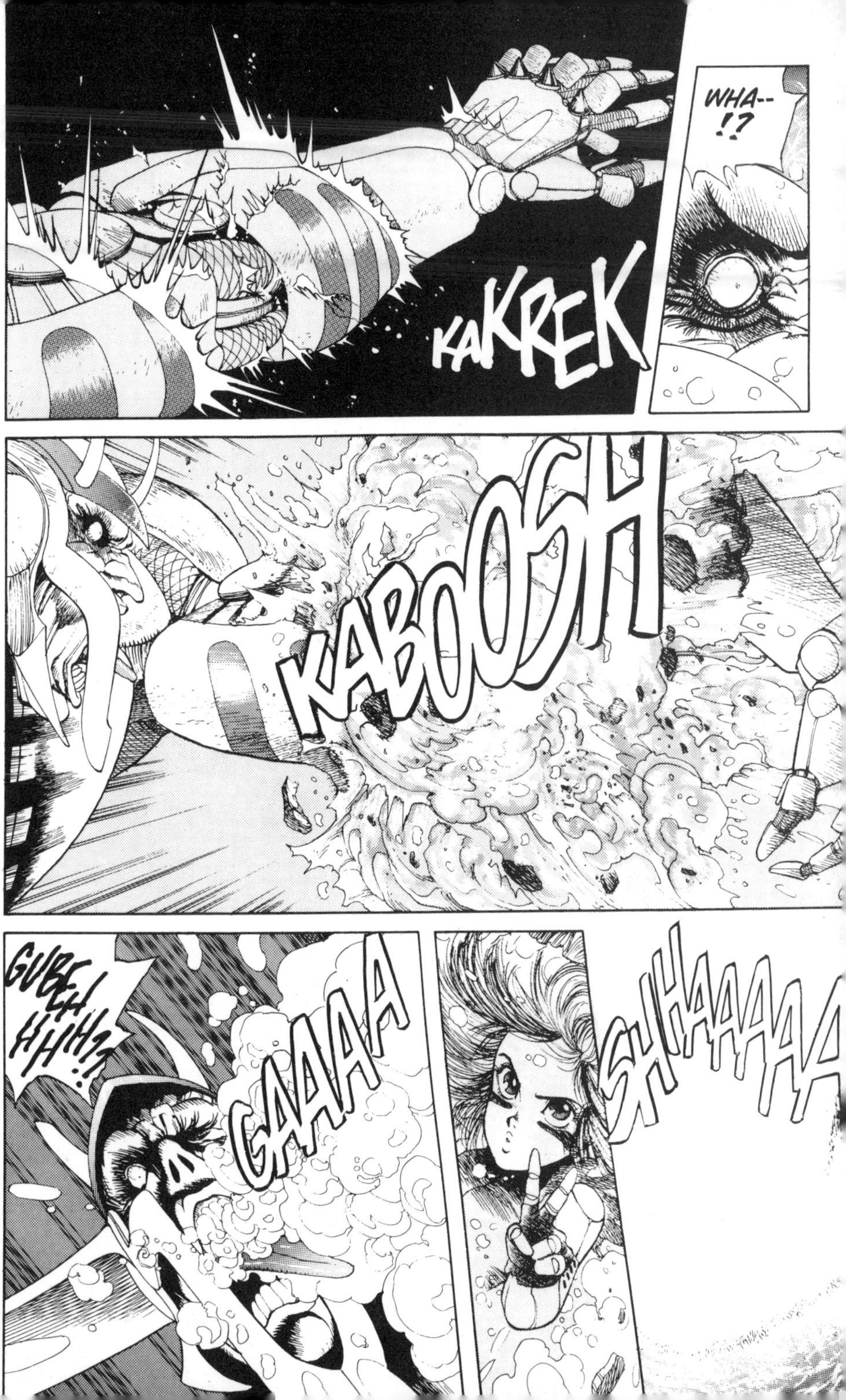
KAKREK
WHA--
!?
KABOOSH
GUBEH
HHH!?!
GAAAA
SHAAAAK

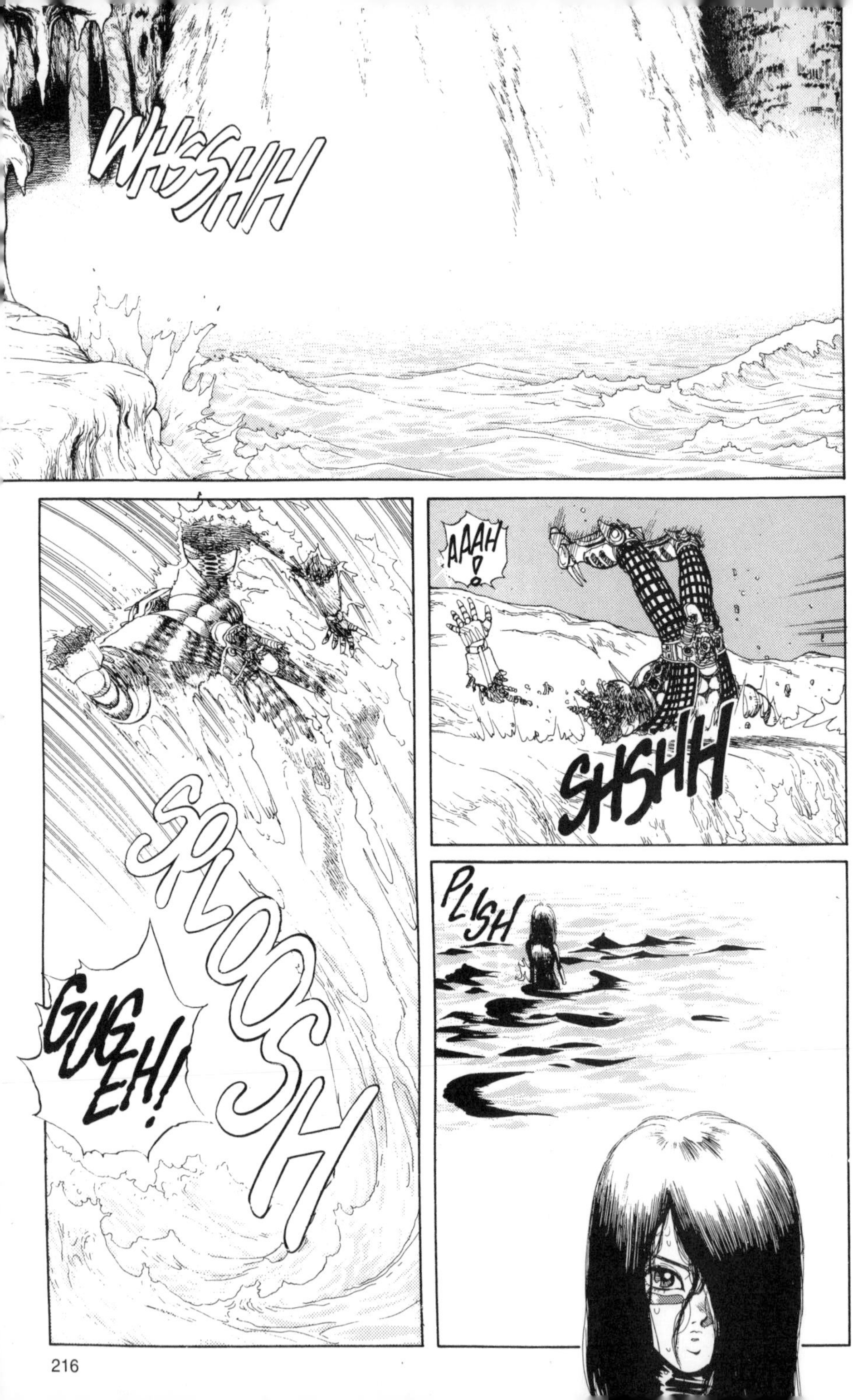
WHSSHH
SPLOOSH
GUGEH!
AAAH!
SHSHH
PLISH

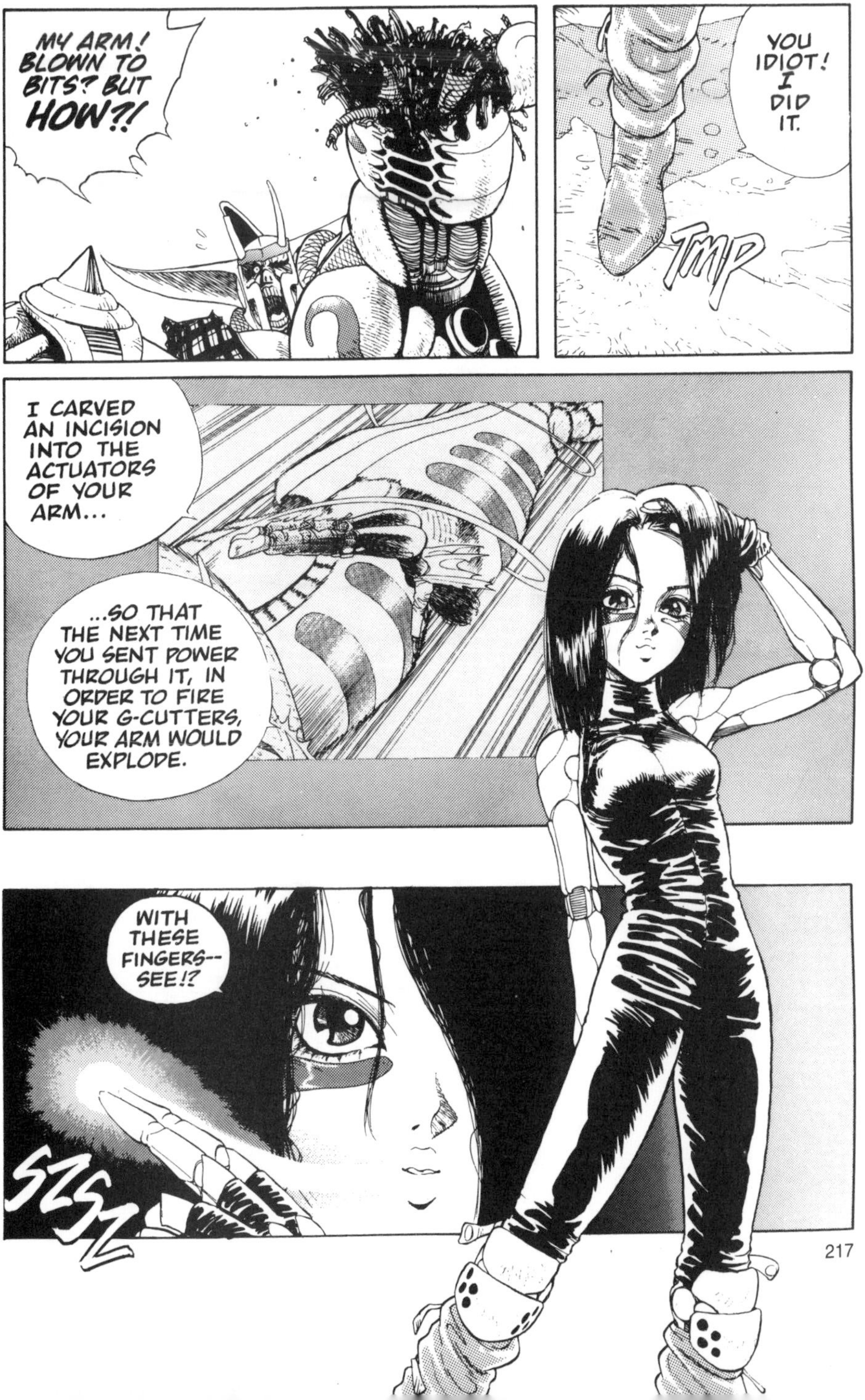
MY ARM! BLOWN TO BITS? BUT HOW?!
YOU IDIOT! I DID IT.
TMP
I CARVED AN INCISION INTO THE ACTUATORS OF YOUR ARM...
...SO THAT THE NEXT TIME YOU SENT POWER THROUGH IT, IN ORDER TO FIRE YOUR G-CUTTERS, YOUR ARM WOULD EXPLODE.
WITH THESE FINGERS-- SEE!?
SZSZ

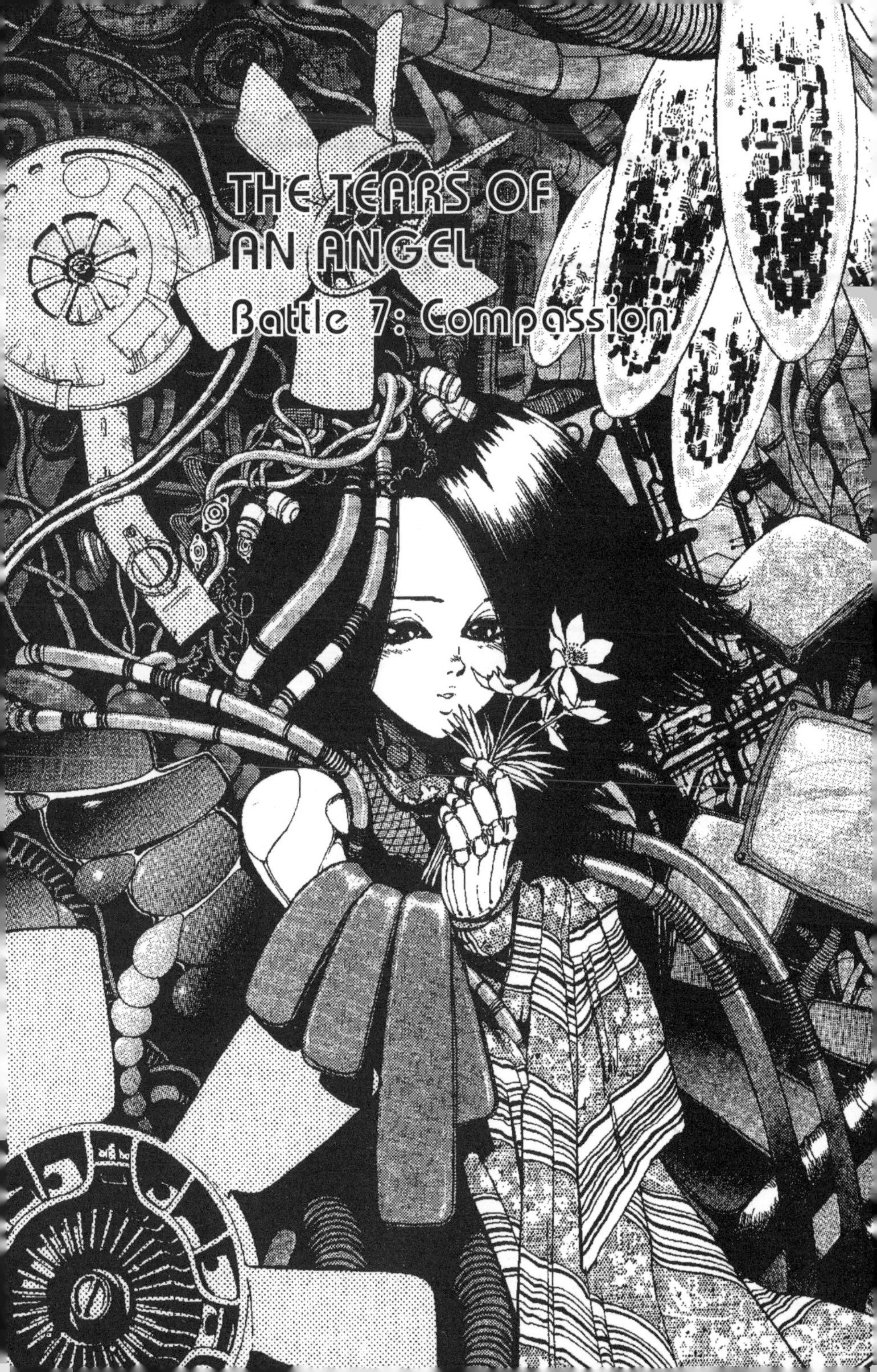
THE TEARS OF AN ANGEL
Battle 7: Compassion

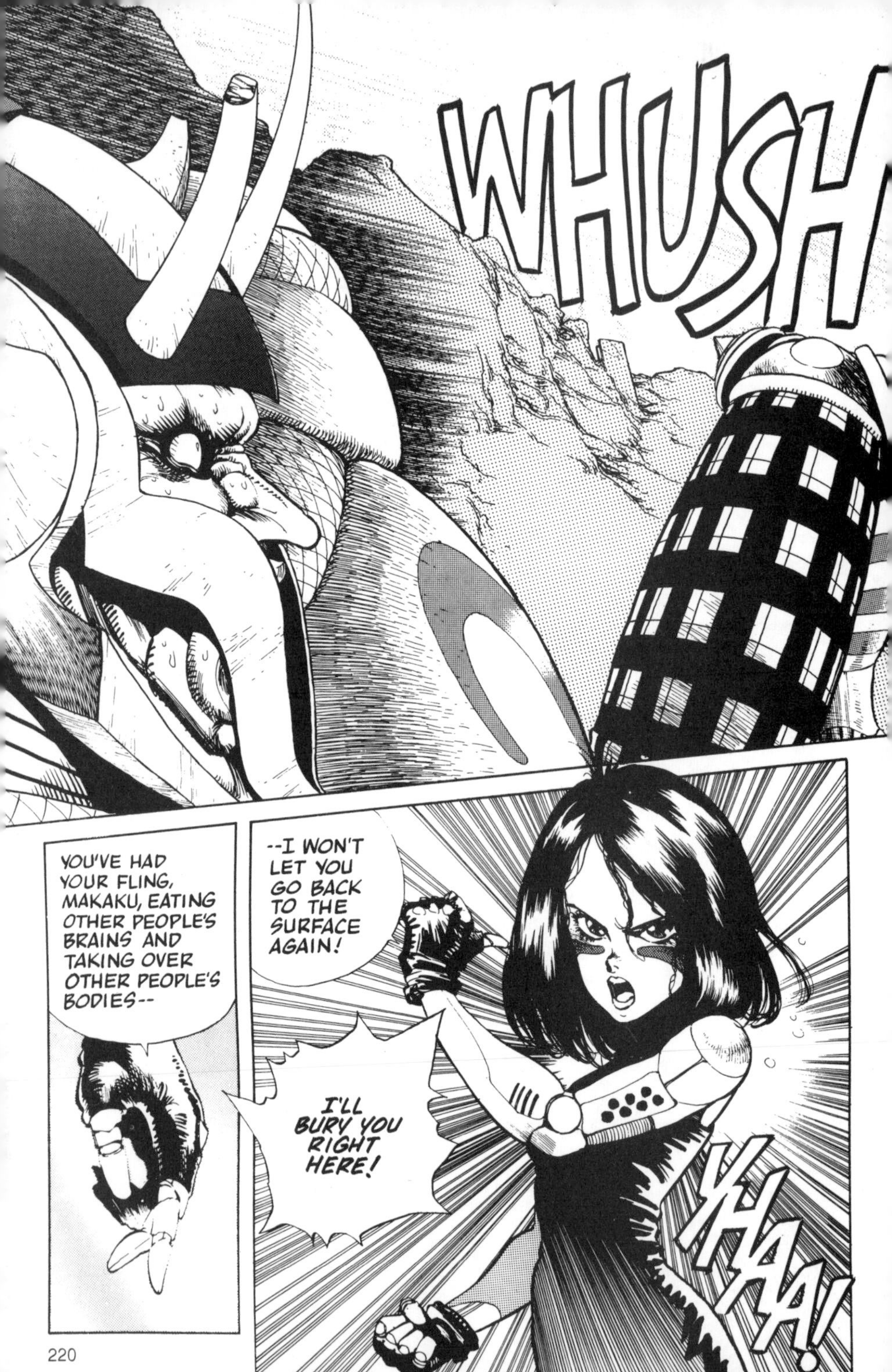
WHUSH
YOU'VE HAD YOUR FLING, MAKAKU, EATING OTHER PEOPLE'S BRAINS AND TAKING OVER OTHER PEOPLE'S BODIES--
--I WON'T LET YOU GO BACK TO THE SURFACE AGAIN!
I'LL BURY YOU RIGHT HERE!
YHAA!

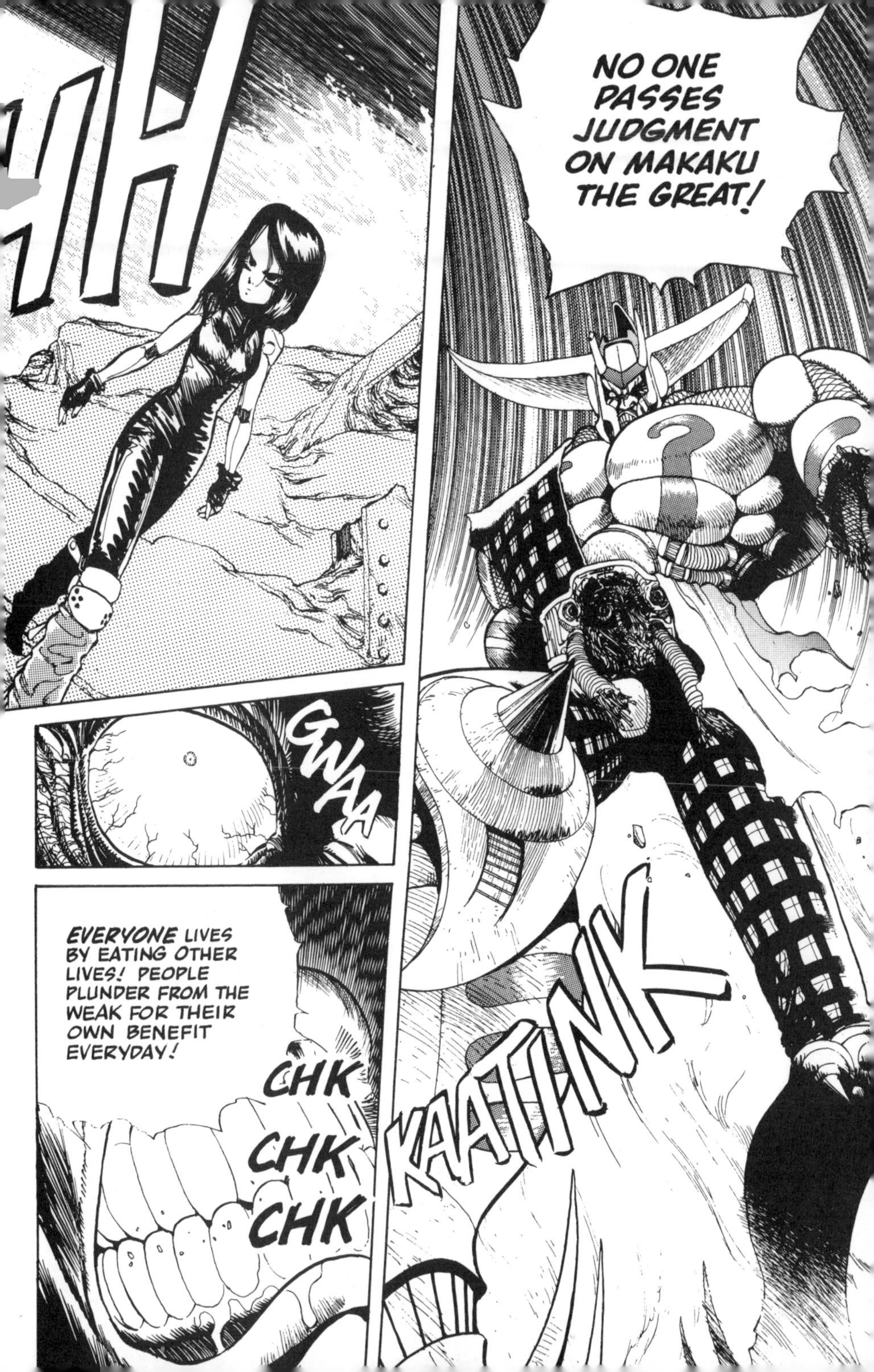
HH
GWAAA
EVERYONE LIVES BY EATING OTHER LIVES! PEOPLE PLUNDER FROM THE WEAK FOR THEIR OWN BENEFIT EVERYDAY!
CHK
CHK
CHK
NO ONE PASSES JUDGMENT ON MAKAKU THE GREAT!
KAATINK

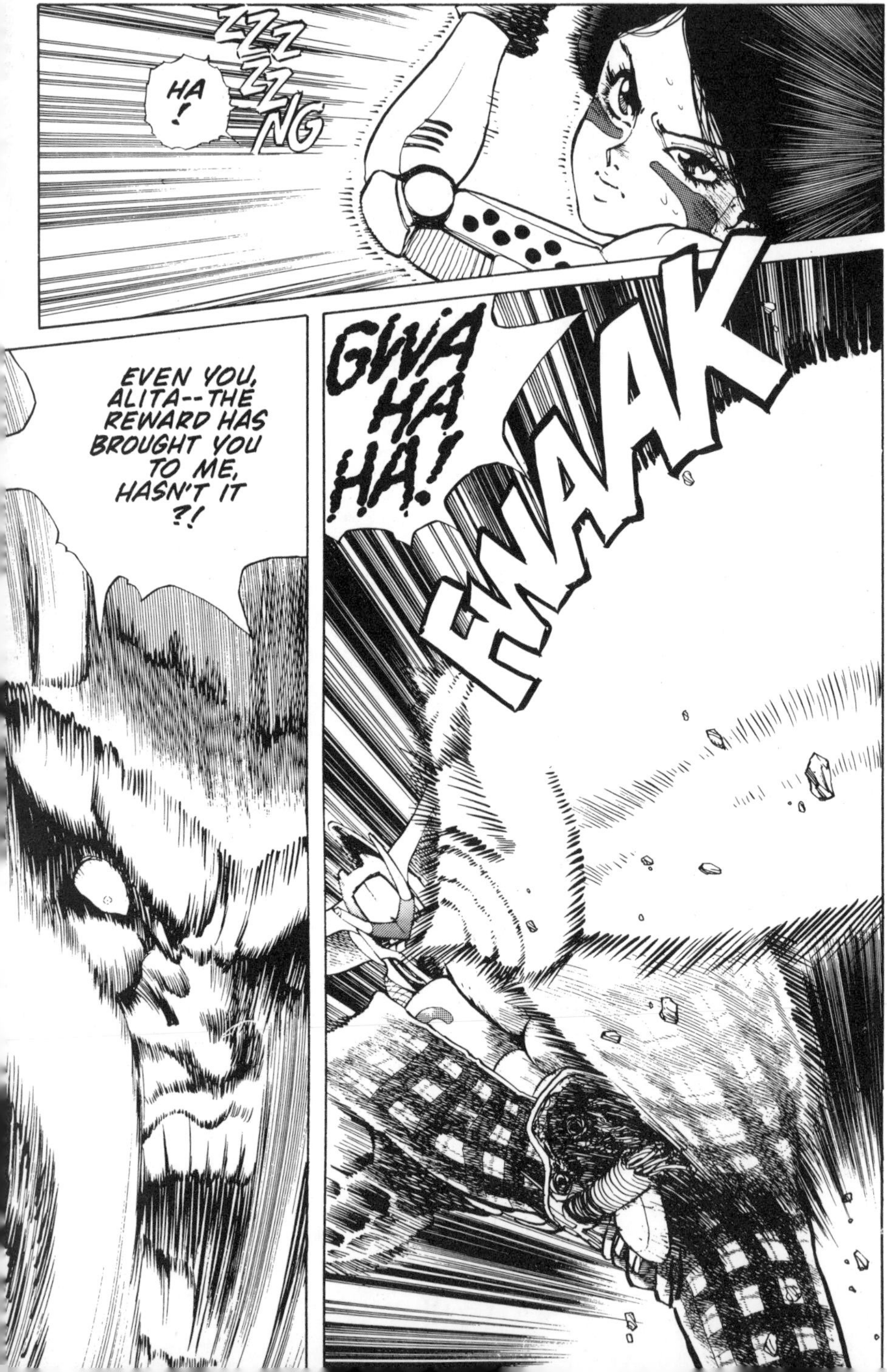
ZZZZZZNG
HA!
EVEN YOU, ALITA--THE REWARD HAS BROUGHT YOU TO ME, HASN'T IT?!
GWA HA HA!
KWAAK

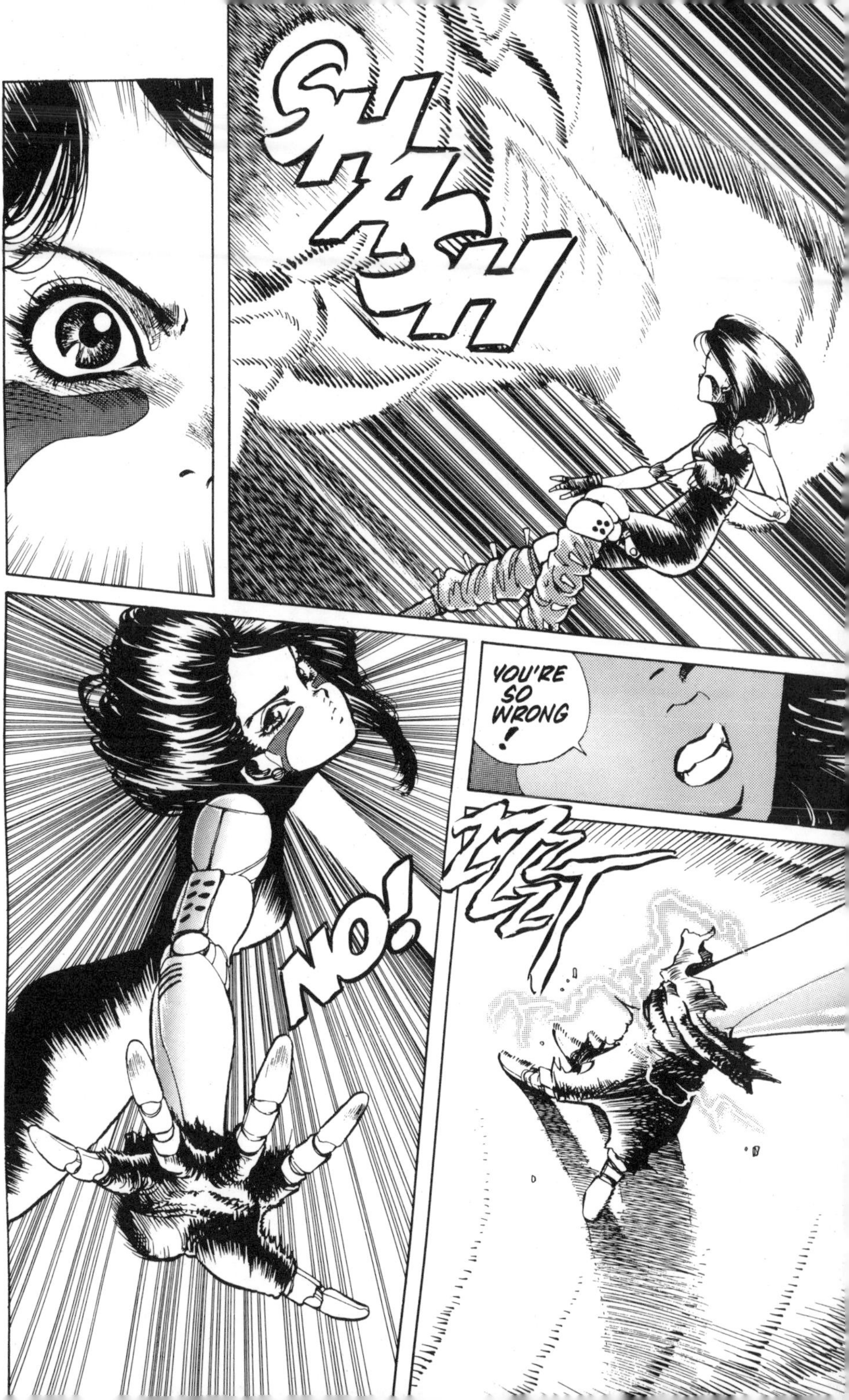
SHAAH
NO!
YOU'RE SO WRONG!
ZZZT

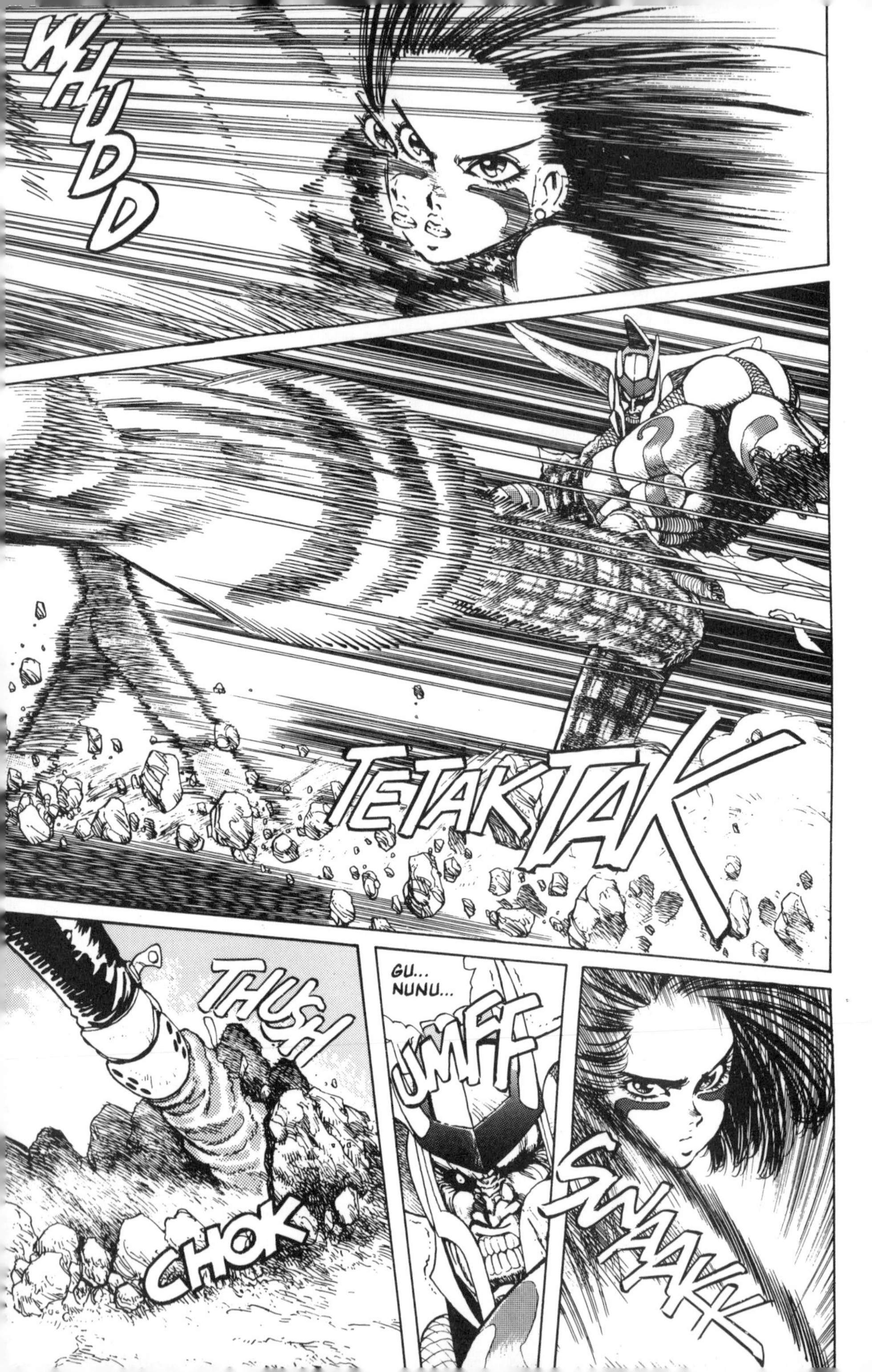
WHUDD
TETAKTAK
THUSH
CHOK
GU... NUNU...
UMFF
SWAKK

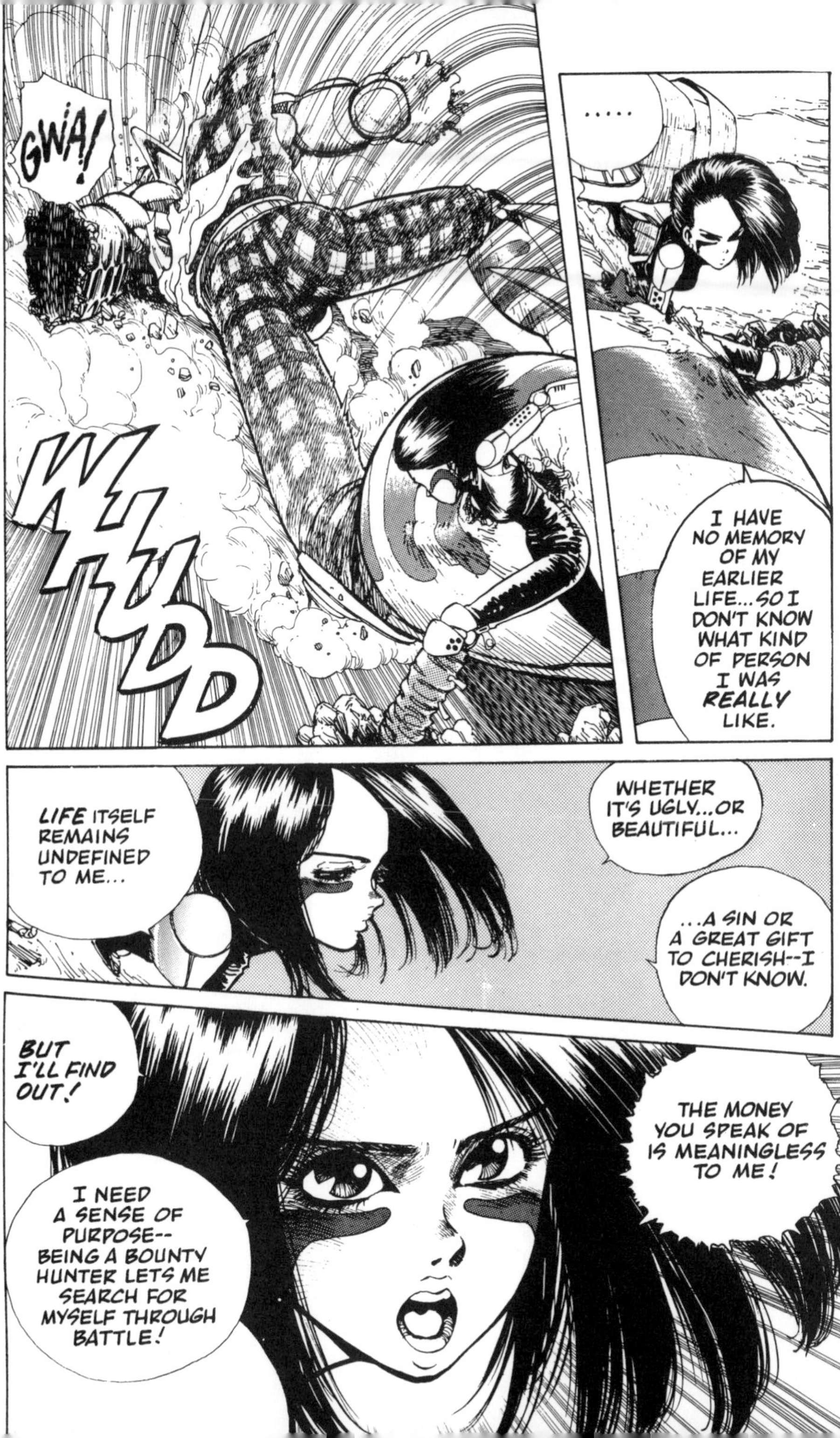
GWA!
WHUDD
.....
I HAVE NO MEMORY OF MY EARLIER LIFE... SO I DON'T KNOW WHAT KIND OF PERSON I WAS REALLY LIKE.
LIFE ITSELF REMAINS UNDEFINED TO ME...
WHETHER IT'S UGLY...OR BEAUTIFUL...
...A SIN OR A GREAT GIFT TO CHERISH--I DON'T KNOW.
BUT I'LL FIND OUT!
I NEED A SENSE OF PURPOSE-- BEING A BOUNTY HUNTER LETS ME SEARCH FOR MYSELF THROUGH BATTLE!
THE MONEY YOU SPEAK OF IS MEANINGLESS TO ME!

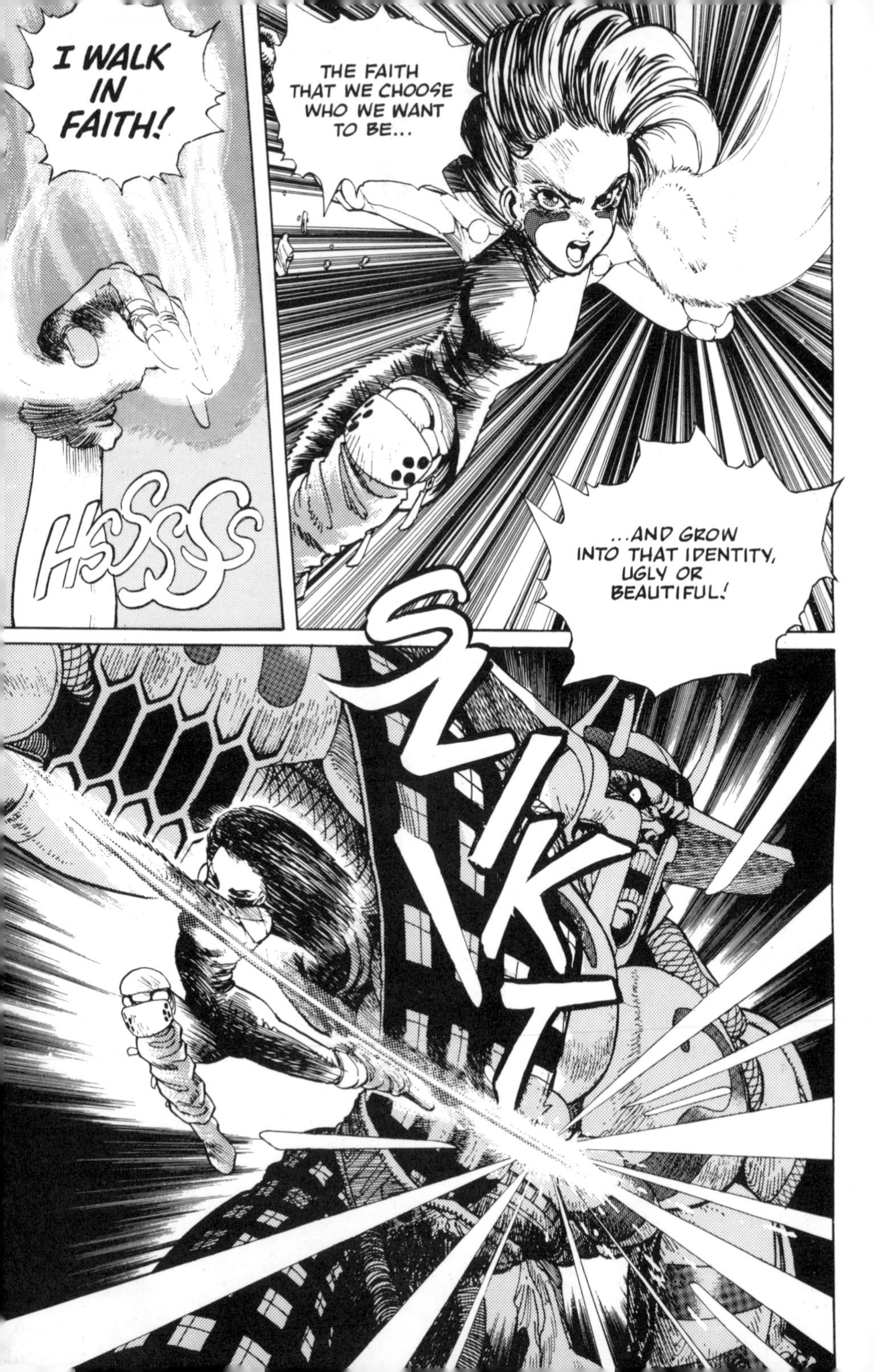
I WALK IN FAITH!
HSSSSS
THE FAITH THAT WE CHOOSE WHO WE WANT TO BE...
...AND GROW INTO THAT IDENTITY, UGLY OR BEAUTIFUL!
SNIKT

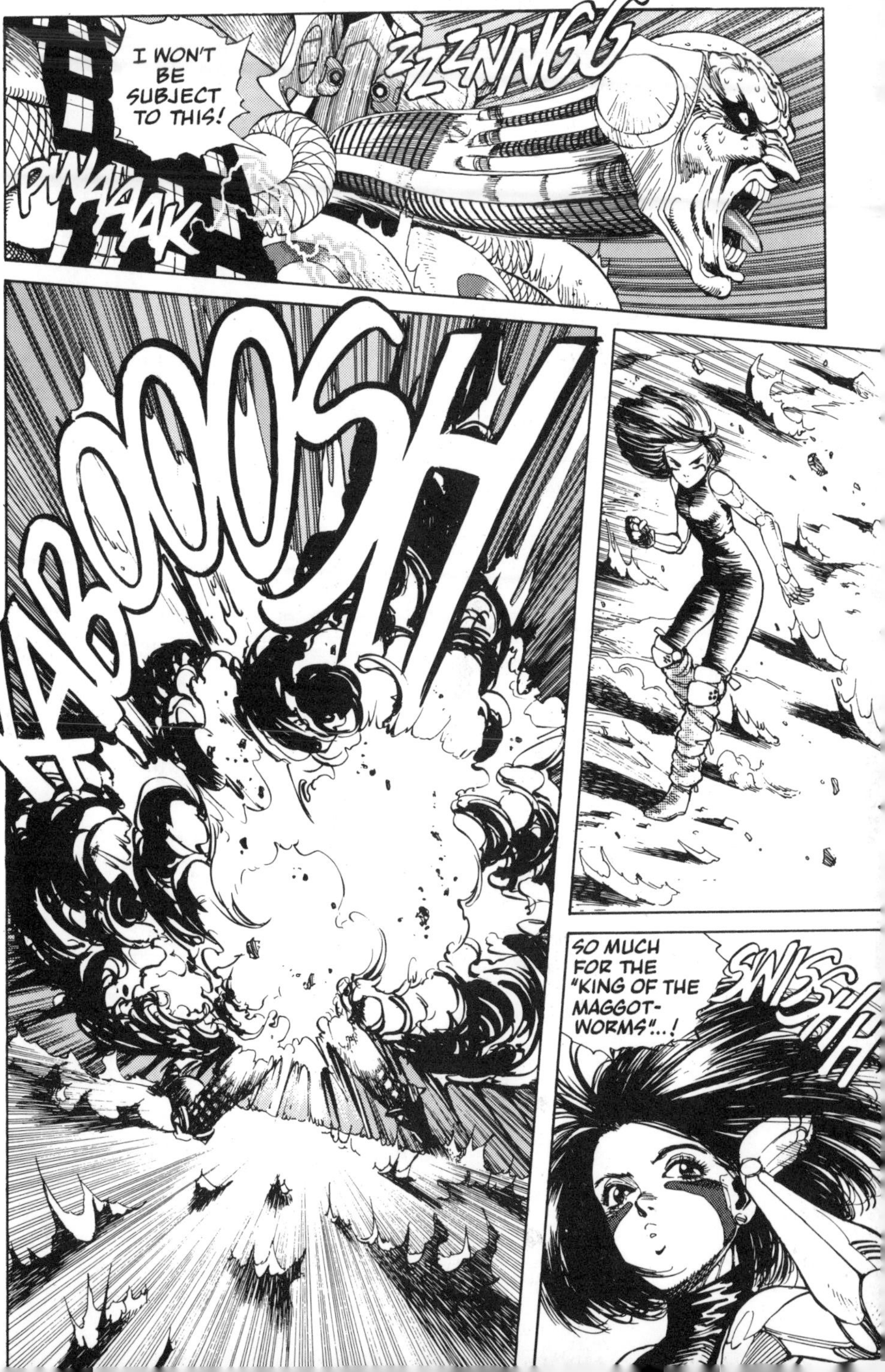

I WON'T BE SUBJECT TO THIS!
ZZZNNGG
PWAAAAK
KABOOOSH
SO MUCH FOR THE "KING OF THE MAGGOT-WORMS"...!
SWISHH

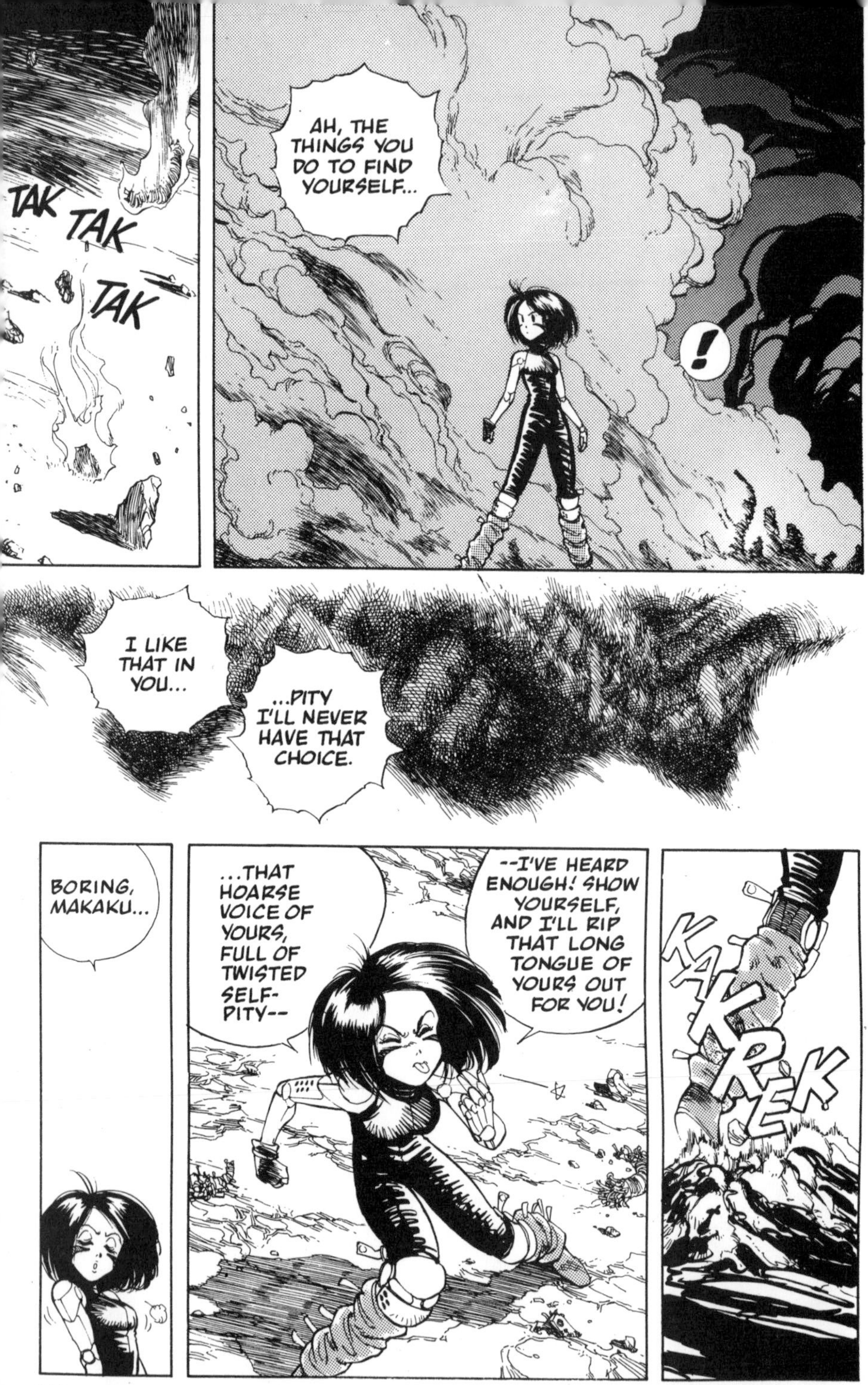
TAK TAK TAK
AH, THE THINGS YOU DO TO FIND YOURSELF...
!
I LIKE THAT IN YOU...
...PITY I'LL NEVER HAVE THAT CHOICE.
BORING, MAKAKU...
...THAT HOARSE VOICE OF YOURS, FULL OF TWISTED SELF-PITY--
--I'VE HEARD ENOUGH! SHOW YOURSELF, AND I'LL RIP THAT LONG TONGUE OF YOURS OUT FOR YOU!
KAKREKREK

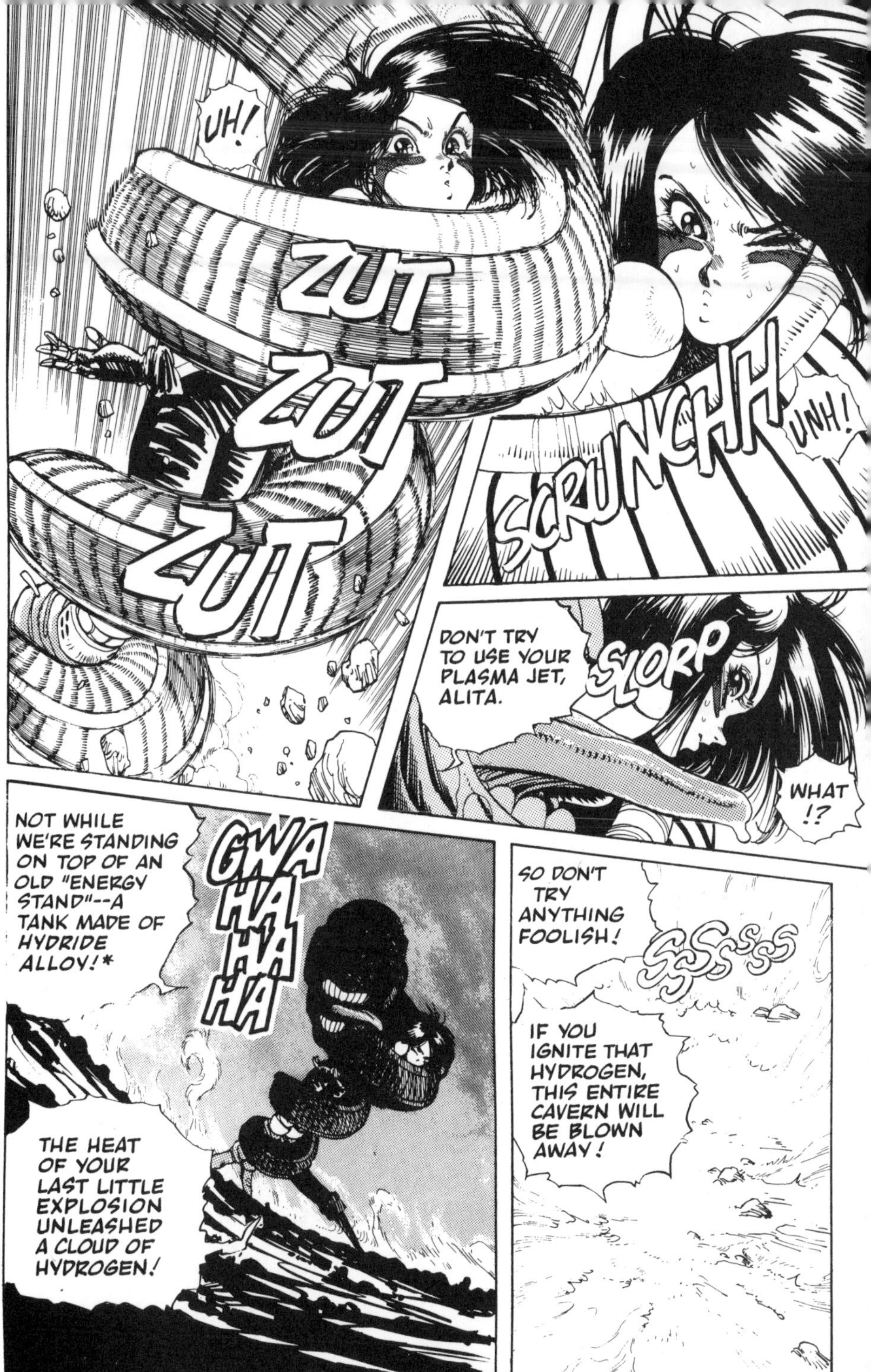
UH!
ZUT
ZUT
ZUT
SCRUNCHH
UNH!
DON'T TRY TO USE YOUR PLASMA JET, ALITA.
SLORP
WHAT !?
NOT WHILE WE'RE STANDING ON TOP OF AN OLD "ENERGY STAND"--A TANK MADE OF HYDRIDE ALLOY!*
GWA HA HA HA HA
THE HEAT OF YOUR LAST LITTLE EXPLOSION UNLEASHED A CLOUD OF HYDROGEN!
SO DON'T TRY ANYTHING FOOLISH!
SSSSSS
IF YOU IGNITE THAT HYDROGEN, THIS ENTIRE CAVERN WILL BE BLOWN AWAY!

* HYDRIDE ALLOY: AN ALLOY THAT ABSORBS AND STORES HYDROGEN GAS. WHEN FORCED TO EXPEL THAT HYDROGEN, THE ALLOY ALSO RELEASES HEAT.

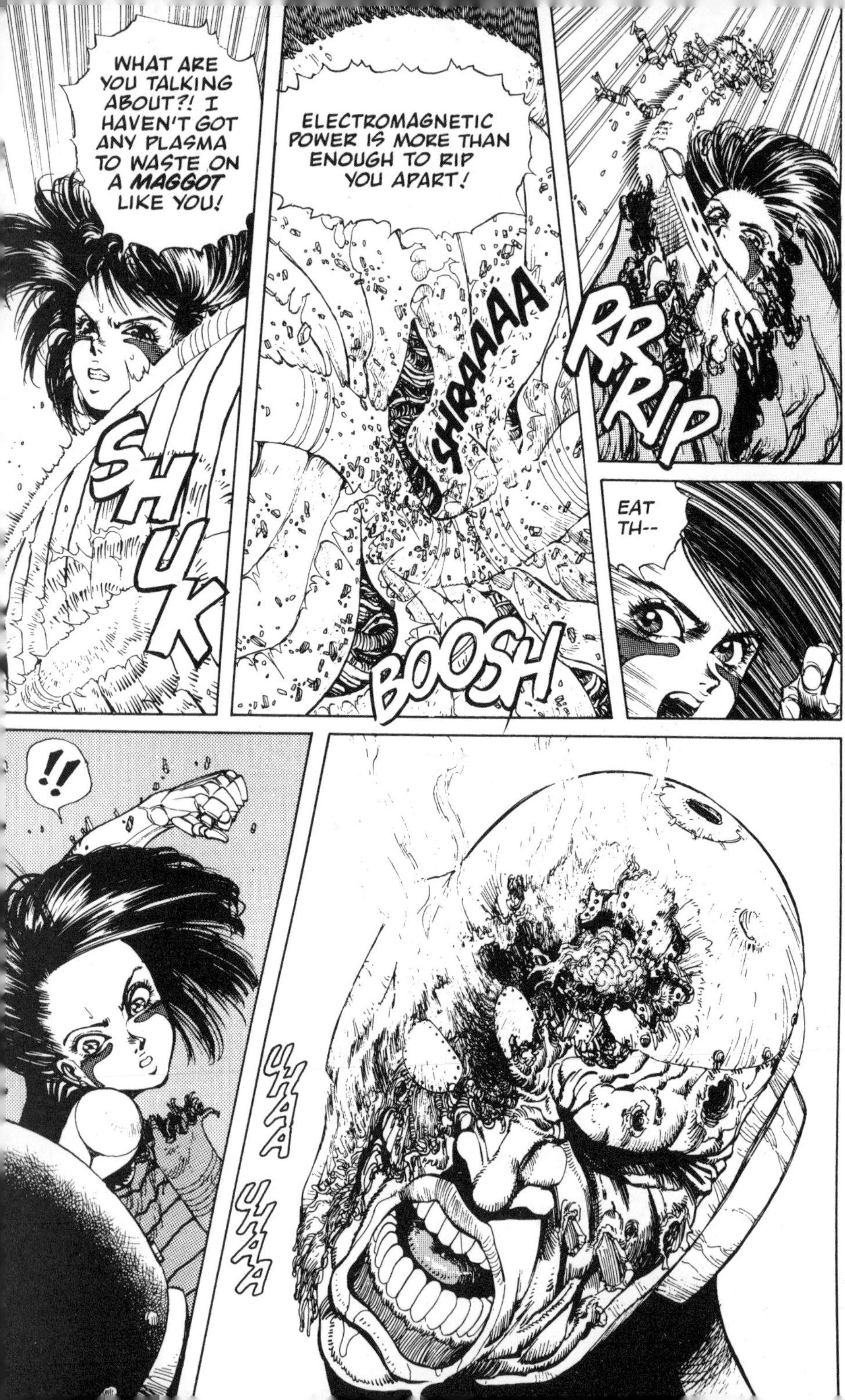
WHAT ARE YOU TALKING ABOUT?! I HAVEN'T GOT ANY PLASMA TO WASTE ON A ***MAGGOT*** LIKE YOU!
SHUK
ELECTROMAGNETIC POWER IS MORE THAN ENOUGH TO RIP YOU APART!
SHRAAAA
BOOSH
RRRIP
EAT TH--
!!
SHAA
SHAAA

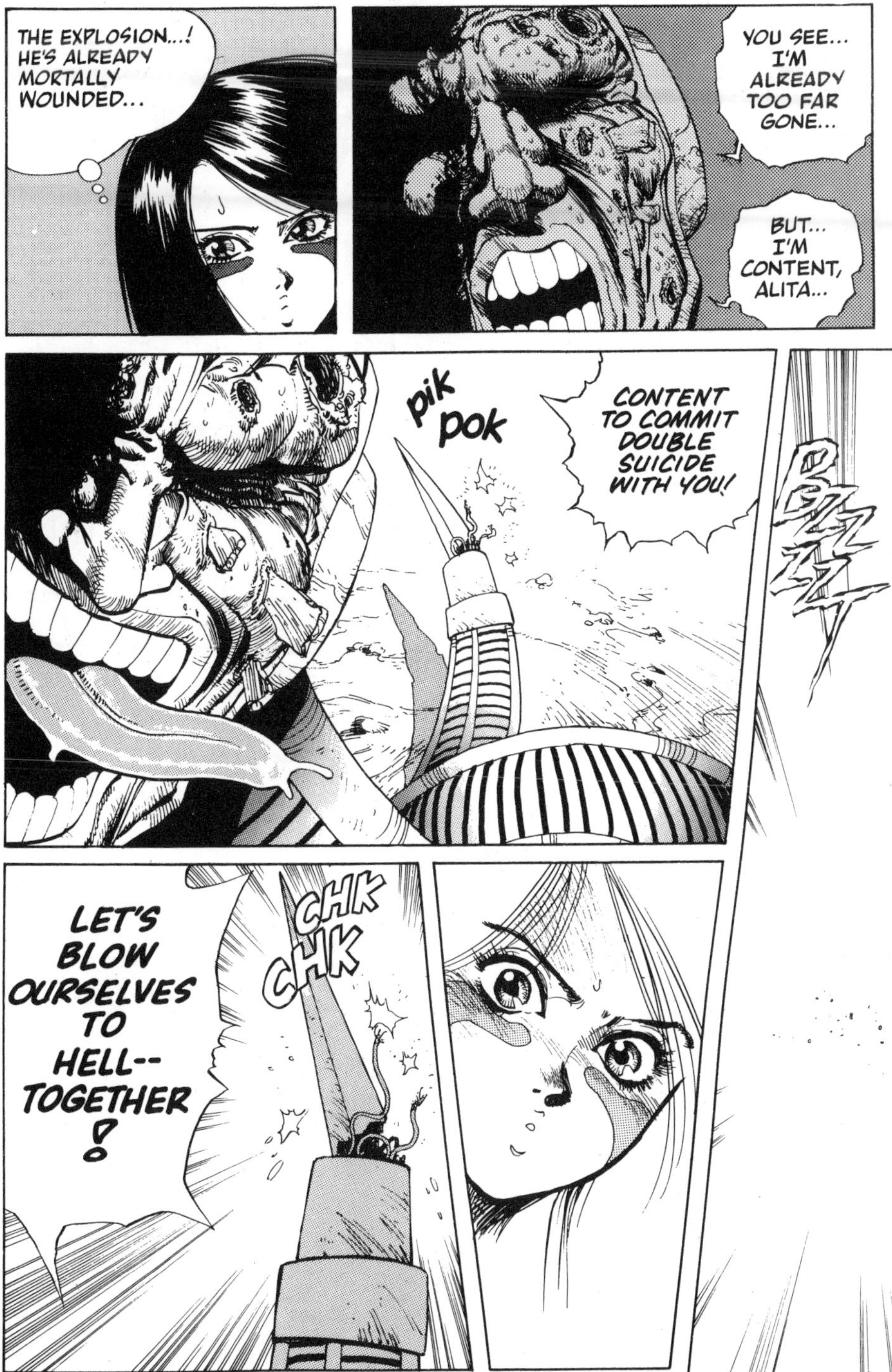
THE EXPLOSION...! HE'S ALREADY MORTALLY WOUNDED...
YOU SEE... I'M ALREADY TOO FAR GONE...
BUT... I'M CONTENT, ALITA...
pik pok
CONTENT TO COMMIT DOUBLE SUICIDE WITH YOU!
BZZZZT
LET'S BLOW OURSELVES TO HELL-- TOGETHER!
CHK CHK

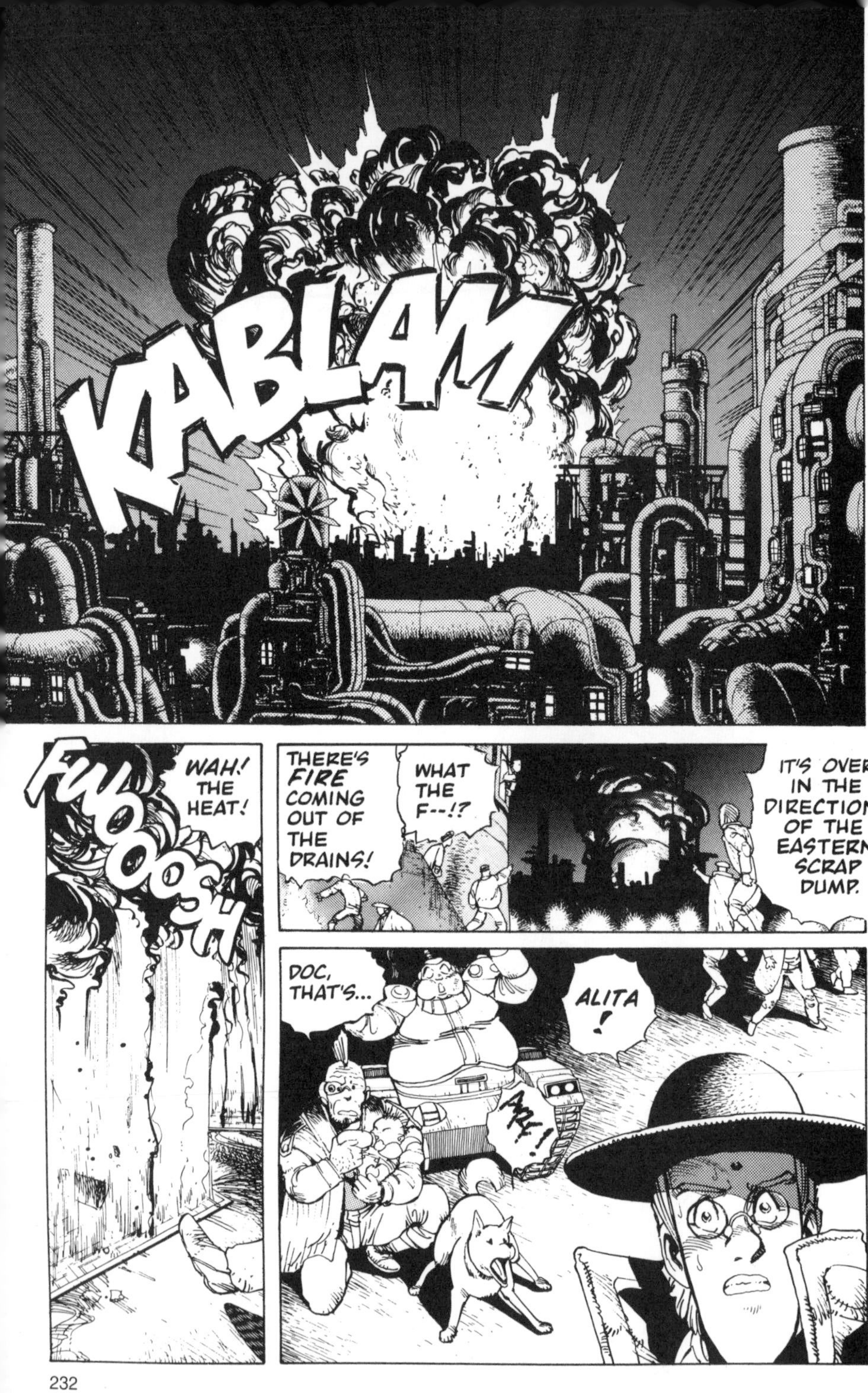
KABLAM
FUWOOOSH
WAH! THE HEAT!
THERE'S *FIRE* COMING OUT OF THE DRAINS!
WHAT THE F--!?
IT'S OVER IN THE DIRECTION OF THE EASTERN SCRAP DUMP.
DOC, THAT'S...
ALITA!
ARF!!

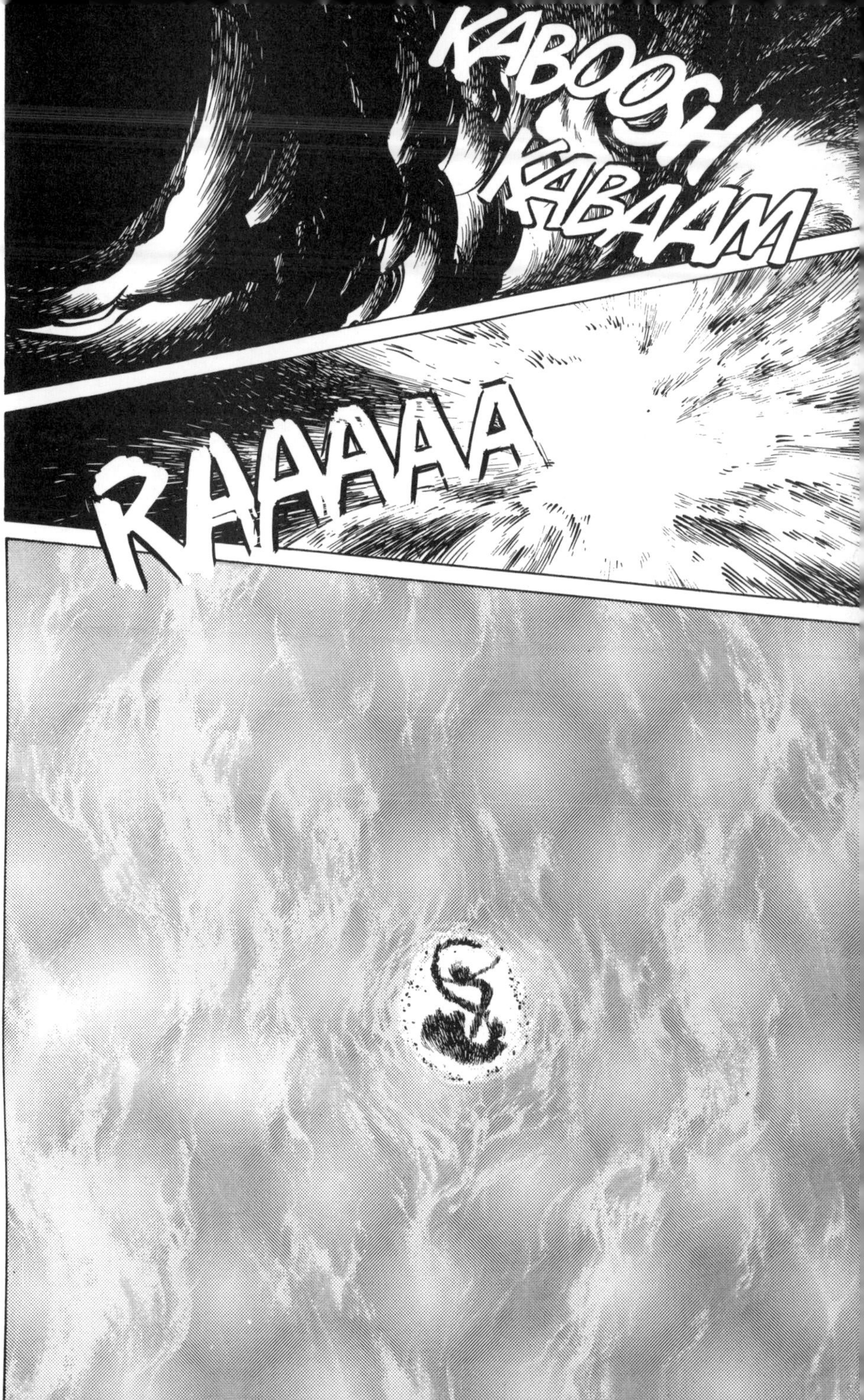
KABOOSH
KABAAM
RAAAAAA

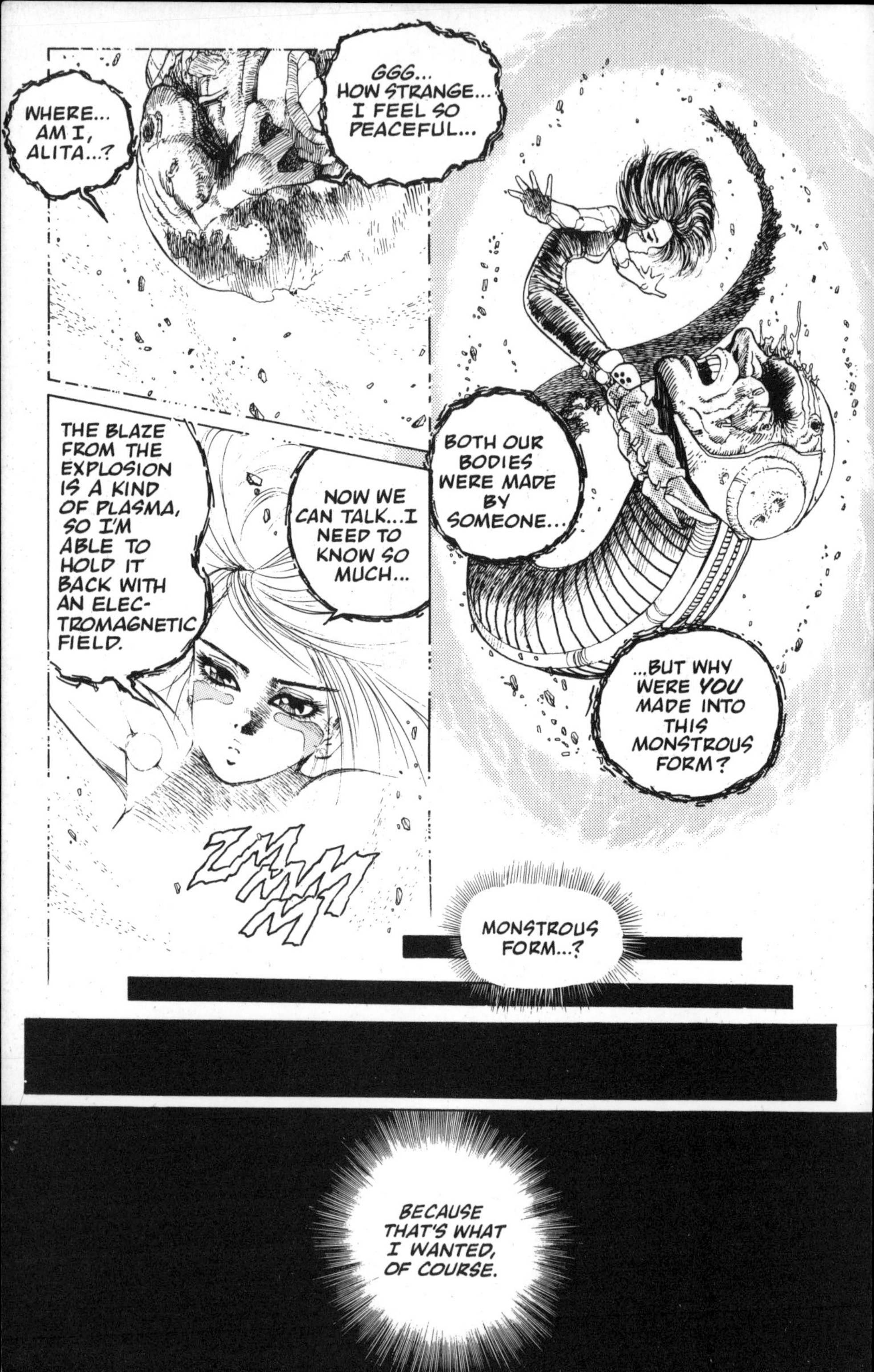
WHERE... AM I, ALITA...?
GGG... HOW STRANGE... I FEEL SO PEACEFUL...
THE BLAZE FROM THE EXPLOSION IS A KIND OF PLASMA, SO I'M ABLE TO HOLD IT BACK WITH AN ELEC-TROMAGNETIC FIELD.
NOW WE CAN TALK...I NEED TO KNOW SO MUCH...
ZMMMM
BOTH OUR BODIES WERE MADE BY SOMEONE...
...BUT WHY WERE *YOU* MADE INTO THIS MONSTROUS FORM?
MONSTROUS FORM...?
BECAUSE THAT'S WHAT I WANTED, OF COURSE.

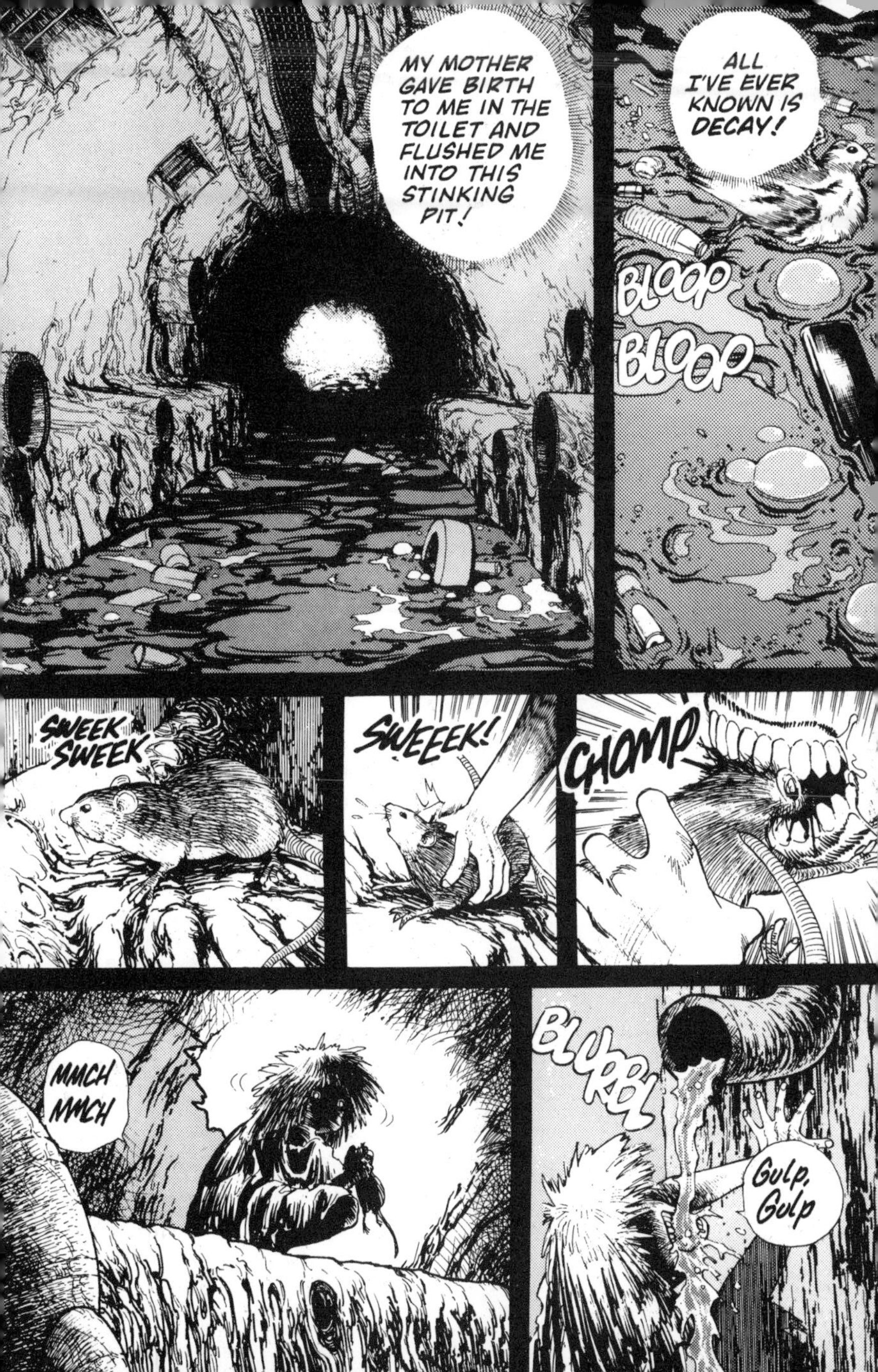
MY MOTHER GAVE BIRTH TO ME IN THE TOILET AND FLUSHED ME INTO THIS STINKING PIT!
ALL I'VE EVER KNOWN IS DECAY!
BLOOP
BLOOP
SWEEK SWEEK
SWEEEK!
CHOMP
MMCH MMCH
BLURBL
Gulp, Gulp

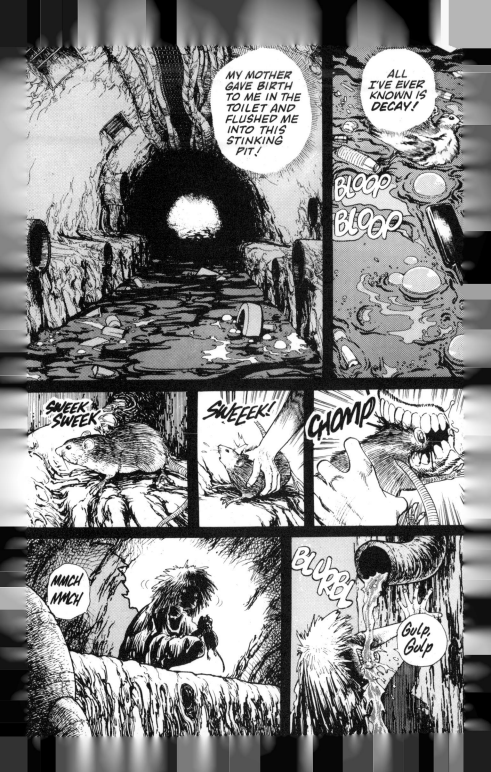

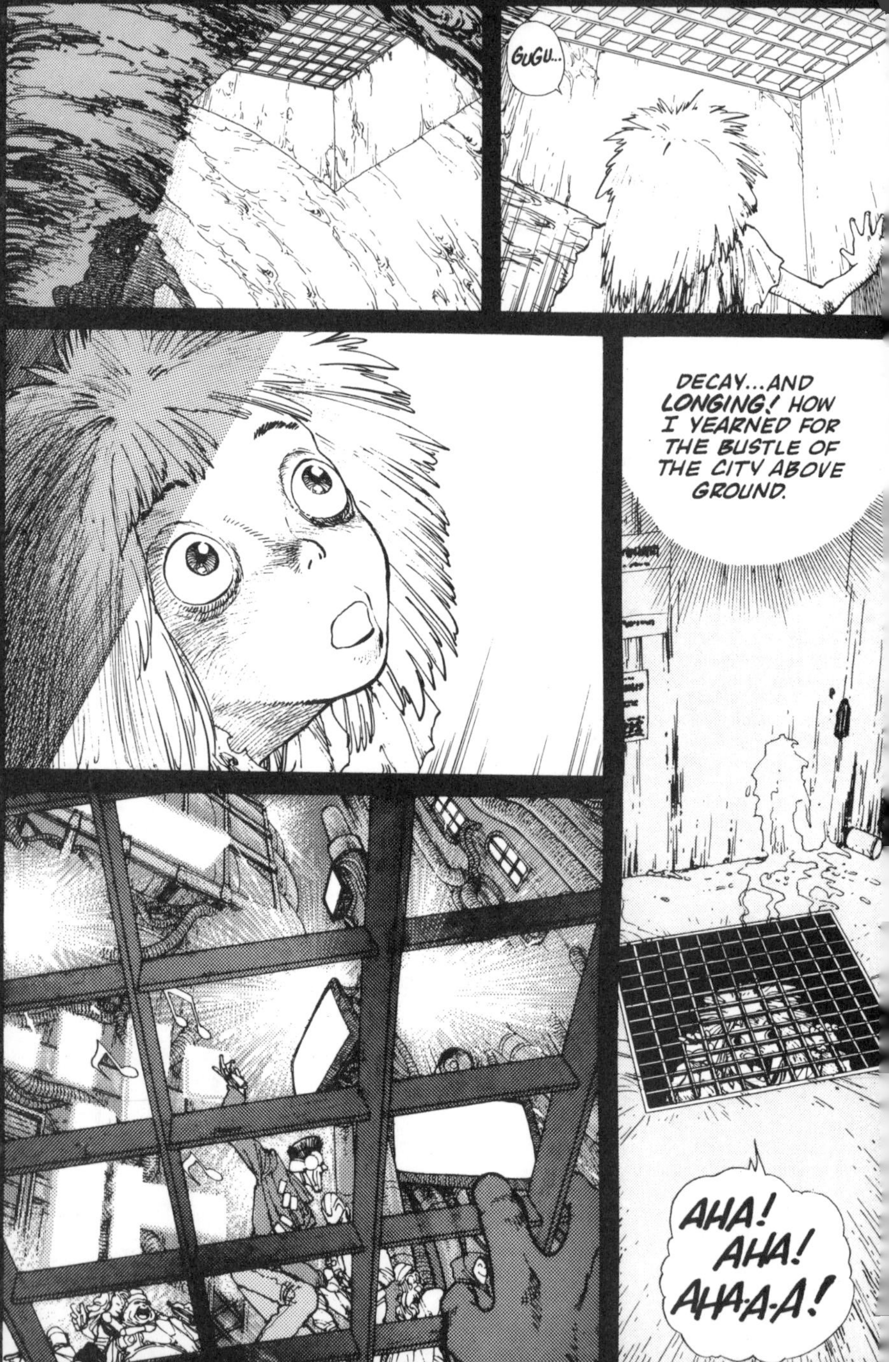
GUGU...
DECAY...AND LONGING! HOW I YEARNED FOR THE BUSTLE OF THE CITY ABOVE GROUND.
AHA! AHA! AHA-A-A!

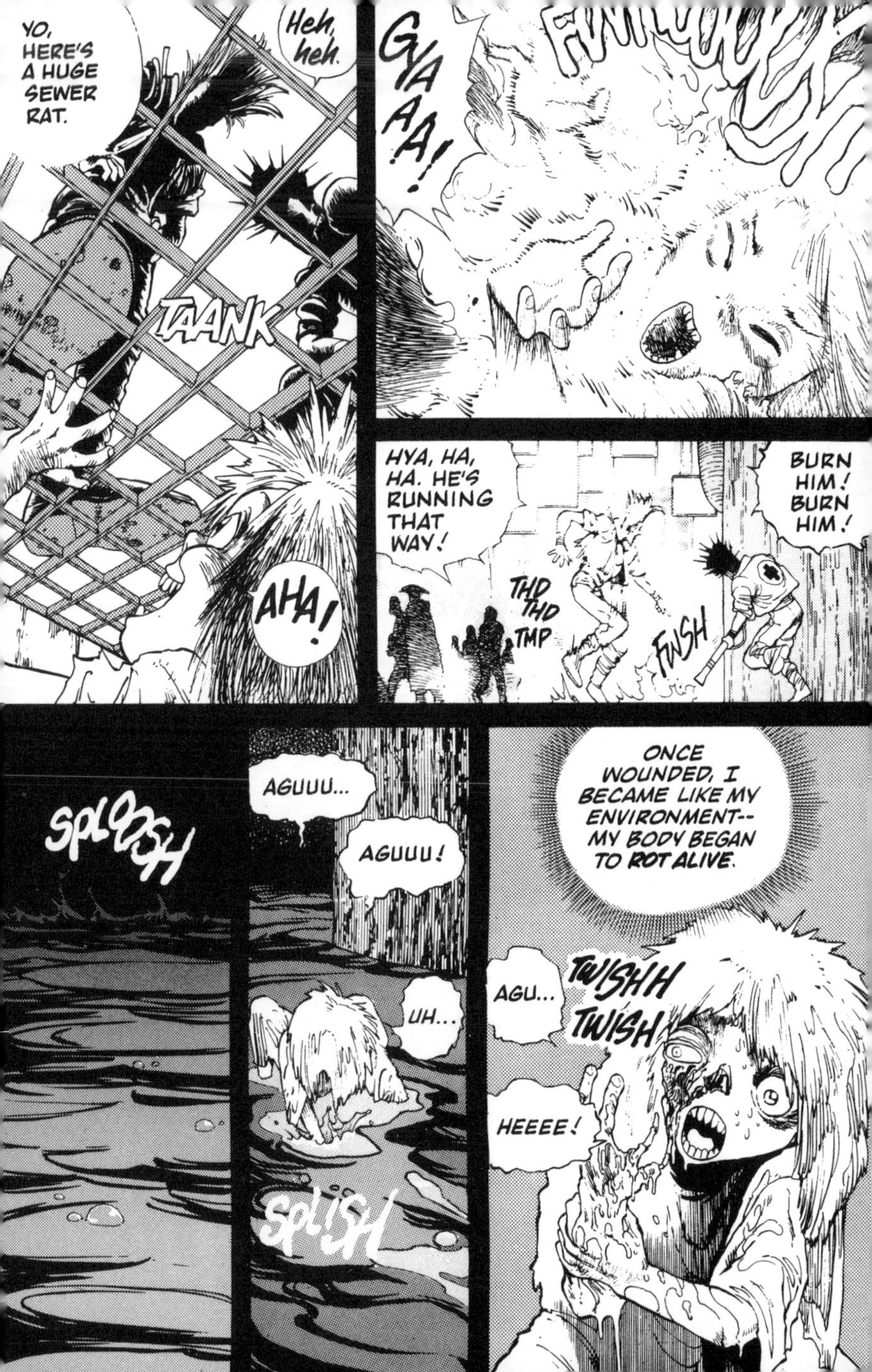
YO, HERE'S A HUGE SEWER RAT.
Heh, heh.
TAANK
AHA!
GYAAAA!
HYA, HA, HA. HE'S RUNNING THAT WAY!
THD THD TMP
FWSH
BURN HIM! BURN HIM!
SPLOOSH
AGUUU...
AGUUU!
UH...
SPLISH
ONCE WOUNDED, I BECAME LIKE MY ENVIRONMENT-- MY BODY BEGAN TO ROT ALIVE.
AGU...
TWISHH TWISH
HEEEE!

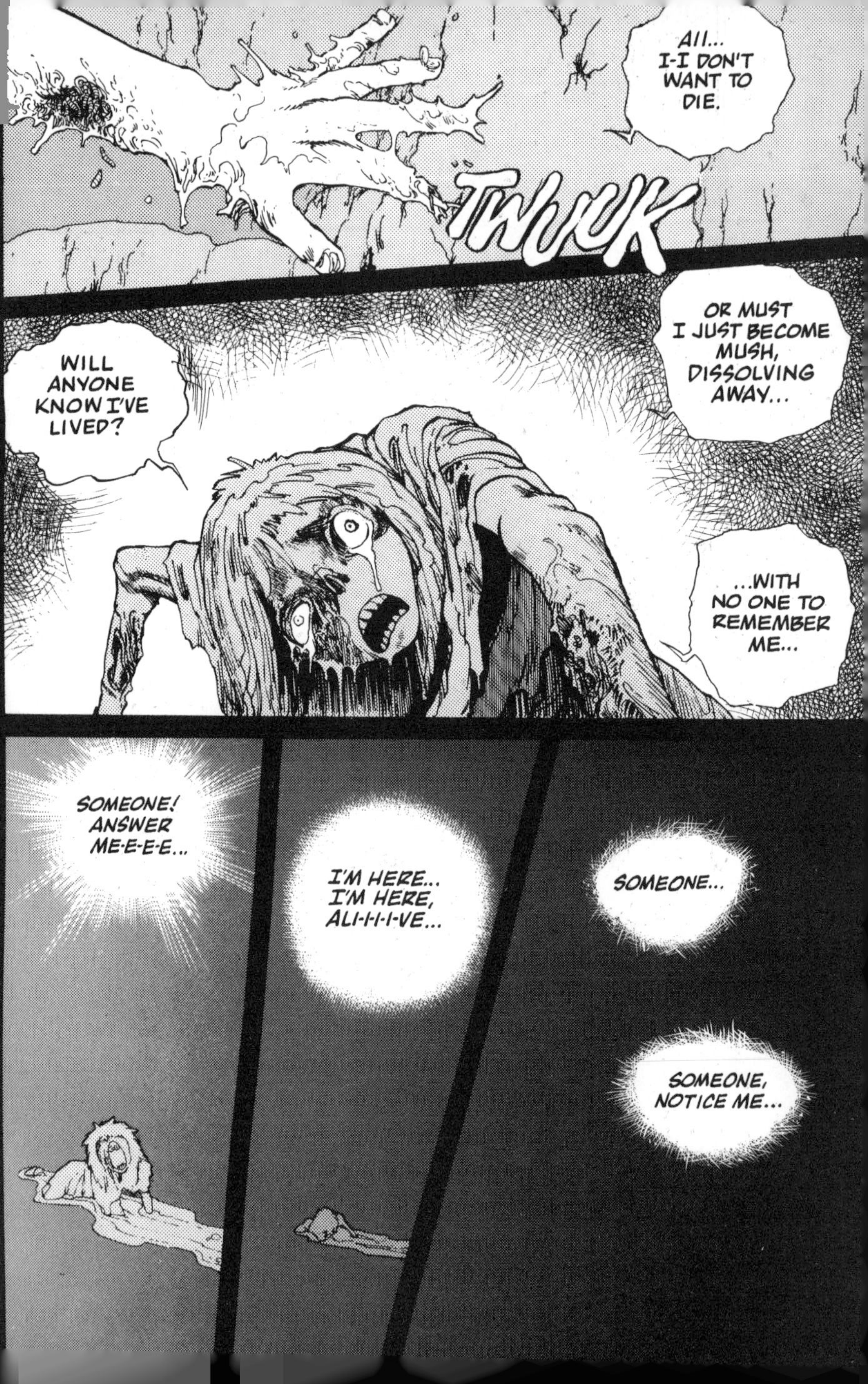
AII... I-I DON'T WANT TO DIE.
TWUUK
WILL ANYONE KNOW I'VE LIVED?
OR MUST I JUST BECOME MUSH, DISSOLVING AWAY...
...WITH NO ONE TO REMEMBER ME...
SOMEONE! ANSWER ME-E-E-E...
I'M HERE... I'M HERE, ALI-I-I-I-VE...
SOMEONE...
SOMEONE, NOTICE ME...

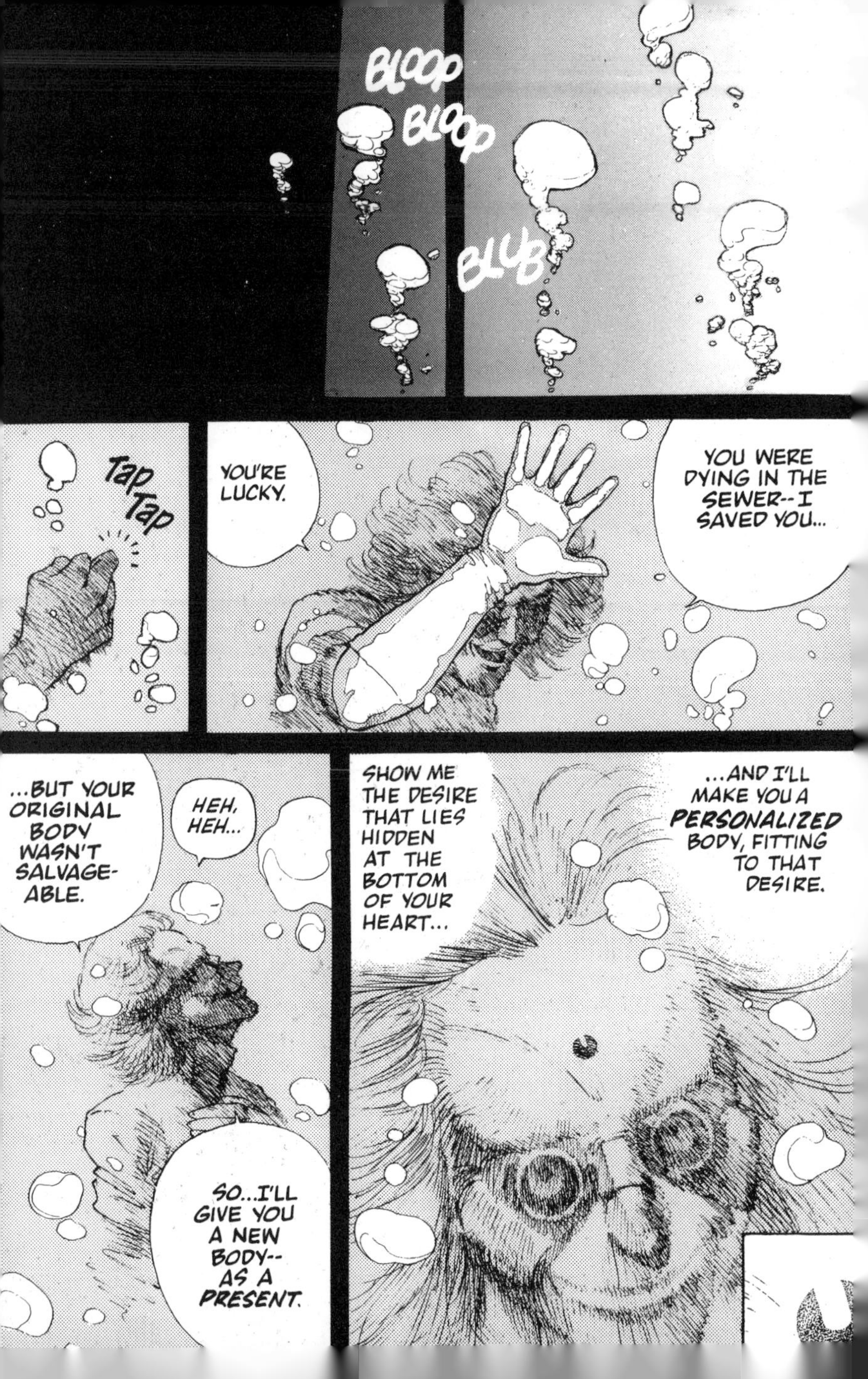
BLOOP
BLOOP
BLUB
Tap Tap
YOU'RE LUCKY.
YOU WERE DYING IN THE SEWER--I SAVED YOU...
...BUT YOUR ORIGINAL BODY WASN'T SALVAGE-ABLE.
HEH, HEH...
SO...I'LL GIVE YOU A NEW BODY--AS A *PRESENT.*
SHOW ME THE DESIRE THAT LIES HIDDEN AT THE BOTTOM OF YOUR HEART...
...AND I'LL MAKE YOU A ***PERSONALIZED*** BODY, FITTING TO THAT DESIRE.

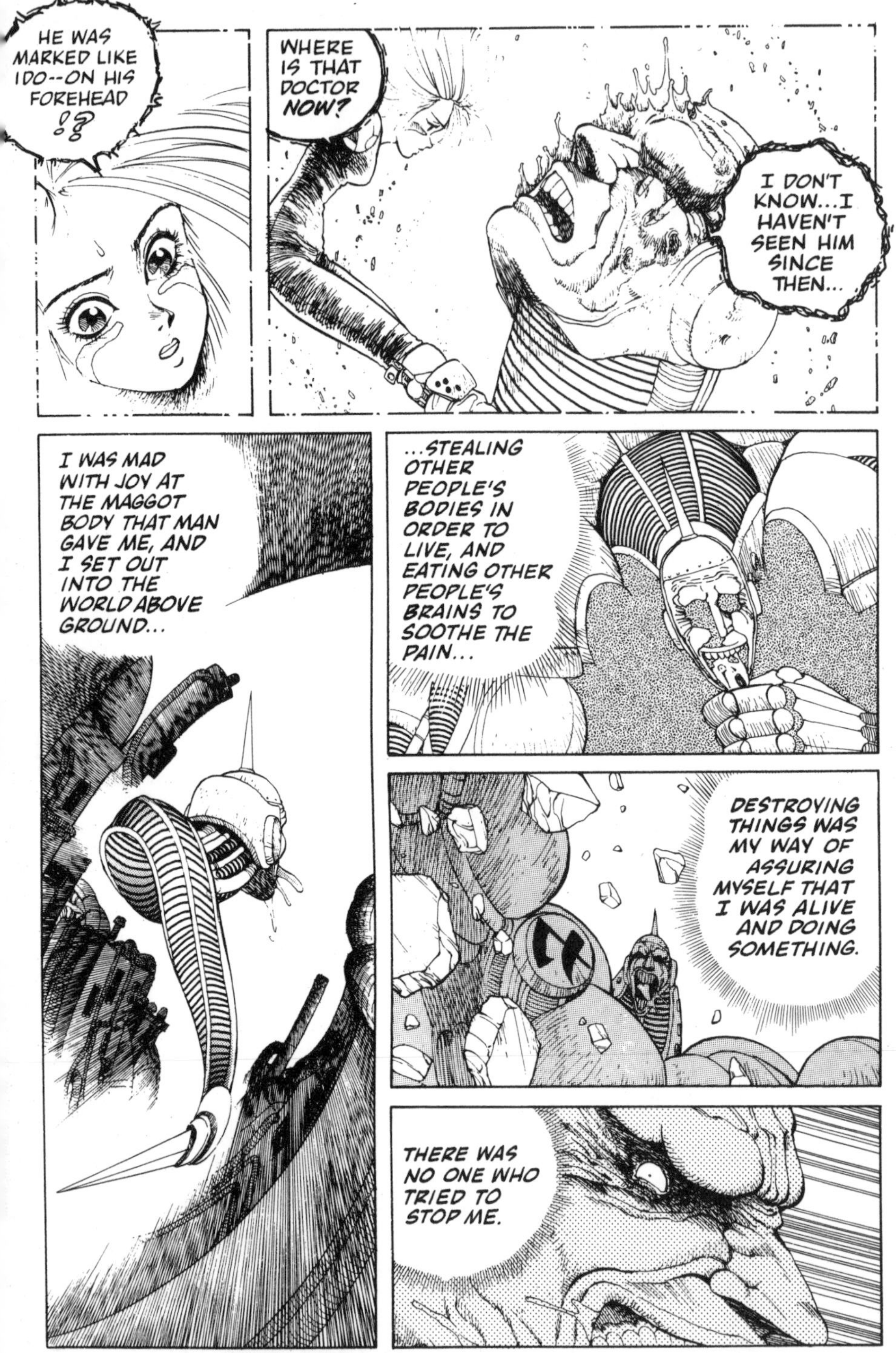
HE WAS MARKED LIKE IDO--ON HIS FOREHEAD !?
WHERE IS THAT DOCTOR NOW?
I DON'T KNOW...I HAVEN'T SEEN HIM SINCE THEN...
I WAS MAD WITH JOY AT THE MAGGOT BODY THAT MAN GAVE ME, AND I SET OUT INTO THE WORLD ABOVE GROUND...
...STEALING OTHER PEOPLE'S BODIES IN ORDER TO LIVE, AND EATING OTHER PEOPLE'S BRAINS TO SOOTHE THE PAIN...
DESTROYING THINGS WAS MY WAY OF ASSURING MYSELF THAT I WAS ALIVE AND DOING SOMETHING.
THERE WAS NO ONE WHO TRIED TO STOP ME.

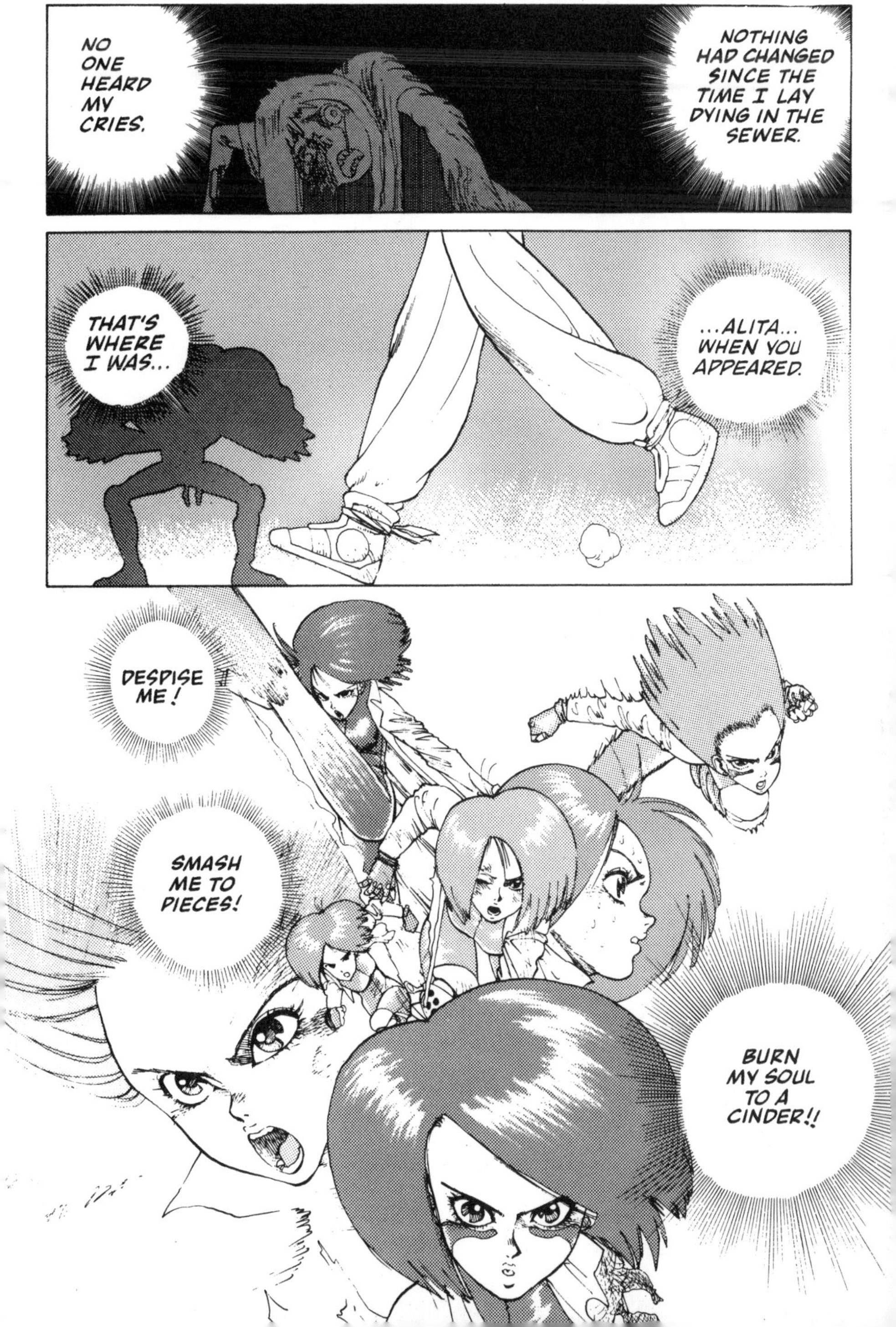
NO ONE HEARD MY CRIES.
NOTHING HAD CHANGED SINCE THE TIME I LAY DYING IN THE SEWER.
THAT'S WHERE I WAS...
...ALITA... WHEN YOU APPEARED.
DESPISE ME!
SMASH ME TO PIECES!
BURN MY SOUL TO A CINDER!!

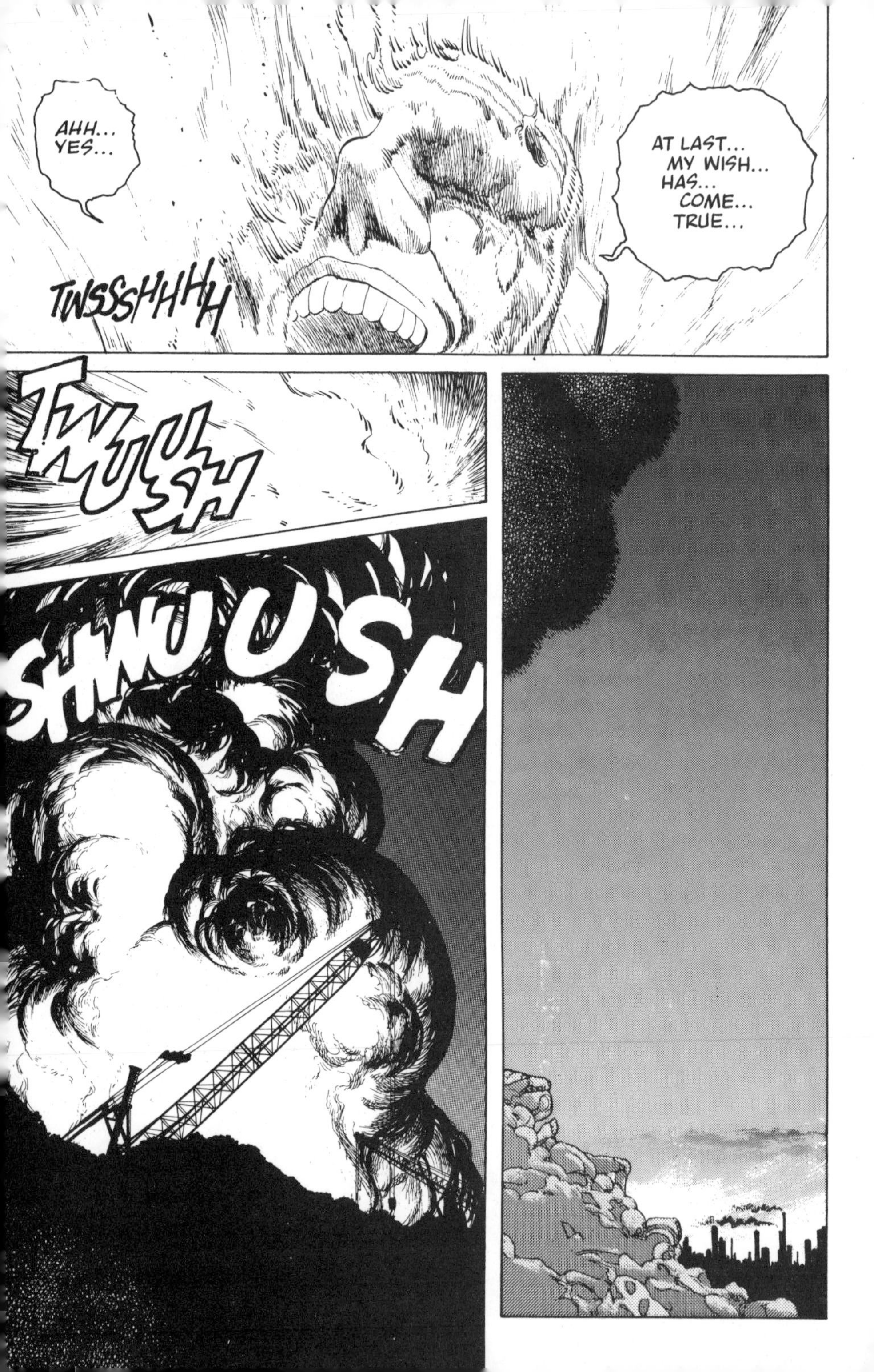
AHH... YES...
AT LAST... MY WISH... HAS... COME... TRUE...
TWSSSHHHHH
TWUUSH
SHWUUSH

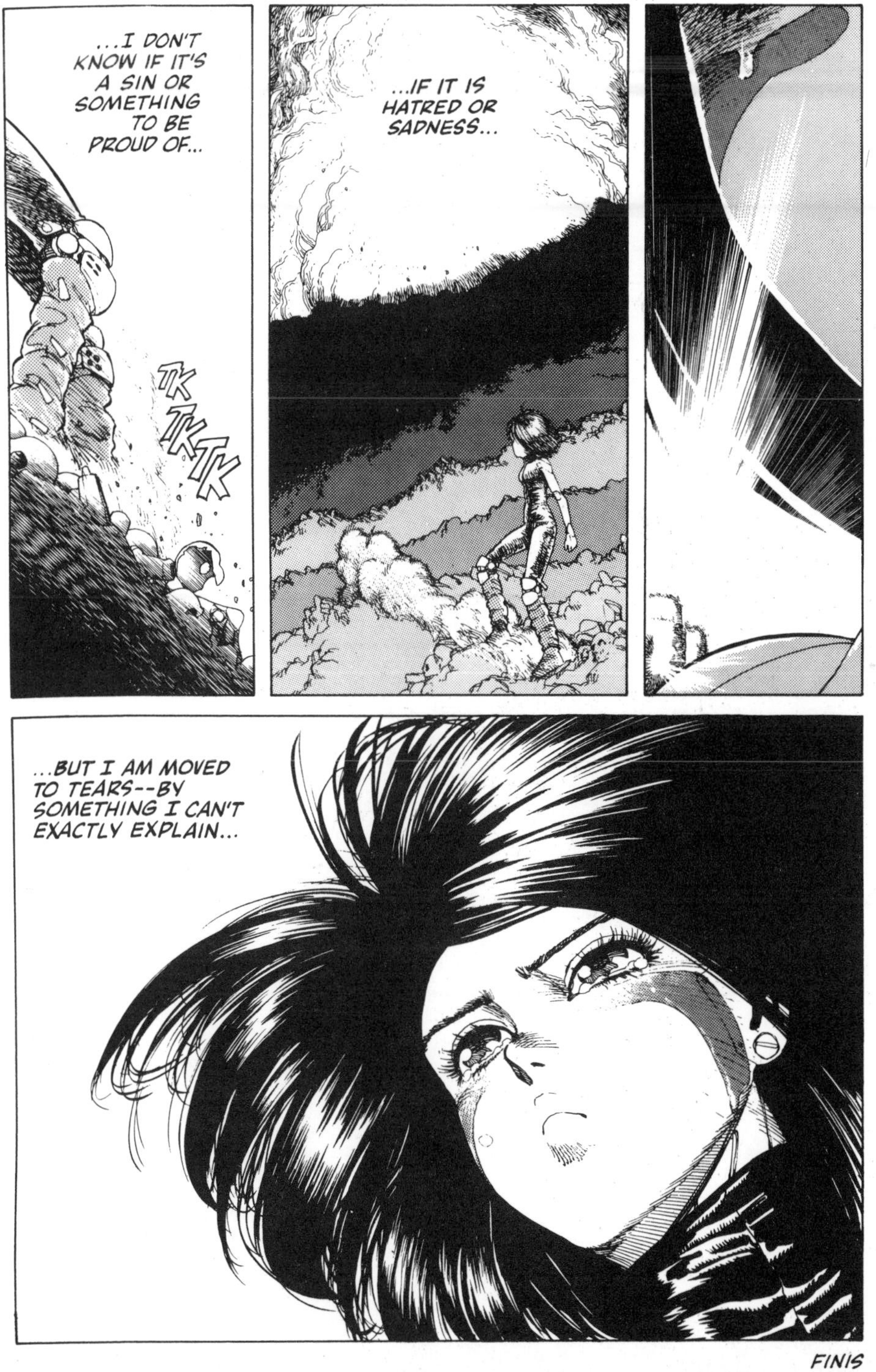
...I DON'T KNOW IF IT'S A SIN OR SOMETHING TO BE PROUD OF...
TK TK TK TK
...IF IT IS HATRED OR SADNESS...
...BUT I AM MOVED TO TEARS--BY SOMETHING I CAN'T EXACTLY EXPLAIN...

FINIS